The Collected Works of
James M. Buchanan

VOLUME 20

Indexes

The Collected Works of

James M. Buchanan

VOLUME 20

Indexes

LIBERTY FUND

Indianapolis

06   05   04   03   02   C   5   4   3   2   1
06   05   04   03   02   P   5   4   3   2   1

Library of Congress Cataloging-in-Publication Data
[The collected works of James M. Buchanan] : indexes.
p. cm. — (The collected works of James M. Buchanan ; v. 20)
Curriculum vitae and comprehensive indexes of the preceding
19 volumes.
ISBN 0-86597-251-6 (alk. paper) — ISBN 0-86597-252-4 (pbk.; alk.
paper)
1. Buchanan, James M. Works Indexes.   2. Buchanan, James M.
3. Economists—United States—Bibliography.   I. Liberty Fund.
HB 119.B67 A2 1999 Index
330—dc21   2001038931

LIBERTY FUND, INC.
8335 Allison Pointe Trail, Suite 300
Indianapolis, IN 46250-1684

Contents

Indexes

Name Index

Aaron, Henry J., **7:** 145 n. 7, 229, 233; **15:** 377 n. 1, 408–9; **16:** 348 n. 4

Abalkin, Leonid, **16:** 253, 254, 260

Abbott, Charles C., **2:** 34 n. 5, 134 n. 1

Acheson, Keith, **8:** 122 n. 8

Ackerman, Bruce A., **11:** 5; **16:** 156

Acton, John Emerich Edward Dalberg (1st Baron Acton), **1:** 28; **3:** 265; **7:** 229; **10:** 73

Adair, D., **16:** 198 n. 13

Adams, H. C., **2:** 82–83

Adams, T. S., **15:** 81

Adarkar, B. P., **18:** 3 nn. 2,3, 12 n. 21, 17 n. 26

Adelman, M. A., **1:** 221 n. 6

Aegidius Romanus, **7:** 32 n. 9, 33 n. 10, 76 n. 7

Ahlbrandt, Roger, **8:** 73 n. 26

Aiken, Henry D., **3:** 315 n. 6

Ainslie, George, **16:** 401–2

Akerlof, George, **12:** 417 n. 3; **17:** 336 n. 10

Albee, Edward, **13:** 87 n. 8

Alchian, Armen A., **1:** 70 n. 11, 383 n. 5, 415; **6:** 34 n. 33, 87; **7:** 29, 229; **8:** 61 n. 6, 147 n. 17; **12:** 7 n. 4, 129, 263, 310 n. 7, 416 n. 3; **13:** 48, 451 n. 2; **14:** 16 n. 21, 440 n. 11; **16:** 29, 173 n. 1; **17:** 17, 61, 364 n. 11; **18:** 213 n. 9, 364; **19:** 96, 235–36, 279

Alexander, Sidney S., **16:** 115 n. 5, 290 n. 6; **17:** 371 n. 19, 376 n. 24, 404 n. 2

Allais, Maurice, **15:** 473 n. 2; **19:** 42, 52, 118

Allen, Edward D., **1:** 123 n. 4, 126 n. 15, **2:** 12, 28

Allen, Peter M., **18:** 291–92, 294 n. 21

Allen, W. R., **12:** 7 n. 4, 129, 310 n. 7

Althusius, J., **1:** 389; **3:** 248, 317; **7:** 187

Amacher, Ryan, **12:** 104 n. 9

Ames, B., **11:** 87 n. 9

Ammon, Alfred, **1:** 30

Anderson, Joseph M., **15:** 377 n. 1

Anderson, Martin, **8:** 165 n. 10

Anderson, Philip W., **18:** 289 n. 3

Anderson, Robert, **8:** 46

Andrews, W. D., **9:** 69 n. 1, 111, 241

Aranson, Peter, **16:** 132 n. 7; **18:** 102 n. 4

Ardrey, Robert, **1:** 343 n. 5

Arena, Celestino, **19:** 33

Arendt, Hannah, **3:** 112 n. 4

Aristotle, **7:** 49 n. 4, 229; **15:** 306; **17:** 116; **19:** 251, 360

Armey, Dick, **11:** 129

Aron, Raymond, **7:** 229

Arrow, Kenneth J.: **1:** xvi, 16, 53–54, 77 nn. 2,5, 79 n. 11, 86 n. 24, 89–102, 256; **3:** 8, 32 n. 1, 337–42; **4:** 122 n. 5; **5:** 118, 119, 191; **7:** 182 n. 10, 217 n. 5, 229; **8:** 101 n. 7; **9:** 7 n. 3, 241; **10:** 85; **11:** 27 n. 4, 28; **12:** 143 n. 3; **13:** 7–8, 43–47, 228 n. 3; **14:** 11–12; **15:** 288 n. 13; **16:** 50, 68–70, 81, 84–85, 90, 201–2, 205 n. 6, 239, 320 n. 4; **17:** xvii, 58, 129, 240, 336 n. 10; **18:** 268 n. 3, 289 n. 3; **19:** 9, 25, 36, 53

Arthur, W. Brian, **12:** 388, 393–95; **18:** 289 n. 3, 296 n. 31

Ash, Timothy Garton, **19:** 240n. 1
Asimakopulos, A., **1:** 94n. 13; **15:** 407n. 1
Atkinson, A. B., **9:** 174n. 6, 241
Augustine, Saint, **16:** 398
Aumann, Robert J., **12:** 145n. 4
Auspitz, Josiah Lee, **17:** 426n. 13
Auster, Richard D., **9:** 241
Averch, H., **13:** 317
Avineri, Shlomo, **7:** 27n. 3, 229; **13:** 172n. 7
Axelrod, Robert, **17:** 229n. 8, 442n. 7
Ayres, Clarence E., **19:** xv, 8, 123–34

Babbit, Irving, **1:** 35
Badger, W. W., **13:** 200n. 4
Bagehot, Walter, **8:** 120n. 5
Bailey, Martin J., **1:** 173; **8:** 63n. 8, 147n. 17; **9:** 150, 151, 152, 154, 157, 241; **12:** 68n. 3, 245–47, 249–52, 257n. 10; **14:** 413n. 6; **19:** 324
Bailey, Stephen K., **8:** 31n. 6
Bain, Joe, **12:** 191n. 1, 195n. 5, 204n. 20
Bakke, Allen, **17:** 347
Banfield, Edward C., **1:** 321n. 6, 344n. 6; **4:** 197–98
Baratz, Morton A., **4:** 273n. 3
Barber, Clarence, **4:** 273n. 4
Barbosa, António S. Pinto, **9:** 228n. 6, 241; **10:** 155n. 3; **15:** xviin. 9; **16:** 409n. 7
Barlow, Robin, **9:** 73n. 5, 241
Barna, Tibor, **1:** 127n. 17, 131n. 28
Barone, Enrico, **4:** 243; **5:** 181; **14:** 7, 101n. 1, 102, 103; **15:** 59n. 1, 68, 70, 71, 79–80, 97, 99, 100, 101, 105; **19:** 32
Barr, James L., **4:** 200–201
Barro, Robert J., **1:** 173; **7:** 198n. 10, 229; **2:** xiii; **8:** 112n. 1, 140n. 13; **11:** 134; **13:** 480n. 11; **14:** xv, 385–90, 392nn. 1,2, 394–95, 403, 406, 408–11, 413–16, 426, 436n. 8, 475–77, 478, 479–80, 483; **15:** 394n. 4, 444n. 5, 446; **17:** 148
Barry, Norman, **1:** 244; **18:** 305–6; **19:** 350n. 5

Bartlett, Randall, **8:** 135n. 7; **13:** 49; **14:** 16n. 23
Bartley, William, **19:** 121
Barzel, Yoram, **13:** 450n; **15:** 322; **17:** 288n. 5
Baskin, Carlisle W., **18:** 28n. 10
Bastable, C. F., **1:** 126n. 13; **2:** 15n. 14, 82–84; **8:** 11; **14:** 72n. 5
Bates, Robert H., **13:** 390n. 1
Bator, Francis, **1:** 62; **15:** xii
Batson, Gladys, **3:** xix
Battalio, Raymond C., **13:** 82n. 6; **17:** 27, 37
Bauer, Peter T., **15:** 428n. 1; **19:** 120
Baumol, William J., **1:** 62, 79n. 12, 91n. 4, 198n. 7; **3:** 43n. 1, 321, 322; **5:** 28, 141, 191; **7:** 52n. 8, 229; **8:** 34n. 9; **9:** 70, 241; **10:** 164; **12:** 385–87; **13:** 421n. 5; **15:** 175n. 2, 239n. 12; **17:** 129; **18:** 289n. 3, 420n. 29
Bayley, John, **17:** 80
Beard, Charles, **3:** 14n. 3, 25
Beavis, D., **18:** 212n. 8
Beck, Lewis White, **1:** 312
Beck, N., **13:** 160n. 6
Becker, Carl L., **7:** 229
Becker, Gary S., **1:** 249; **6:** 85; **7:** 180n. 8, 229; **10:** 57n. 6, 68, 77, 79n. 3; **11:** 124n. 12; **12:** 219–20; **13:** 270, 408n. 14; **14:** 246n. 17, 314n. 12, 458n. 3; **15:** 277n. 8, 466; **16:** 158, 209n. 11; **17:** 59n. 2, 61; **18:** 327; **19:** 60, 96, 102
Bélanger, Gérard, **9:** 162n. 3, 244
Bell, Daniel, **7:** 229
Benhabib, Stephen, **18:** 289n. 3
Benham, Frederick C., **15:** 60; **18:** 10n. 18
Benit, Emile, **14:** 359n. 6
Benn, S. I., **7:** 70n. 2, 229
Benson, G. C. S., **18:** 3n. 1
Bentham, Jeremy, **1:** 257, 298, 309, 389; **19:** 224, 256
Bentley, Arthur, **3:** 10, 11n. 1, 19n. 2, 22n. 9, 123n. 4, 283; **16:** 70
Berardi, S. J., **11:** 87n. 9
Berglas, Eitan, **18:** 148n. 2

Bergson, Abram, **1:** 193, 197, 202; **9:** 17, 241; **16:** 80, 83

Bergstrom, Theodore C., **14:** 7 n. 7

Berkeley, George, **2:** 15

Berlin, Isaiah, **3:** 4, 12 n. 2, 308 n. 2; **16:** 387 n. 6; **17:** 24

Bernholz, Peter, **7:** 229; **16:** 202, 207 n. 9, 330–35, 409, 417, 424–25; **17:** 72 n. 1, 74–75, 78; **18:** 99, 101, 111

Berry, Brian J. L., **18:** 28 n. 10

Besson, J. F., **5:** 94

Bhagwati, Jagdish N., **11:** 107 n. 2; **15:** 161 n. 6, 162 n. 7

Bickel, Alexander, **16:** 111 n. 1, 114, 118

Billings, Josh, **19:** 81

Binmore, Ken, **12:** 39 n. 4; **16:** 206 n. 8; **17:** 94 n. 13

Birdsall, William C., **4:** 205

Bishop, R. L., **16:** 298 n. 15

Black, Duncan, **1:** 50 n. 5, 53, 54; **3:** 132, 331–33, 335 n. 9, 336–38, 341 n. 19, 343; **4:** 146 n. 1; **5:** 117–18, 119, 191; **7:** 182 n. 10, 217 n. 5, 230; **11:** 28; **13:** 7, 9–10, 39, 41–44, 46–47, 58, 179, 182, 227, 228 nn. 2,3, 229 n. 4; **14:** 11–12, 26–27, 75 n. 11; **15:** 360; **16:** 50, 68–70, 320 n. 4; **19:** 42, 52, 118

Blackstone, William, **7:** 28 n. 5

Bloom, Allan, **1:** 444

Blum, Walter J., **15:** 79 n. 17

Bodin, Jean, **7:** 33 n. 10

Bohm, Peter, **15:** 188 n. 5

Böhm-Bawerk, Eugen v., **6:** 11; **16:** 86

Boiteux, M., **12:** 298–99, 302 n. 9, 307

Borcherding, Thomas E., **7:** 203 n. 12, 230; **8:** 73 n. 26; **12:** 265 n. 4; **15:** 440 n. 1

Borda, J. C. de, **3:** 331; **14:** 12

Borgatta, Gino, **4:** 3 n. 1; **15:** 69–70, 73, 97, 101, 102 n. 49, 105

Boskin, Michael J., **15:** 378 n. 2, 450 n. 7

Boss, Helen, **1:** 347 n. 1; **12:** 391

Boswell, James, **18:** 246 n. 4

Bosworth, Barry P., **8:** 87 n. 7; **15:** 377 n. 1

Boulding, Kenneth E., **1:** 30 n. 2, 36 n. 6; **4:** 59 n. 1; **8:** 56–57; **12:** 63–65, 67 n. 1, 191 n. 1, 195 n. 5, 255 n. 6; **13:** 34; **15:** 156 n. 1; **18:** 306

Bowen, Howard R., **1:** 83 n. 20; **4:** ix; **5:** xiii, 45, 140, 182, 191; **13:** 155 n. 2; **14:** 8, 11; **15:** 104 n. 51

Bowen, William G., **1:** 162, 163

Bower, Blair T., **13:** 421 n. 3

Bowley, Arthur L., **16:** 86

Bowman, R. T., **15:** 40, 48

Bowman, Ward S., Jr., **4:** 73 n. 3; **14:** 74 n. 10

Bradford, David F., **9:** 70, 241; **14:** 152 n. 2; **15:** 271, 280 n. 11

Brandis, Royall, **6:** 8 n. 2

Brasca, Cesare, **2:** 22 n. 6, 89 n. 20

Break, George F., **4:** 244; **14:** 71, 103, 285 n. 2

Breit, William H., **1:** 165 n. 2; **6:** xvii; **7:** 145 n. 7, 230; **8:** 11 n. 2, 23 n. 15; **19:** 41, 43

Brennan, Geoffrey, **1:** xvi n. 7, xvii n. 9, xviii n. 11, 6, 22, 25, 392 n. 9; **4:** xi; **7:** 104 n. 3, 230; **9:** xv n. 3, xvi n. 4, 70 nn. 3,4, 101 n. 2, 234 n. 7, 241; **10:** xi n. 1, xx n. 1, 23 n. 1, 53 n. 1, 54 n. 2, 62 n. 8, 95 n. 2, 132 n. 5, 136 nn. 9,10, 137 n. 11; **11:** 64, 118 n. 6, 124 n. 12; **12:** 85 n. 12, 105 n. 10, 271 n. 6; **13:** xii, 53, 80 n. 5, 165 n. 9, 213 n. 1, 273 n. 11, 294, 366 n. 12, 371 n. 18; **14:** xii nn. 2,3, xiv nn. 8,9, xv n. 11, 47 n. 1, 51 n. 3, 67, 98 n. 7, 188 n. 13, 194 n. 18, 204 n. 4, 208 n. 5, 209, 212 n. 1, 214 n. 3, 229–32, 246 n. 18, 247 n. 19, 263 nn. 9,10, 279 n. 5, 287 n. 5, 308 n. 5, 314 n. 11, 325 n. 3, 328 n. 8, 331 n. 9, 337 n. 12, 426 n. 23, 440 n. 13; **15:** xviii n. 11, 392 n. 2, 435 n. 1, 439 n. 4; **16:** xi n. 1, 12 n. 6, 52 n. 3, 162 n. 8, 189 n. 5, 251 n. 15, 278, 311, 322, 368 nn. 8,10; **17:** xviii n. 16, 50 n. 5, 62 n. 7, 68 n. 10, 147, 154 n. 2, 163 n. 8, 267 n. 1, 279 n. 3; **18:** 70 n. 3, 84 n.

Brennan, Geoffrey (*continued*)
  3, 111n. 7, 192n. 4, 288n. 9; **19:** 51, 59, 61,
  62, 100n. 7, 283n. 7, 312n. 5, 334n. 1,
  336n. 2
Brennan, William, **17:** 348
Breton, Albert, **5:** 72, 94, 141, 178; **9:** 204n.
  4, 242; **13:** 49; **14:** 16n. 23; **15:** 265–70,
  280; **18:** 27n. 8; **19:** 98
Bridgeman, P. W., **3:** 143n. 11
Briefs, Goetz, **3:** 287n. 4
Brittan, Samuel, **7:** 230
Brock, William A. **11:** 107n. 2; **14:** 320n. 17;
  16: 441n. 5; **18:** 23n. 1; **19:** 278n. 2
Bronfenbrenner, Martin, **12:** 200n. 16,
  265n. 3
Broome, John, **12:** 278–81
Brown, E. C., **8:** 39n. 1, 86n. 7
Brown, Jerry, **11:** 129
Brown, Robert E., **3:** 14n. 3, 26
Browning, Edgar K., **11:** 168n. 6; **15:** 395n. 6
Brownlee, O. H., **1:** 123n. 4, 126n. 15; **2:**
  12, 28
Brozen, Yale, **12:** 302n. 9, 307
Brunner, Karl, **8:** 97n. 1; **12:** 30–31, 42
Buchanan, Allen, **18:** 71n. 4, 104n. 5
Buchanan, James McGill
  autobiographical essays, **1:** xiii, xv, 11–27
  co-founder of Center for Study of
    Public Choice, **1:** 7, 26
  co-founder of Thomas Jefferson Center
    for Studies in Political Economy, **1:**
    7, 26
  collaborative works, **1:** xxii–xxiii
  collected works, **1:** xi–xiv
  early career, **1:** 7, 16–26
  early politics, **1:** 14–17
  education, **1:** 7, 12–17
  Fulbright scholar, **1:** 17
  military service, **1:** 13–14
  Nobel Memorial Prize, **1:** xiv, 3–7,
    455–68
Buchanan, James McGill, Sr. (father), **1:**
  11–12

Buchanan, John P. (grandfather), **1:** 11
Buchanan, Lila Scott (mother), **1:** 12
Buckley, James L., **18:** 427
Buiter, William, **14:** 392n. 1, 417n. 15,
  424n. 20
Burke, E., **3:** 318
Burkhead, Jesse, **8:** 11n. 5, 163n. 8; **14:** 71
Burns, Arthur, **9:** 159n. 18; **18:** 425n. 32,
  431n. 37
Burstein, Meyer L., **4:** 73n. 3, 82n. 7; **14:**
  74n. 10, 83n. 15
Burtless, Gary T., **15:** 377n. 1
Burton, John, **13:** 40n. 1, 53
Bury, J. B., **1:** 254
Bush, Winston C., **1:** 22, 434n. 3, 436, 439;
  7: 32n. 9, 75, 231; **13:** 141n. 13; **16:** 92n. 3,
  94, 277n. 1; **17:** 303n. 7, 362n. 9, 371n. 19;
  18: 219n. 2, 434n. 3; **19:** xv, 51, 58–59,
  108–9
Butler, Samuel, **18:** 432

Cagan, Phillip, **8:** 62; **9:** 150, 242
Cairns, John Elliott, **1:** 295
Calabresi, Guido, **12:** 170–71, 175, 280; **13:**
  301n. 2, 313n. 12; **18:** 371n. 5
Campbell, Colin D., **13:** 211n. 12; **15:** xviin.
  10, 390n. 1, 407n. 2, 408, 418, 443n. 4
Cannan, Edwin, **6:** 26; **12:** 58n. 6; **19:** 145
Canterbery, E. Ray, **8:** 122n. 7
Cardozo, Benjamin, **17:** 116
Carens, Joseph H., **19:** 236n. 11
Carlson, Keith M., **8:** 69n. 20, 158n. 4
Carlyle, Thomas, **19:** 70, 71n. 5
Carritt, E. F., **1:** 85n. 21
Carroll, Lewis, **1:** 53; **3:** 332, 333n. 7; **13:** 7,
  42; **14:** 12
Carron, Andrew S., **8:** 87n. 7
Carter, Jimmy, **16:** 313–14, 328
Casas Pardo, José, **13:** 90n, 240n. 2
Casinelli, C. W., **3:** 19n. 3
Cassell, Gustav, **18:** 398n. 6
Casson, Mark, **12:** 111n. 2
Chalmers, George, **2:** 81

Chamberlain, Wilt, **17**: xx, 418–22
Chamberlin, Edward H., **6**: 28; **13**: 230n. 6; **16**: 79
Chammah, Albert M., **15**: 227n. 2, 228n. 3
Chant, John F., **8**: 122n. 8
Chapman, Bruce, **15**: 435n. 1
Charnovitz, Diane Windy, **7**: 8n. 1, 231
Cheung, S., **7**: 29, 231
Chickering, Lawrence, **8**: 93n. 12
Chipman, John S., **15**: 167n. 16
Christ, Carl, **17**: 146–48
Christaller, Walter, **18**: 28
Chrysippus, **16**: 384
Churchill, Winston, **17**: 118, 119
Cisneros, Henry, **18**: 144n. 15
Clague, Christopher, **18**: 343n. 3
Clark, Colin, **8**: 71
Clark, Jane P., **18**: 3n. 1
Clarke, Edward H., **15**: 188n. 5
Clinton, William J., **19**: 217, 220
Coase, Ronald H., **1**: 20, 60n. 1, 221, 223n. 7, 261, 262–64, 267, 276; **3**: 54n. 6, 91n. 2; **5**: 72, 177; **6**: xi, xv, xvii, 26–29, 34, 65n. 2, 87; **11**: 85; **12**: 68n. 3, 169–70, 293–95, 335, 336; **13**: 117, 133n. 5, 260, 297–302, 311–12, 357–60, 363, 367n. 14, 386n. 5, 413n. 1, 430n. 9; **14**: 122n. 1; **15**: 122n. 10, 124–25, 132n. 6, 169, 173, 174n. 1, 176, 201n. 8, 218n. 10, 257n. 9, 291n. 16, 308–9, 311, 312; **17**: 17, 114; **18**: 327, 347n. 9, 363, 370, 376; **19**: 41, 43, 54, 112, 120, 136, 145–47
Cohen, Linda, **14**: 331n. 10
Cohen Stuart, Arnold J., **15**: 79
Cohn, Gustav, **2**: 16n. 21
Coleman, James S., **4**: 122n. 5; **13**: 214n. 2; **14**: 431n. 3; **18**: 185
Coleman, Jules L., **10**: 28–29; **11**: 5n. 1; **16**: 166n. 20
Colm, G., **5**: 72
Commons, John R., **5**: 160; **13**: 5–6; **15**: 61; **19**: 8

Condorcet, Marquis de (Marie-Jean Caritat), **1**: 53; **2**: 15, 84; **3**: 331; **13**: 42; **14**: 12
Congleton, Roger D., **1**: xxi, 420; **11**: 46n. 3, 86n. 5, 87n. 8, 169n. 7, 186n. 3, 189n. 2; **12**: 345n. 2, 435n. 1, 440n. 5; **14**: xivn. 8; **17**: xi, xiin. 3, 83n. 2
Conigliani, C. A., **15**: 97, 98
Conrad, Joseph, **17**: 126
Constant, Benjamin, **3**: 256n. 2
Cooper, John R., **4**: 206–7
Cooter, Robert, **1**: 261, 263, 265, 272; **15**: 437n. 2; **16**: 287; **17**: 360n, 361, 372
Corlett, W., **9**: 70, 242
Cornes, R., **11**: 82n. 1, 152n. 6; **13**: 361n. 8
Cosciani, Cesare, **15**: 70, 71, 74, 97, 100; **19**: 32, 33
Coultrap, Will, **18**: 419n. 27
Cowling, Keith, **9**: 242; **12**: 95n. 4
Crain, Mark, **13**: 51, 261n. 3
Crecine, John P., **7**: 230
Cropper, M. L., **11**: 87n. 9
Culyer, A. J., **1**: 265n. 11

Dahl, Robert A., **1**: 76n. 1, 78n. 7, 80n. 14, 83n. 20, 85n. 23, 88n. 27, 96nn. 16,18, 368; **3**: 8–9, 21n. 8, 24, 32n. 2, 155n. 7; **5**: 141; **7**: 220n. 7, 231
Dales, John, **13**: 260
Dalton, Hugh, **1**: 120n. 1; **8**: 10, 153; **13**: 44
Dam, Kenneth W., **9**: 185n. 1, 242
Danzon, Patricia M., **11**: 34n. 10, 163n. 4; **12**: 443n. 8; **13**: 109n. 7; **14**: 96n. 5, 324n. 1; **18**: 285n. 5; **19**: 348n. 4
Darby, Michael R., **8**: 29n. 5
Darden, Colgate, **19**: 39
Davenport, Herbert J., **6**: xv, 18–19, 21, 61n; **12**: 337
David, Elizabeth, **4**: 196
Davies, David G., **8**: 73n. 26
Davis, J. Ronnie, **8**: 39n. 3
Davis, Lance E., **8**: 14n. 10

Davis, Otto A., **1:** 223n. 7, 324n. 7; **3:** xix,
6n. 3, 57n. 8; **4:** 113n. 1, 122n. 5, 199–201;
5: 72, 73, 94, 118, 177, 192; **6:** 65n. 2; **9:**
243; **13:** 420n. 2; **14:** 123n. 3; **15:** 125n.
15,127n. 1, 166n. 13, 169, 237n. 10, 250;
19: 42
Davis, Richard G., **1:** 162, 163
Dawson, John P., **18:** 400n. 8, 419n. 27
De Alessi, L., **13:** 318n. 2
Debreu, Gerard, **14:** 327n. 5
de Finetti, Bruno, **12:** 149n. 7
Defoe, Daniel, **17:** 42
de Gaulle, Charles, **17:** 131
de Jasay, Anthony, **9:** xvii; **11:** 205; **12:** 445;
16: 273, 441n. 4; **18:** 101, 127; **19:** 63, 204,
273n. 7, 312n. 4, 344–45
de Jouvenel, Bertrand, **17:** 119
Delors, Jacques, **18:** 76, 139; **19:** 207
del Vecchio, Gustavo, **2:** 21n. 3; **15:** 73n. 11,
103, 105; **19:** 36
de Maria, G., **19:** 33
Demetriou, P. A., **6:** 92n. 6; **13:** 231n. 8
Demsetz, Harold, **6:** 87; **7:** 29–30, 34n. 12,
231; **11:** 83n. 2; **12:** 263; **13:** 48, 312n. 11,
358n. 1; **14:** 16n. 21; **17:** 364n. 11; **18:**
318n. 8
Denzau, Arthur T., **9:** 30n. 18, 243
de Ruggiero, Guido, **7:** 235
Descartes, René, **19:** xi, xii
Deutsch, Karl, **3:** 149n. 1
de Viti de Marco, Antonio, **1:** 16, 120n. 1,
124–25, 126, 127n. 16, 163; **2:** 16n. 24,
89–94; **4:** 128, 260n. 2; **5:** xiii, 156–58,
160, 181; **6:** 53; **9:** 19n. 1, 243; **13:** 22, 27,
47; **14:** 6, 7, 26, 385n. 1, 411n. 5; **15:** 59,
64–66, 69, 70, 73–78, 84, 85–92, 97–98,
100, 105; **18:** 122; **19:** 29, 30, 32
Devletoglou, Nicos E., **1:** xiii; **6:** 92n. 6; **7:**
231; **13:** 231n. 8, 233, 235; **15:** 428n. 1; **16:**
392n. 11; **19:** 58n. 6
Dewey, Donald, **1:** 221n. 6; **19:** 80
Dewey, John, **3:** 19n. 4; **7:** 214; **19:** 92

Dick, A. R., **13:** 284n. 2
Dickenson, John, **18:** 400n. 8
Dickinson, Henry, **12:** 26
Dickman, Howard, **16:** 28n.
Dietzel, **2:** 16
di Pierro, Alberto, **7:** 193n. 3, 231; **19:** 236
Director, Aaron, **13:** 151; **18:** 327; **19:** 40, 105
Dixit, Avinash, **12:** 395
Dobb, M., **17:** 298n. 1
Dodgson, C. L. *See* Carroll, Lewis
Domar, Evsey D., **2:** 139, 142; **4:** 49; **6:**
91–92
Dorfman, R., **5:** 141
Dorman, Neil A., **5:** 94; **17:** 142–45
Dosser, Douglas, **5:** 73; **15:** 40n. 3, 223n. 16
Downs, Anthony, **1:** 50n. 5; **3:** 9, 120n. 1,
132, 222n. 5, 257n. 3, 343–47; **4:** 121n. 4;
5: 192; **7:** 217nn. 5,6, 231; **8:** 100n. 5, 137n.
9; **9:** 24, 25n. 12, 26, 28, 38, 243; **12:** 104n.
9, 435n. 1; **13:** 11–12, 28n. 2, 47, 170, 213,
227, 228n. 2, 234n. 11, 394n. 4; **14:** 15; **15:**
67n. 8, 360; **16:** 68–70, 185; **17:** 62n. 6;
19: 98, 99, 100
Drazen, Allan, **14:** 415n. 10, 416n. 13,
423n. 18
Drury, Allen, **3:** 123n. 3
Dry, Murray, **18:** xivn. 4
Ducla-Soares, M. M., **11:** 87n. 9
Due, John, **14:** 135–36, 147n. 6
Duesenberry, James S., **8:** 87n. 7
Duguit, Leon, **3:** 318
Dunne, Gerald T., **18:** 401n. 10
Duren, William, **19:** 39, 51
Durkheim, Émile, **16:** 397

Easterbrook, Frank H., **13:** 272n. 9
Easterlin, R. A., **15:** 40, 48
Edgeworth, Francis Ysidro, **1:** 121; **4:** 137; **5:**
16, 77, 181; **15:** 79, 80; **16:** 86; **19:** 29
Edwards, R. S., **6:** 27n. 22
Einaudi, Luigi, **1:** 133, 425; **2:** 89n. 20; **4:**
214, 223, 252n. 9; **5:** 157, 181; **13:** 27; **14:** 8,

112n. 13, 125; **15:** 64n. 5, 65n. 7, 68, 70, 73–75, 78–84, 92, 97–98, 100, 105; **19:** 32, 35–36

Eisenhower, Dwight D., **16:** 347; **19:** 45

Ekelund, Robert B., Jr., **13:** 261n. 3; **16:** 437n. 5

Elazar, Daniel J., **16:** 145n. 25

Ellickson, Bryan, **15:** 280; **18:** 44n. 2

Elliott, James R., **1:** 163

Ellis, Howard S., **1:** 31n. 4; **12:** 311n. 3; **13:** 329n. 8; **15:** 156n. 1, 170

Ellsberg, Daniel, **3:** 141n. 9

Elster, Jon, **1:** 380n. 3; **10:** 82; **11:** 138n. 3; **16:** 403n. 4; **17:** 65, 86n. 7

Eltis, Walter, **12:** 387n. 6

Ely, Richard T., **7:** 231

Enrick, Norbert, **4:** 183–85, 189

Epple, Dennis, **9:** 202n. 2, 243

Epstein, Richard A., **16:** 66

Erhard, Ludwig, **1:** 184

Escarraz, D. R., **5:** 94

Ethier, Wilfred J., **1:** 359; **12:** 365n. 17, 379n. 2, 394–95

Evans, W. N., **11:** 87n. 9

Fairfield, Roy P., **16:** 441n. 6

Faith, Roger L., **1:** 262n. 7; **10:** 36n. 7; **12:** 172n. 8, 183n. 21; **13:** 211n. 13, 215n. 4; **14:** 241n. 15, 255n. 4; **17:** 449n. 11; **18:** xivn. 6, 71n. 4, 103n. 5, 152n. 5, 157n. 7, 161n. 10

Fand, David I., **8:** 75n. 30, 115n. 3

Farr, Helen T., **4:** 273n. 3

Farrell, Michael J., **4:** 246n. 5; **14:** 105n. 7; **19:** 112

Fasiani, Mauro, **4:** 127–28, 130n. 8, 136; **5:** 181; **9:** 19n. 1, 243; **13:** 27, 47; **15:** 70, 71, 74, 75, 84, 92, 96, 101, 102n. 49, 105; **19:** 32

Fehl, Ulrich, **18:** 293n. 17

Feldstein, Martin S., **2:** xiii; **6:** 60n. 6; **8:** 169n. 3; **9:** 111; **14:** 22n. 29, 285n. 3, 302,

390, 392n. 2, 394, 406; **15:** 421–24, 445–46, 448, 451n. 8, 453; **18:** 52n. 10

Feller, William, **13:** 208n. 10

Fellner, William, **12:** 200n. 16, 311n. 3; **13:** 329n. 8; **15:** 156n. 1, 170

Ferber, Robert, **4:** 187–88

Ferguson, Adam, **19:** 289

Ferguson, James M., **1:** 159n. 10; **2:** xiv; **4:** 99n. 1; **6:** 59n. 5, 60n. 6; **8:** 36n. 11, 143n. 14; **14:** 426n. 23, 429n. 1

Ferrara, Francesco, **4:** 128; **5:** 157, 181; **12:** 337; **15:** 60, 62–65, 69, 70, 72, 75, 104, 105; **19:** 32

Ferry, W. H., **13:** 70

Fiorina, Morris P., **13:** 403n. 10

Fisher, Herbert W., **9:** 69n. 1, 243

Fisher, Irving, **4:** 252n. 9; **8:** 88n. 9; **9:** 69n. 1, 111, 243; **14:** 112n. 13; **15:** 83; **16:** 343; **18:** 410n. 17

Fishkin, James S., **12:** 185; **16:** 156, 165n. 16, 166n. 18

Flatters, F., **18:** 148n. 2

Fleming, Macklin, **18:** 431n. 41

Flemming, John, **8:** 172n. 6

Flowers, Marilyn R., **7:** 153n. 12, 231; **11:** 34n. 10, 163n. 4; **12:** 443n. 8; **13:** 109n. 7; **14:** 96n. 5, 324n. 1; **18:** 135n. 3, 285n. 5; **19:** 348n. 4

Foldes, Lucien, **15:** 427–31, 433

Foley, Duncan, **14:** 7n. 7; **15:** 280–81

Foley, Thomas, **13:** 295

Forbes, Jack, **4:** 208–10

Forbes, Steve, **11:** 129

Ford, Gerald R., **18:** 425

Forte, Carmen, **19:** 35

Forte, Francesco, **4:** 139n. 10, 243n; **6:** xvii; **14:** xivn. 7; **15:** xv; **18:** 30n. 13, 38n. 23; **19:** 34–35

Foster, John, **10:** 54n. 3; **13:** 80n. 2; **16:** 365n. 6

Fouillée, A., **3:** 317

Fouraker, Lawrence E., **3:** 105n. 1

Fowler, R. F., **6:** 27n. 22

Frankel, Charles, **4:** 170n. 1

Frankel, S. H., **6:** xvii, 49n. 1

Frankfurter, Felix, **16:** 309; **18:** 402

Franklin, Benjamin, **10:** xv

Frech, H. E., III, **12:** 170n. 3, 174n. 9

Frey, Bruno, **13:** 52; **16:** 8n. 1

Friedland, Claire, **13:** 318n. 2

Friedman, David, **7:** 231; **9:** 202n. 2, 243; **12:** 75n. 6; **15:** 284n. 2; **16:** 16n. 1, 22n. 4; **17:** 433

Friedman, Milton, **1:** 31, 191, 225n. 9; **2:** 20n. 1; **4:** 110, 244; **8:** 3, 43, 91n. 11, 109n. 16, 127n. 11, 147n. 17, 161n. 7, 174n. 9, 179n. 12; **9:** 142n. 7, 150n. 12, 154, 155, 157, 243; **12:** 28, 54–55, 198–99, 200–203, 245, 265n. 6; **13:** 57, 59, 61; **14:** 103, 509–10; **15:** 432; **16:** 238–39; **17:** 300n. 3; **18:** 395n. 4, 408n. 16, 415n. 23; **19:** 10, 13, 119, 324, 342

Frisch, Ragnar, **1:** 210, 211–12, 216n. 3, 218; **2:** 21n. 5; **5:** 118; **10:** 151n. 2; **12:** 31; **13:** 135n. 8, 229n. 4, 240n. 3; **15:** 221n. 15; **16:** 81

Frost, Robert, **3:** xv; **19:** 159

Frowen, Stephen F., **19:** 153

Frye, E. B., **18:** 137n. 7

Fubini, R., **15:** 72, 104; **19:** 33

Fukuyama, Francis, **11:** 208n. 4; **12:** 43; **16:** 267, 435n. 4, 440; **19:** 187, 199–201, 208, 219n. 7, 263, 264, 267, 269, 271, 274, 295, 303

Fullerton, D., **13:** 467n. 1, 479

Furubotn, Eirik G., **7:** 29, 231, 232; **14:** 16n. 21; **16:** 8n. 1

Gabor, André A., **5:** 47; **12:** 304n. 12, 310n. 6

Galbraith, John K., **5:** 137; **12:** 104n. 9

Galton, Francis, **3:** 332

Gangemi, Lello, **15:** 105; **19:** 30, 34

Garvey, Gerald, **13:** 234n. 11

Garvy, George, **8:** 81n. 3

Gauthier, David, **1:** 350; **12:** 346, 438–39; **16:** 134n. 9, 156, 161n. 7, 164n. 13, 165n. 16; **17:** xxin. 19, 222n. 5, 230, 437–44, 446–57, 461–64, 467–68

Gellner, Ernest, **17:** 103n. 5

Gensemer, Bruce L., **4:** 186n. 6

Gerelli, Emilio, **18:** 40n. 27

Germino, Dante, **13:** 172n. 7

Gibson, W. L., Jr., **7:** 236

Gillespie, W. Irwin, **4:** 198–99

Gintis, Herbert M., **12:** 26

Girard, Marcel, **14:** 72n. 5

Glahe, Fred, **19:** 49

Glass, Carter, **16:** 343

Gobbi, U., **15:** 81, 101

Godwin, William, **7:** 220

Goetz, Charles J., **1:** 26; **4:** 38n. 3, 127n. 7, 217n. 1; **5:** 140; **6:** 52n. 3; **8:** 148n. 18; **12:** 401n. 5; **13:** 36, 272n. 10, 419n. 1; **14:** 15n. 17, 239n. 13; **15:** xv, xvin. 6, xviii, 477n. 4; **18:** 45n. 3, 59n. 18, 62n. 20, 148n. 2; **19:** 42, 51, 57

Gold, L. S., **11:** 87n. 9

Goldberg, Victor, **14:** 480–81

Goldfarb, R. S., **13:** 130n. 3

Goldin, Kenneth, **12:** 179n. 20

Goldsborough, Thomas A., **16:** 343–44

Goldwater, Barry, **15:** 454

Gombrich, E. H., **4:** 127n. 3

Gonce, R. A., **12:** 111n. 2

Good, I. J., **13:** 179n. 1

Goode, Richard, **14:** 134n. 1, 147n. 6

Goodell, Charles, **18:** 23n. 1

Goodman, Leo, **1:** 94n. 13

Gordon, David B., **13:** 480n. 11; **17:** 148

Gordon, Donald F., **8:** 88n. 9; **14:** 477, 480, 481–84

Gordon, H. Scott, **12:** 317n. 7, 323; **13:** 57, 59–60, 80n. 3; **17:** 404n. 1, 410n. 5

Gordon, Kermit, **19:** 40

Gough, J. W., **3:** 317n. 9; **7:** 232

Graaff, J. de V., **1:** 61n. 2, 193; **5:** 192; **15:** 109n. 2

Graham, Frank D., **1:** 125n. 9

Gramlich, Edward M., **8:** 58n. 2

Gray, John, **1:** 453n. 2; **16:** 28n. 1; **17:** 120; **18:** 200n. 2, 207n. 5; **19:** 151n. 15

Green, Leonard, **13:** 82n. 6

Greene, Kenneth V., **8:** 144n. 15

Greenspan, Alan, **16:** 56, 310

Greenwood, Gordon, **18:** 6n. 6

Greenwood, Peter, **12:** 174n. 10

Griffin, C. W., **1:** 254

Griziotti, Benvenuto, **2:** 16, 89–94; **8:** 140n. 12; **15:** 61, 82, 89–90, 92n. 35, 105; **19:** 33, 34

Grofman, B., **13:** 209n. 11

Grossman, Herschel, **8:** 82–83

Grotius, Hugo, **7:** 32n. 9, 33n. 10, 77n. 7

Groves, Harold M., **2:** 11, 68; **13:** 44; **14:** 72n. 5

Guerin, Daniel, **7:** 24n. 1, 232

Guidi, Laura, **19:** 31, 33

Gurley, Jack, **19:** 43

Haavelmo, Trygve, **1:** 79n. 12

Haberler, Gottfried, **8:** 40n. 4, 71n. 22, 74n. 28, 177n. 10; **15:** 161n. 6

Habermas, Jürgen, **11:** 5; **16:** 156, 165n. 16, 166n. 19, 167

Hacker, Andrew, **7:** 147n. 8, 232

Hague, D., **9:** 70, 242

Hahn, Frank H., **14:** 109n. 9

Hahn, T. Marshall, **19:** 44

Haig, R. M., **9:** xiii

Hailsham, Lord, **9:** 8n. 4, 243

Hall, Challis A., **12:** 61n. 9

Hall, John C., **7:** 86n. 15, 118n. 2, 232

Hall, Robert E., **11:** 128–29; **14:** 317

Hallet, George H., **3:** 332

Hamilton, Alexander, **3:** 274n. 4; **16:** 42–43

Hamilton, Earl J., **1:** 16–17; **19:** 12, 30

Hamlin, Alan, **19:** 114

Hammond, Peter, **16:** 281n. 6

Hansen, Alvin H., **2:** 10, 11, 12n. 7, 38n. 1; **4:** 273n. 3; **8:** 35n. 10

Hansen, Bent, **9:** 17, 243

Harberger, Arnold C., **9:** 70, 76n. 7, 96, 98, 243; **10:** 66n. 9; **12:** 95n. 4, 96, 212n. 4; **13:** 251

Hardin, Russell, **16:** 28, 31; **17:** 439n. 4

Hardy, C. O., **1:** 169, 410, 411n. 4; **3:** 143n. 13

Hardy, Thomas, **7:** 4; **19:** 11, 84

Hargreaves, E. L., **2:** 15n. 16

Harris, C. J., **1:** 129n. 23

Harris, Ralph, **4:** 193n. 11

Harris, Seymour E., **2:** 3, 11; **15:** 257n. 11, 345n. 8

Harrison, William Henry, **8:** 14

Harriss, C. Lowell, **8:** 68n. 19; **14:** 72n. 5

Harrod, R. F., **1:** 174, 175n. 12; **8:** 80n. 1, 81

Harsanyi, John C., **11:** 8n. 6, 185, 186n. 2; **12:** 14n. 11; **16:** 74n. 10, 103, 294n. 10, 407; **18:** 272; **19:** 280n. 6

Hart, Albert G., **8:** 32n. 7

Hart, Henry M., Jr., **18:** 400n. 8

Hart, Herbert, **18:** xvin. 8

Hartwell, Max, **19:** 118

Hay, George A., **13:** 421n. 6

Hayek, Friedrich A., **1:** 76n. 1, 78n. 9, 153n. 5, 180, 185, 247, 303n. 25, 416, 420, 421, 428; **3:** 7n. 5, 58n. 8, 78n. 6; **6:** xi, xv, xvii, 21–26, 29, 33, 34, 40, 48, 77, 87; **7:** 37n. 13, 117n. 1, 151n. 9, 211n. 1, 232; **8:** 108n. 15, 125n. 10, 177n. 10; **9:** 8n. 4, 132n. 1, 184, 185, 190, 223, 224, 227, 235, 243; **10:** 13, 159; **11:** 64, 200; **12:** 3, 8, 12, 18, 20, 23, 24, 80n. 8, 134, 327–29, 361n. 15, 429–30, 441; **13:** 16, 126, 175; **14:** 196, 203, 250–51, 256–59, 265, 282n. 7, 460n. 7, 488; **15:** 285n. 7, 288n. 12; **16:** 44, 135, 140–41, 143–44, 159n. 4, 162n. 10, 216, 360, 373, 439n. 1; **17:** 32, 83, 101–9, 120, 189n. 2, 200, 203n. 2, 226–27, 425n. 11,

Hayek, Friedrich A. (*continued*)
  439, 441–42, 457, 460, 461, 467; **18:** 85,
  101n. 2, 111, 140n. 13, 172, 178, 179, 183,
  199n. 1, 251, 255, 309n. 57, 310, 311–13,
  316–19,321–23; **19:** xiii, xv, 23, 41, 49, 52,
  112, 113, 116–22, 141, 157, 189, 197, 207,
  210–11, 221, 232, 234, 242n. 2, 250, 262,
  267, 269, 351
Hazlitt, Henry, **17:** xivn. 8
Head, John G., **5:** x, xin. 2, xiii, 27, 28, 45,
  46, 74, 140, 192; **9:** 73n. 5, 243; **13:** 451n.
  1; **14:** 281n. 6; **15:** 210n. 2, 239n. 12
Hearn, William E., **7:** 232
Heckathorn, Douglas D., **16:** 164n. 14
Hegel, Georg Wilhelm Friedrich, **7:** 174n.
  6; **11:** xx; **12:** 478; **13:** 170–72; **14:** 90; **16:**
  244; **19:** 188
Heiner, Ron, **10:** 90n. 7; **13:** 404n. 12; **17:**
  86n. 5
Heller, Walter W., **4:** 61n. 3; **8:** 4, 43nn. 6,8,
  48n. 10, 158n. 5; **14:** 71; **18:** 23n. 1
Helpman, Elhanan, **15:** 437n. 2
Henderson, David, **19:** 270n. 4
Henderson, Elizabeth, **1:** 456; **19:** 37
Henderson, Hubert, **6:** 26n. 21; **12:** 67n. 1
Henderson, J. Vernon, **18:** 148n. 2
Henderson, William, **19:** 29n. 1
Hennipman, P., **13:** 239n. 1
Heraclitus, **1:** 257
Herold, J. Christopher, **3:** 209n. 5
Herring, Pendleton, **3:** 19n. 2, 283
Heyne, Paul, **17:** 154n. 2
Hicks, John R., **1:** 127n. 19, 193, 197; **5:** 47;
  12: 66n. 13, 196nn. 6,8, 256, 259; **15:**
  51–52, 118n. 7; **16:** 79, 298n. 15
Hicks, Ursula K., **1:** 127n. 19; **8:** 22n. 14
Hildreth, Clifford, **1:** 94n. 13
Hinich, Melvin J., **5:** 118; **9:** 243
Hirschman, Albert O., **12:** 49n. 3, 435n. 1;
  14: 441; **16:** 142; **18:** 82, 213n. 9
Hirshleifer, Jack, **5:** 46; **12:** 146n. 5, 298,
  299n. 4
Hitch, Charles J., **4:** 91n. 3

Hitler, Adolf, **17:** 118, 119; **19:** 133
Hobbes, Thomas, **1:** 26, 51, 59, 389, 433,
  439; **2:** 123; **3:** 248, 312, 313; **7:** xiii, xiv, 9,
  32, 33n. 10, 34, 66–67, 86n. 15, 87, 119n.
  2, 165, 186, 227, 232; **9:** 6–7, 13, 243; **10:** 5,
  17, 68, 112, 114n. 3, 117; **11:** 7, 16, 25; **12:** 32;
  13: 53, 59, 74, 175, 411; **14:** 177, 277n. 4,
  278–79; **15:** 3–4, 305; **16:** 26, 47, 91–93,
  215–16; **17:** 18, 46, 123, 191, 302, 305, 381,
  383–85, 457, 463–65; **18:** 167, 170, 218–19;
  19: xvi, 58, 175, 218, 297, 357–58
Hobhouse, L. T., **7:** 232
Hochman, Harold M., **7:** 68n. 19, 232; **9:**
  192n. 3, 244; **11:** 166n. 5; **13:** 129–30,
  148n. 16; **15:** 442n. 3, 490n. 18; **16:**
  278n. 3
Holcombe, Randall G., **13:** 403n. 10; **14:**
  393n. 2, 436n. 8
Holzer, Henry Mark, **18:** 388n. 1, 401n. 12,
  424n. 31
Hoover, Herbert, **8:** 39; **16:** 342
Hotelling, Harold, **2:** 21n. 5; **3:** 342; **9:** 76n.
  7, 244; **12:** 330; **13:** 227
Houthakker, H. S., **5:** 46
Howell, Henry, **13:** 327
Hoyt, William H., **11:** 189n. 2
Hughes, Charles Evans, **18:** 410n. 17,
  418n. 26
Hughes, Howard, **17:** 132
Hughes, Jonathan R. T., **8:** 14n. 10; **16:** 340
Humboldt, Wilhelm von, **3:** 322, 323; **17:**
  466
Hume, David, **1:** 361, 424, 451; **2:** 79–80; **3:**
  312, 313–15, 321; **7:** 27n. 3, 28n. 4, 33n. 10,
  47, 49, 77n. 7, 232; **9:** 42, 244; **10:** 68; **11:**
  38, 39, 55, 56, 71, 141; **12:** 30, 50, 87; **13:** 54,
  88n. 10, 94, 101, 107, 122, 303, 307; **14:**
  365; **15:** 11, 14, 30, 287; **16:** 11, 146; **17:** 46,
  68, 83, 94, 176, 229–30, 357, 457, 461,
  466; **18:** 446; **19:** xii, xiiin. 5, 77, 93, 111,
  223, 289, 357
Humphrey, George, **8:** 46
Humphrey, Hubert, **8:** 93

Humphrey, Thomas M., **8:** 174n. 8
Hunt, Leigh, **19:** 85
Hunt, Lester, **14:** 272n. 2
Huntington, E. V., **3:** 339n. 16
Hutcheson, Francis, **19:** 289
Hutchison, Terence W., **17:** 169n. 13; **19:** 42, 52, 118
Hutt, William H., **6:** 29; **7:** 111n. 6, 232; **8:** 27n. 3, 97n. 1; **12:** 48n. 2, 398n. 2; **16:** 82n. 12, 374, 381–82, 421n. 4; **19:** xvi, 135–52, 218n. 5
Hutton, Graham, **8:** 72n. 25, 75n. 32

Ibsen, Henrik, **13:** 87n. 8
Ingene, Charles, **12:** 174n. 10
Ireland, Thomas R., **7:** 143, 177n. 7, 199n. 10, 232; **13:** 34; **15:** 287n. 11, 483n. 10
Irving, Washington, **17:** 126

Jackson, J. D., **14:** 436n. 8
James, William, **17:** 176–81, 183, 184
Jannaccone, P., **1:** 416n. 5
Javits, Jacob, **8:** 93; **18:** 23n. 1
Jay, John, **16:** 42–43
Jay, Peter, **8:** 172n. 6
Jefferson, Thomas, **1:** 25; **9:** 197, 244; **10:** xv; **16:** 201; **17:** 296; **18:** 256, 257, 258; **19:** 176, 291
Jenkins, H. P. B., **2:** 74n. 4
Jensen, Michael C., **18:** 199n. 1
Jeremias, Ronald, **14:** 203n. 3
Jevons, William Stanley, **6:** 9, 11, 21, 45; **15:** 48; **17:** 29; **19:** 138
Jewkes, John, **15:** 257n. 10, 346n. 9, 360; **19:** 117
Jewkes, Sylvia, **15:** 257n. 10, 346n. 9, 360
Jeze, Gaston, **14:** 72n. 5
Johansen, L., **5:** 27, 139, 192
Johnson, Byron L., **18:** 9n. 16
Johnson, David B., **1:** 137n. 3; **7:** 216n. 4, 232; **9:** 78n. 8, 244; **13:** 34; **15:** 483n. 10
Johnson, Harry G., **8:** 23n. 16, 72, 74n. 29; **9:** 147, 244

Johnson, L. L., **13:** 317
Johnson, Lyndon B., **8:** 4, 52; **16:** 347
Johnson, Nevil, **13:** 52
Johnson, Paul, **17:** 168n. 11; **19:** 111
Johnson, Ronald N., **12:** 184n. 22
Johnson, Samuel, **15:** 441; **18:** 246
Jones, P., **18:** 211n. 8
Jones, Reginald H., **8:** 68n. 19
Jones, William H., **18:** 11
Jorgenson, Dale W., **15:** 377n. 1
Joseph, M. F. W., **15:** 101
Joyce, James, **18:** 289

Kafka, Alexandre, **19:** 41, 54
Kafoglis, M. Z., **5:** 27, 28, 46, 178, 192; **15:** xiv, xvn. 4, xvi, xviin. 9, 127n. 2, 248n. 3, 344n. 7, 357–58, 485n. 14
Kagel, John, **13:** 82; **17:** 27, 37
Kahn, Alfred E., **16:** 394n. 12
Kahn, R. F., **12:** 316n. 6, 323
Kaiser, Joseph H., **3:** 283n. 1
Kaizl, G., **1:** 126
Kaizuka, K., **5:** 179
Kaldor, Nicholas, **1:** 193, 197, 353; **9:** 111; **12:** 353, 387n. 5; **14:** 326; **15:** 83n. 26
Kalven, Harry, Jr., **15:** 79n. 17
Kant, Immanuel, **1:** 67, 312; **3:** 138, 316; **7:** xii, xiv, 150, 155, 174n. 6; **11:** xix; **13:** 35–38; **15:** 306; **17:** xiv, 94, 461; **18:** 292n. 15
Kaplan, Morton A., **3:** 250n. 1
Kapp, K. W., **1:** 62
Karlson, Nils, **19:** 208
Katz, M. L., **12:** 394n. 8
Kaufmann, F. X., **16:** 145n. 24
Kaufmann, Walter, **7:** 232; **17:** 180n. 5
Kazmann, R. G., **13:** 209n. 11
Kearl, J. R., **14:** 215n. 5, 235n. 9
Kearny, John W., **8:** 13–14
Kedourie, Elie, **7:** 232
Keener, B. Nowlin, **18:** 410n. 17, 414n. 22
Keeney, Bob M., **6:** 19n. 8
Kelley, Walt, **3:** 134n. 3

Kelman, Steven, **13:** 79, 80, 81; **19:** 283n. 7

Kemp, Arthur, **19:** 116

Kemp, Murray, **1:** 94n. 13; **15:** 162n. 8, 164n. 11

Kendall, Willmoore, **3:** 258n. 3

Kendrick, M. Slade, **14:** 72n. 5

Kennedy, John F., **8:** 48, 49, 50

Kennedy, Joseph, **1:** 438; **16:** 97

Kershner, Frederick, **19:** 79

Kessel, Reuben A., **7:** 29, 229; **8:** 61n. 6, 147n. 17

Keynes, John Maynard, **1:** 164–78; **2:** 17, 63; **8:** 4, 6, 7, 25, 26, 27, 28, 31, 38, 39, 40, 51, 63, 64, 79, 80, 81, 82, 83, 85, 91, 98, 115, 148, 171, 172, 175, 178; **9:** 129, 244; **10:** 101–2; **12:** 66, 458–59, 462, 466–67, 480; **13:** 40, 53; **14:** 4, 65, 366, 489, 505–6; **15:** 423; **16:** 242–43, 310, 447; **17:** 7–8; **19:** 242, 320–25, 341n. 5

Khrushchev, Nikita, **18:** 107

Kimmel, Lewis H., **8:** 13n. 8

King, Martin Luther, **16:** 174

Kirzner, Israel M., **1:** 30n. 1, 106n. 1; **6:** 34; **12:** 151, 154n, 164, 176n. 13, 424; **16:** 209n. 11; **17:** 34, 36n. 11, 59n. 2, 167n. 10; **18:** 292, 293–94, 298–303, 308–10; **19:** 155, 156, 160, 236

Klaus, Vaclav, **12:** 482

Klein, Benjamin, **1:** 343n. 5; **8:** 74n. 27

Kliemt, Hartmut, **11:** 130n. 19; **13:** 371n. 17, 295; **17:** 215n. 2; **19:** 121

Kneese, Allen V., **5:** 177; **13:** 421n. 3

Knerr, Charles, **8:** 163n. 8

Knight, Frank H., **1:** 11, 15, 16, 29, 31, 36, 63n. 6, 77, 85, 183, 219, 230–40, 251, 253–54, 296, 308n. 35, 325–26, 361, 443, 451; **2:** 30, 31n. 4; **3:** 20n. 6, 97, 103, 111n. 4, 203; **5:** 22, 160; **6:** xvii, 13–16, 18, 21, 22, 39, 45, 70, 79; **7:** ix, xvii, 118, 209, 232; **12:** 24, 27, 55, 110–27, 134, 143–45, 260, 311–15, 323, 400n. 4; **13:** 252n. 1; **14:** 460n. 8; **15:** 44–45, 156n. 1, 160, 243, 422;

16: 80, 85, 120n. 10, 175, 245n. 10, 246, 371; **17:** 18, 25, 116, 120, 132, 139–40, 153n, 169n. 12, 209, 223, 316, 326, 335n. 9, 353, 424n. 10; **18:** 38, 265–66, 323, 339; **19:** xi, xii, xiv, xv, 3–4, 6–16, 19–20, 23–24, 40, 41, 52, 53, 77–93, 109, 111, 117, 118, 123–34, 165, 168, 220

Kochin, Levis, **14:** 390n. 9, 393n. 2

Koestler, Arthur, **16:** 396n. 14

Koopmans, Tjalling, **12:** 24–25, 63n. 11

Kopf, David H., **1:** 161, 163

Koslowski, Peter, **18:** 276n

Kristol, Irving, **7:** 232

Krueger, Anne O., **9:** 40n. 21, 244; **11:** 107n. 2; **13:** 49, 251, 264n. 1; **19:** 105

Krugman, Paul, **12:** 394–95

Kuhn, Thomas, **1:** 46

Kuran, Timur, **16:** 132n. 8

Kuzmak, Richard A., **15:** 377n. 1

Kuznets, Simon, **15:** 41, 48, 49, 51, 56

Kydland, Finn E., **10:** 103n. 6; **13:** 480n. 11; **17:** 148

Lachmann, Ludwig M., **18:** 293, 294n. 20, 297, 301

Laffer, Arthur, **10:** 95

Laidler, David, **8:** 60n. 4

Laird, John, **3:** 20n. 6

Laird, Melvin, **18:** 23n. 1

Lancaster, Kelvin, **12:** 255n. 6; **14:** 104n. 6

Landes, William M., **18:** 338–41

Lange, Oskar, **1:** 185; **12:** 26; **13:** 22, 174; **19:** 113

Laplace, J., **3:** 332

Larsen, Roy, **3:** 284

Laski, Frida, **3:** 318n. 11

Laski, Harold, **3:** 318n. 11

Lau, Lawrence A., **15:** 378n. 2

Lave, Lester B., **15:** 228n. 3

Lean, Jane A., **4:** 186n. 6

Lee, Dwight R., **10:** 101n. 4; **11:** 106n. 1, 119n. 7, 125n. 14, 162n. 2; **12:** 219n, 450n.

12; **13:** 285n. 2, 474n. 5, 476n. 6; **14:** 51n.
3, 310n. 7, 314n. 13, 325n. 3; **16:** 193n. 7,
430n. 2; **18:** xivn. 6, 77n. 8, 136n. 5,
139n. 9; **19:** 206, 262n. 5, 278nn. 2,3,
352n. 7

Lees, Dennis S., **15:** 360

Leijonhufvud, Axel, **8:** 8n. 4, 26n. 2, 27n.
4, 63n. 11

Leland, Simeon E., **18:** 6n. 7; **19:** 6

Lenin, V. I., **1:** 183, 285; **8:** 164; **19:** 101

Leo XIII (pope), **18:** 252–53

Leoni, Bruno, **3:** xix, 9, 24n. 12; **7:** 232; **11:**
13n. 10; **17:** 108n. 12; **18:** 333; **19:** 35, 42,
52, 118

Lepage, Henri, **13:** 40

Lerner, Abba P., **1:** 163, 172, 173, 176, 185; **2:**
10–11, 46, 58–59; **4:** 105; **6:** 23, 26; **8:** 33n.
8, 53n. 12, 153n. 1; **9:** 70, 244; **12:** 26; **13:**
22, 174; **14:** 359, 435n. 7; **19:** 321

Leroy-Beaulieu, Paul, **2:** 15n. 13, 82–87; **14:**
72n. 5

Letwin, Shirley, **17:** 105n. 10

Levine, Michael E., **13:** 183n. 2

Levy, David, **1:** 265n. 11, 355n. 9; **10:** 163n.
8; **11:** 77n. 4; **12:** 112n. 5, 119n. 8, 360n.
14, 417n. 4; **16:** 193n. 8, 198n. 13; **17:** 38n.
12, 86n. 6; **19:** 73, 110

Levy, Ferdinand, **12:** 209

Lewis, C. Day, **17:** 80

Libecap, Gary D., **12:** 184n. 22

Lincoln, Abraham, **18:** 104

Lindahl, Erik, **1:** 124n. 6, 137–38, 426; **5:** xi,
xii, xiii, 27, 46, 93, 139–40, 182, 187; **9:**
xiv; **11:** 29–30, 117, 153n. 9; **14:** 7, 32, 93,
214, 308; **15:** 70

Lindbeck, Assar, **13:** 479n. 10; **14:** 414,
459n. 6

Lindblom, Charles E., **1:** 76n. 1, 78n. 7,
80n. 14, 83n. 20, 85n. 23, 88n. 27,
96nn. 16,18, 368; **3:** 9, 32n. 2; **5:** 141; **7:**
193n. 4, 220n. 7, 231, 233; **16:** 385–86; **19:**
162–64

Lindsay, C. M., **17:** 288n. 5; **19:** 42, 109

Lindsay, Peter H., **8:** 135n. 6

Lippmann, Walter, **3:** 247; **19:** 180, 181

Lipsey, Richard G., **12:** 255n. 6, 310n. 7

Little, Ian M. D., **1:** 89n. 2, 91–92n. 7, 93n.
9, 95n. 14; **4:** 244; **14:** 103n. 3

Littlechild, Stephen C., **18:** 293, 294n. 23,
296n. 29, 297n. 32, 299, 304n. 52, 306n.
56; **19:** 112, 161

Lively, Jack, **9:** 244

Livingston, S. Morris, **8:** 31n. 7

Locke, John, **1:** 51, 389; **3:** 248, 314; **7:** xiii,
xiv, 79, 80, 107n. 5, 121n. 5, 187, 233; **11:** 7;
17: 46, 431, 433, 434

Lomasky, Loren, **14:** 218n. 9, 243n. 16; **15:**
392n. 2; **17:** 379n, 380n. 2; **18:** 89n. 7

Lombra, Raymond E., **8:** 124n. 9

Long, Millard F., **13:** 386n. 6

Lösch, August, **2:** 65n. 5

Lott, L. R., Jr., **13:** 284n. 2

Lucas, J. R., **17:** 49n. 4

Lucas, Robert E., Jr., **8:** 161n. 6, 177n. 10,
189n. 6; **9:** 144n. 8, 244

Luce, R. Duncan, **3:** 149n. 1, 162n. 10,
176n. 2, 178, 180; **5:** 95, 159; **7:** 42n. 17,
233; **15:** 227n. 2, 351n. 14

Macaulay, Thomas B., **16:** 109

MacCallum, Spencer, **1:** 328n. 8

Macfie, A. L., **1:** 295, 298n. 12; **15:** 283n. 1,
290n. 15

Machiavelli, Niccolò, **3:** 43; **4:** 129; **13:** 23,
47; **17:** 51n. 6, 137

Machlup, Fritz, **12:** 255

Mackay, Robert J., **9:** 30n. 18, 243, 244; **13:**
196n. 2

Mackie, John L., **17:** xxin. 19

Macleod, H. D., **1:** 30

Madison, James, **1:** xx, 19, 372, 468; **3:**
24–25, 214n. 2; **9:** 67, 244; **10:** xv; **13:** 23,
46, 109; **15:** 424; **16:** 42–43, 73, 75, 185,
197, 199, 231–33, 430, 441n. 6; **17:** 109,

Madison, James (*continued*)
  359, 466; **18:** 74, 87, 102–3, 117, 146; **19:** 62, 349
Maffezzoni, F., **2:** 89n. 20, 92n. 23, 93n. 25; **15:** 90n. 32, 91n. 34
Magaw, R., **11:** 87n. 9
Magee, Stephen P., **11:** 107n. 2; **14:** 320n. 17; **16:** 441n. 5; **19:** 27n. 2
Magruder, Jeb, **7:** 152n. 10
Maine, Henry S., **3:** 275n. 4; **7:** 16n. 7, 70n. 2, 87n. 17, 233; **16:** 152
Maitland, F. W., **7:** 233
Malinvaud, E., **15:** 188n. 5
Malthus, Thomas, **2:** 4; **6:** 7; **8:** 26–27
Mandeville, Bernard de, **7:** 47; **13:** 122; **15:** 302, 307; **17:** 46; **18:** 446, 448
Mann, F. A., **18:** 401n. 11, 422n. 30, 428n. 35, 431n. 39
Manne, Henry G., **18:** 327
Mannheim, Karl, **17:** 116
Mansfield, Harvey C., Jr., **1:** 242
Mansfield, Mike, **18:** 427
Margolis, Howard, **10:** 163n. 9
Margolis, Julius, **3:** 136n. 4; **4:** 179; **5:** 71, 73, 192; **14:** 71, 72n. 6, 85, 87–88; **15:** 44n. 4, 271n. 1; **18:** 23n, 54n. 13
Markowitz, Harry, **1:** 94n. 13
Marshak, Jacob, **3:** 10n. 16
Marshall, Alfred, **1:** 30, 60, 62, 106, 351, 444–46, 454; **2:** 19; **5:** 33–36, 53–54, 182, 183; **6:** 12–13, 68n. 3; **12:** 54–55, 67–69, 134, 142, 255, 277, 299n. 4, 390, 394; **13:** 40; **14:** 4n. 1; **15:** 104, 156n. 1, 159–60, 170, 213; **19:** 29, 47
Marshall, Ray, **13:** 58
Martin, D. T., **18:** 137n. 7
Martin, Donald L., **7:** 126n. 8, 233
Marty, Alvin L., **8:** 63n. 8
Marx, Karl, **1:** 148, 183, 285, 387; **6:** 5; **7:** 174n. 6, 187; **10:** 163; **11:** 25, 208; **12:** 478–79; **16:** 443–44; **18:** 256; **19:** 167, 188, 265, 267, 276

Masci, **15:** 71
Maser, Steven M., **16:** 164n. 14
Maslow, Abraham, **15:** 364n. 1
Maxwell, James A., **4:** 273n. 3; **18:** 3n. 1
May, K. O., **3:** 155n. 7
Mayer, Lawrence, **7:** 75n. 6, 231
Mayr, Ernst, **18:** 291n. 13
Mazzola, Ugo, **5:** xiii, 181; **14:** 6, 26; **15:** 59n. 1; **19:** 32
McClennan, Edward F., **16:** 163n. 11
McCleod, Neil, **19:** 116
McDougall, Duncan M., **8:** 14n. 10
McGee, John S., **12:** 206n. 1
McGinn, Colin, **17:** 156n. 3
McGovern, George, **7:** 116; **15:** 457
McGrane, Reginald C., **8:** 14n. 10
McGuire, Martin, **7:** 145n, 229, 233; **18:** 44n. 2
McGuire, Thomas G., **9:** 70n. 4, 242; **12:** 105n. 10
McIntosh, Donald, **7:** 102n. 2, 119n. 3, 233
McKean, Roland N., **2:** 102n. 2; **4:** 91n. 3; **5:** 177; **6:** 56n. 4, 87; **7:** 8n. 1, 29, 233; **12:** 177n. 18; **13:** 12–13, 48; **14:** 16n. 21, 389n. 6; **18:** 358, 363
McKenzie, Richard B., **1:** 377, 378; **13:** 222n. 8; **16:** 430n. 2; **18:** 77n. 8, 136n. 5, 137nn. 6,7; **19:** 206, 262n. 5
McKinnon, Ronald I., **4:** 275n. 5
McManus, M., **15:** 114n. 5
McQueen, R., **18:** 7n. 9
Meade, James E., **1:** 163; **2:** 12, 13, 14, 22–24; **9:** 69n. 1, 244; **12:** 316n. 6; **13:** 366n. 13; **15:** 170n. 4; **17:** 298n. 1
Meckling, William H., **1:** 70n. 11; **18:** 199n. 1
Mehra, Rajnish, **12:** 403n. 6
Meiselman, David, **8:** 64n. 13
Melamed, A. Douglas, **12:** 170–71, 175, 280; **13:** 301n. 2, 313n. 12; **18:** 371n. 5
Mellon, Andrew, **8:** 46
Melon, J. F., **2:** 15, 84
Meltzer, Allan H., **13:** 394n. 4

Menger, Carl, **6:** 9, 11; **12:** 426; **17:** 29

Mera, Koichi, **18:** 42n. 28

Meyer, Arthur B., **11:** 86n. 7

Meyer, Lawrence S., **16:** 277n. 1

Meyer, Paul A., **13:** 130n. 3

Meyer, Robert A., **7:** 34n. 12, 234

Meyer, Willi, **17:** 35n. 9, 132

Michael, Robert T., **12:** 220

Michelman, Frank I., **7:** 28n. 4, 58n. 13, 233; **13:** 425n. 7

Mieszkowski, Peter, **18:** 148n. 2

Migué, Jean Luc, **9:** 162n. 3, 244

Mill, James, **16:** 109

Mill, John Stuart, **1:** 126n. 13, 295; **2:** 81; **4:** 252n. 9; **6:** 5; **9:** 3, 16, 69n. 1, 111, 244; **12:** 85, 87; **13:** 54–55, 88n. 10; **14:** 112n. 13, 179–80; **15:** 79, 83; **16:** 11; **17:** 68; **18:** 8n. 12; **19:** 71n. 4, 138, 139

Miller, H. Lawrence, Jr., **1:** 163

Miller, James C., III, **9:** 21, 245; **19:** 42

Miller, John, **1:** 301n. 20

Miller, Merton H., **8:** 42n. 5

Minasian, J. R., **5:** 177; **15:** 259–64

Mints, Lloyd, **1:** 405, 407, 410; **14:** 359; **19:** 40

Mirowski, Philip, **18:** 290n. 3

Mises, Ludwig von, **1:** 78n. 6, 80, 83n. 19, 185, 270n. 15; **3:** 46n. 2, 309n. 3, 316n. 7; **6:** 21–26, 29, 33, 34, 40, 87; **7:** 50n. 6, 236; **12:** 8, 18, 25, 134; **17:** 24n, 25, 28, 32–34; **19:** 113, 118, 121, 157, 221, 232, 234, 250

Mishan, E. J., **4:** 259n. 1; **5:** 73; **12:** 280n. 6; **13:** 130n. 3, 359n. 4, 362n. 10; **14:** 357–60; **15:** 28, 156n. 2, 159n. 4, 179

Mitchell, Wesley C., **13:** 6

Mitchell, William C., **13:** 14n. 11

Modigliani, Franco, **1:** 154n. 6, 160; **6:** 60; **14:** 358n. 3, 363

Moes, John, **3:** xix

Molden, Otto, **19:** 304n

Montemartini, Giovanni, **15:** 59n. 1, 97–98; **19:** 32

Montesquieu, Baron de la Brède et de (Charles-Louis de Secondat), **1:** 51; **7:** 18, 19, 173n. 5, 205, 233; **9:** 245; **18:** 103; **19:** 175, 177

Moore, John, **19:** 42

Moran, Donald W., **15:** 377n. 1

Morgenstern, Oskar, **1:** 65; **3:** 151, 164, 186, 330; **5:** 159; **11:** 43, 93, 122; **12:** 480n. 5; **14:** 312; **16:** 84; **19:** 30

Mosca, Gaetano, **4:** 128; **13:** 47; **15:** 67

Moser, Peter, **16:** 145n. 26

Mosher, Fredrick C., **8:** 39n. 2

Moss, Laurence, **7:** 24n. 1, 233; **17:** 416n. 4

Moynihan, Daniel P., **7:** 233; **19:** 185n. 4

Mueller, Dennis C., **1:** 365n. 7; **7:** 47n. 1, 233; **9:** 242; **12:** 95n. 4, 431n. 8, 438n. 4; **13:** 39n, 45, 185n. 3; **14:** 17n. 25; **17:** 430, 439n. 3

Mueller, Eva, **4:** 196–97, 198n. 16, 202, 203

Mundell, Robert A., **4:** 278, 280n. 7; **12:** 3

Murphy, Henry C., **2:** 28n. 1, 59n. 4, 118n. 2

Murphy, Jeffrie G., **7:** 174n. 6, 233

Murray, R. A., **15:** 70, 97, 98, 99–100

Musgrave, Richard A., **1:** xviiin. 10, 130n. 25, 133, 146n. 7, 160, 324n. 7; **3:** 109n. 2, 110, 198, 202; **4:** ix, 18, 49, 113, 119, 161n. 3, 227, 286n. 1, 296–97; **5:** x, xi, xiii, 11, 27, 28, 45, 48, 72, 93, 94, 140, 182, 184; **6:** 92; **7:** 68, 233, 234; **8:** 32n. 7, 35n. 10, 42n. 5, 86n. 7, 112n. 2; **9:** 17, 204n. 4, 245; **11:** 118n. 5; **12:** 103n. 8; **13:** 129, 148n. 16; **14:** xiii, 6n. 4, 8, 54–68, 93, 308n. 4, 363, 389n. 7; **15:** 39n. 2, 48, 59n. 1, 104n. 51, 208, 211n. 3, 227n. 1, 239n. 12, 265, 360, 462n. 1, 471n. 1; **16:** 279n. 5; **17:** 432; **18:** 26, 30n. 13, 350n. 13

Muskie, Edmund, **8:** 4

Muth, J., **15:** 278n. 8

Myers, Gerald E., **17:** 172, 176–78, 181

Myrdal, Gunnar, **17:** 18, 251n. 1

Nader, Ralph, **8:** 4; **13:** 327; **15:** 310; **19:** 163

Nagel, Thomas, **17:** 33 n. 7, 253

Nanson, E. J., **3:** 331

Neal, Alfred C., **1:** 80 n. 13

Neenan, William B., **4:** 186 n. 6

Negishi, Takashi, **1:** 37 n. 8

Nelson, J. R., **12:** 298 n. 3, 299 n. 7

Nevins, E., **2:** 39

Newcomer, Mabel, **4:** 273 n. 3

Newing, R. A., **5:** 118, 191; **13:** 229 n. 4

Newman, Peter, **5:** 27

Ng, Yew-Kwang, **9:** 70 n. 4, 245

Nichols, Roy F., **18:** 5 n. 5

Niebuhr, Reinhold, **1:** 360 n. 1

Niemi, R., **13:** 200 n. 4

Nietzsche, Friedrich Wilhelm, **1:** 34, 46, 179, 180, 393; **13:** 3; **14:** 361 n. 2; **17:** 114, 180

Nimitz, Adm. Chester W., **1:** 13

Nisbet, Robert, **17:** 375 n. 23

Niskanen, William A., **7:** 204 n. 15, 217 n. 6; **8:** 73 n. 26, 186 n. 2; **9:** 29 n. 17, 30 n. 18, 47 n. 4, 162, 245; **12:** 101–3; **13:** 48–49; **14:** 18, 155 n. 6, 476, 479–81, 484; **15:** 36, 441 n. 2, 480 n. 7; **16:** 99 n. 7; **17:** 61; **19:** 98

Nixon, Richard M., **7:** 152 n. 10; **8:** 3, 52; **16:** 182; **17:** 126, 131, 132; **19:** 179–80, 183

Noll, Roger, **14:** 331 n. 10

Norman, Donald A., **8:** 135 n. 6

North, Douglass C., **7:** 29, 234; **12:** 75–76; **16:** 8 n. 2

Nove, Alec, **1:** 181; **19:** 249 n. 2

Nozick, Robert, **1:** 293, 299, 306; **7:** xiii, xiv, 234; **8:** 178 n. 11; **9:** 205 n. 5, 245; **10:** 129; **13:** 274; **14:** 254 n. 1, 463 n. 11; **16:** 18 n. 2, 24 nn. 5,6, 25, 26, 120, 204 n. 4, 216, 244; **17:** xx, 34 n. 9, 97, 137, 191 n. 3, 249 n. 4, 387 n. 10, 394 n. 13, 401 n. 18, 404 n. 1, 415–36, 449, 457; **18:** 169, 178 n. 1, 179, 183, 195 n. 5; **19:** 59, 83

Nussbaum, Arthur, **18:** 400 n. 8, 419 n. 28, 429 n. 36

Nutter, G. Warren, **1:** 26; **2:** 140; **5:** 95; **15:** 57 n. 14, 144 n. 8, 240 n. 14; **19:** 37, 38, 39–41, 43, 45, 49, 51–56, 118, 165

Oakeshott, Michael, **13:** 175; **18:** 183

Oates, Wallace E., **4:** 275 n. 5; **7:** 47 n. 2, 234; **8:** 144 n. 15, 148 n. 18; **11:** 188 n. 1; **18:** 44 n. 2

O'Driscoll, Gerald P., Jr., **8:** 140 n. 11; **9:** 144 n. 8, 246; **14:** 394 n. 4; **18:** 298 n. 37

Officer, Lawrence H., **12:** 308–10

Ohlin, Bertil, **2:** 30, 63; **19:** 42, 52, 117, 118

Okner, Benjamin A., **14:** 285 nn. 2,4

Okun, Arthur, **8:** 168 n. 2

Oliver, Henry, **3:** 9, 20 n. 5

Olsen, Edgar O., **13:** 130

Olson, Mancur, **1:** xix, xx n. 13, 324 n. 7, 429 n. 1; **4:** 113 n. 1; **5:** 94, 178, 192; **7:** 54 n. 11, 78 n. 9, 234; **9:** 204 n. 4, 245; **12:** 286; **13:** 170 n. 4, 222 n. 10, 394 n. 4; **15:** 240 n. 13, 360; **16:** 88 n. 1, 268, 381; **18:** 343 n. 3; **19:** 144, 190, 209, 229 n. 3

O'Neill, Eugene, **13:** 87

Oppenheimer, J. Robert, **17:** 4

Ordeshook, Peter C., **7:** 235; **8:** 99 n. 4, 100 n. 6; **9:** 243, 245; **13:** 160 n. 6, 170 n. 3, 214 n. 2

Orr, Daniel, **15:** 423–24

Ortega y Gasset, J., **1:** 393

Orton, W. A., **9:** 99, 245

Orwell, George, **17:** 132; **19:** 194, 199

O'Shaughnessy, Brian, **17:** 33 n. 7

Ostrom, Elinor, **11:** 82 n. 1; **16:** 163 n. 12

Ostrom, Vincent, **1:** 255; **7:** 203 n. 13, 217 n. 6, 234; **16:** 145 n. 24

Page, Talbot, **16:** 157 n. 1

Paish, Frank, **13:** 436

Palmer, R. R., **7:** 187 n. 2, 234; **19:** 177 n. 2

Palyi, M., **18:** 405 n. 15

Pantaleoni, Maffeo, **1:** 124 n. 7; **2:** 16 n. 24,

89n. 20; **5:** xiii, 181; **13:** 22; **14:** 6, 7, 26; **15:** 59n. 1, 64–66, 73, 99, 105; **19:** 32

Papi, G. Ugo, **15:** 77n. 15; **19:** 32, 36

Pareto, Vilfredo, **1:** 192; **3:** 8, 92; **4:** 126n. 2, 128, 174, 287; **5:** 11, 15, 45, 79, 88, 89, 91–92, 107, 108, 112, 114, 115, 116, 127, 132, 146, 147, 183, 184, 188, 190; **7:** 4, 10; **9:** 26; **13:** 8, 23, 47; **15:** 61, 63, 66–68, 70, 97, 99, 101–2, 105; **16:** 248; **17:** 5, 115, 116, 117, 126, 129, 136, 138, 140, 141, 237, 259n. 4

Parkin, Michael, **8:** 60n. 4

Parravicini, Giannino, **2:** 14n. 12, 89n. 20; **19:** 30, 31–35

Parry, Stanley, **3:** 317n. 8

Parsons, Talcott, **13:** 17

Pascal, Blaise, **17:** 178, 183

Passmore, John, **7:** 186n. 1, 234; **16:** 146n. 28; **17:** 467

Patinkin, Don, **12:** 57–59, 61–63

Patman, Wright, **16:** 343–45; **18:** 431n. 37

Paul, Ellen Frankel, **16:** 28n

Pauly, Mark V., **1:** 137n. 3; **5:** 73, 178; **6:** xvii; **9:** 78n. 8, 244; **13:** 13n. 11, 185n. 3, 462n. 10; **14:** xivn. 7, 144n. 5; **15:** 483n. 11; **19:** 42

Peacock, Alan T., **4:** 61; **5:** 192; **7:** 205n. 16, 234; **9:** 245; **13:** 149n. 17; **14:** 6n. 4, 54; **15:** 59n. 1; **18:** 350n. 13; **19:** 114

Pechman, Joseph A., **8:** 48n. 10; **14:** 5, 285nn. 2,4; **15:** 408–9; **18:** 23n. 1

Pedersen, Jorgen, **2:** 12n. 7, 38

Peel, J. D. Y., **7:** 234

Pejovich, Svetozar, **7:** 29, 232, 234; **14:** 16n. 21; **18:** 318n. 8; **19:** 120

Pelczynski, Z., **18:** 200n. 2

Peltzman, Sam, **13:** 51; **19:** 59–60

Pence, G. E., **16:** 286

Pennock, J. Roland, **3:** 349; **10:** 68n. 12; **18:** 400n. 8

Pepys, Samuel, **9:** 162n. 2

Perloff, H., **4:** 273n. 3

Perradin, William R. M., **15:** 377n. 1

Perry, Arthur Latham, **1:** 30, 35n. 5

Pesek, Boris P., **9:** 132n. 2, 245

Peston, Maurice H., **8:** 34 n. 9

Peters, G., **18:** 139n. 10

Peters, R. S., **7:** 70n. 2, 151n. 9, 229

Peterson, George E., **13:** 131n. 4; **15:** 471n

Peterson, William H., **8:** 68n. 17

Phelps, Edmund S., **7:** 230, 233; **9:** 158n. 17, 224, 245; **17:** 336n. 10; **19:** 324

Philbrook, Clarence, **1:** 82n. 17; **19:** 116

Phillips, Almarin, **1:** 221n. 6; **15:** 240n. 15; **16:** 389n. 8

Phillips, A. W., **8:** 88n. 9, 173n. 7; **10:** 102

Phipps, Cecil G., **19:** 13

Pierce, Lawrence C., **8:** 22n. 14

Pigou, Arthur Cecil, **1:** 20, 60–74, 121; **2:** 5, 12, 59; **4:** 137; **5:** 166; **6:** 65–76; **9:** 17, 245; **10:** 93; **12:** 58n. 6, 277, 292, 311, 324; **13:** 26, 44, 58, 117, 299, 311–12, 362; **14:** 5, 91; **15:** 44–45, 65n. 7, 78, 79, 156n. 1, 159–60, 170, 342, 344; **18:** 7n. 10, 38; **19:** 16, 29, 129, 146

Pines, David, **18:** 289n. 3

Pinto, **2:** 15

Plant, Arnold, **6:** 26, 29; **19:** 145

Plato, **1:** 289, 290; **3:** 312; **15:** 459; **17:** 116, 293, 295, 310, 320

Plattner, Marc F., **1:** 293n. 3; **16:** 18n. 2

Plott, Charles R., **5:** 73, 118, 192; **7:** 34n. 12, 234; **12:** 68n. 2; **13:** 183n. 2, 203n. 7, 229n. 4; **15:** 167n. 15, 169, 218n. 10, 221n. 15; **16:** 81n. 8; **19:** 42

Poland, Orville F., **8:** 39n. 2

Polanyi, Michael, **1:** 85n. 21, 101, 230–43, 432; **7:** 48n. 3, 234; **10:** 47; **16:** 91; **17:** 98, 153n, 155; **18:** 303n. 51, 305–6, 312; **19:** 41, 52, 118, 262

Polinsky, A. Mitchell, **7:** 64n. 16, 234; **12:** 170n. 6; **15:** 488n. 17; **18:** 47n. 5

Popper, Karl R., **1:** 450; **3:** 46n. 2; **17:** 180; **18:** 292n. 15, 301n. 45; **19:** 121, 122, 277

Portney, P. R., **11:** 87n. 9

Posner, Richard A., **7:** 167n. 1, 234; **9:** 40n. 21, 195n. 4, 245; **11:** 12n. 9; **12:** 31n. 1; **13:** 49, 264n. 1, 267, 404n. 11; **17:** 108n. 13; **18:** 327–36, 338–41

Post, Russell Z., **18:** 400n. 8

Postlethwayt, Malachy, **2:** 15n. 16

Pound, Ezra, **17:** 215

Pound, Roscoe, **7:** 234; **17:** 116

Pred, Allen, **18:** 28n. 10

Prescott, Edward C., **10:** 103n. 6; **12:** 403n. 6; **13:** 480n. 11; **17:** 148

Prest, A. R., **6:** 61n. 6

Price, V. C., **18:** 142n. 14

Prigogine, Ilya, **16:** 146; **18:** 289–90, 291n. 9, 292n. 15, 293n. 16, 303; **19:** 243

Pringle, Robin, **8:** 5

Putnam, Hilary, **17:** 156n. 3

Puviani, Amilcare, **1:** 150, 156, 157–58; **4:** 127, 128–39; **8:** 134n. 5; **13:** 22, 27, 47; **14:** 15, 52; **15:** 70, 71, 92–97; **19:** 32

Quine, W. V., **17:** 103n. 5

Rabushka, Alvin, **11:** 128–29; **14:** 317

Rachlin, Howard, **13:** 82n. 6

Radzicki, Michael, **18:** 290n. 3

Rae, Douglas W., **1:** 281–82, 301n. 20; **7:** 55n. 12, 234; **12:** 185

Rae, John, **15:** 292n. 18; **19:** 71n. 5

Raiffa, Howard, **3:** 149n. 1, 162n. 10, 176n. 2, 178, 180; **5:** 95, 159; **7:** 42n. 17, 233; **15:** 227n. 2, 351n. 14

Ramaswami, V., **15:** 161n. 6, 162n. 7

Raphael, David D., **17:** xin. 1

Rapoport, Anatole, **15:** 227n. 2, 228n. 3

Ratchford, B. U., **2:** 12, 14, 34

Rawls, John, **1:** 23–24, 50, 292, 293, 296, 297, 298n. 13, 299, 301–4, 306, 307–8, 309–10, 432, 465; **4:** 295n. 3; **5:** 160; **7:** xiii, xiv, 10n. 4, 47n. 1, 91n. 18, 221–23, 234; **9:** xxii, 6, 24, 39, 47n. 5, 220, 240, 245; **10:** 35, 36, 115n. 4, 155; **11:** 8n. 6, 11,

185; **13:** 46; **14:** 13n. 16, 35n. 5, 43–45, 152n. 1, 164, 217–18, 236–37, 255; **15:** 486n. 16; **16:** 14, 18n. 2, 26n. 8, 45n. 2, 74, 90–91, 103, 115n. 5, 117, 128–29, 131, 156, 160, 164n. 15, 187, 189, 219, 224, 278, 285–300, 326–27, 407; **17:** 94n. 12, 104n. 9, 165n. 9, 249n. 4, 279n. 3, 314, 326, 333, 353, 355–72, 375–77, 380–81, 384–86, 392–404, 409, 411–15, 425, 432, 433–35, 451–52, 457; **18:** 179–81, 272, 411n. 19; **19:** 59, 83, 150, 280n. 6, 281

Reagan, Ronald, **15:** 389; **19:** 318

Reed, W. R., **13:** 284n. 2

Rees, David, **15:** 280n. 11

Rees, John, **9:** 244

Rehnquist, William, **17:** 349

Reid, John J., **4:** 204–5

Reid, Thomas, **19:** 289

Reynaud, P. L., **15:** 93n. 37

Ricardo, David, **1:** 158, 163, 387; **2:** 15–16, 34–37, 80–82, 89–94, 122–23; **4:** 265; **6:** 5, 7, 61–63; **7:** 161; **8:** 26, 139; **9:** 101; **11:** 34; **14:** xv, 352, 365, 385, 389, 392–95, 409–11, 436n. 8; **15:** 65, 85–90, 444n. 5; **18:** 133

Ricca-Salerno, Giuseppe, **15:** 71; **19:** 32

Ricci, U., **15:** 81

Richard, Scott, **13:** 394n. 4

Richenburg, L. J., **1:** 99n. 23

Richter, R., **16:** 8n. 1

Rignano, E., **4:** 301

Riker, William H., **3:** 23n. 11, 150n. 2; **7:** 138n. 1, 235; **8:** 99n. 4, 100n. 6; **9:** 245; **13:** 47, 160n. 6, 170n. 3, 214n. 2; **14:** 15; **15:** 287n. 11, 360; **17:** 260

Rizzo, Mario, **12:** 149n. 7; **18:** 298n. 37

Roback, Jennifer, **14:** xvn. 11, 436n. 8, 441n. 14; **17:** 213

Robbins, Lionel, **1:** 30, 31, 32, 93, 94n. 12, 153n. 5; **4:** 59n. 2; **5:** 183; **6:** xv, 19–23, 26, 33, 34, 87; **12:** 253, 255–56, 327–28, 330, 473n. 1; **14:** 65; **16:** 79, 83, 104, 239; **17:** 120; **19:** 89, 112, 123, 125, 233

Roberts, Donald J., **14:** 7n. 7

Roberts, Paul Craig, **1:** 432; **7:** 141n. 3, 235; **12:** 136; **14:** 184n. 9, 481–82, 484; **16:** 91; **19:** 42

Robertson, Dennis H., **3:** 27, 28n. 16; **9:** 19–20, 245; **10:** 72n. 14; **12:** 15, 67n. 1, 78; **13:** 62, 125; **15:** 156n. 1, 160; **17:** 96

Robinson, Joan, **6:** 30; **9:** 81n. 9, 245; **12:** 191n. 1, 277; **15:** 159n. 4; **16:** 79

Rockefeller, John D., **1:** 438; **16:** 97

Rodgers, James D., **7:** 68n. 19, 232; **9:** 192n. 3, 244; **11:** 166n. 5; **13:** 130, 148n. 16; **15:** 442n. 3; **16:** 278n. 3

Roesch, Susan R., **8:** 124n. 9

Rogerson, William P., **13:** 390n. 1

Rogge, Ben, **19:** 116

Rolph, Earl E., **2:** 134n. 1; **4:** 89n. 1, 244; **14:** 4n. 2, 71, 103, 389n. 7; **15:** 103n. 50

Romer, Paul M., **12:** 387n. 7, 389, 390, 395

Romer, Thomas, **13:** 196n. 2; **18:** 75n. 5

Roosevelt, Franklin Delano, **1:** 14, 175; **8:** 39, 52; **16:** 342, 344; **18:** 395–96; **19:** 82

Röpke, Wilhelm, **3:** 283n. 1, 286n. 3; **8:** 67n. 16

Rosen, Harvey S., **14:** 152n. 2

Rosenberg, Alexander, **12:** 31n. 2

Rosenberg, Nathan, **1:** 305n. 28; **15:** 295n. 20

Rosenthal, Howard, **13:** 196n. 2; **18:** 75n. 5

Rothbard, Murray, **1:** 299; **6:** 33; **7:** 9n. 2, 24n. 1, 235; **15:** 284; **16:** 16; **17:** 135, 416, 433

Rothenberg, Jerome, **1:** 89n. 2, 92n. 7, 93nn. 9,11

Rousseau, Jean-Jacques, **1:** 100; **3:** 248, 318; **7:** 16n. 7, 34, 86n. 15, 118n. 2, 119n. 4, 140n. 2, 187, 235

Rowley, Charles K., **9:** 245; **11:** 138n. 4; **13:** 149n. 17; **17:** 440; **18:** 212n. 8; **19:** 114

Rudd, Mark, **16:** 174

Ruml, Beardsley, **2:** 130n. 5

Runciman, W. G., **5:** 160

Russell, Bertrand, **7:** 235

Rymes, T. K., **1:** 265n. 10

Samuels, Warren J., **1:** 440; **7:** 67n. 17, 235; **16:** 98–99, 111n. 1, 118; **17:** 110n, 111nn. 2,3,4, 112–14; **18:** 342–46, 350, 355–57; **19:** 162

Samuelson, Paul A., **1:** 37n. 7, 72n. 12, 120n. 2, 136, 137, 193, 197, 202, 324n. 7, 381, 426; **2:** 105; **3:** 110, 192n. 1, 202, 348n. 28; **4:** ix, 11, 113, 119, 227, 286n. 1; **5:** ix, x, xi, xiii, 11, 22, 27–28, 45, 46, 72, 94, 128, 161, 177, 182, 183, 184, 193; **7:** 43n. 18, 235; **8:** 29, 82n. 4, 86, 89n. 10, 173n. 7; **9:** 17, 34, 246; **10:** 54; **11:** 27, 29–30, 69–70, 117, 143n. 1; **12:** 45, 66n. 13, 299, 328; **13:** 80n. 3, 113, 129, 131, 385n. 4, 448; **14:** 9–10, 32, 65, 93, 308n. 2; **15:** xiii, xiv, 44n. 4, 104n. 51, 121n. 9, 124, 144, 166, 193–95, 199, 200n. 7, 215, 221, 227n. 1, 239n. 12, 259–64, 265–66, 271–73, 278–80, 286, 327, 360, 409, 411; **16:** 79–80, 209n. 12, 365n. 6, 366n. 7; **17:** 113n. 7; **18:** 25, 45–46, 52n. 11, 56, 59, 63, 93

Sandler, T., **11:** 82n. 1, 152n. 6; **13:** 361n. 8

Sargent, Thomas, **9:** 144n. 8, 246

Saulnier, Raymond J., **8:** 188n. 5

Saving, Thomas R., **9:** 132n. 2, 245

Savio, Mario, **16:** 174

Sax, Emil, **1:** 124n. 7; **5:** xiii, 45, 181; **14:** 6, 26; **15:** 66, 70

Say, J. B., **1:** 125, 352

Sayers, R. S., **8:** 120n. 5

Scalia, Antonin, **16:** 66

Scarf, Herbert, **12:** 25

Schansberg, D. E., **13:** 284n. 2

Schanz, Georg, **9:** xiii

Schelling, Thomas C., **1:** 252, 336, 343n. 5, 380n. 3; **3:** 153, 154n. 6; **7:** 79n. 11, 154n. 13, 235; **10:** 82; **17:** xxn. 17, 65; **18:** 448n. 16

Schink, George R., **15:** 377n. 1

Schlatter, Richard, **7:** 13 n. 5, 33 n. 10, 76–77, 235

Schlesinger, J. R., **16:** 389 n. 8

Schmid, Al, **17:** 130

Schmidt, Emerson P., **2:** 48 n. 6, 102 n. 2

Schmidt, J. R., **18:** 137 n. 7

Schmölders, Günter, **4:** 127 n. 5, 185–89, 195

Schneider, Friedrich, **13:** 90 n, 240 n. 2

Schneider, Louis, **17:** xi n. 1

Schoeffler, Sidney, **1:** 99

Schopenhauer, Arthur, **19:** 79

Schotter, Andrew, **9:** 144 n. 8, 246; **18:** 318

Schultz, Theodore W., **19:** 6, 12

Schultz, William J., **14:** 72 n. 5

Schumpeter, Joseph Alois, **1:** 37; **3:** 342–43; **8:** 63, 178; **12:** 154 n, 158, 176 n. 13, 424; **13:** 23, 47; **16:** 68–69; **19:** 59, 97

Schwartz, Anna J., **8:** 179 n. 12; **18:** 395 n. 4, 408 n. 16, 415 n. 23

Scitovsky, Tibor, **1:** 154 n. 6, 193, 197; **12:** 191 n. 1, 316 n. 6; **15:** 109

Scott, Anthony D., **9:** 204 n. 4, 242; **18:** 24–25

Scott, Robert E., **13:** 273 n. 10

Scotto, Aldo, **4:** 214 n

Seale, J. R., **15:** 340 n. 1

Seidl, Christian, **17:** 72 n. 1, 75

Selden, Richard T., **7:** 225 n. 9; **13:** 129 n; **15:** xvii n. 11, 455 n. 9

Seldon, Arthur, **4:** 193 n. 11

Seligman, E. R. A., **15:** 81

Selten, Reinhard, **17:** xx n. 17

Sen, Amartya K., **1:** 382; **11:** 27 n. 4, 92 n. 10; **13:** 110, 170 n. 3, 414; **14:** 219; **16:** 202, 205 nn. 6,7; **17:** xvii, 71–79, 386; **18:** 268 n. 3; **19:** 151

Senior, Nassau, **2:** 30; **4:** 69; **6:** 7

Sensini, G., **4:** 126 n. 2; **15:** 102 n. 49

Shackle, G. L. S., **1:** 177, 251, 257, 258, 287 n. 5; **6:** 35–36; **8:** 8 n. 4, 103 n. 11; **12:** 143, 147, 150, 163, 278 n. 3, 335 n. 5; **16:** 288 n. 5;

17: xvii n. 2, 38–39, 44, 69, 172, 176, 181–83; **18:** 293, 294, 295–97, 298; **19:** xvi, 112, 153–61, 247 n. 5

Shand, A. H., **18:** 296 n. 30

Shapiro, C., **12:** 394 n. 8

Shapley, L., **3:** 180

Sharp, Ansel M., **4:** 273 n. 3; **5:** 94

Shefrin, H. M., **1:** 380 n. 3; **9:** 24 n. 6, 246; **17:** 65

Shepsle, Kenneth A., **11:** 95 n. 12; **13:** 403 n. 10

Sherman, Roger, **6:** xvii

Shipley, J. J., **13:** 130 n. 3

Shoup, Carl S., **1:** 163; **5:** 46, 73; **9:** 246; **13:** 451 n. 1; **15:** 48, 210 n. 2, 223 n. 16

Shubik, Martin, **3:** 149 n. 1; **5:** 141; **15:** 242 n. 16

Shughart, W., **11:** 169 n. 7

Shultz, George P., **18:** 431 n. 37

Shultz, W. J., **1:** 129 n. 23

Sidgwick, Henry, **1:** 60

Siegan, Bernard, **16:** 364

Siegel, Jeremy J., **9:** 158 n. 17, 246

Siegel, Sydney, **3:** 105 n. 1

Silone, Ignazio, **16:** 386 n. 4

Silver, Morris, **9:** 241; **13:** 61 n. 4

Simms, C. C., **19:** 5–6

Simon, Herbert A., **3:** 20 n. 7; **12:** 12

Simons, Henry C., **1:** 126 n. 14, 133, 169, 310, 405, 407, 443; **2:** 112, 133, 162–63; **4:** 227, 298; **9:** xiii, 246; **13:** 44; **14:** 189 n. 15, 359, 363; **15:** 60, 84 n. 27, 104; **18:** 20 n. 30, 305–6, 327, 339; **19:** 40, 88, 108, 117

Singer, Marcus George, **1:** 311 n. 1, 321 n. 5; **5:** 94; **17:** 143

Singer, Peter, **7:** 212 n. 3, 235

Sirkin, Gerald, **1:** 365 n. 8

Sjaastad, Larry A., **9:** 147 n. 10, 246

Skidelsky, Robert, **8:** 26 n. 2

Smith, Adam, **1:** xxii, 28, 29, 35, 37, 104, 114, 186, 251, 292–96, 297, 298–301, 303, 304–8, 309–10, 348, 357, 387–88, 389,

415, 458; **2:** 80, 81; **3:** 22, 248, 312; **4:** 137; **6:** 3, 5–7, 39; **7:** 48, 117, 214–15, 235; **8:** 3, 12; **9:** 20, 36, 160, 218, 246; **10:** xvi, 4, 16, 17, 60; **11:** 60, 206; **12:** 28, 32, 35, 337, 349, 350, 363, 369, 377–78, 385–86, 387, 392, 399–400, 429–30, 439, 481; **13:** 16, 54, 62–63, 122, 123, 299; **14:** 326, 485, 489; **15:** 9, 157, 263, 282–97, 302–3, 306–7, 315, 440; **16:** 3, 5, 27, 41, 47, 146, 245 n. 9, 315, 354, 430; **17:** xi, 25–28, 33, 45 n. 2, 46, 82, 96, 100, 101, 102, 235, 293, 295, 310, 320, 327, 409 n. 4, 411 n. 6, 449, 452, 453, 457, 466; **18:** 69, 76–77, 109, 128, 133, 172, 184, 198, 199, 210, 227, 263, 264–67, 271, 273–74, 307, 446, 449; **19:** 40, 71 n. 5, 134, 139, 148, 173, 176, 184, 185, 189, 191, 195, 230, 266, 289–303, 314, 315, 357, 358–59, 361

Smithies, Arthur, **8:** 32 n. 7, 80 n. 1

Snavely, T. R., **19:** 39

Snider, Delbert A., **12:** 255 n. 5

Snow, Arthur, **11:** 119 n. 7; **14:** 310 n. 7

Snyder, Richard C., **3:** 149 n. 1

Sohmen, Egon, **2:** 65 n. 6

Solow, Robert M., **8:** 89 n. 10, 173 n. 7

Solzhenitsyn, Alexandr, **17:** 427–28; **19:** 163

Sopper, William E., **11:** 86 n. 6

Southern, R. W., **7:** 236

Sowell, Thomas, **7:** 236; **17:** 467; **18:** 311, 312, 321, 323

Spann, R., **13:** 322 n. 5

Sparks, Gordon R., **9:** 73 n. 5, 241

Sparks, John, **18:** 401 n. 9

Spence, Michael, **17:** 334 n. 8, 336 n. 10

Spencer, Herbert, **5:** 22; **12:** 454; **13:** 70; **16:** 85; **18:** 167

Spencer, Roger W., **8:** 69 n. 20

Spengler, Joseph J., **1:** 80–81; **17:** 128–29

Spinoza, B., **1:** 389; **3:** 312, 313; **7:** 186, 187

Sprague, O. M. W., **2:** 87

Sprinkel, Beryl, **8:** 164 n. 9

Sraffa, Piero, **11:** 134 n. 2

Staaf, Robert, **12:** 26, 171 n. 7, 187; **15:** 6; **18:** 137 n. 6

Starosolskyj, W., **3:** 67 n. 2

Stein, Herbert, **8:** 49 n. 11, 156 n. 2; **19:** 320 n. 1

Steiner, Peter O., **5:** 46; **12:** 298–99, 301 n. 8, 308–10

Stengers, Isabelle, **18:** 289 n. 2, 290

Stern, N. H., **9:** 174 n. 6, 241

Steve, Sergio, **19:** 30, 32

Stevenson, Charles L., **1:** 236 n. 7

Stewart, Dugald, **19:** 72 n. 5

Stigler, George J., **1:** 28, 201, 249, 253–54, 351 n. 3; **3:** 115 n. 5; **4:** 182 n. 1; **6:** 83 n. 1; **7:** 180 n. 8, 229, 236; **8:** 135 n. 8; **10:** 57 nn. 6, 7, 79 n. 3; **12:** 44, 74–75, 124 n. 9, 137, 220; **13:** 51, 134 n. 7, 151, 318 n. 2; **15:** 156 n. 1, 292; **16:** 284 n. 7; **17:** 308 n. 12; **18:** 44 n. 1, 211 n. 7, 327; **19:** 59, 73, 105, 120, 276, 301

Stiglitz, Joseph E., **12:** 395; **14:** 414 n. 7, 415 n. 11, 424 n. 20

Stigum, B., **12:** 151 n. 8

Stockfisch, J. A., **2:** 21 n. 4; **15:** 81, 156 n. 2

Stolper, Wolfgang F., **15:** 166

Strawson, Peter, **17:** xiii

Streissler, Erich, **17:** 34 n. 9; **19:** 124 n. 2

Strotz, Robert H., **1:** 158 n. 9; **4:** 249 n. 7; **5:** 46, 193; **12:** 307 n. 14; **14:** 109 n. 10, 424 n. 19; **16:** 388 n. 7

Stuart, C., **13:** 471 n. 4

Stuart, J., **2:** 15

Stubblebine, William Craig, **1:** xvii n. 8, xxii, 20, 262 n. 6, 266 n. 12; **4:** 193 n. 10; **5:** x, 72, 177, 178; **12:** 170 n. 2, 293 n. 6, 358 n. 12; **13:** 131 n. 4, 147 n. 15, 367 n. 14; **14:** 85 n. 16, 122 n. 1; **15:** xi, xvi n. 6, 127 n. 1, 160 n. 5, 197 n. 6, 215 n. 8, 244 n. 1, 294 n. 19; **17:** 218; **18:** 369 n. 1; **19:** 42

Sugden, Robert, **17:** 229 n. 8; **18:** 211 n. 8; **19:** 114

Surrey, Stanley, **14:** 5

Sweetser, W., **11:** 186 n. 3

Tabatoni, Pierre, **15:** 67 n. 8

Tannian, F., **15:** xvi n. 6

Tarascio, Vincent, **17:** 123

Tartini, Giuseppe, **8:** 138

Taussig, M., **15:** 408–9

Taylor, Gordon Rattray, **7:** 119 n. 3, 236

Taylor, Overton H., **19:** 42, 52, 118

Taylor, Philip E., **2:** 59; **14:** 72 n. 5

Taylor, Richard, **7:** 14 n. 6, 236

Telser, Lester, **15:** 187 n. 4

Terborgh, George, **8:** 68 n. 18

Terrell, T. P., **18:** 200 n. 2

Thaler, Richard, **1:** 380 n. 3; **9:** 24 n. 6, 246;
    17: 65

Thatcher, Margaret, **18:** 76, 129; **19:** 202

Thin, Tun, **1:** 130 n. 25

Thirlby, G. F., **1:** 153 n. 5, 263 n. 8; **4:** 59 n. 2;
    6: xi n. 1, xv, xvii, 26, 29–34, 45; **12:**
    334–36; **19:** 112, 113 n. 1

Thomas, Robert Paul, **7:** 29, 234; **16:** 8 n. 2

Thompson, Earl, **5:** 178–79, 192; **7:** 95 n. 19,
    236; **9:** 178, 206 n. 7, 246; **13:** 34; **15:** 263;
    16: 197 n. 12; **18:** 380 n. 9

Thompson, Perronet, **9:** 181, 246

Thünen, Johann H. von, **16:** 430

Thursby, Vincent, **3:** xix

Tideman, T. Nicolaus, **1:** 362 n. 3; **13:** 147 n.
    15, 179 n. 1, 432 n. 10; **15:** 188 n. 5

Tiebout, Charles M., **3:** 115 n. 5; **5:** 178; **9:**
    201, 204 n. 4, 246; **11:** 190 n. 3; **14:** 17 n. 24,
    226 n. 11; **15:** 477; **17:** 430 n. 2; **18:** 26,
    44–48, 136 n. 5, 148

Tinbergen, Jan, **9:** 17, 247

Tisdell, C., **16:** 386 n. 5

Tobin, James, **8:** 82, 83, 86 n. 7; **12:** 61 n. 9;
    14: 361–64, 392 n. 1, 395 n. 6, 474–75,
    482–83

Tocqueville, Alexis de, **14:** 519; **17:** 132

Tollison, Robert D., **1:** 20 n. 8; **9:** 40 n. 21,

242; **10:** 73 n. 15, 134 n. 8; **11:** 46 n. 3, 87 n.
    8, 138 n. 4; **12:** 93 n. 3, 271 n. 6, 389 n. 2,
    423 n. 5; **13:** 25 n, 51, 166 n. 10, 185 n. 3,
    214 n. 3, 264 n. 1, 353; **14:** 20 n. 27, 31 n. 3,
    235 n. 8, 466 n. 14; **16:** 160 n. 6, 437 n. 5;
    17: 451 n. 12; **19:** 15, 42, 60, 106 n. 12,
    260 n. 4, 273 n. 6

Toma, Eugenia F., **11:** 189 n. 2

Torto, Raymond G., **8:** 124 n. 9

Tower, Edward, **9:** 150

Treacy, G. C., **18:** 252 n. 6

Triffin, Robert, **18:** 431 n. 38

Trollope, Anthony, **13:** 263

Truman, David B., **3:** 10 n. 15, 12 n. 2, 22 n.
    9, 270 n. 2, 283

Tuerck, David G., **7:** 133 n. 10, 196 n. 7, 236;
    9: 190 n. 2, 247; **11:** 130 n. 18; **14:** 96 n. 6;
    18: 355 n. 15

Tullock, Gordon, **1:** xii, 6, 7, 19–20, 22–23,
    26, 39, 40 n. 10, 50 nn. 3,5, 60 n, 146 n. 7,
    163, 223 n. 7, 282 n. 3, 307 n. 32, 362 nn.
    3,4, 364–65, 421, 438; **3:** x, 9, 132 n. 1,
    257 n. 3; **4:** 90 n. 2, 117 n. 3, 206 n. 24,
    220 n. 2, 259 n. 1, 289, 299 n. 5; **5:** 27, 73,
    95, 118–19, 159, 178, 192; **6:** xvii, 74 n. 5,
    87, 89 n. 3; **7:** xiii, xiv, 10, 19, 32 n. 9, 33 n.
    11, 55, 84 n. 12, 91, 104 n. 4, 129 n. 9, 144 n.
    6, 180 n. 8, 182 n. 9, 183 n. 11, 197 n. 9,
    204 n. 14, 211 n. 1, 217 n. 6, 221 n. 8, 226 n.
    10, 231, 236; **8:** 104 n. 12, 122 n. 6, 137 n. 9;
    9: 10 n. 6, 40 n. 21, 47 n. 5, 147 n. 10, 204 n.
    4, 242, 247; **10:** xi n. 2, 7, 15 n. 4, 23 n. 1,
    32 n. 5, 73 n. 15, 134 n. 8, 150 n. 1, 155; **11:**
    8 n. 7, 22 n. 2, 46 n. 3, 51, 68 n. 1, 87 n. 8,
    125 n. 15, 185; **12:** 93 n. 3, 104 n. 9, 185 n.
    24, 389 n. 2, 423 n. 5, 435 n. 1, 446 n. 11; **13:**
    xii n. 1, xiii, 10–12, 16, 24, 31, 34, 39 n, 44,
    45–46, 47–48, 49, 63–70, 75, 109 n. 8,
    134 n. 7, 145 n. 14, 151, 166 n. 10, 170, 194,
    211 n. 12, 213, 214, 227, 228 n. 2, 230 n. 5,
    231, 234 nn. 10,11, 244 n. 6, 251, 262 n. 4,
    264 n. 1, 267, 268 n. 5, 271 n. 8, 282 n. 1,

303n. 4, 346, 368n. 16, 402n. 10, 404n. 11, 450n; **14:** 13, 18, 34n. 5, 44, 102n. 2, 152n. 1, 154n. 4, 215n. 4, 229n. 2, 255, 260n. 8, 315n. 14, 425n. 22, 466n. 14, 494; **15:** xv, xvi, 115n. 6, 131n. 5, 230n. 4, 252n. 7, 274, 297, 322, 360, 396n. 7, 403n. 12, 463n. 3, 486n. 15, 487n. 17; **16:** xin. 1, 20n. 3, 26n. 9, 45n. 2, 61n. 3, 68n. 2, 71, 72, 87n, 88n. 1, 97, 102, 103, 128, 131, 150n. 3, 160n. 6, 185, 187, 218, 219, 249n. 13, 270n. 5, 284n. 7, 308, 319n. 3, 323n. 6, 327n. 9, 357n. 2, 394n. 13, 407, 456n. 3; **17:** xiin. 4, xvn. 9, 61, 62n. 6, 121, 127, 129, 142n, 165n. 9, 246n. 3, 249n. 4, 253, 261, 267n. 1, 279n. 3, 288n. 5, 304n. 9, 308n. 12, 353, 361n. 6, 375n. 22, 411, 435n. 9; **18:** 181n. 2, 182n. 3, 190n. 3, 219n. 2, 271n. 5, 272, 279n. 2, 286n. 7, 305n. 53, 327, 336n. 8, 353n. 14, 380n. 8, 411n. 18, 425n. 33, 433n. 1, 434n. 2; **19:** xiv–xv, 24, 37, 41, 43, 44, 51, 54–60, 95–107, 142n. 7, 174n. 1, 236, 260n. 4, 273n. 6, 280n. 6
Tumlir, Jan, **16:** 145n. 26
Tuomela, Raimo, **17:** xviiin. 15
Ture, Norman B., **8:** 68n. 19
Turvey, Ralph, **5:** 72, 177; **6:** 61n. 6; **15:** 127n. 1, 218n. 10
Tyler, John, **8:** 14

Ullman-Margalit, E., **17:** 441n. 5
Usher, Dan, **10:** 130n. 2; **16:** 251n. 15; **17:** 326; **18:** 288n. 9

Vanberg, Viktor J., **11:** 23n. 3; **12:** 435n. 1, 440n. 5; **13:** 359n. 3; **14:** xvin. 12; **16:** 128n. 2, 131n. 6, 134n. 9, 136n. 12, 140nn. 13,14, 141n. 15, 146nn. 26,27, 164n. 13, 169n. 29, 186nn. 2,3, 360n. 4, 408n. 6; **17:** xvin. 10, 83n. 2, 459; **18:** 192n. 4, 313, 319; **19:** 59, 121, 213n. 2, 280n. 5, 308nn. 1,2, 346n. 3

Van Buren, Martin, **8:** 14
van den Haag, E., **7:** 236
Van Doren, Carl, **3:** 214n. 2
Vassilakis, S., **1:** 358n. 10; **12:** 353n. 7
Vaubel, R., **18:** 82n. 2, 134n. 2, 137n. 7, 139n. 11
Vaughn, Karen I., **16:** 169n. 29; **18:** 302n. 48
Veblen, Thorstein, **13:** 5–6; **19:** 8
Vibert, Frank, **18:** 140n. 12, 142n. 14, 146n. 18
Vickrey, William, **1:** 150, 151n. 12, 152, 154, 156, 158, 160, 162; **6:** 60; **12:** 255n. 6, 310n. 7; **13:** 34; **14:** 358n. 3, 363
Vinci, Felice, **15:** 93n. 36
Viner, Jacob, **1:** 29, 297; **12:** 328n. 6; **15:** 289n. 14; **19:** 10, 51, 52–53, 59
Vining, Rutledge, **1:** 23, 33, 202n. 11, 212, 431–32; **3:** 80n. 7, 209, 330n. 3, 348; **5:** 159–60; **7:** xvii; **16:** 72, 90, 211n. 14, 251n. 15, 410n. 9, 420n. 3; **17:** 18, 256, 315, 316, 325, 353; **18:** 28n. 11; **19:** 14, 39
Voltaire, **2:** 15, 85
von Neumann, John, **1:** 65; **3:** 151, 164, 186, 328n. 2, 329, 330; **5:** 159; **11:** 43, 93, 122; **12:** 480n. 5; **14:** 312; **16:** 84; **17:** 7

Wachter, Michael L., **8:** 169nn. 3,4
Wade, Larry L., **13:** 170n. 3
Wagner, Adolph, **1:** 124n. 8; **2:** 16, 29; **4:** 227
Wagner, Richard E., **1:** 21, 176n. 13; **2:** xiin. 3, xiii; **6:** xvii; **7:** 47n. 2, 236; **8:** 16n. 11, 20n. 12, 36n. 11, 73n. 26, 134n. 3, 143n. 14, 145n. 16, 184n. 1; **9:** 236n. 8, 242; **10:** 62n. 8; **13:** 23n. 5, 40n. 1, 53; **14:** xiin. 2, xvin. 12, 20n. 27, 31n. 3, 184n. 9, 366n. 1, 430n. 1, 445, 456n. 1, 483n. 3, 490n. 3, 494, 520n. 1; **15:** 487n. 17; **16:** 13n. 7, 55n. 4, 345n. 3; **17:** 89n. 9, 318; **18:** 53–54, 56n. 16, 62n. 21, 63; **19:** 42, 51, 59, 60, 61, 341n. 4
Wagstaff, J. V., **4:** 184–85, 189
Wallace, D. H., **5:** 46

Wallace, George, **7:** 116, 219; **19:** 177, 179
Wallace, Neil, **9:** 144n. 8, 246
Wallich, Henry C., **8:** 55n. 13
Walras, Léon, **6:** 9; **12:** 254; **15:** 66; **17:** 29
Warburton, Clark, **1:** 225n. 9
Ward, Frank, **1:** 42
Wares, W., **12:** 171n. 7, 187
Warren, Earl, **17:** 115, 116, 358; **18:** 340
Washington, George, **3:** 214n. 2
Watrin, C., **17:** 34n. 9
Weaver, Carolyn L., **9:** 30n. 18, 243, 244; **13:** 196n. 2; **15:** xviin. 10, 386n. 4, 392n. 3, 406n. 14
Weaver, Richard M., **8:** 7n. 3
Weber, Max, **1:** 78n. 8; **12:** 433; **13:** 48; **16:** 107
Weber, Warren E., **8:** 73n. 26, 148n. 18
Wegehenkel, Lothar, **1:** 274n. 17
Weibull, Jörgen W., **14:** 414n. 7, 459n. 6
Weidenbaum, Murray, **18:** 142n. 14
Weingast, Barry R., **11:** 95n. 12; **13:** 403n. 10
Weintraub, Robert, **16:** 343–45
Weintraub, Sidney, **12:** 191, 195–96, 199n. 14
Weisber, H., **13:** 200n. 4
Weisbrod, Burton A., **1:** 251; **4:** 21n. 3; **5:** 73; **6:** 56n. 4; **13:** 386n. 6; **18:** 45n. 3, 63n. 22
Weitzman, Martin, **1:** 353; **12:** 348n. 4, 353
Weldon, J. C., **1:** 92n. 8; **5:** 72; **15:** 265–70, 280, 407n. 1
Weldon, T. D., **1:** 33; **3:** 4, 5, 63; **17:** 252
Wellisz, Stanislaw H., **5:** 73; **13:** 420n. 2
West, E. G., **8:** 36n. 11, 143n. 14; **15:** 284nn. 3,7, 292
Whately, Richard, **1:** 29–30, 35
Whinston, Andrew, **1:** 223n. 7, 324n. 7; **4:** 113n. 1, 122n. 5; **5:** 72, 73, 94, 177, 192; **6:** 65n. 2; **13:** 420n. 2; **14:** 123n. 3; **15:** 125n. 15, 127n. 1, 166n. 13, 169, 237n. 10, 250; **19:** 41, 43, 54
White, Charles P., **1:** 13; **19:** 5
White, Michael D., **12:** 426n. 2
Whitehead, Alfred North, **1:** 252

Wick, Warner, **1:** 312n. 3
Wicken, Jeffrey S., **18:** 291
Wicksell, Knut, **1:** 4, 5, 15, 16, 20, 74, 98, 125, 126n. 12, 127n. 20, 134, 135, 138–40, 141, 142, 144, 145, 147, 192n. 2, 204, 217–18, 269, 323n. 7, 362n. 2, 421, 431, 432, 455–57, 458, 459, 460, 461, 463–64, 465–66, 468; **2:** 16, 127n. 4; **3:** x, 8, 83, 197, 291, 348; **4:** xix–xi, 113n. 1, 114–16, 173, 241, 287–89; **5:** xi, xii, xiii, 7, 9, 10, 27–28, 45, 88–91, 93, 95, 127, 128, 131, 132, 135, 137, 140, 146, 147, 148, 154, 155, 157, 181–82; **7:** 11, 50, 68, 111n. 6, 124, 127, 188–90, 236; **8:** 12, 82; **9:** xiv, xxii, 6–11, 46, 182, 183, 235, 247; **10:** 48; **11:** 22, 23, 68, 117, 153n. 8; **12:** 281, 445; **13:** 10, 20–22, 24, 40, 109, 110, 133, 241n. 4, 302n. 3; **14:** xi–xii, 6, 7, 9–13, 21, 26–27, 33, 35, 62–63, 74n. 8, 93, 95, 153n. 3, 154–55, 214, 229, 233n. 6, 256, 259, 265, 306, 308–9, 471; **15:** 67, 70, 98, 104, 105, 342, 462–63, 468n. 7; **16:** 9–10, 71–73, 82–83, 101–2, 105, 270, 273, 308–10, 317–21, 369; **17:** 239, 245, 307; **18:** 350–52; **19:** xvi–xvii, 3–4, 9, 23–24, 29, 36, 37, 53, 54, 56, 60, 136, 140–43, 146n. 11, 244, 245, 329–30
Wicksteed, Philip Henry, **1:** 41; **2:** 30; **3:** 17; **6:** xv, 13, 15, 17–18, 19, 20, 21, 22, 26, 30, 40, 73; **10:** 41; **12:** 72–73, 337
Wieser, F. von, **6:** 11, 13
Wildavsky, Aaron, **7:** 236
Willard, Charles H., **18:** 400n. 8
Willett, Thomas, **6:** xvii; **12:** 104n. 9; **13:** 185n. 3; **19:** 42
Williams, Alan, **5:** 178; **15:** 236n. 7; **18:** 45n. 3
Williams, Bernard, **17:** 433
Williams, C. Arthur, **4:** 141n. 12
Williamson, Oliver, **5:** 46; **12:** 307n. 15
Williamson, R., **15:** 333n. 9
Willis, R., **15:** 277n. 8
Wilson, James Q., **1:** 321n. 6; **4:** 197–98
Wilson, Thomas, **8:** 120n. 5

Wintrobe, Ronald, **19:** 98
Wiseman, Jack, **1:** 153n. 5, 248, 251; **4:** 59n.
    2, 61; **6:** xi, xv, xvii, 34; **7:** 205n. 16, 234;
    12: 334–36; **16:** 143n. 20, 145n. 24; **18:**
    293, 294, 295nn. 24,25,26,27, 297, 298n.
    35; **19:** xv, 110–15
Witt, Ulrich, **18:** 200n. 3, 293n. 17
Wittfogel, Karl A., **3:** 348
Wolff, Christian, **3:** 317
Woodward, Susan, **12:** 416n. 3; **18:** 213n. 9
Worcester, Dean A., Jr., **12:** 95n. 4; **13:**
    330n. 8; **15:** 156n. 2
Wright, David McCord, **2:** 12–14; **19:** 39, 52
Wunderlich, Gene, **7:** 236

Yeager, Leland B., **8:** 8n. 4, 190n. 7; **13:**
    140n. 12; **18:** 34n. 19, 412n. 20; **19:** 39, 41,
    43, 51, 54

Yeats, William Butler, **18:** 76; **19:** 101
Yohe, William P., **8:** 123n. 8
Yoon, Yong J., **11:** 162n. 3; **12:** 406n. 9,
    453n. 1; **14:** xivn. 9, 326n. 4, 328n. 7,
    336n. 11; **19:** 299n. 4
Young, Allyn, **1:** 353; **6:** 81, 83; **12:** 352n. 6,
    382, 386; **14:** 326; **15:** 156n. 1, 160; **19:**
    79, 86
Young, Leslie, **11:** 107n. 2; **14:** 320n. 17; **16:**
    441n. 5; **19:** 278n. 2

Zardkoohi, Asghar, **14:** 203n. 3, 393n. 2,
    436n. 8
Zeckhauser, Richard, **5:** 94
Zelenitz, Allan, **9:** 202n. 2, 243
Zlabinger, Albert, **19:** 121
Zohlnhöfer, Werner, **8:** 172n. 5

Subject Index

ability-to-pay theory of taxation, **4:**
  156–57; **5:** 158
absolute(s), relatively absolute. *See*
  relatively absolute absolute(s)
abstinence, **2:** 30; **6:** 7, 8
  from spending, **4:** 69–70
abstraction
  Homo economicus as, **12:** 6–10, 71,
    73–77, 128
  necessity of, **12:** 70–71
academic freedom, **7:** 156
academic settings, **1:** 25–26
accounting and inflation, **8:** 68
accounting examples, **2:** 50–57
adjudication by government, **7:** 114
administrative-decision model, **13:** 307–11.
  See also neutrality, allocational
affluent society, **1:** 293
agenda control, theory of, **11:** 29
aggravative fiscal systems, **1:** 128
aggregate capital formation, **1:** 160–61
aggregate demand in Keynesian model, **8:**
  83–84
aggregate rent (Knight), **12:** 323
aggregate sacrifice, learning and least, **4:**
  137; **5:** 157
aggregate social calculus, **1:** 72, 162,
  195
aggregate supply
  in Keynesian model, **1:** 168; **8:** 83–84
  in Phillips-curve models, **8:** 87–88

agreement
  analysis of, **5:** 104, 108, 121, 123, 124, 128,
    135–36
  cartel, majority rule voting for, **13:** 341
  compensation to secure, **16:** 116–17
  constitutional (*see* constitutional
    agreement)
  in constitutional choice (Rawls), **16:** 160
  in constitutional economics, **16:** xii
  constitutions formed by, **11:** 5
  contractarian interpretation of, **16:**
    28–29, 159–60, 165–71
  contractarian sharing principles
    emerging from, **17:** 452
  costs of, **3:** 98; **5:** 9, 10, 22, 80, 169
  criterial and epistemological, **11:** 5n. 1
  as criterion, **3:** 7; **11:** 5
  in Crusoe-Friday model, **17:** 361–66
  in discourse, or dialog, notion, **16:**
    155–56, 165–71
  on efficiency, institutional change for,
    13: 345–54
  efficiency and, **10:** 28–29; **16:** 113–14
  emergence and enforcement, **16:** 91–93
  exchange: as basis for, **7:** 23–24; role in,
    5: 102; **16:** 247–48
  fairness defined by, **17:** 314–15, 325, 410
  on fiscal rules, **5:** 152
  on markets, **1:** 219
  morality, **1:** 86
  multilateral, **5:** 9

agreement (*continued*)
on Pareto efficiency, **16:** 374–75
on Pareto optimality, **16:** 374–75
on Pareto-relevant reform, **16:** 374–75
in politics, **16:** 155–71; **17:** 165
preconstitutional (Rawls), justice from,
   16: 74
on preventing economic reform, **16:**
   377–78
public goods, consumption of, **5:** 121
on public policy rules, **16:** 73–74
required compensation for, **16:** 116–17
rules, alternative, **17:** 325–26
rules, with uncertainty about, **16:** 162
rules and, **3:** 78; **16:** xii
in rules emerging from, **16:** 165–70
in social contract theories, **16:** 155–56,
   159–60, 165
in social interaction, **19:** 306–7
in social interaction theory, **12:** 239
in taxing-spending choice (Wicksell),
   19: 142
taxpayers, related to transfer taxes, **14:**
   242–43
between traders, **17:** 166
trading of, **5:** 16, 32
truth tested by, **16:** 175–76
uncertainty of, **16:** 162n. 10
behind veil of ignorance, **16:** 103, 187; **17:**
   364–66
behind veil of uncertainty, **16:** 187
in voluntary exchange, **19:** 141, 150–51
Wicksell's focus on, **19:** xvii
See also voluntary exchange
Agricultural Adjustment Act (1933)
   Thomas Amendment, **18:** 403
   unconstitutionality of, **18:** 355
Alfred Nobel Memorial Prize in Economic
   Sciences, **1:** xiv–xv, xxii
   acceptance lecture, **1:** 455–68
   press release, **1:** 3–7

allocation. *See* resource allocation;
   resource allocation theory
allocationist-maximization paradigm:
   catallactic-coordination paradigm,
   differences from, **19:** 6–7
allocationists
   defined, **19:** xvii
   market failure diagnosed by, **19:** 137
   normative emphasis, in modern, **19:**
      147–48
   of orthodox economics, **19:** 9
allocative efficiency, **1:** 267–68; **11:** 12
altruism, **1:** xx, 4–5, 48, 329–45; **4:** 198; **10:**
   68–69; **19:** 104–5
American dream, mythology of, **1:** 439
amortization of public debt. *See* public
   debt, retirement of
anarchists
   contractarians and, compared, **16:**
      18–21, 27
   individual rights, boundaries to, **16:**
      23–25
   libertarian, criticisms of, **16:** 21–23
   student revolutionary, **16:** 178–79
anarchy, **1:** 51, 59, 293, 299; **7:** 7; **11:** 7
   barriers to, **17:** 431
   conditions for, **17:** 99, 377; **19:** 198
   constitutional, **1:** 372; **7:** 10, 19; **18:** 182;
      19: 177–79
   constitutionalist-contractarian, **16:** 27
   contractual social order, **16:** 19–21
   counterculture, quasi-anarchistic, **19:** 179
   equilibrium and, **7:** 75–76; **17:** 100–101
   Hobbesian, **7:** 12–13, 16, 32–33, 42, 73,
      108, 165–66, 186–87; **9:** 6–7, 13; **10:** 30;
      17: 302–4, 362–65, 369, 380–84; **18:**
      175; **19:** 317
   as ideal, **7:** 5–9, 117–18
   interaction, **7:** 72–76
   Leviathan, **1:** 21–22
   libertarian, **15:** 283–84

limits of, **7:** 5–8

Lockean variants of, **16:** 26

moral order in, **7:** 8

ordered, defined, **7:** 215; **17:** 191, 229, 438, 463; **19:** 58, 174–75

potential for, **19:** 179

property rights distribution under, **7:** 31–32; **19:** 174

Rawlsian, **17:** 370–71

rights in, **15:** 4

romantic version, **7:** 11

rules under, **15:** 4–5

social contract as alternative to, **17:** 405, 408

studies of, **19:** 58–59

See also anarchists; Hobbesian jungle; moral anarchy

anti-federalism, **18:** 75

Anti-Federalists, **18:** xiii–xiv, 103

antitrust laws, **11:** 103

arbitrage opportunity, **2:** 152–53; **12:** 151–52, 164–67, 424

Articles of Confederation, U.S., **18:** 102–5, 146–47

artifactual constraints, **19:** 306

artifactual man

defined, **1:** 255

natural man and, **1:** 246–59

artifactual political economy, **19:** 239

assets, owned and non-owned, **1:** 156–61

association and exchange behavior, **1:** 35

asymmetry

between external economies and diseconomies, **15:** 173

of Keynesian policy, **8:** 86

in reciprocity in money economy, **12:** 413–14

of tax and expenditure analysis, **4:** 94–95

auction method

argument for, **13:** 260

not applied, **13:** 261

ownership rights, of assigning, **13:** 257–62

rent seeking, **13:** 260

Austrian economics, **1:** 47–48; **6:** xi, 20, 23, 87; **8:** 134n. 4; **13:** 71–72, 76

of business cycle, **8:** 71n. 22, 108n. 15, 177n. 10

entrepreneurial choice (Kirzner), **19:** 156, 160

Knight's criticism of, **19:** 89

neo-Austrian economics, **1:** 251

Austrian school. *See* Austrian economics

autarky, extra-market, **18:** 236–38

authoritarianism

constitutional order, as alternative to, **16:** 180

opposition to, **1:** 231

paradigm of, **16:** 17–18

authority

logic of, **16:** 16–19

principle of, **1:** 298

rational deference to, **16:** 190–91

rules versus, **1:** 224–25

autobiography

conceptions of a person in, **19:** 66–70

as subjective record, **19:** 15

truth in, **19:** 64

autonomy

competitive federalism, efficacy under, **18:** 72–76, 86–88

federal system, for subunits of, **18:** 95–96

individual, range and scope of, **18:** 106

balanced budget, **1:** 170, 173; **8:** 16–21; **14:** 496

classical rule, **8:** 11

constitutional amendment, proposed, **14:** 451, 493–94, 500–516; **16:** 58–59, 310

as constitutional constraint, **11:** 137–38

balanced budget (*continued*)
  constitutional proposal, **8:** 9
  as constitutional rule, **8:** 183–89
  over cycle, **8:** 154–55
  decision making and, **8:** 12
  fiscal constitution and, **8:** 96–97
  fiscal decision and, **8:** 184–85
  at full employment, **8:** 42–43, 53–55,
    157–62
  at high employment, **8:** 42–43, 47–48
  at hypothetical income, **8:** 42–43
  Keynesian bias, **8:** 101–6
  Keynesian rejection, **8:** 32–33
  multiplier and, **2:** 76–77; **8:** 34n. 9
  as procedural constraint, **9:** 183, 235–36
  rules for, **8:** 8, 153–66; **14:** 102, 105, 110,
    270, 500–501
balanced-budget multiplier, **2:** 76–77; **8:**
  34n. 9
  as procedural constraint, **9:** 183,
    235–36
balanced-budget rule, **4:** 102, 105; **8:** 8,
  153–56; **14:** 500–504
  at full employment, **4:** 110
  institutional choice of, **4:** 270
balance sheets
  individual, **2:** 41, 50–57
  national, **2:** 33
bargaining
  behavior strategy in, **5:** 92
  Coasian solutions, **1:** 355; **13:** 358–59,
    367n. 14
  competition and, **3:** 103–4
  determinants, **5:** 17, 102
  difference principle and, **16:** 294–95
  efficiency and, **3:** 104–5
  externalities, in private response to, **13:**
    358–59
  in fiscal decision, **4:** 117–20
  game, **5:** 77, 89
  intraexchange, **12:** 356
  markets and, **3:** 103, 104

  maximin solution, Rawlsian, **16:**
    291–96
  model, **3:** 100–103; **16:** 296–304
  in political exchange, **18:** 186
  under property and liability rules, **12:**
    171
  range, **3:** 98–100; **14:** 255
  in trade, **5:** 77, 82
  unanimity rule and, **3:** 60, 69, 107
  behind veil of ignorance, **16:** 294–95,
    300–301
Barro neutrality theorem
  consumption and savings streams
    under, **14:** 411–13
  defined, **14:** 410
  public debt issue under, **14:** 409–13
  rational expectations in, **14:** 408–9
  Ricardian equivalence theorem,
    difference from, **14:** 409–13
  saving under, **14:** 411–13
barter economy
  buyers and sellers in, **12:** 411–12
  exchange in, **5:** 117; **12:** 411–12
  inefficiencies in, **12:** 412
behavior
  amoral, **17:** 208
  analysis of, **1:** 322–24
  association and exchange, **1:** 35
  of bureaucracy, **13:** 12; **14:** 15–16, 85–86
  of bureaucrats, **13:** 48–49, 63–70
  certainty, degree of, **1:** 76–77
  Christian hypothesis, **13:** 33–34
  of citizens toward bureaucrats, **14:** 524
  coercion, degree of, **1:** 82–84
  in complex society, **17:** 49–51
  constitutional choice, **1:** 367–73
  constraints in, **16:** 156–57; **17:** 93–94
  cooperation and conflict, **1:** 361
  cooperative, as form of morality, **17:**
    230–31
  dichotomy versus consistency, **1:** 70
  economic (*see* economic behavior)

economic interest, contrary to, **17:** 228–31

endogenous constraints on, **17:** 92–94

ethical rules and constraints, **1:** 356, 357

in exchange, **17:** 81–91; **18:** 229–30

fiscal institutions, effect of, **14:** 17–19, 27–30

Homo economicus model, **12:** 6–10, 71–73, 87–89, 128; **17:** 49–51

immoral, **17:** 208

imposing constraints on future, **16:** 403–7

labor and, **1:** 346–59

legal institutions, effect on, **12:** 286–87

limits on, **1:** 329–45

logic of, **1:** 66–67

market and, **1:** 35–42, 75–88, 346–59; **12:** 439; **13:** 72–73; **17:** 81–87, 208, 243

models of, **1:** 64–65, 67–68

moral, **17:** 208

under moral anarchy, **17:** 190–91

moral norms, in accordance with, **14:** 48

nature of alternatives, **1:** 81–82

in nonmarket situations, **14:** 478

normative (Rawls), **1:** 432

norms for in voluntaristic ethics, **5:** 94

numbers and, relevance of, **1:** 318–22

oligopoly, **15:** 240–42

opportunistic, **17:** 81–87, 92–93, 228–31

political, **1:** 40, 62, 67, 196; **14:** 490; **16:** 152, 154; **19:** 314

political institutions, effect of, **13:** 13; **14:** 19–20, 30–31

political rules, among alternative, **1:** 19, 22

politicization to impose preferences on, **13:** 413–18

politics and, **13:** 418

power relations and, **1:** 84–85

in prisoners' dilemma game, **12:** 132–33

promise-keeping, **14:** 524

in public goods production, **5:** 24

resource utilization and, **1:** 272–73

responsibility, degree of, **1:** 79–81, 257, 334, 340, 343

revolutionary (Tullock), **19:** 101–3

rules of, **1:** 313, 334, 344; **18:** 317–21

samaritan's dilemma and, **1:** 329–45

self-control, economics of, **1:** 380

social choice and, **16:** 201–3, 204, 207

socialism and, **1:** 70

social participation, degree of, **1:** 77–79

symmetry of, **13:** 108–10

in two-person society, **17:** 48–49

of unrestricted monopsony, **13:** 321

utility-maximizing, **17:** 99–101

voluntary, **1:** 41, 182, 198, 244, 266, 268, 275; **7:** 52–55

voter (*see* voter behavior)

See also choices; collective choice; individual choice; rational choice behavior models

behavior strategy, **1:** 272–73, 330–45, 450

absence of, **5:** 44

in adjustment process, **5:** 14, 76, 169

in bargaining, **5:** 89, 92

disturbing equilibrium, effect of in, **5:** 24

limitation on, **5:** 78

in small-number case, **5:** 81, 88, 122

beliefs

conflicts over, **17:** 162

in confronting reality, **17:** 155–56, 159–60

error in, correction of, **17:** 156–57

evaluations and, **17:** 159–62, 172

function of, **17:** 171

generalization of, **17:** 155–56, 161

of individuals, **17:** 155–57, 159–61

religious, **17:** 158–59, 177, 179–83

rules of politics in, **17:** 163

in scientific process, **17:** 156–57, 174–75

benefit-cost analysis. *See* cost-benefit analysis

benefit principle of taxation, **2:** 121–22; **3:** 291–93; **5:** 157

benefits
of collective action, **1:** 5, 380–81, 389, 424–25
costs and, **15:** 16, 200–202
of defense, **4:** 192
discounting and (Barro), future, **14:** 389
divisibility of, **4:** 18
of education, **4:** 192–93
in externalities, **15:** 16
government, **14:** 253, 499
indivisibility of, **4:** 112
in majority rule voting, costs and, **13:** 194
monopoly, capitalization of, **12:** 214–15
objectivity in identifying, **12:** 19
present-value, **12:** 212–13
of public expenditure, **4:** 65–69, 189–94
public goods, **15:** 227–43
social security, **15:** 451–53
spillover: exclusion from, **5:** 60; from saving, **12:** 464
stochastic, **11:** 177–78

benefit theories, early, **1:** 124

benevolent despots, **9:** 14
political models, **1:** xvi, 15–16, 72, 74, 144, 203, 362, 456; **9:** 7, 220
Wicksell on, **1:** 15–16, 74, 144, 362 n. 2, 456

benevolent dictator, **14:** 176

benevolent fiscal authority, **14:** 91, 99–100

benevolent fisc model, **14:** 90–92, 97–100

benevolent paternalism, **1:** 284

benevolent political agents, **19:** 332–34

benevolent self-interest in work, **1:** 357–59

benign deity, Smith's, **1:** xxii

bequests
public debt, **14:** 415–17
as value transfers of value, **13:** 265
See also fiscal transfer; intergenerational transfers; public debt financing

bias
capitalization, differences in, **4:** 66–69
public sector, and deficit finance, **8:** 106–9

bicameralism, **3:** xvi, xix, 231–46

bifurcated man, **1:** 68

biography, **19:** 66 n. 2, 72–73

black markets, **12:** 419

bonuses, veterans', **4:** 204–5

borrowing, **1:** 170, 171–72; **2:** 47; **4:** 98–103. *See also* debt; public debt

borrowing, corporate
burden of payment, **14:** 437
external and internal, **14:** 436, 438
principles of, **14:** 438–39

borrowing, internal: accounting, **2:** 41

borrowing, public
budget deficit, **14:** 446
current consumption, **14:** 124–25, 462, 519
exchange in, **14:** 343–44, 353–55, 357–62
from individuals, **14:** 108
internal and external, **14:** 353–55
national accounting fallacy, **14:** 352–55
public finance principles, classic, **14:** 496
public spending, **14:** 351, 358–60, 373–75, 446–47
the state and, **14:** 436
taxation and, equivalence to public debt, **14:** 436–38

Bronson v. Rhodes (1869), **18:** 389 n. 2

budget, balanced. *See* balanced budget

budgetary ratio in general-fund financing, **4:** 75, 77–79

budgetary theory, **2:** 127–28

budget deficit, **8:** 3–4
actions to reduce, **14:** 499
budget imbalance (1969 to early 1990s), **14:** 495–96
creation of, **14:** 463–64
debt-financed, **8:** 138–47; **14:** 360, 446–50, 492 n. 4

democracy and, **8:** 5
financing, **8:** 34–35; **17:** 88–89
fiscal choice and, **4:** 97–98; **8:** 138–47
government growth and, **8:** 71–73; **14:** 480–81
in Great Depression, **8:** 38–40
inflation and, **8:** 59–60
interest rates, impact on, **14:** 448
investment and, **8:** 68–69
after Keynes, **8:** 57–59
Keynesian policy and, **8:** 34
monetary expansion and, **8:** 124
monetary pressures and, **8:** 117
money creation and, **8:** 110–28, 147–49
money supply and, **8:** 118–20; **14:** 479–80
after 1960s, **8:** 51–52
in non-Keynesian setting, **8:** 105
passive, **8:** 38–40
public sector bias and, **8:** 106–9
budget management in unstable economy, **8:** 96–97
budget principles, **8:** 6
budget reform, Congress and, **8:** 162–64
Budget Reform Act (1974), **8:** 162–64; **16:** 57 n. 5, 310
budgets and budgeting
  balanced budget (*see* balanced budget)
  bias and, **7:** 197–204
  built-in flexibility, **4:** 41–42, 149
  constitutional economics applied to, **16:** 13–14
  decision-making, and piecemeal, **7:** 193–94
  earmarked and general-fund revenues, allocation of, **14:** 76–86
  efficiency and, **7:** 194, 195
  fiscal choice and, **4:** 97–111
  fiscal theory (Musgrave), **14:** 55–59, 65
  general-fund, **4:** 82; **5:** 75
  government, and fiscal illusion, **4:** 135
  government, sectors of, **14:** 94–95, 100

Keynesian macroeconomic theory, **14:** 65, 496, 506
majority rule voting and, **7:** 128, 192–93
politics and, **8:** 95–96
size: regulation and, **5:** 36; **9:** 195; taxation and, **11:** 125
transfers in, **11:** 162–63
See also budget deficit; earmarked revenue; public debt
budget surplus
  debt retirement and, **8:** 189–90; **14:** 469
  democracy and, **8:** 102–4
  full employment and, **8:** 48, 158–59
  locational rents and, **9:** 201
  migration, effect on, **18:** 40–42
  mobility costs and, **9:** 209–10
burden
  of bureaucracy, **15:** 33–35
  cost and, **6:** 50: theory of, **1:** xviii, 150–63, 467; **8:** 36 n. 11, 143 n. 14
  excess (*see* excess burden)
  of freedom, **1:** 127–32
  of inflation, **2:** 77–78, 106–7; **8:** 62–66
  of monopoly restrictions, **12:** 212–13
  primary real, **2:** 5, 6, 8–9, 26, 32
  of private debt, **2:** 46
  of public debt (*see* public debt burden)
  public debt issue and postponement of, **14:** 362–64
  transfer, **2:** 7, 8–9, 12–13, 34
  of war, **2:** 106
  See also taxes
bureaucracy
  attitude toward, **16:** 348–50
  burden of, **15:** 33–35
  control of U.S., **16:** 104–5
  decision-making and, **7:** 127; **15:** 33–35
  defined, **15:** 33
  discretion in: market order, effect of, **16:** 257, 259; with political pricing, **16:** 257–58
  dismantling of, **16:** 350–52

bureaucracy (*continued*)
  economic approach to, **16:** 107
  economic incentives in, **19:** 235–36
  efficiency and, **8:** 73n. 26
  Federal Reserve Board and, **8:** 127
  franchise and, **7:** 197–204
  frustration with, **7:** 116
  government, U.S., **19:** 177–78, 183
  growth of, **16:** 348–50
  individual choice behavior in, **13:**
    48–49, 63–70
  maximizing behavior of, **14:** 15–16, 85–86
  maximizing units in, **14:** 16
  monetary authority and, **8:** 122–23
  opposition to, **16:** 359
  organizational behavior, **13:** 12
  political pricing, **16:** 257–58
  politicians and bureaucrats, **13:** 11–13,
    62–70
  politics of, **19:** 97–99
  power, **9:** 28–30
  prices, role in, **16:** 257–59
  rents and, **7:** 197–204
  restrictions of, **19:** 192–94
  in socialist economy, **19:** 192–93, 237
  spending, role in, **15:** 456
  theories of, **1:** 50, 56–57; **3:** xviii; **7:** 217n.
    6; **9:** 162; **13:** 48, 62–69: agenda,
    bureaucracy control of, **9:** 29–30;
    economic theory of, **19:** 97–99;
    modern theory of, **13:** 47–49
bureaucrats
  allocational neutrality theorem, **13:**
    308–9
  behavior, **13:** 63–70
  in Coase's model of the state, **13:** 312
  motivation of, **13:** 48–49, 65–66
  in Pigovian model of the state, **13:** 312
  politicians and, behavior of, **13:** 11–13,
    62–70
  public choice role, **13:** 120
  self-interest, **13:** 12

business accounting, inflation in, **8:** 68
business administration, **3:** 308n. 1
business cycles
  Austrian theory, **8:** 71n. 22, 108n. 15,
    177n. 10
  budget balance and, **8:** 154–55
  political, **13:** 4, 51–52
business decisions, costs in, **6:** 26–29
buyers
  in barter economy, **12:** 411–12
  in command economy, **12:** 417–20
  consumers and, as sellers, **13:** 389–91
  demands of, **12:** 192–95
  expectations of, **12:** 232–33
  interests of, **18:** 210
  liberty for, **18:** 205
  under marginal evaluation curve, **12:**
    197–200
  in market space, **13:** 230–31
  in money-goods exchange, **12:** 412–14
  price change, **2:** 219–20
  price discrimination among, **5:** 37–38
  producers and sellers as consumers
    and, **13:** 389–91
  quantity discount mechanism, **12:**
    204–5
  quantity discount transactions, **12:**
    200–202
  of substitute public goods, **18:** 203–4
  in two-dimensional market space, **13:**
    230–31
  in vote market, **13:** 214–26
  See also consumers

candidates and elections, Downs on
  theory of, **3:** 343–47
capacities, or endowments
  differences, **17:** 301–2, 330–31
  distribution of, **17:** 298–302, 311, 326–27
  economic equality in premarket
    assignment, **17:** 300
  equal and differing, **17:** 286–89

equal-capacities hypothesis, **17:** 295
   identity in, **17:** 283–85
   increase or decrease in, **17:** 284
   nontaxability of, **17:** 322–23
   preferences in, **17:** 283–89, 299–302
capital
   consumption of, **1:** 159, 160–61; **9:** 109;
     14: 414–15, 490
   creation, **1:** 160–61; **14:** 376–77: **15:** 294:
     saving and, **9:** 99
   investment, **1:** 248; **14:** 370–73
   nature of law, **7:** 136–64
   norms related to, **14:** 489
   permanence of, **12:** 465
   political economy and, **14:** 329–34
   productivity through, **12:** 463
   public debt and, **2:** 121; **8:** 11, 18–19; **11:**
     135–37; **14:** 78–80
capital budgets, **2:** 130 n. 5; **4:** 268; **11:**
   136–37
capital formation, **1:** 160–61; **4:** 69–70
capital gains, **4:** 141–42; **11:** 127
capital goods, **7:** 156–60; **12:** 463–64
capital-income relationship, **2:** 66
capital investment, **2:** 121; **4:** 266–68; **7:** 21
capitalism, **1:** 368
   ethics of, **13:** 151
   Knight's ethical criticism of, **12:** 127
   Marxist-socialist critique of, **1:** 183–84
   See also markets
capitalization
   bias differences in, **4:** 66–69
   of future taxes, **2:** 35, 43, 89–90
   of interest receipts, **2:** 43
   of monopoly benefits, **12:** 214–15
   of payments stream, **2:** 155–56
   of public expenditure benefits, **4:** 65–69
   of taxes, **2:** 43, 89–90; **6:** 63–64: fiscal
     choice and, multiperiod, **4:** 65–69;
     Italian fiscal theory and, **15:** 81–83;
     public debt and, **4:** 131–32, 266–68;
     on wealth, **4:** 29

capital outlay, **8:** 11, 18–19
capital shortage, **8:** 68–71, 87 n. 7
capital taxes, **9:** 114–16, 178, 230; **11:** 127; **14:**
   375–76
   defense and, **9:** 178
   inflation and, **9:** 115–16
   Leviathan and, **9:** 107
   public debt and, **14:** 375–76
capital value
   consumption of, **14:** 447
   debt issue, relationship to, **14:** 368–73,
     376–77
   default, effect of, **14:** 378–80
   of moral constraints, **14:** 461–62
   public debt, with creation of, **14:**
     376–77, 456
   restoration of, **14:** 381
   as revenue source, **9:** 99
cartels
   advertising-marketing: effect of, **13:**
     339–40; of firms, **13:** 338–44
   costs, **13:** 390–97
   democracy and, **11:** 103; **13:** 397–98
   European Union, conditions in, **18:** 146
   formation game, **13:** 404–5
   incentives to make, **13:** 408
   industries and, **13:** 391–409
   as institutions, **13:** 339–44
   interindustry interaction, **13:** 343–44
   majority rule in, **13:** 341
   market sharing, **13:** 339–40
   output restriction, **13:** 339–40
   political effectiveness, **13:** 390–96
   price fixing, **13:** 339–40
   problems of, **13:** 342–43
   rents and, **13:** 403–6
   rent seeking and, **13:** 398–402, 403
   restrictions on, **13:** 389–99
   rules, internal, **13:** 340–42
   sizes, limited, **13:** 403
   under supranational government, **18:** 136
   unanimity rule in, **13:** 341

catallactic paradigm
  allocationist-maximization, difference
    from, **19:** 6–7
  exchange in, theory of, **19:** 7–9
catallactic perspective
  Buchanan's conversion to, **19:** 4, 24, 122
  of competitive society, **12:** 117, 125
  for economic interaction, **16:** 60
  economic order in, Knight's criticisms
    of, **12:** 117–23
  economics, approach to, **13:** 15–21
  of economic theory, **12:** 480
  exchange, focus on, **12:** 116–17
  externalities in, relevant, **12:** 121
  of markets, **19:** 7–9
  maximizing perspective, difference
    from, **12:** 115–16
  political economy, versus, **1:** 29, 35
  politics, applied to, **13:** 18–21; **16:** 62–63
  revival of, **16:** 240
  as science of exchange, **13:** 16–17
  symbiotics, **1:** 35–36
Center for Study of Public Choice, **1:** 7, 26,
    419; **19:** 44–45, 108–10
central banks
  European Union nations, **18:** 112; **19:**
    207
  monetary expansion by national, **18:**
    124–25
  in nation-states, **18:** 124
central government
  defense and, **9:** 206
  European Union, functions in, **18:** 124,
    132, 134
  fiscal systems in, **18:** 3–22
  interest groups, effect on, **18:** 134–37
  New Deal and, **16:** 339–42
  public goods, provision of, **18:** 4–7,
    35–42
centralization
  economic activity, control over, **18:**
    91–92

federalism, under competitive, **18:**
    72–76, 86–88
  fiscal, pressures, **18:** 139
  of political exchange paradigm, **1:** 24,
    26–27, 29, 34, 35–36, 49, 181–82, 384,
    456, 460–61
  of political power, **18:** 134–37
  pure democracy and, **1:** 76
  See also decentralization; European
    Union; federalism, competitive;
    markets
central place theory, **18:** 28–29
central planning, Hayek's critique, **16:** 140
certainty
  in decision making, **1:** 76–77
  individual choice in, **12:** 145–49
  structures of, **12:** 144–45
  See also uncertainty
ceteris paribus
  data in pound of, **12:** 53
  equivalence, **12:** 56
  in macroeconomic analysis, **12:** 59–65
  misuse of, **12:** 56–58, 61
  partial equilibrium variables in, **12:**
    53–54, 66
  use of (Boulding), **12:** 64
  variables, as restriction on, **12:** 53–55
charity, economics of, **13:** 34
choice, institutional
  economic ignorance in, **19:** 219–20
  understanding of, **19:** 212–15
choice calculus
  of individual, **4:** 216, 293–94: analysis
    of, **4:** 222–23; fiscal policy and, **4:**
    269–81; public debt and, **4:** 258–68;
    taxes and, **4:** 227–57
  progressive tax and, **4:** 38–42, 148–66,
    227–42
  of taxpayer, **4:** 12–14, 90–95, 172–73,
    216: currency creation, effect of, **4:**
    106–8; functional finance, effect of,
    4: 108–9; public debt issue, effect of,

4: 99–102; under taxes, **4:** 35–42, 48–54

uncertainty, effect of (*see* choice under uncertainty)

choices

among alternatives, **12:** 26–27, 114; **16:** 202

of belief: James, **17:** 183; Pascal, **17:** 183; Shackle, **17:** 183

under bureaucratic discretion, **16:** 258

under certainty, **12:** 145–49

as commitment, **19:** 159–60

consequences of, **12:** 297; **19:** 159

constitutional (*see* constitutional choice)

constraints on, **9:** 239–40; **14:** 505; **16:** 156–57; **17:** 60–61, 63–66, 81–87, 91–94, 463; **19:** 245

consumer and voter, differences in, **13:** 162–69

cooperative morality, in Gauthier's, **17:** 461–62

cost and, **6:** 17, 19, 20, 37–48

creative and reactive, **19:** 154–56

between debt forms, **2:** 62–63

defined, **17:** 172: neoclassical, **19:** 154–55; by Shackle's, **19:** 153–61

democratic, **15:** 347–49

in economics, **5:** 143–44; **6:** 40; **19:** 125–26

economic theory, in subjective, **17:** 36–38

electoral, **13:** 293–95

exit options as, **18:** 97

expectational, **18:** 295

of experts in markets and democracy, **16:** 135–39

among fiscal institutions, **14:** 34

of idleness, **12:** 368–70

implementation, with lagged, **16:** 399, 407–9

individual (*see* individual choice)

interest- and theory-components in, **16:** 158

intertemporal, **14:** 462–63

labor, in allocation of (Smith), **19:** 300–302

in laissez-faire economy, **15:** 9–11

legal uncertainty (*see* choice under uncertainty)

logic of, **6:** 40; **12:** 4–9, 14–18

in market and political exchange, **16:** 249–50

in market economy, **12:** 34–35; **17:** 316–17; **18:** 268–70; **19:** 249

market order, informed by, **19:** 214

market size, influencing, **12:** 378–79

minimax principle of, **13:** 122, 124

Mises's theory of, **17:** 33

necessity of, **17:** 172–74

noneconomic elements in, **12:** 12–21

norms for, **12:** 5

opportunity cost in, **6:** 16; **12:** 285–86, 337–38

political, **10:** 18; **11:** 27–28, 72–74; **17:** 273–74; **18:** 82–85

among political rules and institutions, **17:** 262–63

politicization of, **18:** 68

preference for, **16:** 156–57

properties of, **12:** 144

public and private choice outcomes, **14:** 478–79

public choice, private choice distinct from, **13:** 29–30

in public choice analysis, **16:** 46–47

in radical subjectivism, **18:** 294–96

risk and uncertainty, **12:** 279

of rules, **10:** 11–13, 33–34

within rules, **3:** 110

rules (Wicksell), made within, **16:** 9–10

with scarcity, **16:** 239; **19:** 223

scientific, **17:** 174–76

under Sen's liberalism rule, **17:** 72–79

choices (*continued*)
    Shackle's interpretation, **17:** 181–83
    social, **13:** 43–44
    among social states, **11:** 27
    spending-versus-saving, **12:** 461–65
    in temporary preference theory, **16:** 401–2
    time preference, **16:** 399–401
    under uncertainty (*see* choice under uncertainty)
    unethical or immoral, **12:** 370
    utility maximization in, **13:** 116; **15:** 362–63
    in valuation of a life, **12:** 278–81
    voluntariness of, contractarian interpretation of, **16:** 165–66
    voting, **10:** 86
    work-leisure, **12:** 345–49
    See also costs; individual choice; opportunity cost(s); preference
choice under uncertainty, **4:** 107–8; **12:** 296; **17:** 38, 172–73
    alternatives, **12:** 145
    Arrow on theories of, **1:** 77 nn. 2,5
    debt and currency creation, **4:** 107–8
    entrepreneurial, **12:** 150, 163
    excise tax and, **4:** 253
    individual choice behavior and, **14:** 113–16
    inflation and, **8:** 67–68
    Knight on, **12:** 143–45, 151
    legal, opportunity costs and, **12:** 296
    progressive tax and, **4:** 236–38
    public debt and, **4:** 263–64
    risk and, **12:** 142, 279; **19:** 87–88
    Shackle's theory of, **12:** 143, 150, 163
    taxes and, **4:** 253
citizens
    citizenship linked to residency, **14:** 440
    debt obligation, as holders of, **14:** 520
    political agents, behavior related to, **14:** 524

City Bank Farmers Trust Co. v. Bethlehem Steel Co., **18:** 419 n. 28
civil law, **11:** 83–85
civil order
    collective organization, ensured by, **14:** 228
    secession to provide, **14:** 242–43
    valued product under, **14:** 233
civil society, **1:** 253–54
    individuals' behavior in, **13:** 410–13
    social interdependencies in, **13:** 410–13
claims. *See* capacities, or endowments
classical liberalism, **11:** xx
    fiscal targeting and, **11:** 206
    generality and, **11:** 111
    limits of, **19:** 147–51
    means testing and, **11:** 206
    support of, **1:** 231
classical politics, conception of, **1:** 234
class interest in politics, **3:** 26
Clay Committee, **2:** 27
Clinton administration, **19:** 201
closed economy, fiscal policy in, **4:** 270–72
clubs
    collective decision making in, **13:** 135–36
    costs and benefits in, **15:** 200–202
    emergence of, **5:** 170
    fiscal, formation of, **18:** 63
    goods and services, club-type, **5:** 167, 170
    locational fixity, in absence of, **18:** 47–48
    optimal size, **15:** 205 n. 11
    public goods in, **15:** 195–207
    quantity with sizes of, **15:** 202–3
    sharing in, **15:** 194, 201–5
club theory, **7:** 47
    consumption in, **15:** 194–207
    of cooperative membership, **15:** 193–94
    costs in, **15:** 200–202
    goods and services in, **15:** 194

membership margin, determining, **15:** 194–207

optimal exclusion theory in, **15:** 208

property rights and, **15:** 208–9

coalitions, majority

    constitutional constraints on, **19:** 351–52

    costs imposed by, **16:** 395

    effect of shifts in, **16:** 395

    fiscal policy of, **16:** 271

    generality principle, selections under, **19:** 354

    market game, **16:** 272–73

    payoff structure, **16:** 271–74

    political approval, **19:** 348–49

    restrictions from, **16:** 377–79

    support for, disappearance of, **19:** 352

    tax base of, **9:** 187–88

    taxes, imposition of, **16:** 271

coalitions, models of, **18:** 149–61

coalitions, special interest, **16:** 269–76

Coase theorem, **1:** 264, 265, 267, 272, 276

    analogues to, **13:** 430; **15:** 174–75; **19:** 146

    applicability, **18:** 363

    assumption of, **18:** 364

    attention to, **12:** 335

    contractarian reconstruction of, **1:** 262–64

    externality applied to, **18:** 369–73

    institutional setting, **13:** 300–301

    legal rights under, **12:** 293

    liability under, **13:** 300; **18:** 363

    modification of, **13:** 413

    ownership rights under, **12:** 291; **15:** 308–18; **19:** 249

    prisoners' dilemma payoff structure with, **16:** 150–52

    property rights in, **12:** 291, 293–94; **13:** 300; **15:** 174–75

    resource allocation under, **18:** 370

    rights in, **19:** 146

    summary of, **12:** 154–55, 293–96; **13:** 298; **18:** 370

See also neutrality, allocational; social cost theory

codes of conduct (Hayek), **12:** 361n. 15, 441

coercion

    in decision making, **1:** 82–84, 204, 341, 389, 461

    freedom from, **16:** 225

    in governing, **9:** 10–11, 192–96

    majority rule and, **7:** 56

    in minimal state, **17:** 432

cognition

    with full information, **12:** 149–50

    information brings (Knight), **12:** 144–45

    See also certainty; uncertainty

collective

    exchange paradigm of, **1:** 24

    as organism, **3:** 31–32

    rules of behavior in, **1:** 344

    self-interest in, **17:** 255–57

    social rationality and, **1:** 93, 102

collective action

    Arrow's critique of, **1:** 53–54

    benefits of, **1:** 5, 380–81, 389, 424–25

    competition in, **15:** 35–37

    constitutional and postconstitutional, **1:** 145–46

    contractarian concept of, **13:** 302–3

    costs of, **3:** 44, 68–70; **16:** 392–94

    decision rule and, **3:** 206–7; **16:** 218–19

    definition of and justification for, **15:** 4

    effect of, **1:** xix, 311–28, 361, 362

    explicit, **15:** 29–35

    external costs of, **3:** 64–68

    external diseconomy, against, **15:** 184

    external economies of, **15:** 130–32, 138–43

    externalities of, **3:** 64–68, 89; **15:** 17–19; **18:** 57–60

    for externalities within the law, **15:** 20–21

    freedom, **16:** 392–94

    through government, **15:** 13–14

collective action (*continued*)
  individual choice (Ferrara), **15:** 63
  individuals in, **13:** 17–18, 304–5; **19:** 346
  justification for, **15:** 4; **16:** 69–71
  kinds of, **16:** 222
  within laws, **16:** 218–20
  libertarian socialist, view of, **19:** 167–68
  limits of, **1:** 70
  logic of (Olson), **16:** 268; **19:** 190
  with majority voting, **13:** 42–43; **15:**
    30–32
  modeling, **1:** 256–57
  monopoly practices, to control, **15:**
    23–24
  optimality and, **1:** 225–27, 228
  origin of, **15:** 5
  ownership under, **15:** 308–18
  political economy of, **15:** 25–37
  preference for, **1:** 87
  in prisoners' dilemma, **16:** 149–50
  private preferences as reason for, **13:** 42
  property rights with and without, **13:**
    304–5
  proposals for, **15:** 307–8
  public bads without, **15:** 310
  range, **3:** 200–209
  without relevant externality, **15:** 134–35
  transaction costs, to reduce, **15:** 13–14
  voting franchise, implications for, **13:**
    130–33
  See also collective; consensus; majority
    rule
collective agreement, **5:** 121, 126, 144–46
collective choice, **1:** 53, 73, 95, 100, 198, 199,
  201, 202, 204, 212, 238; **2:** 50, 117–29; **15:**
  442; **17:** xv–xviii
  alternatives for, **13:** 106–7; **16:** 132
  Arrow on, **1:** 53–54, 79 n. 11, 86 n. 24
  constitutional, **14:** 43–45, 73
  for constitutional experts, **16:** 136–39
  costs and, **3:** 206–7
  decision making and, **1:** 225–27, 341–43

dilemma in, **13:** 92–93
discounting in, **2:** 122–23
in electoral model, **13:** 293–95
factors resulting in, **14:** 73
fiscal theory, as problem of, **15:** 104
free markets and, **1:** 100–102
individual choice, **1:** 53, 62, 64, 75–78,
  236, 246–59; **4:** 173–80; **13:** 4–5; **14:**
  117, 525–26, 527; **15:** 351–52
information in, **4:** 181–83
institutions for, standard or uniform,
  14: 116–17
Italian theorists, contribution to
  concept of, **15:** 97–100, 104
limiting rules, within, **18:** 170
majority cycle: decision for binding, **13:**
  186–92; establishment and
  discontinuance of, **13:** 181–86
with majority rule, **13:** 195, 239–48
multiperiod, **4:** 64–69
objects of, **5:** 121
political, **19:** 216
in prisoners' dilemma, **16:** 149–50
process, **5:** 130–31, 140: in Anglo-Saxon
  fiscal theory, **15:** 67
public debt and, **2:** 119–29
public investment, of voters-taxpayers
  considering, **13:** 382–86
public services, **14:** 83–86
rationality of, **13:** 212
responsibility in, **3:** 38
rules and, **1:** 421–23, 448–50; **5:** 174:
  Wicksell on, **1:** 15, 23, 217–19; **3:** 6,
  63–84
social interaction and, **17:** xvii–xviii
in socialist philosophy, **18:** 106–7
taxpayers and, **13:** 382–86
theory, **3:** 3; **4:** 3–5; **5:** 117
unanimity requirement and, **1:** 15, 23,
  217–19; **3:** 6, 63–84; **13:** 303–4; **16:** 150
  (*see also* Wicksellian economics)
uncertainty in, **3:** 37

unproductive, **2:** 66, 81
welfare spending, **15:** 456–57
See also behavior; individual choice
collective consumption, private supply of,
  13: 464–65
collective-consumption goods. *See* public
  goods
collective economy, **17:** 283–92
collective goods. *See* public goods
collective laws, **15:** 5
collective market, external economies in,
  15: 130–32
collective order, unanimity and, **10:** 26
collective outcomes
  buying/selling votes to influence, **13:**
    214–26
  derived from individual behavior, **13:**
    174
  effects of, on rules, **4:** 201–7
  from political behavior, **14:** 21
collective rationality in social choice
  theory, **16:** 84
collective redistribution, insurance and, **3:**
  193–99
collective services. *See* public services
collective transfers, **19:** 104–5
collectivist-socialist view, **19:** 188–89, 195,
  214–15, 228–29, 238, 260
collectivization
  allocation-maximization paradigm, **19:**
    214
  individual behavior, **16:** 396n. 15
  monopolistic restrictions with, **19:**
    255
  process, **16:** 397
  under socialism, **19:** 226–29, 231–33
  in social order, **16:** 178
Colwyn Committee, **2:** 16–17, 87–88
command economy
  asymmetric reciprocity in, **12:** 417–20
  market economy, transition to, **12:**
    420–25

Commission on Money and Credit, **4:**
  108
commitments
  government repudiation of, **14:** 526
  government's, adherence to, **14:** 530–32
  of government to pay, **14:** 343, 353–55
  justice and, **10:** 111–16
  promise-keeping of government, **14:**
    524
Committee on Social Insurance
  Terminology, **4:** 141n. 12
committees and elections, Black on theory
  of, **5:** 117
commodities, taxation of, **4:** 255–66; **9:**
  68–70, 96–98; **11:** 128
commodity models, **1:** 409–15, 416
commonality, **7:** 25–28; **11:** 57–58; **18:** 220
common facilities
  private ownership with resources on, **13:**
    257–58
  right to use, **15:** 309–11
common law, **9:** 194; **12:** 176–78; **19:** 139
common property, **10:** 16
  exchange in, **18:** 226–34
  externality and, **7:** 73–74; **18:** 220
  government role in, **15:** 13–15
  law enforcement and, **18:** 224–25
  ownership of, **15:** 14, 309–18
  privatized, **18:** 227–29
  rule of law in, **18:** 222–26
  sharing of, **18:** 227–29
commons, the
  access to, **18:** 210–11
  externalities in, **3:** 58
  interdependence with shared, **18:** 217
  ownership of, **12:** 404–5
  partition of, **18:** 222–26
  privatization of, **18:** 216, 217, 220–29
  as property, **18:** 216, 220–22
  resources on, use of: specialized, **13:**
    255–58; unspecialized, **13:** 252–55
  user decisions, **12:** 326

commons, tragedy of the, **11:** 55, 82; **13:**
    252; **18:** 216, 220–22
    rules change to overcome, **12:** 289–92
communitarianism, **1:** 390–91
community, motivational force of, **1:**
    363–66
compensation
    defined, **1:** 197
    just, **9:** 193
    for loss of life, **12:** 279–80
    to secure agreement, **16:** 116–17
    unanimity and, **3:** 90–91
    in welfare economics, **1:** 196–202; **3:**
        90–91
compensation principle, **1:** 193, 197–98, 200
competition
    bargaining and, **3:** 103–4
    catallactic perspective of Knight's view
        of, **12:** 117–23
    citizens, protection of, **18:** 145
    collective action and, **15:** 35–37
    competitive economic order:
        characteristic of, **5:** 79; emergence of,
        5: 77; Knight on evaluation of, **12:**
        110–27
    constitutional, **16:** 135, 142
    contractarianism and, **1:** 273–75
    for deference with contemporaries, **16:**
        199
    demand side of, **18:** 239
    disciplinary pressure of, **18:** 93
    in distributional game, **16:** 148–50
    in economic order (Knight), **12:** 117–23
    electoral and party, **1:** 50, 55–56
    enforcement of, **1:** 220–24; **11:** 103
    equilibrium in, **1:** 348, 350, 358
    exploitation of forces of, **18:** 92
    among governments, **9:** 216–17; **11:** 191
    imperfect, **1:** 87
    individual liberty and, **18:** 258
    in industry (Marshall), **12:** 277
    in information industry, **16:** 196

interdependence in absence of, **5:** 82
interparty (Downs-Riker), models of,
    14: 15–16
    Knight on, **1:** 36, 325–26, 361
    in market economy, **18:** 69; **19:** 261
    monopolistic, **12:** 390–91, 395–96; **13:**
        336–37
    monopoly power, effect on, **12:** 206–7
    among nations, **19:** 205–6
    among nation-states, **18:** 123–30
    objectivist versus subjectivist-
        contractarian conceptions of, **1:**
        273–75
    party, majority rule and, **9:** 26
    perfect, **13:** 335: Knight's, **1:** 36–37, 78,
        296, 322–26, 361; **19:** 87
    political, **8:** 98–100; **16:** 136–37
    among politicians, **8:** 98–100
    scarce goods and, **16:** 258–59
    under socialism, **19:** 255, 261
    among states in a federalism, **18:** xii,
        70–72
    in supranational federalism, conditions
        for, **18:** 123–27
    tax, prisoners' dilemma and, **9:** 200; **18:**
        145–46
    Tiebout, **11:** 191
    welfare theory and, **1:** 61
    See also European Union, proposed;
        federalism, competitive; markets
Condorcet paradox, **7:** 182
conflict model, taxpayers in, **14:** 48–50
conflict resolution
    adjustments to, **13:** 413–14
    majoritarian institutions and, **13:**
        415–17
    politics and, **13:** 414–17; **16:** 380; **17:**
        163–64
    through voting, **13:** 414–15
conflicts
    advance commitment and, **1:** 336
    over beliefs, **17:** 162

distributional, **10:** 15; **16:** 379–80
in Hobbesian anarchy, **7:** 12–13, 16
interclass, **1:** 387
in politics, **1:** 385–86; **17:** 162–64
property rights, **13:** 411–13
congestibility, **18:** 49, 55, 60
conscription, **9:** 193
consensus, **1:** 99–100, 204–7
contractual-consensus test (Wicksell), **1:** 269, 431, 432, 466
for political change (Wicksell), **19:** 143
See also unanimity
consent, tacit, **10:** 115–16
consent principle, **17:** 128
conservatism, reformist, **19:** xii–xiii
consociationalism, **16:** 145
Constitution, U.S., **1:** 367
balanced-budget, proposed amendment, **8:** 184–89; **14:** 451, 493–94, 500–516
Bill of Rights in, **19:** 177
constraints, **14:** 252; **16:** 58–59
due process, **9:** 11–12, 193–94; **16:** 51, 67; **17:** 305
enforcement under, **18:** 141
erosion of, **13:** 52–53; **18:** 182
failure of, **13:** 52–53
Federalists, role of, **18:** xiii
fiscal powers, **14:** 252–53, **16:** 52–53, 310–11; **18:** 146, 410–15
government in, role of, **19:** 176–77
history of, **16:** 231–34
New Deal changes to, **18:** 399–410
reform of: need for, **7:** 209–28; **10:** 14; **13:** 61; **16:** 58–59, 64, 104; **17:** 148–49; **19:** 180–81; questions about, **16:** 104
revolution prospects for, **7:** 209–28
secession, right of, **18:** 103
separation of powers in, **19:** 177, 349–50
structure, Madisonian, **1:** 19; **18:** 102–3

constitutional agreement
compliance and renegotiation problems, **16:** 163
in contractarian framework, **16:** 165–71
in discourse, or dialogue, framework, **16:** 155–56, 165–71
interest-based obstacles to, **16:** 128
on rules, **11:** xx, 5, 67–68
rules furthering interests, with ignorance of, **16:** 189
stability and fairness of, **16:** 162–64
truth judgment in interpretation of, **16:** 166–69
constitutional attitude, **4:** 301–2
constitutional change
free riders and, **10:** 33, 41, 160–62
rules and, **10:** 153–54
constitutional choice, **1:** 238–40, 341, 367–73; **3:** ix, 110; **4:** 218–22; **9:** 5–6, 37–41, 70–71, 219; **17:** 278
agreement in (Rawls), **16:** 160
authority to make, selecting a well-informed, **16:** 190–91
bargaining range in, **14:** 255
constitutional politics, of individual in, **13:** 405
defined, **1:** 255; **16:** 157–59
excise tax, of specific, **4:** 243–57
of fiscal institutions, **4:** 116–20, 294
of fiscal policy, **4:** 269–81
generality as constraints of, **1:** 419–28
generality in, **4:** 225–26
implementation, **16:** 403–9
individuals in, **16:** 73
information in, **16:** 186–89
knowledge-problem, **16:** 129–30, 188
limits of reason, **16:** 130, 132, 139–43
neocontractarian approaches, **16:** 128
in politics, **16:** 308
postconstitutional, **16:** 21, 44–46, 308
problem of, **16:** 147

constitutional choice (*continued*)
  process, interpretation of, **16:** 155–56,
    165–70, 187
  of progressive income tax, **4:** 227–42
  of public debt, **4:** 258–68
  rational ignorance theory in, **16:** 130,
    132–39
  rules and, **7:** 90–92; **16:** 11–12, 45,
    127–28
  self-interest and, **3:** ix, 95–96
  stability in, **16:** 164–65
  subconstitutional, **16:** 127–28
  among tax bases, **14:** 158–71
  among tax institutions, **14:** 34–35,
    151–74
  tax limits, related to, **14:** 229–49
  in transitional economies, **3:** x
  unanimity in, **16:** 10, 220–21
  veil of ignorance, under Rawls's, **16:** 129
  veil of uncertainty, behind, **16:** 187–88
  voluntary, **16:** 165–70
  See also constitutional preference; rules
constitutional convention, Rawlsian, **11:**
  194n. 6
constitutional design, **10:** 14
  inequalities generated by, **17:** 322–24
  limits in, defining, **17:** 275–76
  public choice theory in, **17:** 276–79
constitutional economics, **1:** 378–85,
  390–93; **10:** 4–5; **19:** 329
  agreement in, **16:** xii
  applications, **16:** 12–14
  constraints examined by, **16:** 4
  Homo economicus on, **16:** 10–12
  individual choice behavior in, **1:** 383–84;
    16: 10–12
  precursor to, **16:** 9–10
  public choice, emergence from, **16:** 7–8
  public choice theory and, **1:** 377–95
  rationality and, **1:** 391–92
  rule making in, **16:** xii
  unanimity, test in, **16:** 10

  See also constitutional political
    economy; political economy, Virginia
    school of
constitutionalism, **1:** 377–95; **7:** 10; **17:** 124
  Buchanan's interest in, **1:** xxi, 4, 19–20,
    22, 24–25, 50, 133, 145–47, 255,
    366–67, 419–20, 431–41
  Calculus of Consent and, **1:** xxi, 19–20,
    22, 23, 39
  constitutional politics and, **1:** 384–86
  contractarian, **1:** 465–68; **18:** 179–81
  defined, **1:** 51–52, 238, 239–40, 431, 447;
    16: 89–90; **18:** 175–78
  development of, **1:** 187–88
  entrepreneurship and, **1:** 187
  ethics of, **1:** xx, 368–73
  as generality, **11:** 61–64
  monetary predictability and, **1:** 396–418
  noncontractarian, **10:** 24–25
  student demands, response to, **16:**
    182–83
constitutional majoritarianism, **11:** 25–26
constitutional order, Madisonian, **1:** 372
constitutional political economy, **1:** 19–20,
  22, 23, 24; **3:** ix; **11:** 67–68
  Calculus of Consent and, **1:** 19–20, 22, 23
  contractarianism as precursor to, **1:** 387,
    388–90
  contractarianism perspective in, **19:** 60,
    62–63
  contractarian philosophy of, **19:** 59–60
  defense of, **1:** 393–95
  defined, **1:** 145–46, 238, 377–95; **19:** 97
  emergence of, **19:** 244–46
  field of, **16:** xi–xii
  generality and, **1:** 419–28
  intellectual traditions of, **1:** 15–16,
    386–90, 455–57
  Lakatosian classification, **1:** 390, 450
  naturalistic fallacy and, **1:** 394
  nonconstitutional political economy
    versus, **1:** 379–84

normative foundations, **1:** 442–54

normative purpose of, **19:** 362

perspective, **1:** 393–95

political economy of policy, replaces,
   19: 24–25

public policy issues of, **19:** 60

reform, **1:** 463–68

rules and, **1:** 70, 72–73, 237–40, 255,
   377–78, 384–86, 420, 447–48,
   455–68

Smith, associated with, **19:** 302–3

variable institutions in analysis using,
   16: 330–31

Wicksell's contribution to, **19:** xvi

wisdom, loss of, **1:** 371–72

constitutional preference, **16:** 134–35

alternative rules, reflecting tradeoffs
   among, **16:** 127–28

in constitutional convention model, **16:**
   186

of individual, **16:** 186–87

interest- and theory-components, **16:**
   128, 155, 159, 169, 186–87

See also constitutional choice

constitutional reform, **10:** 14

anticonstitutionalist mind-set in, **16:** 361

"churning state," as escape from, **19:** 63

for competitive federalism, **18:** 73–74

as contractual process (Buchanan), **19:**
   xiii

evolutionist perspective on, effect of, **16:**
   360–61

of fiscal policy, **16:** 52–56

Hayek's advocacy of, **18:** 321, 323

opposition, sources of, **16:** 357–59,
   363–65, 370

path dependency of, **18:** 72–75

rules and constraints in, **16:** 46–47, 64

self-enforcement in, **18:** 132

unanimity rule in, **16:** 270

constitutional revolution, **7:** 7, 187,
   209–28; **10:** 149–65

of New Deal, **18:** 385

possibility of, **18:** 183–84

constitutional rules, **1:** 70, 72–73, 238–40,
   255; **3:** 110; **4:** 116–20

budget balance required by, **19:** 342

collective choice processing by, **14:** 73

contractarian view of, **18:** 179–81

control of private sector through, **16:**
   105

for decision making and power to tax,
   16: 309

defining economic interaction, **16:** 259

failure of, **16:** 410–11

fiscal constraints, in need for, **16:** 309

fiscal institutions, to select, **14:** 43–45

generalized, **19:** 282

laissez faire, **19:** 266–67

majority voting cycle, to stop pure, **13:**
   184

in making collective decisions, **16:**
   307–8

for a market regime, **16:** 259–61, 267

of New Deal era, **16:** 346–47

ordinary politics within, operation of,
   16: 231

political action, to define, **14:** 503–4

political agent subject to, **19:** 338–40

political pressures, immunity from, **17:**
   343–44

politics, limits on, **17:** 275–76

politics within, **14:** 381–82

public choice model of fiscal choice, **14:**
   153

to reduce majority rule exploitation, **16:**
   273–74

reform using: exit feature, **16:** 269–70;
   generality concept, **16:** 270–76

as relatively absolute absolutes, **16:** 66,
   230–31

tax constitution, in "good," **14:** 254–56

tax response model, two-person, **14:**
   126–28

constitutional rules (*continued*)
 unanimity rule, **16:** 270
 See also fiscal rules; rules
constitutions
 agreements: formed by, **11:** 5; on meta-
  constitution, **16:** 144–46
 constitutional contract, terms of, **16:**
  278–79
 as constraints (*see* constraints,
  constitutional)
 as contract, **7:** 37, 40–41, 42–43, 69–95
 defined, **9:** 5–6; **14:** 431; **16:** 43–45, 410
 domain of, **9:** 21–25
 economic theory of political, **13:**
  45–46, 48
 enforceability of, **9:** 13–14
 European Union, for proposed, **18:**
  100–101, 104–5, 109, 111–12
 failure of, **13:** 52–53
 federal, **9:** 200–214
 fiscal exchange in, elements of, **18:**
  190–91
 fiscal institutions in theory of, **14:**
  20–24
 generality and, **11:** xx
 ideal (Wicksell), **14:** 11
 implementation of, lag in, **16:** 407–12
 imposed changes, **7:** 105–8
 for individual, **3:** 97
 individual behavior within, **16:** 12
 individual choosing, **16:** 415–16
 individuals' interactions, as rules for,
  14: 271
 institutions, theory based on choice of,
  14: 13
 interpretation of, by eighteenth-century
  intellectuals, **19:** 347
 logical basis, **9:** 6–8
 majority rule voting and, **7:** 57
 monetary, **9:** 131–32, 153–59
 necessity for, **4:** 301–2; **19:** 174
 organizational decisions, procedures
  for, **14:** 442

 Pareto criterion and, **3:** 94
 political, **13:** 11; **16:** 68–69
 as public capital, **7:** 156–60
 public choice analysis, **13:** 87–89
 rationality and, **3:** 81
 rights and laws under, **19:** 174–75
 as rules, **3:** 6; **7:** 90–92, 172–80; **9:** 5,
  8–9; **10:** 9: for changes in rules of, **16:**
  379; for individuals' interactions, **14:**
  271; organizational decisions,
  defining procedures for, **14:** 442
 socialist countries, of former, **16:**
  215–17, 234
 of a society, **14:** 271–72
 structure and taxation and, **11:** 115
 sumptuary, **13:** 418
 theory of, **3:** 63–84, 311; **14:** 13 (*see also*
  voting rules)
 of welfare state, **11:** 172–74
 Wicksell's unanimity rule, **14:** 259–60
 written, **19:** 176–77
 See also Constitution, U.S.;
  constitutional reform; economic
  constitution; fiscal constitution;
  monetary constitution; political
  constitution
constraints
 artifactual, **19:** 306
 in choice behavior, **16:** 156–57
 choice of, **19:** 306
 collectivities, imposed by, **19:** 241
 constitutional (*see* constraints,
  constitutional)
 as contingencies, **9:** 100
 electoral, **9:** 9, 12, 20–32, 38–39
 endogenous, on behavior, **17:** 92–94
 equal treatment promoted by, **17:**
  338–41
 ethical rules and, **1:** 311–28, 356–57,
  367–73
 on exercise of rights, **18:** 209
 fiscal (*see* constraints, fiscal)
 on fiscal constitution, **16:** 108–9

in fiscal policy, **13:** 473–74

formal, absence in Hobbesian anarchy of, **17:** 381–82

on government, **16:** 56–57

on government decision makers, **13:** 53, 313–14, 473–74

institutional, **13:** 53–54; **18:** 270–74

interdependence among, **9:** 182

Leviathan without, **14:** 179–80

on liberty, **18:** 209–11

on majority rule voting, **7:** 190–94; **11:** 114–25

majority voting, **7:** 190–94

market economy, **17:** 82–84

under market rules, **17:** 81–87

moral, **14:** 461–62

on outlay and revenue, **9:** 233–34

on political agents, **19:** 334–43

political choice, rules related to, **14:** 500–501

political economy, subject to change in, **16:** 250–51

politically imposed, **19:** 197

political process, **14:** 482–83

preferences, distinct from, **17:** 160n. 5

procedural, **9:** 182–84

on procedures, **9:** 235–36

on process, **9:** 183–84

public choice theory and, **1:** 462–65

on public expenditure, **14:** 260–61

in rational choice model, **17:** 55, 60–66

rational choice of, **17:** 463

on ratio proposals, **9:** 233–34

as rules, **10:** 20; **18:** 270–74

self-imposed in exchange relationship, **17:** 82–84

self-seeking with, **17:** 45–46

substitutability among, **16:** 308

on taking power, **9:** 193–95

taxation, with generality in, **14:** 310–11

on taxation of wealth, **9:** 110

on tax base, **9:** 48–55, 231–33

on tax discrimination, **11:** 113–14

on tax rates, **9:** 48–55

temporal, **19:** 246–47

term limits, imposed by, **13:** 283–84

See also choices; government; individual choice

constraints, constitutional, **13:** 53–54; **14:** 251–53; **17:** 273–74, 277–78; **18:** 175

budget balance and, **11:** 137–38

constitutional convention, Rawlsian, **11:** 194n. 6

constitutional economics, examined by, **16:** 4

democracy, requirement in, **19:** 347–49

fiscal constitution, in proposed, **14:** 482–83

fiscal rules, to change, **14:** 494

franchised members, to safeguard interests of, **14:** 443–44

on government (Hobbes), **16:** 47–52

laws as, **16:** 221–22

on majority coalition, **19:** 351–52

on politics, **12:** 436–37

on tax discrimination, **11:** 114

constraints, fiscal

absence of, on spending and taxation, **14:** 253

generality in, **9:** 45, 185–90

on government, **14:** 154–64

logic of, **14:** 251–52

migration and, **9:** 200–203

need for, **16:** 309

ratio-type proposals, **14:** 262

over tax base, **14:** 262–64

taxes, with maximum-rate limits of, **14:** 260–61

on tax revenues, **14:** 261–62

in U.S. law, **14:** 252–53

constructive institutionalism, **1:** 229

constructivism

constitutional, **17:** 463–65

of Hayek, **18:** 313, 319

constructivism (*continued*)
Hayek's criticism of, **18:** 323
moral, **17:** 460–63
consumer choice
household production function, in
terms of, **12:** 219–20
revealed preferences theory of, **13:**
167–69
supply functions, with down-sloping,
12: 191–95
voter choice, difference from, **13:**
162–64
consumer interests
with efficiency criteria for regulated
firms, **13:** 327–30
with general inflation, **13:** 323–26
monopsony interests of, **13:** 332
monopsony power of, **13:** 319–20
as political representation, **13:** 318
public regulation, in theory of, **13:** 316
regulatory agency, capture of, **13:**
322–23
consumers
of collectively financed goods
(Wicksell), **19:** 141
human capital, acquisition of, **12:** 220
of monopolist's product, **12:** 207–9
monopoly or monopsony, in curve of
unregulated, **13:** 320–21
monopoly theory, adjustment to price
change in, **12:** 221–35
producers and sellers as, **13:** 389–91
public good units of production,
availability of, **15:** 267
regulated firm, in long-run average-cost
curve of, **13:** 319–21
consumer sovereignty, **1:** 55
Hutt on, **19:** 139–41, 147–51
in market economy, **15:** 363
consumer surplus, **5:** 24, 39; **9:** 53, 86–87
consumption, **7:** 47
in club theory, **15:** 194–207

collective goods, joint consumption of,
13: 451, 455–59
domestic (nonmarket utilization), **1:**
348–49
of external diseconomies, **13:** 426–31
external economies, of services with, **15:**
245–56
goods and services, in private exchange
of, **15:** 211
in market exchange, **19:** 229–31
private supplement of collective, **13:**
464–65
production and, **1:** 161, 346–47, 348–49,
415; **5:** 33; **19:** 221–24
production requirement of, **19:** 222–25
under socialism, **19:** 226–29, 231–33
uniformity, **13:** 452–54
consumption, public
under Barro neutrality theorem, **14:**
411–13
borrowing to finance, **14:** 24–25, 462,
519
debt financing, **14:** 369, 376–77, 458, 490
debt financing (Keynes), **14:** 457,
459–61, 496
norms related to, **14:** 496
public choice theory, prediction from,
14: 471
public goods consumption, equivalence
in, **14:** 39–41, 75–76
under Ricardian equivalence theorem,
14: 411
See also goods and services; public
goods
consumption loan, **2:** 47–48
consumption spending, **2:** 67–71
consumption tax, **2:** 67–71; **4:** 42–43; **9:**
49, 111; **11:** 128
consumption units
external economy or diseconomy in
supply of, **15:** 216–17
joint supply, **15:** 212–13, 217–22, 267

of public good, **15:** 267

in public goods theory, **15:** 274

contractarianism

    Buchanan's interest in, **1:** xix, 24–25, 39, 50, 51, 204, 269–70, 429–31, 465–68; **17:** xx

    competition and, **1:** 273–75

    constitutionalism and, **1:** 465–68

    constitutional political economy, as precursor to, **1:** 387, 388–90

    democracy and, **16:** 221–23

    exchange and, **1:** 262–64

    existing institutions, to evaluate, **17:** 1–4, 249

    foundations, **11:** 20–24

    generality and, **11:** 207–8

    Hobbesian, **17:** 380–84

    individualism and, **10:** 23–24

    participation and, **11:** 6

    as perspective, **10:** 23–37

    Rawlsian, **17:** 380–81, 384–95, 404

    sharing principles emerging from agreement, **17:** 452

    tax theory and, **1:** xviii

    See also social contract

contractarian perspective, **10:** 23–27; **19:** xiv–xv

    agreement, interpretation of, **16:** 159–60, 165–71

    anarchist perspective compared with, **16:** 19–21

    arguments against, **16:** 113–18

    choice, interpretation of voluntariness of, **16:** 165–66

    classical liberalism in, principles of, **16:** 39–41

    of constitutional order, **18:** 179–81

    in constitutional political economy, **19:** 60, 62–63

    constraints on and limits to, **16:** 111–15

    democracy, relation to, **16:** 221–23

    distributive justice, **17:** 408–11

    to economic interaction, **16:** 60

    economists' understanding of, **16:** 121

    of fairness, **16:** 165; **17:** 314–18

    freedom of exchange in, **19:** 150–51

    goods and services, evaluation of voluntary exchange of, **16:** 36–39

    institutional arrangements, consensus on, **17:** 249

    legitimate law in, perception of, **17:** 407–8; **18:** 179–81

    logical analytical structure, discourse in, **16:** 121

    majority rule derived from, **16:** 218–19

    in monetary system, U.S., **18:** 386–87

    neocontractarianism, **16:** 128

    normative economics and, **17:** 246–47

    of political equality, **16:** 219–23

    political-legal order as, **16:** 222–23

    politics, model of, **16:** 215

    politics-as-exchange in, **13:** 19–20

    pseudocontractarian position, **16:** 114–15, 118

    in public choice theory, **13:** 87–89

    as public philosophy, **16:** 122–23

    Rawlsian, **16:** 160

    state, limits on, **16:** 217–18

    of taxation, **9:** 221–24

    of tax system, **14:** 269–71; **16:** 314

    utility maximization paradigm, difference from, **16:** 85

    welfare economics, as superior to, **17:** 246–47

    of Wicksell, **17:** 245–47

    See also catallactic perspective; social contract

contractarian process, **11:** 7

contractarian-subjectivist perspective, **1:** 262, 270

    Wicksellian consensus test and, **1:** 269, 431, 432, 466

contracts, **10:** 23–37

    alienability through, **18:** 226–29

contracts (*continued*)
  Coase, critique of, **1:** 262–64
  constitutional (*see* contracts,
    constitutional)
  as continuing instrument, **7:** 96–115
  contractual criteria, Wicksellian, **14:**
    228–29
  in Crusoe setting, **7:** 118–20
  debt instruments, obligations in, **14:**
    367–68
  defection, **7:** 83–88
  disarmament, **7:** 76–77
  economic basis, **7:** 98
  economics as science of, **16:** 86
  efficiency and, **7:** 38, 40
  enforcement, **7:** 83–88, 122, 131–33, 168
  ethics and, **7:** 96–99
  European monetary constitution,
    under proposed, **18:** 111–12
  exchange and, **1:** 264, 265, 267, 272,
    275–76, 463–65
  of fiscal exchange, **14:** 93–94
  freedom of, **1:** 221
  government commitments, **14:** 530–32
  Hobbesian, **10:** 31; **16:** 215–16; **17:** 380–84
  hypothetical, **16:** 115–16
  indirect, **7:** 58–63
  between individual and sovereign
    (Hobbes), **18:** 193
  postconstitutional, **7:** 37n. 13, 38, 40, 41,
    42–43, 44, 46–68
  private, government restrictions on, **18:**
    419–22
  property rights, to exchange, **16:** 260
  in public goods, **7:** 40–41
  Rawlsian, **7:** 221–23; **16:** 286–87
  renegotiation and, **7:** 97–98
  in restraint of exchange, **16:** 33; **18:** 210
  in rights, **7:** 28–31
  slavery, **7:** 77–78; **18:** 171
  social, **7:** 43, 187; **11:** 5, 8
  stages, **7:** 37

  theory of democracy, **16:** 220–21
  trade and, **7:** 78–83
  violations, **7:** 35–36
  See also social contract
contracts, constitutional, **7:** 37, 40–41,
  42–43, 57, 69–95; **16:** 21–23
  enforcement of, political role in, **17:** 274
  European federal union, in proposed,
    18: 99–105
  externalities produced by, **17:** 128
  Hobbesian, **17:** 380–84
  monetary rules, **18:** 411–15
  potential, defined, **16:** 278–79
  Rawlsian, **17:** 380, 385–88
  state authority in, limits of, **18:** 171
  transfers and redistribution under, **16:**
    278–84; **17:** 434–35, 464–68
  See also social contract
contract theory, **3:** xvi, 7, 248–51, 310,
  319–21
  of the state, **1:** xix, 24–25, 39, 50, 51, 204,
    269–70, 387, 388–90, 429–41,
    465–68; **7:** 10; **16:** 87–88
contractual-consensus test (Wicksell), **1:**
  269, 431, 432, 466; **12:** 281; **14:** 228–29
cooperation, **1:** 36, 38, 40, 361, 385, 386
  in Crusoe-Friday model, **17:** 362–63
  in Gauthier rule, **17:** 442–43
  in politics, **3:** 266
cooperative group, formation of, **5:** 169
coordination, spontaneous. *See* order,
  spontaneous
corporation income tax. *See* income tax,
  corporate
cost-benefit analysis, **6:** 54, 56
  Broome on, **12:** 279
  of punishment, **7:** 169–72
cost curves and flexibility, Stigler on, **12:** 137
costs
  of agreements, **3:** 98: multilateral vis-à-
    vis bilateral, **5:** 9; negotiating, **5:** 22,
    169; *n*-person, **5:** 10, 80

burden and, **6:** 50
in bureaucratic choice, **6:** 89–90
in business decisions, **6:** 26–29
choice and, **6:** 20, 23, 37–48:
    subjectivist approach, **12:** 8–9, 17–18
in classical economics, **6:** 3
in club theory, **15:** 200–202
of collective decisions, **3:** 68–70; **16:**
    392–94
of collective organization, **3:** 44
of crime, **6:** 84–86
of debt-financed outlay, **6:** 59–63
of decision making, **3:** 45, 67–70,
    97–116; **4:** 117, 217–19, 288
in deer-beaver model, **15:** 159–60
dictatorship and, **6:** 55
dimensions, **6:** 41
as displaced value, **6:** 20
in economic theory, **6:** 3–16
entrepreneurship and, **6:** 18
ephemeral, **6:** 30
equilibrium and, **6:** 46–48
of exit option, **18:** 235–36
external, **3:** 45, 64–68
in externalities, **15:** 16
externality and transaction, **3:** 90
forward-looking, **6:** 41
of group decision-making, **5:** 144–46,
    148–52
incidence, **6:** 46
institutional structure and, problems
    of, **1:** 222–23
interdependence, **3:** 48, 52
of joint supply of consumption units,
    15: 213
of law enforcement, **7:** 168
of legal restrictions, **7:** 141
location, **6:** 41
majority coalition, imposed by, **16:** 395
in market equilibrium, **6:** 77–78
meanings, **6:** xiv, 42–46
measurability, **6:** 41

minorities, of exploiting dissident, **5:**
    150
nonmarket value and, **6:** 15
objective, **6:** 24
in objectivist theory, **12:** 8
pain and, **6:** 8, 44
political structure and, **6:** 53–55
pricing rules and, **6:** 31
private, **6:** 65; **15:** 122
production, theory of, **6:** 5–6, 17
profit maximization and, **6:** 27–28
property rights, for enforcement of, **18:**
    373–79
public debt and, **6:** 59–63
in public finance theory, **6:** xiv
of public goods, **6:** 49–64
of punishment, **7:** 167–69
quasi-rents and, **6:** 80–81
real, **6:** 7, 44–45: doctrine of, **2:** 30; of
    public goods, **4:** 88–89
realization, **6:** 41
resource allocation with differing, **12:**
    311–26
sacrifice and, **6:** 8, 43–44
social, **6:** 2, 65–76; **15:** 122
in socialist calculation, **6:** 87–89
sunk, **6:** 45–46
in tax incidence, **6:** 50–52
of unanimity, **3:** 69
voting, **4:** 121–23
in welfare economics, **6:** 25
See also opportunity cost(s); social cost;
    transaction costs
cost theory
    Hayek on, **1:** 153n. 5
    London School of Economics, **6:** 17–36;
    12: 327
    public debt and fiscal illusion, **1:**
    150–63
    Robbins on, **12:** 327–28, 330
Council of Economic Advisers, **8:** 31, 168;
    19: 318–25, 330

crime and criminal activities, **11:** 184
    corruption in public officials, **9:** 9
    cost of, **6:** 84–86
    criminal monopolies, objections to, **18:**
        442–46
    in reaction-curve construction, **18:**
        433–41
"crowding-out," **8:** 69
culturally evolved man, Hayek on, **1:** 247
currencies
    creation, **4:** 98, 103–8
    devaluation (1934), **18:** 405–6
    of nation-states in supranational
        federalism, **18:** 124
    U.S., before 1933, **18:** 388–89
    See also money

Davenport-Samuelson principle, **17:** 113
debt
    anti-inflation, **2:** 111–14
    burden of (*see* public debt burden)
    classical form of, **2:** 26
    classical theory of, **2:** 9–10, 81
    corporate outlays, to finance, **14:** 438–39
    cost and, **6:** 59–63
    creation, **2:** 29, 98
    criteria for choice between forms of, **2:**
        62–63
    deflation, **2:** 112
    external, **14:** 447–48
    internal, **2:** 8–9, 26, 58–66: as money
        creation, **2:** 99, 101, 104–5, 132
    marginal, **2:** 18, 67–68
    state and local, **2:** 134
    supramarginal, **2:** 19
    wartime, **2:** 104–10, 132; **4:** 61–62
    See also borrowing, corporate; public
        debt
debt burden. *See* public debt burden
debt finance. *See* public debt
debt instruments
    as contractual obligation, **14:** 367–68

of public debt, **14:** 346–47
    purchase of, **14:** 357–58, 438, 446, 448
debt issue. *See* public debt issue
debt measurement
    local government debt, **2:** 151–54
    national debt, **2:** 154–59
    private debt, **2:** 149–51
debtor-creditor, symmetry, **2:** 43
debt purchasers, banking system as, **2:**
    104–5
debt theory
    extended to rational expectations, **14:**
        478
    in Italian fiscal theory, **15:** 85–92
    Keynesian economics and, **14:** 475–76
    methodology of, **2:** 18–25
    new orthodoxy of, **2:** 5–17, 26, 50
    pre-Keynesian, **2:** 79–94
    unemployment and, **2:** 96–97
decentralization, **3:** 114–15
    consociationalism, **16:** 145
    federalism, **16:** 145
    political, **15:** 35–37
    of private ownership, **16:** 260–61
    socialist countries, in former, **16:** 227
    territorial and nonterritorial, **16:** 145
    See also European Union; federalism;
        goods and services
decision making
    affluence and, **1:** 343
    alternatives in, **1:** 76–77, 81–82
    centralized, and pure democracy, **1:** 76
    certainty in, **1:** 76–77
    choice in, logic of, **12:** 19
    coercion in, **1:** 82–84, 204, 341, 389, 461
    constitutional, **17:** 255–57, 260–64
    in contractarian model, **17:** 270
    costs, **3:** 45, 67–70, 97–116; **4:** 117,
        217–19, 288: agreement and, **3:** 98;
        collective choice and, **3:** 206–7;
        group size and, **3:** 112–13; majority
        rule and, **3:** 108

democratic, **1:** 134; **8:** 7–8; **17:** 273
generality in, **1:** 23, 419–28
institutions, choice among, **17:** 263–64
majority decision, **17:** 164–65
participation in, **1:** 77–79
in Pigovian model, **13:** 311–12
planning model of, **1:** 136–38
political (*see* decision making, political)
preference ordering in, **12:** 5, 7, 18
from single- to multi-party, **12:** 183–84
decision making, collective, **1:** 225–27,
    341–43; **5:** 92, 93; **12:** 19–20
in clubs, **13:** 135–36
cost, **3:** 206–7
discounting and, **2:** 122–23
efficiency of, **13:** 465
individuals in, **5:** 138–39; **13:** 4–5; **15:**
    351–52
of individuals through government, **13:** 4
inefficiency predicted, **13:** 465
in large groups, **5:** 109, 185
majority rule voting in, **13:** 194
market organization and, **5:** 138–39
rational choice in, **16:** 84, 394–95
self-interest in, **17:** 255–57
welfare economics and, **15:** 546–47
See also decision-making models,
    collective
decision making, government: fiscal, **14:**
    258–60
decision making, political, **1:** 234–37; **17:**
    252–55
analysis of, **5:** 7
economics extended to, **17:** 20
efficiency of, **13:** 313–15
fair and just institutions of, **17:** 327–29
ideal in, cost of, **5:** 9–10
in individualist-contractarian model,
    17: 270–71
individual self-interest in collective, **17:**
    255–57
majority rule voting in, **17:** 261–63

private-goods sector, analogy to, **5:** 7
in public choice theory, **13:** 113–14
unanimity in, **17:** 257–58
as voluntary "political exchange," **5:** 7
decision-making models, collective, **4:**
    143–57
model of fiscal decisions, **14:** 197–211
progressive taxation and, **4:** 149–66
    passim
tax-prices in, **4:** 149–51
Wicksellian, **15:** 462–63, 467
decision-making rules
analysis, **3:** 63–84, 308
coalition industries under democracy,
    13: 396–400
distributional elements in, **5:** 132
empirical studies of, **4:** 205–7
fiscal rules and, substitution between, **5:**
    153–56
ideal, distance from the, **5:** 9
neutrality of, **4:** 152–54
of politics, **13:** 19–20
transfer of value, power of, **13:** 271–73
as "workable unanimity," **5:** 9
See also majority rule voting; unanimity
    rule
decision theory (Shackle), **12:** 335 n. 5
deer-beaver model, **17:** 26
production: by competitive industry, **15:**
    157–60; with external diseconomies,
    15: 160–67
defense
benefits of, **4:** 192
capital taxes and, **9:** 178
central government and, **9:** 206
of conditions for status quo, **17:** 258
of constitutional political economy, **1:**
    393–95
of political institutions, **1:** 21
of private property, **1:** 319; **6:** 87; **18:**
    252–54
of scientific freedom, **1:** 230–43

deference
   competition with contemporaries for,
      16: 199
   conditions for, **16:** 193–98
   costs, **16:** 197–98
   posthumous, **16:** 198–99
   theory, **16:** 185–86, 189–91
deficit finance, **1:** 171, 172, 176; **11:** 131–40
   monetary pressures and, **8:** 117
   money creation and, **8:** 110–28
   in non-Keynesian setting, **8:** 105
   public sector bias and, **8:** 106–9
   spending, **8:** 96–97
   See also budget deficit; public debt
deflation and debt, **2:** 112
delegation-of-decision rule, **5:** 103, 107
demand
   aggregate, in Keynesian model, **8:** 83–84
   Bailey's contribution to theory, **12:** 246,
      250–51
   demand-for-money rents, **13:** 50
   government, models of, **13:** 58–59
   labor-supply curve, **12:** 254, 256, 259
   law of, **12:** 5, 129–31
   monopoly theory, quantity demand in,
      12: 221–35
   price elasticity of, **12:** 219–20, 246–47
   for public goods, **8:** 130–31
   supply and, **12:** 57–59, 254–55 (*see also*
      Smithean economics)
demand curve
   Friedman and Bailey, compared, **12:**
      248 n.4
   Friedman's interpretation of
      Marshallian, **12:** 54–55, 198–99,
      200–203, 245
   Hicksian, **12:** 56
   income allocation, Crusoe model of, **12:**
      247–50
   market equilibrium curve, **12:** 57–58
   Marshallian, **12:** 54–55

for money (Patinkin), **12:** 57–59, 62–63
   price elasticity, application of, **12:**
      246–47
   Robbins on, **12:** 253, 255–56
   usefulness of, **12:** 58
   See also monopsony
demand theory, **1:** 53, 55, 352–53
democracies, Western
   as modern welfare states, **19:** 350
   politicized sectors of, **19:** 204–6
   See also European Union
democracy
   budget surpluses and, **8:** 102–4
   cartels and, **11:** 103
   conception of, **1:** 200
   constitutional (*see* democracy,
      constitutional)
   constitutional change and, **10:** 149–65
   contractarianism and, **16:** 221–23
   defined, **1:** 99; **16:** 220
   electoral process and, **9:** 8–9
   equality in, **11:** 57
   ethics of, **3:** 265–81; **13:** 151
   experts and, **7:** 125–28
   fiscal exchange paradigm and, **1:** 147–48
   in former socialist countries, **16:** 225–28
   generality in, **1:** 427–28
   individualism and, **3:** 100; **7:** 4–5
   individualist, **3:** 4, 100
   Keynesian economics and, **8:** 95–109
   Madisonian theory of, **3:** 24
   majority, role of, **16:** 361
   majority voting in, **13:** 110
   myths of, **13:** 86
   political, institutions of, **16:** 49
   political equality under, **16:** 220, 225
   within politics, **14:** 381–82; **17:** 275–76
   public good and, **7:** 217
   punishment rules and, **7:** 184–85
   pure, and centralized decision making,
      1: 76

reform with constitutional rules, **13:** 418
representative, **3:** 120, 212–22, 233; **9:** 21
social choice and free markets, **1:**
  89–102
time horizon and, **8:** 166
unconstrained, **7:** 204–6
democracy, constitutional, **17:** 266–67,
  273–74, 279–80; **19:** 344
  limits to, **19:** 349–53
  modern, out of control, **19:** 350
  normative, **17:** 279
  parameters for, **16:** 229
  political discipline, as guarantor of, **19:**
    347
  political exchange in, **18:** 195
  public choice model of, **19:** 273
  structure of, **18:** 335–36
  U.S. structure as, **16:** 225–26
democracy, direct, **3:** 120
  cartel coalition in, **13:** 397–98
  defined, **13:** 396
  model, **13:** 403
  political decisions under, **13:** 398
democracy, majoritarian, **10:** 48–50; **11:**
  19–34, 114–15
  distributional politics of, **19:** 200–206
  participatory, **11:** 3–4; **14:** 310–15
  political activity in, **19:**353
  political coalitions in, **19:** 348–49
  politics of, **19:** 316
  U.S. as, **19:** 350
  See also majority; majority rule voting
democratic model, analysis of, **4:** 181–211
democratic politics, interpretation of, **1:** 21
democratic process, **1:** 21
democratic revolution, **7:** 187
demogrants, **10:** 135, 140–42; **11:** 161–64
depoliticization. *See* privatization
depression
  budget deficits and, **8:** 38–40
  public debt and, **2:** 95–103

public expenditure in, **4:** 104–5
  See also Great Depression
deregulation, move in U.S. toward, **13:**
  124
developing (underdeveloped) society, **1:**
  294
dialogue. *See* discourse, constitutional
diamond-water paradox, **17:** 29
difference principle of distribution
  (Rawls), **14:** 44; **17:** 384
  constitutional level, acceptance on, **17:**
    xix–xx
  contractual agreement, emergence
    from, **17:** 38
  departure from, **16:** 287–88
  Hobbesian interpretation of, **17:** 374–77
  in many-person setting, **17:** 369–72
  of primary social goods, **17:** 412–13
  redistribution under, **17:** 326
  rules or institutions, choice of, **16:**
    285–88
  statement of, **17:** 355
  veil of ignorance, agreement from
    behind, **17:** 365–66
  veil of ignorance bargaining, emergence
    from, **16:** 294–95
  violation of, **1:** 307
diminishing marginal utility, **2:** 138–39
disarmament, **4:** 62; **7:** 76–77
discount, quantity
  buyer exploitation in, **12:** 204–5
  motivation for, **12:** 205
  profit-maximizing rate, **12:** 203–4
  sales promotion effects, **12:** 191–95, 205
discounting
  collective decisions, **2:** 122–23
  future benefits (Barro), **14:** 389
  future taxes, **2:** 35–36
  future taxes (Barro), **14:** 388–90
  interest payments, **2:** 90
  in politics, **10:** 92–107

discourse, constitutional, **16:** 131, 133
  agreement and fairness concepts in, **16:** 166–71
  Habermas's theory, **16:** 166–69
  limitations, motivational and cognitive, **16:** 131–32
discretion, bureaucratic
  market order, effect of, **16:** 259, 267
  with political pricing, **16:** 257–58
discrimination, **11:** 11
  intertemporal, **11:** 131–40
  law, limited by, **11:** 67
  under majority rule, **14:** 310
  by a monopoly, **13:** 320–21, 333–35
  offer schedule and, **9:** 92–93
  perfect, **9:** 82
  political, **11:** xix, 14–16, 67, 68
  regional, **11:** 188, 192–93
  in spending, **9:** 190
  in taxation, **11:** 113–14, 119–20
  in taxes and excess burden, **9:** 86
  in tax-prices, **9:** 38, 87–88, 185
  in tax structure, **9:** 84–94
  See also price discrimination
diseconomies in competitive ownership, **12:** 323–24 (*see also* external diseconomies)
distribution
  allocation and, **7:** 67–68
  under anarchy, **19:** 174: Hobbesian anarchy, **7:** 16, 32–33, 42, 165–66, 186–87; **17:** 303
  classical views on, **2:** 30
  consensual change and, **10:** 152–55
  contractual, **16:** 278–80
  distributive game, legislation as, **13:** 282
  distributive norm, **15:** 435
  equity in, **15:** 133
  of gains-from-trade, **15:** 472–82
  of income, **18:** 11–12
  justice in, **1:** 304–8; **17:** 247–48
  under majority rule, **3:** 151

  in market exchange process, **17:** 298
  as norm, **18:** 287–88
  politics of, **19:** 200–206, 271–73, 277–83, 344–45
  postmarket, **17:** 299
  premarket, **17:** 298–302, 311, 326–27
  rights, **16:** 117–22, **18:** 211–12
  rules and institutions, **10:** 15; **17:** 248
  under socialism, **19:** 236, 249–50, 311
  tax load, **1:** 122–32
  under welfare state, **19:** 255–56
  See also difference principle of distribution (Rawls); redistribution; transfers
distribution, natural, **7:** 19, 31–33, 75
  boundaries, **16:** 91–94, 96–98
  factors modifying, **16:** 94–96
distributional formulas, probabilistic, **11:** 179
distributional paradoxes (Boulding), **12:** 63–65
distributional rules and efficiency, **11:** 158
  legislative office, played by those seeking, **13:** 283–88
distributive justice, **10:** 126–48; **17:** 289, 311–13; **19:** 311–12
  in contractarian perspective, **17:** 408–11
  criticism of, Nozick's, **17:** 417–22
  entitlement theory of (Nozick), **17:** 424–30, 432–36
  equal-treatment principle, **17:** 334–38
  in social philosophy, **17:** 247
  in system of natural liberty, **17:** 327
divisibility spectrum (scale), **5:** 163, 168, 178
dominance
  majoritarian, **3:** 178; **11:** 29–31, 39–41, 120–22
  Paretian, **11:** 52
donor cooperatives
  government analogues to, **13:** 136–39

income redistribution, voluntary, **13:** 135–36

    See also clubs

draft, military, **9:** 193

drainage, external, **2:** 62

due process, **9:** 193, 195

duopoly model (Stackelberg), **11:** 98: stagflation, **1:** 169; **8:** 79, 175–77

duopoly theory, **9:** 28

    clustering theorem: challenge to, **13:** 231–33; of Hotelling, **13:** 227–28

    restrictions in, **13:** 238

    in two-dimensional market space, **13:** 230–33

dynamic models, **12:** 66 n. 13

earmarked revenue

    allocation of, **14:** 76–86

    constitutional, **14:** 91, 98–99

    defined, **14:** 72, 91

    in fiscal exchange model, **14:** 90–92, 94, 97–100

    in fiscal institutions, **14:** 98–99

    in fiscal transfer model, **14:** 96–97

    as institution, **14:** 92, 100

    normative theory of, **14:** 73

    for social security trust fund, **14:** 22–24

    theory of, **14:** 72

    for trust-fund accounts, **14:** 72–73

earmarked taxes

    analysis of, **4:** 71–86

    hypothesis, as illustration of, **4:** 177, 179

    ignorance of liability of, **4:** 72

    individual choice of, effect on, **4:** 23–26

earmarking, **9:** 162, 177–80

    for debt service, **2:** 127

    in fiscal exchange model, **14:** 93–95

    fiscal process and, **14:** 72–73

    normative analysis of, **14:** 90

    of revenues, **14:** 72, 91

tax liability under, **4:** 72

as tie-in sales, **14:** 75–86

easy budgets and tight money, **8:** 44–45; **13:** 435–49

economic analysis

    constitutional and orthodox, **16:** 3–4

    failure of, **1:** 381–84

    levels of, **16:** xi

economic behavior

    corroboration, **12:** 15–16

    defined, **1:** 40

    in game of derivation of policy norms, **12:** 14–18

    Knightian sense of, **12:** 133

    logic of, **12:** 128

    market behavior, morality of, **12:** 439

    noneconomic and, compared, **12:** 132

    objectivity in, **12:** 8

    rules and institutions, **1:** 23

    science of: abstract, **12:** 6–11, 19, 128; Alchian approach in, **12:** 129–32; predictive, **12:** 10–12, 125

economic constitution

    defined, **16:** 339

    during Great Depression, **16:** 350

    before New Deal, **16:** 339

    New Deal policies under, **16:** 345–47

economic growth

    classical theories of, **12:** 387

    debt retirement and, **2:** 140–42

    endogenous theories of, **12:** 387, 389

    enhancement of, **12:** 390

    political efficiency and, **11:** 53

    taxation and, **11:** 125

    transfers and, **11:** 163–64

economic ignorance, **19:** 208–9

    choices made in, **19:** 215–17

    example of, **19:** 217–18

    in institutional choice, **19:** 219–20

economic integration

    advantages of, in European Union, **18:** 132

economic integration (*continued*)
  effect of, **18:** 122–23
  monetary reforms necessary for, **18:** 110,
    111–12
  supranational, national sovereignty
    under, **18:** 119–23
  See also European Union
economic interdependence
  in the economy, **12:** 52
  Walrasian, **12:** 66
economic man. See *Homo economicus*
economic motivation in politics,
  empirical tests of, **4:** 194–202
economic order
  competitive: Knight's criticism of, **12:**
    117–24; welfare properties of, **13:**
    387–88
  efficiency-enhancing function, **12:** 113
  five functions of, Knight's, **1:** 31; **12:**
    111–13
  See also efficiency; markets
economic planning. *See* budgets and
  budgeting
economic policy
  macroeconomic, **19:** 325–28
  nondiscriminatory political treatment
    in, **13:** 409
  planning, **8:** 92–94: Keynesian
    economics and, **8:** 81
  political process, emerging from, **14:**
    483–84
  political setting, **8:** 79–80
  reform of, **1:** 15
  stabilization policy, instruments of, **13:**
    435–37
  theory: Keynesian, **19:** 60–61, 320–25;
    public choice critique of, **19:** 333–34
  See also fiscal policy; macroeconomic
    policy
economic problem, **10:** 3
  Robbins's definition of, **1:** 30
  technological problem and, **1:** 33

economic process, circular-flow, **15:** 40
economic reform
  agreement on, preventing, **16:** 377–78
  conditions for, **16:** 382–83
  defined, **16:** 372
  ideology as motivation for, **16:** 383
  market order in postwar Europe and
    Japan, **16:** 381–82
  politicized interference, to remove, **16:**
    376–79
  Wicksell, advocated by, **1:** 463–64
economic relationship: distinct from
  political relationship (Tullock), **13:** 66–68
economic rent
  creation, **1:** 106
  defined, **1:** 104–6
  dissipation, **1:** 105, 106–7
  governmental action and, **1:** 108–11
  origins of (Tullock), **13:** 66–68
  political allocation without, **1:** 111–12
  without social return, **1:** 107–8
  See also rent seeking
economics
  Austrian (*see* Austrian economics)
  classical: Keynesian interpretation, **8:**
    25–29; Marxian extension of, **18:**
    254–55
  contributions to: engineering, **17:** 9,
    12–13; humanities, **17:** 9, 13–14; law,
    17: 9, 14–15; other disciplines, **17:**
    8–10, 12–16; political science, **17:** 9,
    15–16
  development of, **16:** 146; **17:** 8–12, 16–19,
    22; **19:** 124–25
  of disorder, **19:** 194–97
  education in, **16:** 354–55
  focus of: inappropriate, **16:** 239; what it
    should be, **16:** 240
  Founding Fathers, as understood by, **19:**
    176–77
  ignorance of, **19:** 208–9, 215–20
  incentive structure in, **19:** 235–36

after Marshall, **12:** 480

mathematical perspective in, **19:** 46–49, 124

natural science, distinct from, **12:** 48–49

neoclassical: choice analysis of, **19:** 155, 156; defined, **1:** 191; Knight's contribution to, **19:** 88–89

objective attitude in, **17:** xiv–xv

orthodox, **1:** 378–85; **16:** 4, 108–9: criticism of, **1:** 40–42, 64, 211

politics: applied to, **12:** 49–50; relationship to, **17:** 166

predictive power of, **6:** 37–40; **12:** 472; **16:** 353

professional specialization in, **17:** 20

public aspect of, **12:** 44–45

relationships, political and economic, **13:** 66–68

rights of decision, economic value of, **13:** 313–15

after Robbins, **1:** 256, 383

Robinson Crusoe–style, **19:** 125–26

rules in, importance of, **16:** xi–xii

subjective elements of, **12:** 8, 27; **17:** 25–32

Virginia program in, **19:** 52–54

welfare (*see* welfare economics)

See also constitutional economics; economic theory; economists; Keynesian economic theory; neoclassical economics; political economy

economic science, **1:** 457; **6:** 37–40; **7:** 24; **13:** 16–21, 57–59, 68–69; **17:** 4–7, 21–22, 40–41, 47–48, 50, 53–54, 97

analysis of "might be's," **12:** 50

challenges for, **19:** 208

defined, **19:** 230

emergence of, **19:** 296

flexibility of, **12:** 137

Homo economicus defined in, **12:** 72–73

hypotheses and predictions from, **19:** 200, 208, 263–75, 295, 328–29

limitations of (Knight), **19:** 91

Marshallian, **12:** 134

model of man used in, **12:** 83

natural science and, compared, **19:** 200–202, 215–16, 218–19, 293–94

"product" of, **12:** 47

publicness of, **12:** 47–49

Smith's creation of, **19:** 289–96

teachings of, **19:** 208

understanding of: lack of, **19:** 219–20; minimum, **19:** 214–15

economic stabilization and debt retirement, **2:** 143–48

economic system. *See* economic order; markets

economic theory

of bureaucracy, **19:** 97–99

catallactic focus of, **12:** 480

charity in (Tullock), **19:** 104–5

of choice, **1:** 355

classical, **17:** 25–30

of constitutions, **1:** 45, 50, 51–52; **3:** 7

defined, **1:** 47–48, 58–59

economic science distinct from, **12:** 72

equilibrium fallacy, **12:** 23

in explanatory sense, **3:** 4; **12:** 134–36

game theory, **12:** 480

of income transfers, **12:** 136

Knight's conception of, **19:** 90–91: Stigler on, **12:** 44

marginal-utility theory, **17:** 29–30

Marshallian time and, **1:** 444–46, 454

mathematical tools of, **12:** 479

Mises's interpretation of, **17:** 32–34

mutually exclusive domains for, **17:** 35–39

neoclassical, **17:** 30

open system in, **13:** 25–28

of organizational-institutional order, **12:** 472

of political constitutions, **13:** 45–46

economic theory (*continued*)
  of politics, **13:** 23, 41–44, 50–51, 54; **19:**
    59 (*see also* public choice theory)
  positive or predictive, **12:** 134–35,
    137–38; **17:** 28, 34–37
  quantification and objectification of, **12:**
    327–31
  scientific progress in, **12:** 479
  socialism in, **12:** 471–72
  spontaneous order, principle of, **19:**
    166–68
  subjective, **17:** 25, 28–31, 36–39
  subjective-value, **17:** 29, 31–32, 34
  subjectivist-contractarian perspective, **1:**
    262, 266, 267, 273–75: costs, **1:** 153–55,
    157, 158, 159; maxims, **1:** 312, 313,
    314–22; objectivist versus, **1:** 276
  teleological foundations of, **1:** 245, 250,
    256–58, 458
  traditional, values set at margins in, **14:**
    479
  transaction costs in, **12:** 137
  two domains of, **17:** 37
  Wicksell's attempt to extend to public
    sector, **1:** 458
economies, Western
  competitive federalism in, **19:** 207
  politicized, **19:** 203–9
  post-socialist democratic, **19:** 258–60
  transfer activities of, **19:** 237–38
  See also European Union
economies of scale
  external, **12:** 389–91
  locational, **11:** 148–49, 152
  See also increasing returns
economists
  allocational perspective, **19:** 7, 136–38
  catallactists, **19:** 7
  choice: modeling of, **16:** 399–400;
    understanding of, **19:** 246
  contractarian logic, understanding of,
    16: 121

contractarians, **16:** 112–14, 121
  in cross-disciplinary fields, **17:** 20–21
  elitism of, **17:** 241–42
  gains-from-trade methodology of, **19:**
    136–38, 148
  general equilibrium theorist, **12:** 27
  institutionalists, **13:** 5–6
  Knight's credentials as, **19:** 82
  macroeconomic structure, failure to
    look at, **16:** 243 n. 7
  man's behavior, models of, **17:** 46
  moral philosophers and, compared, **19:**
    70–72
  moral responsibility, **19:** 128
  natural, **19:** xiv–xv, xvi, 95: Tullock as,
    19: 95–107
  observers, **13:** 5–6, 9
  property rights theorists, **13:** 48
  public policy role, **16:** 101–2
  role, **1:** 28–42, 191–92, 454; **17:** 21–22:
    Knight on, **1:** 29; social, **12:** 42–43
  scientists, **12:** 30–43
  social engineers, **12:** 46, 50; **17:** 239–41
  socialism, idea of, **19:** 242–43
  social reformers, **18:** 447 n. 15
  social welfare function, using, **16:** 81–83
  tasks, **17:** 6–7
  taxes, proposals for constitutional limits
    on, **16:** 311
  tools and theorems, **17:** 5–7
  training of modern, **12:** 27
  victims of "fatal conceit," **19:** 218
  See also political economists, role of
economy, international: taxing power and,
  9: 197–98
economy, the
  competitive, **16:** 240–41
  as constitutional order, **16:** 418–21
  distributional conflicts, as setting to
    resolve, **16:** 379–80
  fine-tuning of, **1:** 174; **8:** 97
  functions of (Knight), **18:** 265–67

institutional interactions, as set of, **13:** 5

institutional structure of, **16:** 239

laissez faire in, principle of, **18:** 274

under maximizing paradigm, **16:** 242–43

migration in, **18:** 29–32

order, as an, **16:** 238

politicization of: factors limiting, **19:** 206; increased, **19:** 139

rules and institutions, defined by, **18:** 274–75

socialization in, spectrum of, **19:** 237

social welfare function, in terms of, **16:** 248

spatial structure of, **18:** 28

structure, order, rules, and interactions in, **16:** 239; **18:** 28, 267–70, 274

underground, **18:** 319–21

See also exchange; market economy

education, **4:** 199–200, 206–7

awareness of benefits of, **4:** 192–93

consumption externality in, **5:** 64–69, 73

publicly financed, **5:** 36

efficiency, **1:** 26, 38, 39, 60, 62, 74, 75, 110, 149, 192, 193–96, 208, 221, 245, 260, 261, 262–63, 264–66, 273–77, 298–99, 300, 301, 306, 389, 398–400, 403, 426–27, 457, 462–63; **3:** 172

agreement and, **10:** 28–29; **16:** 113–14

auction method, argument for, **13:** 260

bargaining and, **3:** 104–5

barter economy inefficiencies, **12:** 412

of collective decision-making, **13:** 313–15, 465

conditions for, **5:** 45

of contract, **7:** 38, 40

criteria for, defining, **13:** 334–35

defined, **1:** 267–68; **11:** 12

of distributional rules, **11:** 158

economic and political, **11:** 52–53

in economic order, **12:** 113

equity and, **10:** 128

of final equilibrium, **5:** 45

in financing, **15:** 462–63

fiscal institutions, in mix of, **4:** 290–94

generality and, **11:** 11–13, 52–53

general taxation: in argument for, **14:** 305–6; of requirement for, **14:** 309–10

goods and services: collectivization of partial, **13:** 457, 465; private and government-provided, compared, **13:** 450–65

institutional change for, agreement on, **13:** 347–54

in joint production, **5:** 60

justice and, **4:** 295–97

in knowledge-information industry, **16:** 197–98

in laws and cost-sharing, **7:** 142

least-price-distortion as norm for, **5:** 157

of markets and market economy, **16:** 5, 253–54, 260

in modern law-economics discourse, **11:** 12

normative implications of, **5:** 8

of organizational hierarchies, **13:** 64–65

orthodox criteria of, **5:** 69

in outlay, **9:** 47–48

ownership rights, in assignment of, **12:** 290–91

Pareto, **10:** 22; **11:** 83, 88–90, 143

as policy norm, **12:** 405

political, **11:** 52–54, 100, 158, 194

pressure toward, **5:** 169

presumptive, **1:** 194–95, 199–200, 205

in private-goods world, **5:** 6, 7

problems of government, **15:** 143–45

of profit seeking, **13:** 277

promotion of, by money commodity, **5:** 74

property rights and, **7:** 27–28

in public goods world, **5:** 7, 149, 185

public sector (Samuelson), **14:** 9–10, 32

regulated firms, criteria for, **13:** 327–30

efficiency (*continued*)
  in resource allocation, **13:** 334–35
  social contract and, **7:** 51
  socialists' argument for, **12:** 18
  in taxation, **9:** 45; **11:** 113–30
  Tiebout, **11:** 191
  unanimity and, **7:** 50
  value scale for, **1:** 194–95
  from voluntary exchange process, **5:** 7
  Wicksellian, **11:** 143
  See also inefficiency; optimality
efficiency, decision-making
  defined, **18:** 322
  excess burden analysis and, **4:** 54–55
  of invariant tax-price, **4:** 23–27
  as norm, **18:** 285–88
  in public sector, **8:** 73n. 26
  in taxation: excise tax, **4:** 52–54; general
    sales tax, **4:** 50–52; income tax, **4:**
    30–42, 46–49; indirect taxes, **4:**
    44–46; old tax, **4:** 61; various tax
    devices, **4:** 42–43; wealth tax, **4:**
    27–29
  voluntary agreement, emerging from,
    18: 322–23
egalitarians and social justice, **1:** 364–65
Eisenhower years and economic policy, **8:**
  45–47
elasticity
  of demand: excess burden and, **9:** 76;
    for public goods, **8:** 107; for real
    balances, **9:** 142; for tax base, **9:** 54,
    61, 76, 167
  of import demand, **2:** 64
  income, **5:** 14, 152; **9:** 167
  of revenue, **4:** 63–64
  tax exportation and, **9:** 199
elections
  candidates and, Downs on theory of, **3:**
    343–47
  committees and, Black on theory of, **5:**
    117

electoral choice model, **13:** 293–95
electoral fallacy, **16:** 48–49, 222; **17:** 465,
  467; **19:** 347, 350–51
electoral process, democratic, **17:** 267–71
elitism, **1:** 289–90, 291
elitist assumption of Keynes, **8:** 80
eminent domain, **9:** 193
employment
  fiscal policy and, **8:** 167–79
  full, **1:** 168–70: budget balance at, **4:** 110;
    8: 42–43, 53–55, 157–62; budget
    surplus at, **8:** 47–48, 158–59; fiscal
    policy and, **8:** 167–79; of labor
    supply, **1:** 169; objective under
    Keynesian economic theory, **16:** 346
  high, budget balance at, **8:** 42–43,
    47–48
  in Keynesian theory, **1:** 168–70; **8:**
    170–72
  labor, productive and nonproductive,
    12: 377–78
  of nonlabor resources, **12:** 371–73
  See also unemployment
Employment Act of 1946, **8:** 31, 40
employment model: equal treatment
  principle in, **17:** 331–34
  constraints on employer to promote,
    17: 338–41
  violation of in alternative, **17:** 334–41
endowments. *See* capacities, or
  endowments
Enlightenment, **3:** 304
  Scottish, **1:** 293–95
entitlements protected by
  liability rule, **12:** 170–76
  property rule, **12:** 170–76
entrepreneurs, **12:** 160–62
  activity, factors reducing, **12:** 184–87
  arbitrage opportunities, **12:** 151–52,
    164–66, 424
  constitutional, **16:** 138–39
  efforts of, **18:** 320

heterogeneous input combination, in
model of, **12:** 262–65
Kirzner's theory of, **18:** 298–304
as owners (Kirzner), **12:** 164
political, **16:** 133; **19:** 191, 203, 209,
348–49
potential, **16:** 253
profit-seeking of, **19:** 279
property and liability rules, actions
under, **12:** 173–76, 180
risk-taking, **12:** 162–64
supply-side (Schumpeter), **12:** 424–25
tax, **18:** 319–21
entrepreneurship
in allocative process, **12:** 159–60
Austrian theory of, **12:** 151
in command and market economies,
12: 422–24
constitutionalism and, **1:** 187
cost and, **6:** 18
defined by Kirzner and Schumpeter, **12:**
424–25
economics of, **19:** 235–36
inflation, effect of anticipated, **12:**
165–68
Kirzner's theory, criticism of, **12:**
164–65
modeled as discovery, **18:** 303
organizational forms in, **18:** 299, 307
relative certainty in, under conditions
of, **12:** 163
rent seeking and, **1:** 105, 106–7
under socialism, **19:** 251
uncertainty related to, **12:** 150, 163
environment
controls, **9:** 194–95
law, **11:** 86–88
quality of, and public bad, **7:** 153–54
epistemology, **1:** 450–51
equality
actuarial, **11:** 181–82
in anarchy, **7:** 75–76
attributes of, **17:** 282–83
in choice of rules, **3:** 80
contract and, origins of, **7:** 70–71
in democracy, **11:** 57
in labor time, **11:** 60
under law, **7:** 16; **9:** 185; **11:** 9–11, 13–14;
16: 275
among participants in game, **3:** 80
political (*see* equality, political)
in rights and claims, **7:** 114
of tax rules, **14:** 252–53
as value premise, **16:** 19, 24, 27
view of libertarian anarchist, **16:** 24
See also inequality, personal
equality, economic
achievement of, **17:** 297–98
in premarket assignment of capacities,
17: 300
equality, political, **14:** 37; **16:** 219–22; **17:**
297–98
effective and nominal, **17:** 271
in electoral process, **17:** 270–72
exercise of, **17:** 310
equal liberty. *See* natural liberty
equal-preference model, **4:** 156–57
equal-treatment principle, **17:** 331–43
equilibrium
analysis, **12:** 53–57, 66
conditions for, **12:** 370–71
cost and, **6:** 77–78
entrepreneurship, in Kirzner's theory
of, **18:** 298–303
in markets, **18:** 304–8
neoclassical, **18:** 292–98
political, **10:** 18–19; **13:** 473–75
in stationary economy, **12:** 158–60
in tax analysis, **9:** 96–98
in tax institutions, **4:** 59
theory, contributions of, **12:** 479
equilibrium, competitive
allocative efficiency of, **12:** 405–6
idealized, **12:** 347–49

equilibrium, competitive (*continued*)
  market, in extent of, **12:** 379–81
  theory, **12:** 347–49
equilibrium, independent adjustment, **5:**
  15, 16, 25
equilibrium, Nash, **11:** 55–59, 61–62, 65,
  89, 91, 92, 93–94
equilibrium, trading
  algebraic statement, **5:** 19–22, 70
  analysis, **5:** 35, 36
  characteristics, **5:** 18, 21–22, 26, 29,
    49–50, 56
  conditions, **5:** 22, 42, 63, 76, 118
  determination, **5:** 31
  establishment, **5:** 16, 31
  full, **5:** 36
  interpretation, **5:** 19
  path to, **5:** 77
  position, **5:** 30
  predictions, **5:** 77
  price, **5:** 78
  in private goods, **5:** 51
  in public goods, **5:** 25, 30, 48, 51, 55, 56,
    61–62, 69
  shattering, **5:** 107
  states of, **5:** 32
  strategic behavior, disturbance by, **5:** 24
equilibrium analysis, partial: variables in,
  12: 53–54
equilibrium theory, constrained, **1:** 169
  Hayek on, **12:** 327–29
equirevenue comparison
  commodity taxation and, **9:** 68–70
  with maximum revenue model, **9:** 68
  tax reform and, **9:** 225–26
  for tax theory, **9:** 42–43
equity
  counterequity models of tax reform
    and, **14:** 288–98
  debt retirement, **2:** 137–38
  horizontal and vertical arguments, **4:**
    296; **9:** 43–45, 57, 69, 227; **14:** 213

equity principle, **18:** 7–13
  implications of adopting, **18:** 19–22
  political hierarchy, applied to, **18:** 12–13
  transfers, leading to system of, **18:** 13–19
equivalence theorem. *See* Ricardian
  equivalence theorem
establishmentarianism, **17:** 122, 123–24
estimates
  awareness, distinction from, **4:**
    188–89
  of personal income tax, **4:** 183–84
  public expenditure, benefits of, **4:**
    189–94
  of withholding, **4:** 184–85
ethical rules and constraints, **1:** 311–28,
  356, 357, 367–73
ethics
  Christian, **6:** 72–74
  of contract, **7:** 96–99
  of democracy, **3:** 265–81
  efficiency and, **3:** 265–81
  ethical values, Stigler on, **12:** 74–75
  generalization principle in, **5:** 90, 94
  law and, **7:** 150–52
  normative, **1:** 236–37
  in Pigovian economics, **6:** 71–74
  pressure groups and, **3:** 293–94
  in society, **7:** 220
  trade and, **3:** 267–70
  voluntaristic, norms for behavior in,
    5: 94
  of work, **1:** 355–57
European Union
  central government functions of, **18:**
    132, 134
  competitive federalism, **18:** 94
  constitution for, **18:** 76
  currencies in, **19:** 207
  decentralization in, **18:** 139
  federal system for, advantages of, **18:**
    87–88
  monetary constitution for, **18:** 110–12

national central banks and currencies
in, **19:** 207
revenue sources, **18:** 139–40
reverse revenue sharing in, advantages
of, **18:** 145–46
reverse revenue sharing scheme for, **18:**
138–46
single currency in, **18:** 94
subsidiarity issue in, **18:** 143–45
tax rates in, harmonization of, **18:** 146
See also federalism, supranational
European Union, proposed
competition in, **18:** 109–10, 112
constitutional guarantees for, **18:** 115–17
constitution for, **18:** 100–105, 109–12
developments under, **18:** xiv–xv
East Germany, separate in, **18:** 114
effectiveness of, **18:** 115–17
federalism in, **16:** 269–70; **18:** 79, 88; **19:**
206–7
free trade guarantees for, **18:** 114–15
potential for, **18:** 113
requirements for, **18:** 108
evaluations
beliefs, different from, **17:** 159–62
of marginal consumer, **13:** 382
of marginal taxpayers, **13:** 382–86
necessity of, **17:** 171
precede choice, **17:** 172
evolution
common property, exchange in
privatized, **18:** 226–34
cultural (Hayek), **16:** 141, 143; **18:** 317
evolutionary synthesis theory for
economics, **18:** 291–93
of law (Hayek and Nozick), **18:** 179, 183
organized constitutional, **16:** 144n. 22
processes of, **18:** 290–93
of property rights, **11:** 93–94
in social process, **7:** 211
evolutionists as constitutionalists, **16:** 238;
18: 179

excess burden, **1:** 127–32; **5:** 174, 175; **6:** 50
analysis: decision-making efficiency
and, **4:** 54–55; Italian fiscal theory
and, **15:** 74–75; of traditional public
finance, **4:** 43, 54–55
discrimination and, **9:** 86
elasticity of demand and, **9:** 76
inefficiency, **5:** 174
majoritarian rotation, **11:** 34
taxation, **11:** 116, 125; **14:** 285–314
exchange
agreement in, **5:** 102; **16:** 247–48
asymmetric reciprocity in, **12:** 413–16
barter economy idealized, **12:** 411–12
barter system of, **5:** 117
as basis for agreement, **7:** 23–24
behavior in: dependence on, **18:** 229–30;
opportunistic, **17:** 81–87; rules of,
adherence to, **17:** 87–91
bilateral, **5:** 78, 144
in borrowing from government, **14:**
343–44, 353–55, 357–62
catallactic paradigm, **12:** 116–17
catallactics as science of, **13:** 16–17
in command economy, **12:** 417–20
common property of, evolution in
privatized, **18:** 226–34
complex beneficial, **15:** 13–15
as compromise, **5:** 102
constitutional rules, in change of, **16:**
220–21
continuous dealings, as discipline of, **12:**
439–40
contractarian distributional, **16:** 34–36
contracts in restraint of, **16:** 33; **18:**
210
cost of, **5:** 75
deference as indirect, **16:** 193–95
defined, **16:** 240
demand and supply in, **12:** 254
in economic process, **12:** 33; **17:** 166–67
economics as science of, **13:** 16–21

exchange (*continued*)
  economists as specialists in, **16:** 112–14, 121
  enforced, **16:** 221
  equilibrium in, **12:** 293; **16:** 240–41
  equivalence to production, **12:** 116
  ethics and, **3:** 267–70
  failure of, **5:** 80
  fiscal (*see* fiscal exchange)
  free exchange principle, **13:** 403, 406
  gains from, **18:** 234–35
  in game theoretic framework, **16:** 240–41
  indirect, **7:** 57–63
  among individuals, **13:** 17–18; **18:** 186
  as an institution, **16:** 30
  liberty in, **18:** 206, 210
  market (*see* market exchange)
  in maximization framework, **12:** 116
  maximizing paradigm and, distinction between, **16:** 242–43
  model of, **19:** 135–36: taxation and, **11:** 117–18
  money in idealized, **12:** 412–13
  moral content of (Gauthier), **17:** 452–53
  motivations, **17:** 16
  network of, expansion of, **12:** 369
  opportunistic behavior in, **17:** 81–87
  Pareto criterion in, **13:** 134–35
  political (*see* political exchange)
  principle, **13:** 403
  property rights and, **7:** 22–24; **16:** 260
  in public choice perspective, **13:** 18–19
  in public goods, **7:** 46
  reciprocity in, **12:** 410
  rights as basis for, **7:** 15
  rules of, **1:** 265, 275
  self-interest in (Smith), **19:** 358
  simple, **5:** 12, 29, 31
  simple and complex, **15:** 11–12, 16–17
  subjectivist's theory of, **12:** 23
  transaction costs, **15:** 175
  transfer of rights in, **16:** 29–31
  in transfers of value, **13:** 264–65
  unanimity and, **7:** 50–52
  voluntary (*see* voluntary exchange)
  in votes, **3:** 270–74
  See also politics
exchange paradigm, **1:** 24, 26–27, 29, 34, 35–36, 49, 181–82, 384, 456, 460–61
exchange rates
  fixed, **2:** 65
  flexible, **2:** 64–65
  monetary policy and, **8:** 126
exchange values, **10:** 28–29
  in neoclassical theory, **17:** 30
  in predictive theory, **17:** 31
excise tax, **4:** 52–54
  choice of taxed commodity under, **4:** 255–56
  fiscal illusion and, **4:** 131
  individual awareness of, **4:** 187
  institutional choice of, **4:** 243–57
  revenue elasticity of, **4:** 63
  tie-in sales of public and private goods under, **4:** 54
  uncertainty and, choice of, **4:** 253
exclusion, **5:** 36
  law and, **7:** 39
  public goods and, **7:** 47, 52 n. 10; **9:** 208–9
  from spillover benefits, **5:** 60
  unanimity and, **7:** 52–55
exclusion principle, **5:** 48; **14:** 59–61
exclusion rights
  assignment and enforcement of, **18:** 370–73
  fiscal equalization as substitute for, **18:** 38–40
exit options, **11:** 33
  in competitive federalism, **18:** 97, 129, 133–34
  control, as means of, **18:** 82
  costs, **18:** 235–36

individual lacks, **18:** 171–72

internal and external, **14:** 241n. 15

in market economy, **18:** 236–39, 258

private property rights, dependence on, **18:** 230–31, 234

property rights without, **18:** 236–37

socialist system, absence in, **18:** 250, 254

from taxes, **18:** 258

See also internal-exit model

expectations

inflationary, **8:** 90–91; **9:** 144–49

in neoclassical theory, **18:** 295

rational models, **8:** 111n. 1

rules and, **10:** 110–11, 115–16

in subjectivist theory, **18:** 295

expediency criterion, **1:** 313, 314–15

expenditure, abnormal, **2:** 149

expenditures. *See* government spending; public expenditure

expenditure tax, **2:** 67–71; **4:** 42–43; **9:** 49, 111; **11:** 128

experts

constitutional, **16:** 135–39

in markets, **16:** 135–39

in representative democracy, **16:** 136–39

See also deference; rational deference theory

exploitation

in distributional game, **16:** 148–50

of forces of competition, **18:** 92

of the many by the few, **16:** 270

in market exchanges; **16:** 269

in politics, **16:** 269, 275

potential for, **18:** 230

protection against, **18:** 84, 92, 239, 247–49, 258

reduction of, **11:** 33; **16:** 273

of taxes, **9:** 198–99

in two-party political game, **16:** 271–72

external diseconomies, **12:** 316, 323–24; **17:** 98–99, 142

activity generating, **14:** 124–29; **15:** 344

common property in use of, **18:** 220

damages from, **14:** 126

external economies and, asymmetry between, **15:** 173

inframarginal, **15:** 111–12

internalization of, **13:** 255–56, 259; **18:** 441

law-enforcement-induced, **18:** 441

in less-than-unanimity rule, **14:** 13

marginal, **15:** 111

in model of market failure, **18:** 279–80

of monopolist, **15:** 173

with nonspecialized resources, **13:** 252–55

in outmigration, **18:** 49

output- and input-generated, **15:** 163–67

Pareto-relevant, **15:** 114, 160–62, 215–17

penalty tax or regulation of industry producing, **13:** 420–26

politicization of, **18:** 279–85

product-generated, **13:** 426–30

removing to internalize commonality, **18:** 220

in rent-seeking theory, **13:** 253–55

with specialized resources, **13:** 255–58

technological and pecuniary, **12:** 316–17

valuation of, **15:** 186–88, 227–28, 231–32, 238–39

external drainage from income, **2:** 62

external economies, **5:** 15, 30, 60, 63–64, 72; **14:** 129; **15:** 127; **17:** 142–44; **18:** 49

activity generating, **15:** 344

adjustment to: collective market, **15:** 130–32; individual market, **15:** 128–29

in British National Health Service, **15:** 344

collectivization in presence of, **15:** 127

in consumption, **5:** 33, 46, 64, 68–69, 71

external diseconomies and, asymmetry between, **15:** 173

under independent behavior, **5:** 60

inframarginal, **15:** 111, 113

external economies (*continued*)
  from investment and capital formation,
    15: 294
  marginal, **15:** 111
  Marshall on, **12:** 390
  Pareto-relevant, **15:** 114, 215–17:
    conversion to irrelevant, **15:** 148–51
  public goods, in supply of, **15:** 245–56
externalities (external effects)
  analysis, **1:** 69
  in budget decisions, **7:** 193
  in collective action, **3:** 64–68, 89; **15:**
    17–19
  common property and, **7:** 73–74
  in commons, **3:** 58
  in consumption (*see* external
    economies)
  contractual changes, produced by, **17:** 128
  costs or benefits in, **15:** 16
  decision rules and, **3:** 62
  defined, **15:** 15–16
  degree of, **5:** 21, 70
  elimination of, **1:** 262
  extended taxonomy, **15:** 176
  external, **13:** 358, 362
  fiscal: collective internalization of, **18:**
    57–60; conditions for, **18:** 49
  fiscal behavior, evaluation of, **18:** 53–54
  in group-choice situation, **5:** 117
  impact of, **1:** 60, 62, 63, 65, 68, 71–72, 73,
    78, 101, 199, 221–22, 260, 262, 263,
    269–70, 299–300
  inframarginal, **15:** 111, 113, 115–16
  institutional, **1:** 364; **18:** 285
  intergenerational, **11:** 97–100
  internalization of, **1:** 328; **12:** 132, 169,
    355–62; **13:** 364; **17:** 224–26; **18:** 63
  interpersonal and intertemporal, **16:**
    394–95
  interpretation, **13:** 361–62
  joint-consumption relationships as, **15:**
    175–76, 178

  in jointness of production (*see* external
    economies)
  in joint supply, **15:** 215–17, 267–68
  among jurisdictions, **9:** 206
  large-number, **5:** 166
  law and, **7:** 136
  locational (Marshall), **12:** 394
  majority rule and, **3:** 89
  in majority voting, **3:** 145–46, 200–201
  marginal, **15:** 12, 111, 114–15, 122
  markets for exchange of, **15:** 132
  merger and private response to, **13:** 359
  negative, correcting for, **13:** 358
  neutrality theorem (Coase), **12:** 293–96
  nonexchange interdependencies as, **12:**
    292
  nonexclusion as characteristic of, **5:** 67
  nonreciprocal, **11:** 90–92
  nonseparable, **15:** 250
  nonsymmetrical reciprocity, **15:** 151–55
  optimality in mix, conditions for, **15:**
    210–11
  Pareto equilibrium, in full, **15:** 121–25
  Pareto optimality and, **3:** 190–99
  Pareto-relevant, **1:** 262, 263, 350:
    illustration of, **15:** 117–20; influence
    on allocative outcomes, **15:** 156–60
  Pareto-relevant and Pareto-irrelevant,
    12: 361–62; **15:** 114–17, 126, 244; **17:**
    217–20; **18:** 316, 369–73
  Pigovian, **5:** 166; **14:** 121–23
  political, **15:** 32
  political and economic, distinction
    between, **12:** 185
  political corrections of, **13:** 359–61
  political organization and, **3:** 288–89
  political responses, expected patterns
    of, **13:** 362–63
  politicization to correct (Pigou), **12:**
    292–93
  in politics, **3:** 44–47
  potentially relevant, **15:** 112–13

predictions in theory of, **12:** 135
private and political responses to, **13:**
 358–61
property rights and, **7:** 30–31
pure, **5:** 96
reciprocal, **11:** 8, 82, 88–90; **15:** 126–27
relevant and irrelevant, **15:** 112–13
rights, with assignment of, **18:** 209–11
in simple and complex exchange, **15:**
 16–17
small-number, **5:** 166
Smith's conception of, **15:** 283–88
social order and, **3:** 61
tax- and benefit-side, **18:** 36–38, 48–57
in taxes, **8:** 132 n. 2
in tax response, **4:** 56; **9:** 57
technological and pecuniary,
 distinction between, **12:** 177–78; **17:**
 455
trade as institution to internalize, **12:**
 169
voluntary exchange, influence on, **16:**
 37–38
welfare economics and, **1:** 196–200
in work-leisure choice, **12:** 353–55
work-supply, **1:** 353–55, 358, 359
See also external diseconomies; external
 economies
externality problems, **11:** 82
externality theory
 external economy or diseconomy in, **15:**
 217
 optimality, conditions for, **15:** 217–18
 small- and large-number interactions
 in, **15:** 174–75
external public debt, **2:** 9–10, 11, 26, 58–66
external trade, **11:** 104–7
extraordinary tax, **2:** 35, 88–94

factor endowments, **18:** 234–35
fair chances criterion, **17:** 329–49
Fair Labor Standards Act, **1:** 302

fairness, **1:** 308, 465
 of constitutional arrangements, **16:**
 162–63, 166–71
 in constitutional design, **17:** 322–24
 costs, **17:** 343
 criteria of justice, **9:** 6; **10:** 35
 criterion to evaluate, **16:** 44–45, 103, 188
 defined by agreement, **17:** 314–15, 325,
 410
 as equal treatment for equals, **17:** 333–38
 justice as, **7:** 221–23; **10:** 35; **17:** 408–14
 Knight on, **1:** 308 n. 35
 in political rules, **17:** 327–29
 Rawls's definition, **16:** 103
 rule of law and, **11:** 13–14
 in rules, **10:** 21
 in rules emerging from agreement, **16:**
 165–70
fair rules games, **17:** 314–18, 329–30
fallacy
 of composition, **2:** 3–4, 50
 methodological, **2:** 50
false analogy, **2:** 8–9, 15, 38–39
falsification, **6:** 5, 10, 37–40
fame, **16:** 198
fatal conceit, **1:** 180
 economists as victims of, **19:** 218
 socialism as, **18:** 310; **19:** 120–21, 189,
 267–69
 See also socialist economies
federal debt. *See* public debt
federalism, **11:** 188–91, 195; **12:** 236
 argument for, **18:** 84–86
 competitive (*see* federalism,
 competitive)
 competitive politics of U.S., **16:** 32
 criticism of, **18:** 5–6
 economic freedom in, **18:** 97
 enforcement of, **18:** 102
 European: opposition to, **18:** 88;
 potential, **18:** 72
 exit option in, **18:** 70–72

federalism (*continued*)
  fiscal, **7:** 47
  fiscal constitution and, **9:** 203–12; **18:**
    7–13, 21
  fiscal transfers in, equalizing, **18:** 42–43
  of Founding Fathers, **19:** 176–77
  freedom of trade and, relationship
    between, **18:** 77–78
  idealized, **18:** 86
  idea of, **19:** 175–76
  Madison's conception of, **18:** 102–3
  market, as analogue to the, **18:** 68–72
  migration under, incentives for, **18:**
    29–32, 38
  partitioned sovereignty, **18:** 80, 82–84
  political structure in, **18:** 69–70, 77,
    79–80
  in post–Civil War U.S., **19:** 177
  power, reduces and divides, **18:** 88
  provision of public goods under, **18:**
    27–42
  in Switzerland, **19:** 175–76
  taxation and regulation under, **14:** 264
  territorial decentralization under, **16:** 145
  units of, conditions for shifting among,
    18: 93–94
  See also European Union; government,
    federal
federalism, competitive, **18:** xii–xiii
  constitutional reform for, **18:** 73–74
  constitutional structure for, achieving,
    18: 75–76
  efficacy of, **18:** 129
  European central banks in, **18:** 109–10,
    112
  under European Union, **18:** xiv–xv, 78
  exit option in, **18:** 82–83, 97, 133
  function of, **18:** 93
  normative theory of, **18:** 80–82
  political structure, as appropriate, **18:** 92
  reverse revenue sharing, to enforce, **18:**
    142–43

  self-enforcing, **18:** 138
  theory of, **18:** 69–72
federalism, supranational
  advantages and disadvantages, **18:**
    132–34, 145–46
  competition in, conditions for, **18:**
    123–27
  economic integration into, effect of, **18:**
    122–23
  membership in, **18:** 128–30
  national sovereignty under, **18:** 119–27
  nation-states in, **18:** 123–25
  transfer spending under, **18:** 126–27
  See also European Union
Federal Reserve Board
  bureaucracy and, **8:** 127
  political controls and, **8:** 126–27
  Treasury, 1951 accord with, **8:** 44
fees, fiscal illusion and, **4:** 133
Feldstein model
  financing of pension payments, **15:** 445
  social security reduces saving under, **15:**
    446
finance, government
  local, applied to public goods theory, **5:**
    178
  pure, **1:** 119–33
  theories of, **1:** xvii–xviii, 93n. 10
  welfare economics and, **1:** 120–32, 137
  See also general-fund financing; public
    finance
fire protection, **4:** 74–81
firms
  advertising, investment in, **13:** 337–38
  in advertising cartel, **13:** 338–44
  in industries with imposed penalty
    taxes, **13:** 420–23
  in industries with regulation, **13:**
    423–24
  regulated: efficiency criteria for, **13:**
    327–30; monopsony solution for, **13:**
    320–21; returns to, **13:** 318–20

rent-seeking, **13:** 398–402

theory of: individual unit in organized market economy, **13:** 64–65; locational rents in, **18:** 58

See also industries

fiscal authority

benevolent, **14:** 91, 99–100

constrained Leviathan, **14:** 97–100

fiscal choice

debt-financed deficits and, **8:** 138–47

democratic, **4:** 175–80

information and, **8:** 135–36

institutions and, **8:** 130–31

institutions of, **5:** 142–43, 148

levels of, **4:** 215–26

rational ignorance and, **8:** 137

tax institutions and, **8:** 131–38

See also individual choice

fiscal constitution, **1:** 145–47; **5:** 149, 151, 155; **8:** 23–24, 180–93; **9:** 181–82, 237–38; **16:** 58–59

argument for, **16:** 320–21

budget balance, rule of, **16:** 352

constraints on, **16:** 108–9

criteria, **14:** 254–56

defined, **14:** 272; **16:** 314

in federal state, **9:** 214–15

foundations for, **14:** 252

Hayek's change to, **14:** 265

in international economy, **9:** 200–203

after Keynes, **8:** 52–53

Keynesian economics and, **8:** 23–24, 32, 79; **16:** 352–53

for long-term economic growth, **14:** 271–73

political excess, to control, **14:** 482–83

reform in, **16:** 422–24

revenue earmarking, **14:** 98–99

tax constitution, **9:** 45

See also constraints, fiscal; taxation; taxes; tax reform; tax system

fiscal decision

strategic bargaining in, **4:** 117–20

two-sidedness of, **4:** 90

fiscal drag, **8:** 47–48

fiscal exchange, **11:** 117–18

attributes, **1:** 136–39

failure, **16:** 319

between individual and government, **18:** 187–89

intertemporal, considerations in, **14:** 521–22

model, **14:** 92–95, 97, 99–100

paradigm, **1:** 133–49

requirements, **18:** 189–92

taxes in, **14:** 38–39, 213–16; **16:** 317–18

Wicksellian paradigm for, **1:** 134, 138–40, 142, 144, 145, 147, 192n. 2; **14:** 11

fiscal history, pre- and post-Keynesian, **8:** 5–6

fiscal illusion, **1:** 148; **4:** 9, 125–42; **8:** 131–35

defined, **1:** 150–63

Keynesian economics and, **8:** 142

in public spending, **4:** 135

in taxation, **4:** 130–35

fiscal institutions

earmarked revenue as, **14:** 91

modification, **14:** 33–34

private sector, effects on, **14:** 17–18, 27–28

public sector, effects on, **14:** 18–19, 28–30

quasi-permanence of, **14:** 102–3

rules and (*see* rules: fiscal institutions and)

taxation and debt issue as, **14:** 352–55, 357–64

in theory of constitutions, **14:** 20–24

transfers of income and wealth by, **14:** 41–43

fiscal instruments, individual choice of, **14:** 108–18

fiscal irresponsibility, **8:** 51–52

fiscal justice, **4:** 295–97
fiscal liability, **8:** 19
fiscal marginalism, defined, **1:** 119–20
fiscal policy
   activist, **1:** 172, 173, 174
   anti-recession, **13:** 447
   bias in, **13:** 437–38, 449
   budget deficits and, **4:** 102–3
   in closed economy, **4:** 270–72
   constitutional consideration of, **4:**
     269–81
   constraints in, **13:** 473–74
   criterion for, **15:** 336
   exchange rates and, **4:** 278–81
   ideal, **13:** 440–41
   as instrument of stabilization, **13:**
     435–37, 448
   after Keynes, **14:** 506
   Keynesian, **14:** 505–6; **19:** 60–61
   of majority coalition, **16:** 271
   migration, effect on, **18:** 41–42
   monetary policy and, **19:** 341–42
   municipal, **15:** 335–38
   national debt and, **14:** 349–50
   in partially open economy, **4:** 278–81
   politics and, **8:** 171–72; **13:** 439–40
   for private citizen, **4:** 277–78
   tax institutions and, **4:** 108–9
   tax-rate and, **13:** 473
   transfers, equalizing, **18:** 42–43
   in wholly open economy, **4:** 272–77
   Wicksell's theory of, **16:** 9–10
   See also budgets and budgeting;
     Proposition 13 (California); public
     debt financing; public debt issue;
     taxation
fiscal principles, **8:** 180–93
   classical, **8:** 10–24
fiscal process
   benevolent fisc model, **14:** 90–92,
     97–100
   constrained Leviathan model, **14:**
     97–100

earmarking, **14:** 72–73
fiscal exchange model, **14:** 92–95, 97,
   99–100
   fiscal transfer model, **14:** 95–97
   with and without unanimity rule,
     14: 95
   See also fiscal transfer
fiscal prudence
   collective, norms for, **14:** 488
   Keynesian theory, overturn by, **14:**
     489–90
   of Victorian norms, **14:** 461–62, 489
fiscal psychology, **4:** 186
fiscal reality, **1:** 140–43
fiscal record, pre-Keynesian, **8:** 10–24
fiscal reform, **4:** 299–302; **8:** 8–9
fiscal residuum, **1:** 127
fiscal responsibility
   Keynesian, **8:** 3
   principles of, **8:** 3, 6, 10–24; **18:** 20–21
   private-public analogy, **8:** 3, 9
fiscal rules
   agreement on, **5:** 152
   balanced budget and, **14:** 500–504
   generality in, **14:** 250–51, 256–58
   Hayek's "general rules," **14:** 256–57
fiscal spending: budgets and money, **8:**
   44–45
fiscal systems
   aggravative, **1:** 128
   classification of, **1:** 128–29
   equalitarian (redistributive), **1:** 128–29
   equity principle and, **18:** 7–13
   function of, **18:** 11–12
   government units in, **18:** 3–22
   migration in, incentive for, **18:** 29–32
   state-local, **18:** 4n. 4
   status quo, **1:** 128
   See also federalism, competitive
fiscal theory, Anglo-Saxon, **2:** 21; **15:** 100,
   102
   social or collective choice process,
     participation in, **15:** 67

taxation in: incidence of, **15:** 103; neutral tax system, **15:** 78; sacrifice theories of, **15:** 65, 79–81

fiscal theory, Italian, **2:** 16, 21, 35–36, 88–94; **4:** 127–38
  classical, **15:** 65–66
  contribution of, **15:** 59–62, 97–100, 101–2, 104
  cooperative state model (de Viti), **15:** 69–70
  dualism, **15:** 69–71
  excess burden analysis, **15:** 74–75
  Fascist ideology on, influence of, **15:** 71
  of Ferrara, **15:** 63–64
  fiscal account in, **15:** 65, 74–79
  fiscal process (de Viti), economic theory of, **15:** 66
  general equilibrium theory on, influence of, **15:** 66–67, 72–73
  goal of, **15:** 72
  government activity in, **15:** 76–77, 84
  marginal-productivity theory of distribution applied to (de Viti), **15:** 77–78
  methodology, **15:** 72
  productivity theory of state expenditure (de Viti–Einaudi), **15:** 73–79
  public debt theory in, **15:** 85–92
  public spending theory (Pantaleoni), **15:** 65–66
  ruling class in, **15:** 67, 70–71
  sacrifice theories, criticism of, **15:** 79–81
  scientific or positivistic, **15:** 68–69
  sociopolitical theory (Borgatta), **15:** 70–71
  strengths and weaknesses of, **15:** 103
  tax capitalization in, **15:** 81–83
fiscal theory, orthodox, **1:** 125
fiscal transfer
  critique of, **1:** 143–45
  under debt issue and taxation, **14:** 352–55, 357–64

earmarked revenue under model of, **14:** 96–97
  model, **14:** 95–97, 99–100
  transfer of taxes, **14:** 242–43
  See also intergenerational transfers
fixed exchange rates, **2:** 65
  fiscal policy and, **4:** 278–79
fixed institutions: fiscal choice under, **4:** 289–93
flat-rate tax, **1:** 425; **11:** 114, 126, 128
flexibility, revenue: of tax instruments, **4:** 269–70
flexibility and cost curves, Stigler on, **12:** 137
flexible exchange rates, **2:** 64–65
  fiscal policy and, **4:** 279–81
Flint v. Stone Tracy Co., **18:** 18 n. 28
forecasts
  "new economics" and, **8:** 31
  post–World War II errors, **8:** 31–40
foreign trade
  generality and, **11:** 104–7
  rent seeking in, **11:** 107
Founding Fathers, **1:** 51, 373; **3:** 25, 298
  constitutional attitude of, **16:** 309
  constitutional perspective of, **16:** 42–43
  wisdom of, **1:** 255
franchise and bureaucracy, **7:** 197–204
freedom, **15:** 9–11
  burden of, **1:** 127–32
  of citizens from coercion, **16:** 225
  economic, **18:** 97
  of entry and exit, **18:** 236–40
  indivisibility of, **16:** 392–94, 396
  Knight on, **1:** 85
  moral order and moral community, differences in, **17:** 195
  scientific, defense of, **1:** 230–43
  of speech, **18:** 208
  of trade, **18:** 77–78, 97
  See also liberty
freedom of choice, **1:** 258–59
  among alternatives, **18:** 216–17

freedom of choice (*continued*)
    defined, **1:** 85, 88
    instances of, **13:** 68
    logic of, **1:** 66–67
    in market economy, **1:** 182–83; **18:**
        200–204, 239–40
    scientific versus political, **1:** 237
    See also behavior; constitutional
        political economy; individual choice;
        markets; politics; rules
free enterprise, **1:** 101, 296
    Knight's critique of, **1:** 296
free exchange principle
    considered constitutionally, **13:** 403
    in constitutional politics, **13:** 406
free markets, **1:** 202, 282, 346–59
    social choice and democracy and, **1:**
        89–102
    See also markets
free riders, **5:** 26, 30, 83–86, 90, 187; **7:**
    47–50; **9:** 10, 23
    argument, **4:** 113–14
    choice of, probabilistic approach to, **5:** 85
    in constitutional change, **10:** 33, 41,
        160–62
    constitutional rules, eliminated by, **4:**
        116–20
    external diseconomies, valuation of, **15:**
        186–88, 227–28, 231–32, 238–39
    individual behavior under income tax,
        analogy to, **4:** 37
    in joint-supply exchanges, **15:** 217
    motivation, **5:** 88
    oligopoly behavior and, compared, **15:**
        242
    preferences, concealing true, **15:** 186–88,
        227–28, 231–32, 238–39
    problem, **1:** 39, 263, 268–72, 322, 323–24;
        5: 25, 74, 92, 94–95, 122, 186: Wicksell
        on, **1:** 323n. 7
    in public goods interaction, **15:** 227–28,
        231–32, 238–39, 243

terminology, **5:** 83
transaction costs, responsibility for, **15:**
    12–13
Wicksellian proposals and, **4:** 114–16,
    123, 287–89
free trade, **1:** 218–19
    generality and, **11:** 101–12
frictional burden, **2:** 7, 8–9, 12–13, 34. *See
    also* burden
Friday (Crusoe's friend), **17:** 42–46,
    48–49, 362–64
Friedman demand curve, **12:** 193,
    198–200
full employment
    budget balance and, **8:** 157–62
    budget surplus and, **8:** 48
    fiscal policy and, **8:** 167–79
Full Employment Act (1946), **8:** 31, 40; **16:**
    346
full neutrality
    of decision rule, **4:** 152–63 passim
    departures from, **4:** 162–63
functional finance, **1:** 172, 173; **4:** 108–9; **8:**
    53–54, 153n. 1
future generations, **2:** 26–37
    public debt and, **8:** 20: claims against,
        14: 441; effect on, **12:** 211–12

gains-from-trade, **1:** 140, 198, 208, 218–19,
    229, 264, 323, 358, 361; **3:** 248; **5:** 15–16;
    12: 356
    distribution of, **15:** 472–82
    methodology of economists, **19:** 136–38,
        148
    monopolist, **12:** 206
    in private goods, **15:** 472–75
    in public goods, **5:** 80, 81, 83, 108, 184:
        local, **15:** 475–77; national, **15:** 478–82
    Smith on, **12:** 369, 430–31
gains-from-trade perspective
    classical liberal adherence to, **19:** 148
    of Coase, **19:** 146–47

of Hutt, **19:** 136–40, 145–47
of Wicksell, **19:** 141
games
   of coordination, **10:** 11
   fair rules games, **17:** 314–18, 329–30
   n-person cooperative games, **1:** 41, 65
   political: of cartel formation, **13:** 404–5;
      in incumbency model, **13:** 284–87
   rules of, **10:** 8–10; **16:** 44
   strategy and, **10:** 8–9
   See also rules
game theory, **1:** 23, 40, 65, 212, 217–18,
   238–39, 369–71, 431–32, 436–37,
   448–50; **3:** xix, 307, 8 n. 1; **5:** 84, 159, 178;
   17: 7
   competitive equilibrium theory, **12:** 6
   core in, **7:** 42 n. 17
   in economics, **12:** 480; **16:** 240
   as forerunner, **3:** 326–31
   majority rule and, **3:** 149–71
   as mathematics, **16:** 84, 86, 237, 240
   natural distribution of goods, **16:** 95–96
   paradigm, **16:** 108
   payoff structure, **16:** 271–72
   solution concepts of, **12:** 27–28; **16:**
      80–81, 85
   See also prisoners' dilemma
Gauthier rule, **17:** 442–43, 452
general-fund financing, **4:** 71–86
   geometrical analysis of, **4:** 75–81
   imputed outlay under, **4:** 80–81
   tie-in sales, analogy to, **4:** 72–73, 83 n. 7
general impossibility theorem, Arrow's, **1:**
   xvi, 16, 54, 91–92, 256, 431
   critique of, **1:** 89–102
generality, **11:** xix
   applications of, **1:** 424–26
   "bad" politics and, **11:** 65
   classical liberalism and, **11:** 111
   constitutionalism and, **11:** 61–64
   constitution and, **11:** xx
   as constraint in taxation, **14:** 310–11

contractarianism and, **11:** 207–8
in decision making, **1:** 23, 419–28
difficulties in application, **11:** 59–60
efficiency and, **11:** 11–13
ex ante, **11:** 177–78, 194
foreign trade and, **11:** 104–7
free trade and, **11:** 101–12
illustrations, **11:** 35–54
implications of, **11:** 199
intertemporal, **11:** 174–75
law and, **11:** 10
in law and politics, **11:** 3–16, 66–67
in legislation, **3:** 290–93
limited, **11:** 180
majority rule, violated by, **11:** 38
market restriction and, **11:** 9, 101–12
modern democracy and, **1:** 427–28
political agenda and, **11:** 66–78
political efficiency and, **11:** 52–53
in politics, **11:** 14–16
public goods and, **11:** 58
reciprocation and, **11:** 8
redistribution and, **11:** 159–75
rent seeking and, **1:** 426–27; **11:** 46 n. 3,
   53 n. 6, 122–23
Ricardo theorem and, **11:** 134–35
in rules, **3:** 21, 78; **7:** 177–78; **9:** 184–90
service levels, origins of uniform, **11:**
   192
in spending, **9:** 190
summarized, **11:** 199
in taxation, **9:** 45, 185–90; **11:** 113–30; **14:**
   310–11; **14:** 315–18
tax legislation (1993), reversal in, **14:** 319
in Tax Reform Act (1986), **14:** 318–19
of tax structure, **14:** 305–6
unnatural, **11:** 69
generality principle, **1:** 312–13, 319, 340–41;
   7: 150–51, 155; **11:** xix–xx
   applied to politics, **19:** 282–83, 345,
      352–54
   defined, **19:** 350–51

generality principle (*continued*)
   Kantian, **1:** 312, 340
   pork-barrel spending under, **19:** 352–53
general sales tax, **4:** 50–52, 251
general welfare, **1:** 120–22
general will, **3:** 12
   of Rousseau, **1:** 100; **3:** 318
George Mason University, Center for
   Study of Public Choice, **19:** 110
Germany, **18:** 113–14
   economic recovery of, **1:** 184
gifts as transfers of value, **13:** 265
gift tax and fiscal illusion, **4:** 133
gold
   changes in U.S. monetary system
      related to, **18:** 385–87
   under New Deal, **18:** 395–410
Gold Reserve Act (1934), **18:** 396
gold standard, **1:** 405, 412, 413, 414, 417
   concept of, **18:** 389–95
   Great Britain's departure from (1931),
      18: 388
   in international monetary order, **18:**
      388–95
goods
   bads and, **18:** 447
   claims and rights, nominal and real, **13:**
      139–40
   command economy, shortages in, **12:**
      417–20
   distribution of, post-exchange, **16:** 247
   in individual utility function (Alchian),
      12: 129–32
   in joint supply production, **15:** 217–22
   joint supply theory, in Marshallian, **15:**
      213
   in market process, **18:** 307–8
   merit, **16:** 264
   in money-goods exchange, **12:** 33–34,
      412–14
   nonexcludable, locational dimension
      of, **18:** 63

nonprivate, **15:** 265
nonrival and nonexcludable, **15:** xii
order as, imposition of, **16:** 88
in Pareto criterion analysis of transfers,
   13: 139–49
public or collective, **12:** 45; **13:** 452,
   459–61
scarce, rent seeking in competition for,
   16: 258–59
substitute, sellers of, **18:** 201–3
sumptuary, **16:** 267
valuation, **12:** 155–58
See also capital goods; private goods;
   public goods; public goods and
   services
goods and services
   collective: compared with market, **13:**
      451–64; consumption uniformity
      under, **13:** 452, 454, 457
   decentralization in provision of,
      15: 36
   material and immaterial (Ferrara), **15:**
      62–63
   modes of provision, **13:** 451n. 1
   in mutually exclusive categories, **13:**
      463–64
   optimal quantity, **12:** 99; **15:** 202–3
   partial collectivization, **13:** 457
   partially divisible, **5:** 166–67; **13:** 451
   political institutions, provided by, **12:**
      99; **13:** 451–55
   price elasticity demand, **15:** 343–44
   in theory of clubs, **15:** 194
   tradeable and nontradeable, **1:** 348–49,
      352, 457
   utility function with public and private,
      15: 195–96
   valuation of, **12:** 99
   voluntary exchange of, **16:** 36–39
See also consumption, public; private
   goods and services; public goods and
   services

"good society"
  defined, **1:** 240–41
  justice and, **1:** 237–40
  standards for, disappearance of, **1:** 451
government
  as adjudicator, **7:** 114
  as agent, **18:** 188–89
  as artifact, **9:** 4
  benevolent dictator, **14:** 176
  borrowing from individuals, **14:** 108
  budget deficit to growth, relation of, **14:**
    480–81
  collective action through, **15:** 13–14
  as collectivity of maximizers, **14:** 15
  competition, **11:** 191: state-level, **18:**
    69–72
  constitutional contract and, **7:** 107
  constraints on, **1:** 51–52, 57–59, 186–88;
    9: 13; **13:** 53: free enterprise, **19:** 176;
    Hobbes on, **16:** 47–52; power to tax,
    16: 51–52; procedural and
    quantitative, **16:** 56–57; revenue
    maximizing, **14:** 154–64; taking
    power, **16:** 51
  contractual commitments, adherence
    to, **14:** 530–32
  control through constitutional rules, **16:**
    105
  cutting size of, **17:** 126, 131–32
  debt financing, **14:** 455
  defined, **13:** 3–4
  demand-driven models of, **13:** 58–59
  distributional policies of, **17:** 306–9
  efficiency of, problems of, **15:** 143–45
  exchange between individual and, **18:**
    192–94
  expanding, conditions for, **17:** 309–10
  financing of, **1:** 119–32, 170–73
  financing property rights enforcement
    costs, **18:** 379–81
  financing public programs with debt,
    17: 88–89

fiscal illusion, creation of, **15:** 92–97
fiscal or monetary policy, choice of, **13:**
  435–40, 446–47
free enterprise, limited by, **19:** 176
GNP, share in, **7:** 205
growth, **7:** 205–6; **9:** 30–31
Hobbesian perspective, **14:** 177–78
individual behavior in, **13:** 6–7
institutional interactions, as set of, **13:** 5
intervention: in private sector, **13:** 306;
  in U.S. by, **19:** 177–79
law enforcement role of, **18:** 434; **19:** 175
limited, **9:** 13; **19:** 176
local: behavior of, Tiebout's model of,
  18: 163; expenditures, empirical
  studies of, **4:** 207–10; finance, applied
  to public goods theory, **5:** 178;
  macroeconomic policy and, **4:**
  272–77
market failure and, **7:** 216; **13:** 113
modern anarchists and, **7:** 108; **8:** 3–4
monopoly, **9:** 13
in moral anarchy, **17:** 190–91
in moral community, **17:** 192–96
in moral order, **17:** 191–92, 194–96,
  200
New Deal centralized, **16:** 339–42
as paradox, **7:** 116–35
political decentralization, **15:** 35–37
political process in study of, **13:** 6–7
politics in business of, role of, **13:** 4
power to tax, **14:** 177–81: constitutional
  limits on, **16:** 51–52
prior commitment, repudiation of, **14:**
  526
private ownership right, creation of, **13:**
  253–55
as productive process, **7:** 124
promise-keeping behavior, **14:** 524
property rights and, **7:** 107
public debt: defaulting on, **14:** 519–20;
  issuance of, **13:** 442–43

government (*continued*)
  public sector growth, **16:** 309
  rent seeking and, **1:** 108–11
  restraints, **16:** 57
  revenue maximization, constraints on,
    14: 154–64
  role of: assigned in U.S. Constitution,
    19: 176; Coase's theory of social cost,
    13: 297–98; Keynesian analysis, **19:**
    321–22; political exchange, **18:** 188–89
  services, production of, **11:** 149–50
  size of, **3:** 113–14; **7:** 130; **14:** 261
  Smith on, **15:** 296–97; **19:** 184
  spending by, **1:** 170–73
  supply of services, **15:** 342–44
  taking power of, limits on, **16:** 51
  tax-rate, tax-revenue utility function,
    model of, **13:** 468–73
  unjust, **1:** 303
  urban, fiscal strategy of, **15:** 335–38
  as voluntary exchange, **9:** 7
  See also borrowing, public;
    bureaucracy; commitments;
    decentralization; fiscal policy;
    interference, politicized; Leviathan;
    political systems; public debt; public
    expenditure; rules; state, the;
    unanimity rule (Wicksell)
government, federal
  central and subordinate units of, fiscal
    systems in, **18:** 3–22
  in competitive federalism, **18:** 70–72
  in federal system, **18:** xii, 69–72
  guarantees, **18:** xii
  power of U.S., increase in, **18:** 91
government action
  amounts (Italian fiscal theory),
    determination of, **15:** 76–77
  implicit ownership to, **15:** 309–18
  intervention: with market failure, **15:**
    xi–xii, xiv–xv; public goods
    interpretation of, **15:** 291–92

governmental grants, alternative theory
  to, **9:** 212–14
governmental sector and inflation, **8:**
  71–72
government failure, **7:** 217
  defined, **13:** 116
  Homo economicus construction of, **13:**
    118–21
  public choice as theory of, **13:** 113–14, 173
government purchases, **2:** 97
government role
  in commonly held property, **15:** 13–15
  monetary framework, to provide, **15:**
    24–25
  moral anarchy, in climate of, **17:** 197
  moral order in U.S., in erosion of, **17:**
    197–98
  resources, in efficient use of, **15:** 16–17
government spending
  domain of, **9:** 190–92
  empirical tests of, **4:** 202–5
  growth, **7:** 205
  income taxes and, **14:** 334–36
  national income and, **8:** 58
  paradigms in analysis of tax-spend
    process, **14:** 213–15
  regulation and, **9:** 195–96
  taxing and spending decisions,
    separation of, **4:** 87–88
  theory, **2:** 116–19
  uniformity in, **9:** 190
  See also public expenditure
Gramm-Rudman-Hollings legislation, **15:**
  382, 385, 387; **19:** 61
grants, theory of, **9:** 212–14
Great Britain
  industrial revolution in, **1:** 293
  socialist experiments in, **1:** 184
  See also National Health Service, Britain
Great Depression
  economic constitution revised during,
    16: 350

monetary policy during, **16:** 342–47
New Deal economic policy during and
after, **16:** 339–42
Greenspan Commission (National
Commission on Social Security
Reform), **15:** 388–89
Gresham's law in politics, **10:** 68–73
group choice. *See* decision making,
collective
group size and decision costs, **3:** 112–13

hailstorm tax, **5:** 157
Harberger triangles, **12:** 96
Head Money Cases, **18:** 18 n. 28
head tax, **4:** 14; **5:** 90
Hegelian epoch, concept of state after, **1:**
183
heterogeneity, **12:** 261–62. *See also* inputs,
heterogeneous
hierarchies, organizational: efficiency of,
13: 64–65
Hobbesian contractarianism, **10:** 31; **16:**
215–16; **17:** 380–84
Hobbesian jungle, **1:** 22, 51, 59, 433, 439; **10:**
5, 11
anarchy in, **7:** 12–13, 16, 32–33, 42, 108,
165–66, 186–87; **9:** 6–7, 13; **10:** 30; **17:**
302–4, 362–65, 369, 380–84; **18:** 175;
19: 317
cooperation in, lack of, **18:** 206
individual and sovereign in, contract
between, **18:** 193
liberty in, absence of, **18:** 205–6
nature in, state of, **18:** 218–22
rational behavior in, effect of private,
18: 182
Hobbesian natural adjustment
equilibrium, **1:** 434
Hobbesian sovereignty, **7:** 165–66, 208
Homo economicus, **1:** 49, 363, 366, 392, 456,
459–60; **3:** 16; **6:** 38, 49, 88; **9:** 19; **16:**
10–12

Alchian's version of, **12:** 128–38
behavior of, abstract economic, **12:**
6–10, 71, 73–77, 128
in classical political economy, **10:** 53; **12:**
83–85
complex society, behavior in, **17:** 49–51
in constitutional analysis, **10:** 55
in constitutional design, **12:** 81–84
defined, **17:** 49, 50
in exchange, **10:** 40–41
existence of, **19:** 126–29
hypothesis, **17:** 229
limited model, **13:** 121–22
limits of, **10:** 161
as model of man, **12:** 82
moral philosophy, in eighteenth-
century, **17:** 46
perspective of, **19:** xiv
in politics, **10:** 56–57; **13:** 83–85: in
economic theory of, **19:** 54–55, 59
politics-as-exchange paradigm,
combined with, **13:** 23
predictive power of, **12:** 137
in public choice theory, **13:** 80–83;
19: 9
relevant domain of, **13:** 121–22
rules, in evaluation of, **10:** 54
social interaction, in model of, **19:**
130–32
Stigler's conception, **12:** 74–75
Tullock's idea of, **19:** 54–55
two-person exchange, behavior in, **17:**
48–49
utility function of, **13:** 116–17
homogeneity
defined, **12:** 261–62
forced, allocative effects of, **12:** 276
pricing homogeneous inputs, **12:** 261
See also inputs, heterogeneous;
production: factors of
human capital
acquisition of, **12:** 220; **14:** 402–3

human capital (*continued*)
  nonhuman and, **7:** 105
  theory, **1:** 248–49
human nature, **12:** 50
  Buchanan's conception of, **1:** xix,
    246–59
  capacities, differentials in, **1:** 295, 304,
    306, 308
  exchange (and profit) as part of, **1:** 29,
    37, 104, 357, 387–88
  Knight on, **1:** 251, 253–54, 451
  in politics, **3:** 266
  of rules, **1:** 451–52
  self-interest and, **3:** 27–30
hyperinflation, **9:** 150, 152
hypotheses of individual behavior in
  collective choice, **4:** 177–80
hypothetical consent in social contract
  theory, **10:** 115

idealism
  political, **1:** 285–86
  in political theory, **3:** xvi
  rejection of, **1:** 17
ideal (perfect) situations, Knight on, **1:**
  63n. 6
identity
  in capacities or endowments, **17:**
    283–85
  in preferences, **17:** 283
idle balances, and debt creation, **2:** 98
idleness
  for aesthetic purposes, **12:** 375–76
  defined, **12:** 367–68
  involuntary, **12:** 366, 368
  spillover effects of, **12:** 368–71
  See also work ethic; work supply
ignorance
  constitutional convention, of voting in,
    16: 189–91
  in decision-making process, **4:** 157–58,
    181–83

decision to vote, in determining, **4:**
  122
rational, **9:** 24–25
in Rawlsian sense, **16:** 160, 189
See also rational ignorance; veil of
  ignorance
illusion. *See* fiscal illusion
immigration
  effect of, **17:** 212–13
  open markets as substitute for, **17:** 214
  tolerance for, **17:** 213
impossibility theorem of Arrow, **1:** xvi, 16,
  54, 89–102, 256, 431; **3:** 337–42; **8:** 101n.
  7; **10:** 85; **13:** 43–45; **16:** 81, 84, 90, 239; **17:**
  58; **19:** 25–26
  critique of, **1:** 89–102
imposta grandine, **4:** 223
imputed outlay, **4:** 80–81, 85
incentives
  absent or perverse, **19:** 235–36, 360, 363
  cartelization, of industries to seek, **13:**
    408
  choice settings, relevance in, **19:** 242
  in debt finance, **8:** 144–47
  economic, **19:** 235–36
  with full ownership rights, **19:** 360
  legal institutions, influence of, **12:**
    290
  in markets and government
    organizations, **13:** 120, 124
  money and command economies,
    differences in, **12:** 410
  penalty tax or direct regulation, of
    industries with, **13:** 420–24
  of politicians, **19:** 327
  in politics, **19:** 279, 284
  with property ownership, **19:** 360
  savings, **12:** 467
  socialism, incompatibilities under, **19:**
    250–51, 360
  in welfare state with transfers, **19:** 257,
    259

income
  allocation in saving/interest-rate
    analysis, **12:** 247–51
  backbending labor-supply curve, effect
    in, **12:** 256–58
  demand curve for, **12:** 256–57
  fluctuations in individual's expenses
    and: excise tax and, **4:** 248–54;
    progressive income tax and, **4:**
    229–38; public debt and, **4:** 264
  full, **14:** 232, 243–44
  government, adjusted, **4:** 95
  levels of, **1:** 294–95, 304–5
  personal, as indicator of demand for
    public goods, **4:** 157
  political, **7:** 197–204
  taxation of, **14:** 334–36
  as tax base, **11:** 127–28
  transfer: economic theory of, **12:** 136; by
    fiscal institutions, **14:** 41–43; in
    quantity discount transactions, **12:**
    200–202
  utility of, **1:** 294
  See also money income; wages
income effect, **5:** 18, 43
income effect feedback
  importance of, **5:** 38
  incorporation of, **5:** 40, 46, 128
  introduction of, **5:** 31
  neglect of, **5:** 24n. 1, 26, 29, 31, 40, 62,
    128
income redistribution
  constitutional requirements, **13:** 140–41
  impure, **13:** 149
  Pareto criterion, **13:** 135–36
  Pareto norms for politically
    determined, **13:** 136–39
  Pareto-optimal, **13:** 129, 135
  political setting for, **13:** 133–39
  through voluntary cooperatives, **13:**
    135–36
incomes policy, **8:** 93

income tax, corporate
  direct or indirect, **4:** 46
  fiscal illusion and, **4:** 134, 141
  incidence of, **4:** 50; **8:** 138
  individual choice under, **4:** 14–15,
    46–50
  liability, riskiness of portfolio as
    affecting, **4:** 49
  profits tax, **4:** 47, 134
  rate changes of 1964, **4:** 202
  revenue elasticity, **4:** 63–64
income tax, personal, **5:** 152; **8:** 147nn.
  17,18; **9:** 49, 60, 101, 114–16, 155–57
  averaging in, **4:** 141
  collective decision-making model and,
    4: 148–51
  comprehensiveness in, **9:** 226
  exemptions under, **4:** 256–57
  geography, based on, **18:** 18
  liability under, estimates of, **4:** 183–86
  progressive, **4:** 38–42, 148–66 passim,
    227–42
  proportional, **4:** 30–38, 148–66 passim
  rate changes of 1964, **4:** 202
  revenue elasticity, **4:** 63
  tax rate under, **4:** 33–35
  withholding of, **4:** 138–39
  See also progressive tax
income transfer
  beneficiaries of, **13:** 151
  distribution, **13:** 141–47
  political, **13:** 151
  to the poor, **13:** 130–31
  voting rights of people receiving, **13:**
    130–33, 139
increasing returns
  external economies model, in
    Marshallian, **12:** 389–90
  generalized, **1:** 351–53, 358; **12:** 391–93,
    395–96
  monopolistic competition model, **12:**
    390–91, 395–96

increasing returns (*continued*)
  in neoclassical general equilibrium
    models, **12:** 389
  in positive feedback models (Arthur),
    12: 393–96
incrementalism, policy, **7:** 210–27
incumbency model, **13:** 284–87, 293
incumbency/nonincumbency dilemma,
  13: 283–88
independence
  maximal, **18:** 217
  with privatization of the commons, **18:**
    221–29
  See also interdependence
independent adjustment. *See* equilibrium
indifference curve, **12:** 26
individual choice, **1:** xvi, 16, 19, 66–67, 196,
  238–40, 246–59; **17:** xvi
  alternatives in, **1:** 81–82; **13:** 94–110; **17:**
    56–57
  analysis of, **1:** 322–24
  British National Health Service under
    model of democratic, **15:** 347–49
  Buchanan's view, **17:** xvi–xviii
  in bureaucracy, **13:** 48–49, 63–70
  with certainty, **1:** 76–77; **14:** 108–13
  Christianity, prescribed by, **13:** 33–34
  in civil society, **13:** 410–13
  in classical economics, **16:** 11
  coercion, degree of, **1:** 82–84
  in cognitive certainty and uncertainty,
    12: 145–49
  in collective choice, **1:** 53, 62, 64, 75–78,
    236, 246–59; **14:** 527
  collective outcomes derived from, **13:**
    174
  conditions for, **19:** 155–56
  in constitutional constituency, **16:**
    132–35
  in constitutional economics, **1:** 383–84;
    16: 10–12
  of constitutional experts, **16:** 135–39

  of constitutional rules, **14:** 255
  constraints on, **17:** 60–63; **18:** 268–69,
    274
  cooperative patterns of, **15:** 227–28
  economic model of, **13:** 30–32
  ethical rules and constraints, **1:** 311–28,
    356–57, 360–73
  external diseconomy, effect on, **14:**
    124–29
  externalities and, **13:** 29–30; **14:** 122–33;
    15: 128–29
  of *Homo economicus*, **13:** 15–16, 21–24,
    79–85
  information in, **13:** 9
  of institutional rules, **14:** 235
  intertemporal interdependence of, **17:**
    284
  Kantian hypothesis of, **13:** 35–38
  with Knightian uncertainty, **12:** 151
  labor and, **1:** 346–59
  in large-number electorate, **17:** 62–63
  limits on, **1:** 329–45
  among local governments, **18:** 61
  locational fixity, in absence of, **18:**
    46–47
  logic of, **1:** 66–67
  in market order, **1:** 35–42, 75–88,
    346–59, 462–65
  in markets, **13:** 72–73, 162–64; **17:**
    62–63
  migration and, **18:** 36–38
  modification, **13:** 413–14; **15:** 306–7
  noneconomic models of, **13:** 32–34
  numbers, relevance of, **1:** 318–22
  open system, **13:** 26–28
  in political process, **13:** 85–87, 414–15
  political rules, among alternative, **1:**
    19, 22
  power relations and, **1:** 84–85
  preferences, **13:** 162–67
  private services, in demands for, **15:**
    350–52

private (subjective) maxims, **1:** 312, 313, 314–22
public bads, producing, **15:** 302
in public choice theory, **13:** 26, 29–30
in public goods interaction, **15:** 228–43
of public services, **14:** 75–88; **15:** 350–52
rational choice models of, **17:** 55–58
responsibility, degree of, **1:** 79–81, 257, 334, 340, 343
samaritan's dilemma and, **1:** 329–45
Shackle's theory of, **12:** 143
social (collective) choice and, Arrow on, **1:** 53–54, 79 n. 11, 86 n. 24
in social interactions, **13:** 411–12; **17:** 56
social participation, degree of, **1:** 77–79
symmetry, **13:** 108–10
among tax instruments, **14:** 102–8
theory of, **13:** 6
with uncertainty, **14:** 113–16
with uncertainty (Shackle) **12:** 150
utility function, **1:** 286
utility-maximizing private, **15:** 303–4
veil of ignorance, behind, **14:** 255, 527–28
in voting and the market, **1:** 16, 20, 64–66, 69, 75–88, 89–102; **5:** 137–39, 141
in voting behavior, **13:** 162–67
welfare economics and, **1:** 20
See also behavior; fiscal choice; *Homo economicus;* political choice; preference; rational deference theory; rational ignorance theory
individualism, **7:** 3–4, 11
autonomy and, **1:** 390, 391, 392–93
Buchanan's interest in, **1:** xix, 48–49, 468
during Cold War, **19:** 202–3
collectivism and, **19:** 199–200
contractarianism and, **10:** 23–24
democracy and, **3:** 100; **7:** 4–5
epistemic, **1:** 281–84, 289–91
in ethical choices, **1:** 327

foundations of, **1:** 281–91
government finance and, **1:** 122–32
Hayek on, **1:** 76 n. 1, 78 n. 9
idea, as an, **19:** 248–49
methodological, **3:** xvi, xvii, 3, 11–15, 316–17; **16:** 8–9; **17:** xv–xvi, 55–58: public choice theory and, **1:** 24, 48–49, 390–91, 456, 457–58
normative, **1:** 281–91; **3:** xvii; **11:** 21; **16:** 61–62
in public choice theory, **1:** 48–49
socialism and, compared, **1:** 181–82
social rationality and, **1:** 93
of student revolutionary, **16:** 178
in utilitarianism, **1:** 94
value premise of, **16:** 19, 24, 27
of values, relativism and, **17:** 169–70
individualist-democratic model, **4:** 174–77, 282–83
empirical tests of, **4:** 194–202
Italian analysis and, **4:** 128–38 passim
progressive income tax and, **4:** 240–42
public interest and, **4:** 221–22
individualistic approach to fiscal theory, **2:** 117–18
individualistic tradition, **2:** 29
individual rights
defined, **16:** 23–25
of individual choice, **16:** 202–5
under majority rule, **7:** 55–56
political role in enforcement of, **17:** 274
individuals
alternatives, weighing, **16:** 399–402
behavior: in the economy, **13:** 5; imposing constraints on future, **16:** 403–7; in political institutions, **13:** 13
beliefs of, **17:** 155–57, 159–61
as borrowers, **14:** 414–15
choice setting, in Wicksellian, **16:** 73
in collective-choice process, **15:** 351–52
collective decisions of, **13:** 4–5; **14:** 525–26

individuals (*continued*)
  in constitutional choice, **16:** 73
  constitutional preference of, **16:** 159–70
  defined by: allocationist, **19:** 138; in
    exchange perspective, **19:** 137–38
  ethical-social change, contribution to,
    19: 19–21
  in exchange model of politics, **18:** 186–96
  in fiscal exchange model, **14:** 92–95
  government: interaction with, **13:** 4–5;
    lending to, **14:** 108
  information, investment in, **16:** 191–99
  interdependence, conditions for, **18:** 217
  interests of, derivation of, **17:** 160–61
  lexicographic preferences, **15:** 370
  liberty to secede, **14:** 220
  in majority rule voting, **14:** 74–75
  in market order, **17:** 244
  in markets, **13:** 72–73
  in moral community, **14:** 488
  moral order, autonomy in, **17:** 195
  organization, as members of an, **14:**
    430–31
  political action, debt-related, **14:** 477
  politics: in economic theory of, **13:**
    41–44; markets and, **13:** 26; as
    participant in, **17:** 166
  in predictive theory of politics, **17:** 254
  under Ricardian equivalence theorem,
    14: 410–11
  rights of, **16:** 23–25, 202–3
  in socialism, **18:** 249–51
  state: dependence on the, **18:** 170–71; as
    members of the, **14:** 431–32; in
    relation to the, **18:** 168–71
  taxation, in models of, **14:** 103–8
  in totalitarian society, **18:** 169
  "true" preferences of, **14:** 61–62, 86–87
  in utility maximization of Arrow, Black,
    Downs, and Schumpeter, **16:** 68–70
  value, as source of, **10:** 25–27; **17:** 267–73
  values and interests of, **16:** 61–62

indivisibility spectrum, **5:** 49
industrial revolution, **1:** 293–94
industries
  in cartel coalition, **13:** 391–409
  competition in (Marshall), **12:** 277
  under constitutional rule, **19:** 282
  external diseconomy and, **13:** 420–24
  penalty tax or direct regulation,
    incentives with, **13:** 420–24
  political protection, **13:** 388–89
  regulated firms in, **13:** 318–21
  socialized, **19:** 252–55, 259
  See also firms
inefficiency
  allocational, **5:** 174
  distributional, **5:** 174
  excess-burden, **5:** 174
  generality constraint, with absence of,
    14: 313–15
  rent-seeking, **13:** 277
inequality, personal, **7:** 71–72
  in constitutional design, **17:** 322–24
  Gauthier rule, **17:** 452
  origins of contract and, **7:** 71
inflation, **8:** 3
  anticipated, **8:** 61–62, 91; **12:** 165–68
  budget deficits and, **8:** 59–60
  burdens of, **2:** 77–78, 106–7; **8:** 62–66
  business accounting, **8:** 68
  as capital tax, **9:** 115–16
  as counterfeiting, **8:** 148; **10:** 101–4
  debt default through, **14:** 470
  discriminatory tax levied under, **14:** 380
  expectations, **8:** 90–91; **9:** 144–45
  fiscal illusion and, **4:** 132
  government, size of and, **8:** 71–72
  hyperinflation, **9:** 150, 152
  income taxes and, **9:** 155–57
  informational requirements, **8:** 148
  institutional framework and, **8:** 63–66
  Leviathan, as strategy for, **9:** 152
  in monetarist paradigm, **8:** 115

monetary policy and, **8:** 43–45; **14:** 452

money balances, as tax on, **9:** 135–44

national debt, relation to, **14:** 452–53

open, **2:** 106

political effects, **8:** 64–65

politics and, **8:** 171–72

predicted, **8:** 90–91

profits and, **8:** 68

public debt and, **2:** 111–14

real wages and, **8:** 175

repressed, **2:** 106

resource allocation and, **8:** 108

revenue-maximizing rate of, **9:** 142–43

saving, effect on, **12:** 468

as taxation, **2:** 77, 106, 132–33; **8:** 114, 147

taxation and, progressive, **8:** 72, 147nn. 17,18

unanticipated, **8:** 61–62

uncertainty and, **8:** 67–68

unemployment and, **2:** 96; **8:** 87–90, 174–77

inflationary trap, **13:** 480 n. 11

information

    cognitive certainty, individual choice in structures of, **12:** 145–50

    collective decision process, of citizens in, **4:** 181–83

    in constitutional choice, **16:** 186–89

    deference to people with, **16:** 186, 189–91

    empirical tests of, **4:** 182–94

    failure of, **13:** 119

    fiscal choice and, **8:** 135–36

    individual behavior (Knight), obtained through, **12:** 144–45

    inflation and, **8:** 148

    investment in, **16:** 191–99

    knowledge industry, **16:** 195–98

    in markets, **8:** 135 n. 8

    perceptions related to (Hayek), **12:** 80 n. 8

    with perfect competition, **13:** 335

    as public good, **9:** 24–25

    rules and, **10:** 10–11, **14:** 274

    uncertainty, role under (Knight), **12:** 145

information asymmetry, **15:** 365

inheritance tax, **1:** 307; **4:** 300–301

    fiscal illusion and, **4:** 133

    Tullock on, **1:** 307n. 32

inputs

    homogeneous, pricing of, **12:** 261

    symmetry in, **11:** 56

inputs, heterogeneous

    in generalized setting, **12:** 274–76

    homogenization of, **12:** 265–69, 275

    model of, **12:** 262–65

    opportunity costs, with different, **12:** 272–73

    production with, **12:** 269–72

    sources of, **12:** 275

    substitutable, **12:** 275

input units, external marginal product of, **14:** 235, 242

institutional analysis

    comparative: concept of *Homo economicus* in, **12:** 84, 98–100; model of man in, **12:** 77–82; task of, **12:** 79

    monopoly and other market organizations, compared, **12:** 89–95

    Pigou's road case, **12:** 311–26

institutional choice, **5:** 49, 158–59, 162, 163, 188–89

institutional economics, **16:** 105–6

institutionalism, constructive, **1:** 229

institutional reform, **1:** 273–74

institutional setting

    in allocative neutrality theorem, **13:** 300–301

    in Coase theorem, **13:** 300–301

institutional structure, effects on allocative outcomes, **15:** 183–88

institutions

    analysis of existing, **16:** 105–7

institutions (*continued*)

anarchist's criticism of existing, **16:** 21–23

behavior in, rules for, **18:** 317–21

British health system, **15:** 341–42

in British postwar reconstruction, **19:** 142–45, 153–54

cartels as, **13:** 339–44

change in, process of, **18:** 90

church as, decline of, **19:** 132–33

for collective choice, **14:** 116–17

constitutional rules, operating within, **16:** 249

constraints by, **18:** 270–74

constraints on, **13:** 53–54

contractarianism to evaluate, **17:** 1–4, 249

Council of Economic Advisers as, **19:** 318–20

decision making and, **8:** 7; **17:** 263–64, 327–29

distribution emerging from, **17:** 248

economic and contractarian, **16:** 116

in economic policy theory analysis, **16:** 331–32

in economy, **13:** 5

economy and government as, **13:** 5

under equal liberty, **14:** 217–18

of exchange, **16:** 112–14

exchange as, **16:** 30

externalities, treatment of technological and pecuniary, **12:** 179–80

in government, **13:** 4

group interests, designed to further, **13:** 53–54

Keynesian policy and, **8:** 82

knowledge of, **16:** 107

legal: behavior, effect on, **12:** 286–87; consequences of choice determined by, **12:** 297; influence on incentives, **12:** 290; spontaneous evolution of (Hayek), **17:** 101–9

market, study of, **12:** 100

minimax principle of design of, **13:** 122–24

mistrust of public, **15:** 389

monopoly restrictions, designed to ensure against, **13:** 333–34

order, in establishing, **19:** 132–33

political choice and, **8:** 129–49

of political democracy, **16:** 49

property rights and, **15:** 176–88

as public goods, **15:** 284–88

as rules, **10:** 18–19

schools as, **19:** 133

slavery, **13:** 66–67; **18:** 104

social, evolutionist theory of, **16:** 360–61

social cost theorem, structure in, **13:** 300–301

social purpose, achieving, **18:** 448

social security scheme, as alternative to, **15:** 394–96

structure of, change in, **13:** 347–54

sustainability of, **16:** 296–304

tax instruments as, **14:** 102–3

theory of policy, relevance for, **8:** 4

veil of ignorance, from behind, **16:** 287–96

well-being as function of (Smith), **15:** 285–86

work supply, affecting, **12:** 357

See also Council of Economic Advisers; fiscal institutions; tax institutions

institutions, political, **11:** 142–43

behavior, effect on, **14:** 19–20, 30–31

choice among, **17:** 262–63

defense of, **1:** 21

distrust of, **1:** 58

efficiency and adaptability of, **17:** 261

fiscal exchange under, **14:** 94–95

fiscal results from (Wicksell), **14:** 33

interaction in, **13:** 165–66

justification for, **12:** 99

legitimacy, **1:** 283–84, 288

majority rule voting as, **17:** 261–62

market and, difference between, **14:** 478–79

public choice analysis of, **12:** 100

reconstruction, **1:** 58–59

study of, **12:** 100

suspension of, **1:** 175

theory of, **1:** 50

theory of policy, relevance for, **8:** 4

See also government; state, the

insurance

collective redistribution and, **3:** 193–99

medical, **11:** 178, 180–82

social, **11:** 181–82

interclass conflict, **1:** 387

interdependence

common property, **18:** 217–22, 227–29

in competition, absence of, **5:** 82

under competitive federalism, **18:** 76–78

in competitive market economy, **18:** 240–41, 268–70

in conflict-resolution decisions, **13:** 416

in constitutional politics, **13:** 406–9

among constraints, **9:** 182

costs and, **3:** 52

of demand and supply of money, **12:** 57–59

in duopoly, **5:** 82

among economic, ethical, and political environments, **12:** 387

ethical, **17:** 224–26

external diseconomies, related to, **14:** 123–25

fiscal, **12:** 344–45, 369; **14:** 326–29

intertemporal, **18:** 376–77

in large numbers, **5:** 81–83

between market choice and information, **12:** 25–26

in market exchange, **18:** 230

in modern economies, **18:** 257

nonexchange, **12:** 291–92

nonfiscal, **14:** 326–29

in oligopoly, **5:** 82

in Pareto criterion analysis of transfers, **13:** 139–49

of parties in Coase theorem, **13:** 297–98

between rules and organization, **3:** 83

in small groups, **5:** 82

social costs and, **3:** 48; **13:** 411–17

tax institutions and revenue demands, between, **14:** 152

interest, rate of, **2:** 71–75

interest groups, **3:** 282–94

centralized government on, effect of, **18:** 134–37

equilibrium **3:** 287–88

minimum wage, focus on retention of, **13:** 58

politics, **3:** 10; **19:** 314–16, 345

profit-seeking, **19:** 104

under protectionist-mercantilist regime, **19:** 316

public services, effect on, **13:** 437–38

regulation on, effect of, **16:** 421–22

tax laws, effect on, **13:** 437–38; **14:** 280–81

See also consumer interests; producer interests

interest rates

with balanced-budget rule, **14:** 513

debt issue on, effect of, **14:** 363

default risk, **14:** 470

inflation and, **14:** 453

monetary policy, in ideal, **13:** 441–42

as price, **2:** 47

public debt and, **2:** 71–75

under restrictive monetary policy, **13:** 446

rise of, conditions for, **13:** 447

Smith's treatment of, **15:** 293–94

interference, politicized

claims, to settle conflicts over, **16:** 380

removal of, **16:** 376–79

interference, politicized (*continued*)
  in voluntary exchange transactions, **16:**
    374–79
intergenerational transfers, **17:** 322–24
  overlapping-generations model (Barro),
    14: 386–87
  public debt financing on, effects of, **14:**
    496–97, 532
internal-exit model
  coalition in, **18:** 149–61
  illustrations, **18:** 154–57
  secession under, **18:** 150–51
  specifications, **18:** 151–54
internalization
  collective, of fiscal externalities, **18:**
    57–60
  of consequences of choice, **12:** 297
  of external diseconomies, **13:** 255–56;
    18: 441
  of externalities, **1:** 328; **12:** 132, 169–87,
    355–62; **13:** 364; **17:** 224–26; **18:** 63
  law in, **12:** 186–87
  opportunity costs with, **12:** 297
  politicization of, **12:** 182–85
  tax-sharing arrangements in, **18:** 58–60
Interstate Commerce Commission, **1:** 302
intertemporal discrimination, **11:** 131–40
intertemporal generality, **11:** 174–75
intervention, government
  degrees of, **16:** 244–48
  to further social objectives, **16:** 261–64
  regulation as, **16:** 421–22
investment
  budget deficits and, **8:** 69
  debt financing crowding out private, **14:**
    448–50
  in law, **7:** 158
  public spending as, **14:** 370–73
  theory, **7:** 159
invisible hand, **1:** 35; **13:** 84
  conversion, **12:** 79–80
  in human interaction, **19:** 164

results of, **17:** 100–101, 103
Smith's conception of, **1:** 35, 458; **19:**
  297–98
state, in Nozick's explanation of the, **17:**
  430–31
iso-benefit curve, convexity of, **5:** 61
iso-cost curve, **5:** 59–61
Italian theory. *See* fiscal theory, Italian
Italy, **18:** 128–30

joint supply, **4:** 224
  conditions of Marshallian, **15:** 211–12,
    267
  determinacy, **5:** 36
  efficiency, **5:** 59–60
  externalities and, **15:** 215–17, 222,
    267–68
  fixity and variability of, **5:** 53–55
  Marshall's theory of, **5:** 33–36, 51, 52–54;
    12: 299 n. 4; **15:** 213–14
  motive to organize, **5:** 63
  nonhomogeneity of consumption and,
    5: 2–53
  predictions and, **5:** 35
  price discrimination of public goods,
    analogous to, **5:** 37–38
  production units, externality mix in, **15:**
    217–22
  public goods as extension of, theory of,
    15: 262
  public goods model, difference from,
    5: 36
  public goods theory and, **5:** 33–36, 46,
    62, 63–65
  unit of, **5:** 50–51, 54
judicial review, **3:** xvi
judiciary
  enforcement and, **7:** 89–90
  as enforcing agency, **18:** 177
  intrusion, **19:** 196–97
  laws and, **7:** 218; **16:** 63–64; **18:** 339–41;
    19: 178

law viewed by U.S., **18:** 178
legal elite and, **7:** 126–27
limits, **7:** 133–35, 206–7
power, usurpation by, **19:** 178, 183
role of, **7:** 89–90; **18:** 338–40: actions
   inconsistent with, **18:** 340–41; in
   Miller et al. v. Schoene, **18:** 354–57;
   normative interpretation, **18:** 177–78
rules and, **16:** 63–67
Warren Court model, **18:** 341
See also Supreme Court, U.S.
justice, **1:** 438, 465
as attitude, **7:** 103–4
commutative, **17:** 312 n. 2; **19:** 311
in conduct, **10:** 108–9
contractarian argument related to, **16:** 117
demands of, **19:** 312–13
distribution and, **1:** 304–8, 438; **16:** 97
distributive (*see* distributive justice)
efficiency and, **10:** 128
entitlement theory (Nozick), **13:** 274
as fairness, **7:** 221–23; **10:** 35; **17:** 408–14
"good society," and the, **1:** 237–40
in holdings or entitlements, **17:** 312–13
liberty and, **17:** 392; **19:** 311
of markets, **16:** 354
maximal equal liberty (Rawls), **14:**
   217–20, 226, 236; **17:** 384
natural liberty and, **1:** 292–310
nonentitlement norms for, **13:** 274
from preconstitutional agreement
   (Rawls), **16:** 74
promises and, **10:** 111–16
as rhetoric, **7:** 104
rules and, **10:** 108–24
social, **1:** 364–65
in taxation, **1:** 15–16, 98, 125, 126, 135,
   141, 142, 144, 455, 456–57, 468; **14:** 213
theory of (Rawls), **1:** 23–24, 288, 292,
   293, 296, 297, 304–8, 432, 465; **7:**
   221–23; **13:** 46; **14:** 217, 226, 236; **17:**
   353, 358–59, 412–14

veil of ignorance, from behind (Rawls),
   16: 103

Kaiser Aluminum Corporation, **17:** 347
Kantian economics
categorical imperative, **1:** 319, 364
criticism of, **1:** 312–13
generalization principle, **1:** 340, 363; **13:**
   35–37
idealized world, **1:** 314, 320
Kennedy economics, **8:** 49–50
Keynesian economic theory, **2:** 17, 95; **8:** 4;
   17: 7–8; **18:** 107
in academics (1950s, 1960s), **19:** 39, 42
academics and, **8:** 25–37
acceptance of, **13:** 22
balanced budget amendment, **13:** 53; **14:**
   505–7, 513
budget deficits and, **8:** 57–59
critique of, **1:** 21, 164–78
currency creation and, **4:** 104–6
debt analysis, **14:** 362–63
debt-burden denial in, **19:** 29
debt-deficit financing, **14:** 457, 459–61,
   496
debt financing, future burden of, **14:** 475
in democracy, **8:** 5, 95–109
economic constitution by, destruction
   of, **16:** 352
economists, impact on, **8:** 28
employment and, **1:** 168–70; **8:** 170–72
excuses, **16:** 55
fiscal and economic policy, effect on, **4:**
   270; **16:** 310, 422
fiscal constitution and, **9:** 236
fiscal illusion and, **8:** 142
fiscal-monetary prudence, overturn of,
   14: 489–90
fiscal policy, **14:** 505–6: criticism of, **19:**
   60–61; mistakes related to, **14:**
   470–71; rules for, **8:** 33–34
fiscal principles, effect on, **8:** 21–22

Keynesian economic theory (*continued*)
full-employment objective of, **16:** 346
as general theory, **8:** 171
individual choices and, **8:** 36–37
influence of, **15:** 102
international consequences, **8:** 73–75
interventionist bias, **8:** 97
Knight's opposition to, **19:** 82
macroeconomics and, **1:** 20–21, 165, 166,
  167–78; **14:** 4, 373–75, 457, 494; **16:** 13;
  19: 26
market equilibrium and, **8:** 26–27
money and, **1:** 167; **8:** 85–86; **14:** 363–64
during New Deal, **16:** 345–46
of policy, **8:** 31–32; **14:** 473, 474, 483–84,
  496–97; **19:** 320–22
political acceptance, **8:** 38–55
political biases and, **8:** 26
political presuppositions, **8:** 5, 79–94
public choice and, **8:** 96
public debt and, **4:** 102–3; **8:** 36; **14:** 433
public debt theory of, **14:** 475–76
public policy, applications to, **14:**
  366–67, 470
public spending without taxation, **14:**
  381
rational constructivism, **1:** 167
revolution, **8:** 3, 6
scientific paradigm, **1:** 165
of stabilization policy, **13:** 437, 448
structural unemployment and, **8:** 97n.
  2, 170
subjectivism, **1:** 177
survey of results, **8:** 56–76
symmetry in application and, **8:** 52
tax reduction (1964), **8:** 50–52
totalitarian government and, **8:** 81n. 3
Victorian attitudes and, **8:** 26n. 2
Keynesian-type unemployment, **2:** 24
Knightian economics
critique of Polanyi's economics, **1:**
  230–43; **7:** 48n. 3, 234; **10:** 47; **16:** 91;

  17: 98, 153n, 155; **18:** 303n. 51, 305–6,
    312; **19:** 41, 52, 118, 262
on empirical work in economics, **12:** 27
idea of economic theory, Stigler on,
  12: 44
influence on Buchanan, **1:** 11, 15, 16, 183
influence on Vining, **1:** 23
knowledge
availability, **12:** 45
choice with, **12:** 152–53
conjectural and hypothetical (Hayek),
  16: 141
constitutional, **16:** 188
incentives for, **16:** 198–99
information industry, **16:** 195–98
pretense of (Hayek), **16:** 140
scientific, public nature of, **12:** 47
society (Hayek), use in, **16:** 135
knowledge-problem
in constitutional choice, **16:** 129–30, 188
horizontal, or cross-sectional (Hayek),
  16: 140
intertemporal (Hayek), **16:** 140
Knowlton v. Moore, **18:** 18n. 28

labor
behavior and, **1:** 346–59
choices in allocation of (Smith), **12:**
  77–78; **19:** 300–302
Fair Labor Standards Act, **1:** 302
income tax and, **9:** 111–12
individual choice behavior and, **1:**
  346–59
negotiations, prisoners' dilemma in,
  17: 91
nonlabor and, **12:** 368, 371–73
nonproductive, **12:** 383
productive and unproductive (Smith),
  12: 377–78; **15:** 295–26; **19:** 301–2
time, equality in, **11:** 60
labor, division of, **1:** 387–88; **10:** 17–18; **12:**
  350, 378

increasing returns from, **12:** 363–64

market, and extent of, **1:** 346–59; **12:** 378; **19:** 299

labor market. *See* markets

labor standard of value, **1:** 415–16

labor supply, **12:** 357–58, 365

full employment of, **1:** 169

heterogeneous input, substitution in model of, **12:** 262–65

markets, impact on, **1:** 346–59

specialization, under increasing returns to, **12:** 379–81

at work-leisure choice margin, **12:** 379

labor-supply curve

backbending, **12:** 254–59

Hicks's backbending, **12:** 256

Robbins's backbending, **12:** 255–56, 259

Laffer curve, **10:** 95; **11:** 125; **13:** 470–78; **14:** 314

laissez-faire economics, **1:** 61, 183, 186, 187, 301; **7:** 117, 214–15; **15:** 9–11

argument for, **12:** 430–32; **16:** 5

constitutional rules and, **19:** 266–67

defined, **15:** 9

faith in, **19:** 314

future for, **19:** 191–92

romantic ideal of, **16:** 244–48

in Smith's work, **19:** 297

land use, Knight on, **12:** 260

large-number dilemma, **1:** 318–22, 324, 326

hypothesis, **1:** 326

utility maximization and small-number settings versus, **1:** 363, 371

large-number model, **5:** 44, 75–84 passim, 98–99, 113–17, 166–67

law enforcement, **11:** 184–85; **16:** 217–18

common property, in privatized, **18:** 224–25

enforcer as referee model in, **7:** 87–88, 120–21

need for, **15:** 18

police protection, **4:** 74–81

politics, role of, **17:** 274

property protection and, **15:** 286

as public good, **18:** 379, 434n. 4

reaction-curve construction for, **18:** 433–41

truth judgment in, **16:** 217

See also crime and criminal activities; property rights: enforcement of; punishment

law of demand (Alchian), **12:** 129–31

laws

adherence to, **19:** 130

antitrust, **11:** 103

changes in, **7:** 162; **12:** 288–89; **16:** 16, 220–21

in changing constitutions, **7:** 137

civil, **11:** 83–84

collective action within, **16:** 218–20

common law, **9:** 194; **12:** 176–78; **19:** 139

as constitutional constraints, **16:** 221–22

contractarian perspective of, **17:** 407–8; **18:** 179–81

in cost-benefit, **7:** 140–42

discrimination and, **11:** 67

of disorder, **19:** 194–97

due process and, **9:** 193, 195

economic discourse in, **11:** 12

economics, contribution of, **17:** 9, 14–15

economics and, intersection of, **1:** 262, 275, 276

economics in context of the (Posner), **18:** 328–37

efficient limits, **7:** 142

of eminent domain, **9:** 193

enforcement of, government's role in, **19:** 175

environmental, **11:** 86–88

equality and, **7:** 17–18; **11:** 9–11, 13–14, 185–86; **19:** 351

ethics and, **7:** 150–52

evolution of (Hayek and Nozick), **18:** 179, 183

laws (*continued*)
  exclusion and, **7:** 139
  externalities and, **7:** 136; **12:** 176–79,
    186–87; **15:** 20
  fact and, **7:** 89
  generality and, **11:** 10
  judiciary and, **7:** 218; **16:** 63–64; **18:**
    339–41; **19:** 178
  law in internalization, **12:** 186–87
  legal philosophy, **11:** xxi
  moral order and, **11:** 13; **17:** 208–9
  moral support of, **14:** 523–24
  nomos and *thesis* (Hayek), **17:** 107–8
  nonexcludability of, **15:** 287
  order and, **11:** 13; **16:** 63, 222–23, 244–45;
    17: 274
  ownership rights and, **12:** 290–91
  in political constitution, **16:** 44
  in politics, **16:** 216–17
  politics and, **11:** 3–16, 66–67
  in property rights, **7:** 22–24
  public bad and, **7:** 152–56
  as public bads, **15:** 288
  as public capital, **7:** 136–64; **18:** 340–41
  as public goods, **7:** 20, 137–40, 144n. 5;
    15: 284–88
  publicness, as embodiment of, **15:** 287,
    291
  public or collective, **15:** 5
  as reciprocal relation, **7:** 136
  reform, **7:** 160–64; **18:** 177
  rights accorded by, **15:** 6–7
  rule of law (*see* rule of law)
  social order, under contractarian, **16:** 62
  social purpose and, **11:** 13–14
  in society, **19:** 174–75
  sources of, **15:** 287
  tax, **14:** 279, 280–81
  theory, **7:** 69–95
  truth judgment in judicial review, **16:** 63
  violation, **7:** 35–36
  well-being as function of (Smith), **15:**
    285–86

  See also judiciary; liability rule; New
    Deal; property rule; Supreme Court,
    U.S.
learning
  constitutional, **16:** 143
  evolutionary, **16:** 144n. 22
  least aggregate sacrifice, **4:** 137; **5:** 157
  legal philosophy, **11:** xxi
legal system: rights in, **15:** 5–7
legislation
  defined, **17:** 108
  protective state and, **7:** 89–90
legislators
  in incumbency model, **13:** 284–87
  as incumbents and challengers, **13:**
    283–92
  incumbents with seniority, **13:** 292–93
  in initial term in office, **13:** 283–84
  as political agents, **13:** 282–83
legislature
  apportionment of, **16:** 115–17
  incumbency dilemma and, **13:** 288–91
  industrial groups, rent seeking by, **13:**
    401–2
  legislative process, distributive game in,
    13: 282
  politics within rules, carrying out,
    16: 64
  tax decisions, control over, **4:** 94
leisure
  in backbending labor-supply curve, **12:**
    257–59
  personal income tax and, **4:** 35
  utility value of, **12:** 371
  valued as a "good," **1:** 349
  See also idleness; work-leisure choice
lending as a market transaction, **2:** 47
less-than-unanimity rule, **4:** 120
Leviathan, **1:** 51; **9:** 33–37, 46–47; **18:**
  xiv–xv
  as actuality and contingency, **9:** 18–20,
    100
  anarchy and, **1:** 21–22

constitutional limits, **7:** 205
without constraints, **14:** 179–80
defined, **7:** 186
majoritarian conception, **14:** 159n. 13
as monolith, **9:** 35–48
monopoly, **14:** 179–81
persistence of, **1:** 179–88
of political process, **14:** xiv
probabilistic, **9:** 108, 148–49
prospects for control, **7:** 207–8; **15:** 459
rational capital taxes and, **9:** 107
as revenue-maximizer, **9:** 33–37; **11:**
 118n. 6; **14:** 97–100
revenues, and use of, **9:** 161–62
in self-government, **7:** 188–89
simple conception, **14:** 159n. 13
socialism and, **1:** 57–59, 179–80, 186–87;
 7: 227–28
state as, **19:** 317
tax institution to constrain, **14:** 154–64
tax reform and, **9:** 219
threat of, **7:** 186–208
time preference and, **9:** 116–17
unconstrained, **9:** 40
in U.S., **1:** 21–22, 367; **7:** 19; **19:** 177–81
in Wicksellian context, **9:** 183, 184
liability
 estimates of, **4:** 183–85, 186
 under public debt, **4:** 260–63, 267; **8:** 19
liability rule
 bargaining under, **12:** 171
 entitlements protected by (Calabresi-
  Melamed), **12:** 170–76
 entrepreneurs' choice of, **12:** 175
 externalities as, common law treatment
  of negative, **12:** 176–78
 limit in law, **12:** 176–77
 property rule, difference from, **12:** 280
 social cost theory, protection under, **12:**
  173–74
 in valuation of a life, **12:** 280
 See also Coase theorem
liberalism, of Hutt, **19:** 147

liberalism rule (Sen), **17:** 72–79
libertarianism, **17:** 328
libertarian socialist, **19:** 7, 166–68
liberty
 absolute and relative (Rawls), **17:**
  386–90
 allocation of, **18:** 204–5
 civil, **14:** 219–20
 constraints on, **18:** 209–11
 defined, **14:** 218–19; **18:** 205–7
 economic development, under Marxist
  model of, **18:** 254–56
 economic prosperity and, **19:** 309–10
 economic welfare and, **18:** 198–99
 equal (Rawls), **14:** 217–20, 226, 236; **17:**
  355–56, 385–86, 413; **18:** 207–8
 as free good, **18:** 204–7
 in free market regime, **19:** 168
 Hayek on, **1:** 303n. 25, 416, 420, 421, 428
 Hobbesian jungle, absent in, **18:** 205–6
 individual evaluation of, **18:** 200–204
 libertarian socialist view, **19:** 7, 166
 market exchange, to choose in, **18:** 69,
  206, 239, 268
 maximal, **14:** 218–20
 natural: Hobbes, **17:** 381–84; Smith, **16:**
  41; **18:** 199, 210; **19:** 148, 289–90, 292,
  296–98, 314, 358–59
 positive and negative, **18:** 211–12
 private property, protected by, **18:** 240,
  246–49, 258–59
 in Rawls's contract, **17:** 384–86
 rents, related to theory of, **18:** 212
 rights differences, from, **18:** 208
 selling of, restricted, **18:** 212–13
 socialism on, restrictions of, **18:** 249–51
 under state's authority, **18:** 170–72
 voluntary exchange, to enter, **16:** 29–32
 See also exchange; exit options;
  federalism; freedom; freedom of
  choice; market economy; natural
  liberty; rights
liberty tax, **7:** 142–43, 146

life cycle
  public debt and, **8:** 145–46
  saving and, **9:** 99
life-cycle model, Ricardian, **1:** 248
limits
  constitutional, **9:** 12–13
  on procedures, **9:** 235–36
  in ratios, **9:** 233–34
  on taking power, **9:** 193–94
  on tax bases, **9:** 231–33
  on taxes, as reform, **9:** 224–28
  of tax limits, **9:** 196
  on tax rates, **9:** 229–31
  on total outlay and revenue, **9:** 233–34
  on use of revenues, **9:** 161–62
Lindahl criterion, **11:** 30
Lindahl equilibrium, **14:** 7, 10, 32
Lindahl prices, **11:** 156
Lindahl taxation, **9:** 43 n. 2; **11:** 29, 153–56
liquidity
  government, **2:** 99
  in Keynesian model, **8:** 84
  payment, **2:** 98
  public debt and, **2:** 112
loans
  consumption, **2:** 47–48
  equivalence between tax and, **2:** 35
  for private investment, **2:** 48
  public, internal and external, **2:** 58–66
lobbying for ownership rights, **13:** 254–55
local government
  debt, **2:** 151–54
  expenditures of, empirical studies of, **4:** 207–10
  macroeconomic policy and, **4:** 272–77
logrolling, **1:** 55; **3:** x, xviii, 22, 123, 211, 220, 234; **7:** 144, 197
  game theory and, **3:** 158–60
  types, **3:** 135–36
London School of Economics (LSE)
  cost theory, Robbins's contribution to, **12:** 327–28, 330

opportunity cost and, **4:** 59 n. 2; **6:** 17–36
loopholes, tax, **7:** 201 n. 11; **9:** 57, 232
lotteries, **11:** 178, 183
luck
  as determinant: of claims in market economy, **17:** 316, 317; of final consumption, **17:** 289
  in the draw, **17:** 330, 341–42
  See also fairness
lump-sum tax, **4:** 25; **5:** 174; **9:** 43, 69; **14:** 122, 393–403
  future liability implied by debt, **14:** 393, 404–6, 410–14
  in Ricardian equivalence theorem, **14:** 393–97

Maastricht Treaty, **19:** 207
  debt and deficit limit, **18:** 125
  provisional, **18:** 129
  See also European Union
macroaggregation, **1:** 383
macroeconomic policy
  Keynesian theory, heritage of, **14:** 457
  of state as an organization, **14:** 444
  See also fiscal policy
macroeconomics compared with microeconomics, **8:** 30
macroeconomic theory, **17:** 7–8
  balanced budget amendment, in opposition to, **14:** 513–15; **19:** 323–25
  Boulding's variables in, **12:** 63–65
  criticism of, Chicago-based, **1:** 169
  disarray (mid-1980s), **19:** 324–25
  interventionist bias, **8:** 30–31
  Keynesian, **8:** 30; **16:** 242–43; **19:** 241–42, 320–25
  models of: Keynes, **1:** 165, 166, 167–78; **12:** 60–61, 366; Patinkin, **12:** 57–59, 61–63; after Robbins, **1:** 383
  no place for, **16:** 237, 242–43
  policy, implications for, **8:** 30

to simplify reality, **12:** 59
variables in macroeconomic analysis,
 12: 59–65
majoritarian cycles, **3:** 333–35; **5:** 99, 115; **11:**
 28, 36–37. *See also* majority
majoritarian democracy, **11:** 19–34, 114–15;
 13: 316
majoritarian exploitation, **11:** 33
 rent seeking and, **11:** 44–46
majoritarianism
 constitutional, **11:** 25
 taxation and, **11:** 113–30
majority
 legislative and parliamentary, **18:** 195
 minority ruled by, **19:** 347–48, 350–51
 outcome, cycling (rotating), **5:** 108, 118,
  131–32
 qualified, **5:** 92, 106, 115; **9:** 235
majority decisions, time periods for, **13:**
 186–92
majority dominance, **11:** 29–31, 39–41,
 120–22
 nonmajority dominance, **13:** 244–47
 Pareto dominance, as analogue to, **13:**
  239–40, 241–44
 subsets, **13:** 242–44
majority rule, **1:** 19, 23, 53, 54, 64–66, 72,
 95–100, 205–7, 226, 271–72, 421–24; **3:**
 x, 149–71; **10:** 19, 48–50; **15:** 30–32
 anticonstitutionalism of, **16:** 361–62
 coalitions, **5:** 112; **16:** 268
 constitutionalist under, **16:** 183
 as constrained, **11:** 114–25
 as constraint, **9:** 10, 25
 in contractarian model, **11:** 24
 costs and, expected, **3:** 89
 cycle and, **9:** 25–26
 decision costs and, **3:** 108
 decision making, in cartel's internal, **13:**
  341
 decision processes under, **19:** 348–49
 decision rules, **5:** 132; **16:** 218–19

defined, **13:** 91; **19:** 347–48
democracy under, **19:** 200–206, 316,
 348–50, 352–53
distribution and, **10:** 131–35
dominance and, **11:** 39–41
election outcome, **19:** 99
extension of, limiting, **19:** 349–53
fiscal constraint and, **9:** 46
game theory and, **3:** 172–89
generality, violated by, **11:** 38
under general taxes, **9:** 184–90
in-period tax adjustments and, **9:** 222
laws, choices related to changes in, **16:**
 220
operation, **9:** 25–26
orthodox model and, **3:** 247–61
Pareto optimality and, **3:** 172–78
party competition and, **9:** 26
political discussion in, **1:** 206–7
politics of, **19:** 348–54
politics under, instability of, **16:** 319–20
public choice theory, in context of, **13:**
 90–91
as qualified, **11:** 119
redistribution and, **3:** 191–93
solution, **5:** 106
surplus and, **9:** 27–28
tax discrimination and, **11:** 119–20
unanimity and, **3:** 254–55; **11:** 39
unanimity rule, replacement by, **16:** 270
voluntary exchange, intervention with,
 16: 39
See also coalitions, majority; majority
 voting, simple
majority rule voting, **3:** x, 7–8, 132–48,
 149–71; **4:** 290–91; **7:** 55–56, 57; **17:**
 261–63
 Arrow's conception of, **13:** 7–8, 228n. 3
 budgets and budgeting and, **7:** 128,
  192–93
 for cartel agreement, **13:** 341
 coercion and, **7:** 56

majority rule voting (*continued*)
  coercive taxes, limits on, **14:** 229–31
  community membership and, **7:** 57
  constitutional contract and, **7:** 57
  constitutional limits on, **13:** 46
  constraints on, **7:** 190–94; **11:** 114–25
  conventional, analogues and contrasts
    to, **13:** 197–200
  costs and benefits, **13:** 194
  cycle, **3:** 333–35; **5:** 99, 115; **13:** 186–92,
    228–29: Black's, **13:** 43–44; **14:** 12;
    pure, **13:** 179–84, 187–88, 193–94
  decision making and, **2:** 131; **13:** 194; **17:**
    261–63
  decisions: binding, **13:** 186–92; group,
    13: 194; taxing and outlay, **14:** 95–97
  defined, **14:** 310
  democracy, as definition of, **19:** 350
  externalities, **3:** 145–46, 200–201; **13:**
    363–65
  as final determinant, **19:** 351
  income distribution determined by, **13:**
    141–47, 149–51
  individuals in, **14:** 74–75
  loss functions and, **7:** 128–29
  median voter in, **14:** 75
  models, **13:** 197–200
  nonpermanent cycle, **13:** 185–86
  Pareto optimality and, **3:** 94
  as political institution, **17:** 261–62
  in prisoners' dilemma settings, **13:**
    91–110
  problems of, **13:** 10
  qualified, **3:** 210–30; **7:** 64
  response to propositions in yes-no
    voting, **13:** 196–200
  social waste and, **3:** 163–66
  spending projects with, outcome for,
    13: 45
  stability, **11:** 51–52
  theory, **13:** 195
  unconstrained, **7:** 63–67, 195–97

  yes-no voting and, **13:** 196–200
  See also decision-making models,
    collective; majority voting, simple
majority superiority
  Pareto nonsuperiority, moves as, **13:**
    243–44
  Pareto superiority, as analogue to, **13:**
    239–40
majority voting, simple, **5:** 92, 99, 101,
  105–9, 114–15, 131–32, 147, 148–49, 156;
  16: 50
Malthusian theory of population, **6:** 7
marginal cost, social, **13:** 329. *See also*
  pricing, marginal-cost
marginal evaluation curve, **4:** 12–13; **5:** 40
  circularity in, **5:** 42
  deficiency of, **5:** 40
  demand curve: difference from, **5:** 42;
    similarity to Friedman, **12:** 198–200
  derivation of, **5:** 41, 47
  error in vertical summing of, **5:** 43
  explained, **12:** 196–201
  tax-prices, relation to, **5:** 137
marginal supply price (Marshall), **12:**
  67–69
marginal-utility economics, **2:** 138–39; **6:**
  9–12
marginal-utility theory of value, **6:** 9
marginal valuation curve (Hicks), **12:** 196
marketability of assets, **2:** 124–25
market choice, **1:** 76; **3:** 33
market codes of conduct (Hayek), **12:**
  361n. 15
market coordination, **12:** 22, 479
market discipline, **19:** 206, 298
market economy
  allocation and distribution under, **19:** 249
  claims in, **17:** 316–17
  command economy to, transition from,
    12: 420–25
  competitive, property rights in, **18:**
    236–40

competitive federalism, extension of
   principles to, **18:** 80–82
competitive process of, **18:** 92
complex order of, **18:** 268
constraints in, **17:** 82–84
decisions of, political economic, **16:** 254
determinants of claims in, **17:** 316–18,
   329–49
efficiency, **16:** 227, 253–54
ethical standards, **19:** 362–63
exit and entrance from, **19:** 296, 360–61
exit options in, **18:** 258
freedoms in, **18:** 97, 203
government, limits power of, **19:** 176
input payments, **14:** 235
institutional framework, **12:** 34–35
within laws and institutions (Smith),
   19: 296–98, 310
monetary stability in, need for, **19:**
   361–62
nonsocialist, socialization in, **19:** 252–53
organization of, reform in, **19:** 356–63
participants in, dependence of, **18:** 236
performance, **18:** 90
political-legal framework, **18:** 69
politicized, **18:** 68, 258; **19:** 191–93
preferences and capacities in, **17:**
   283–92, 299–302
properties of, **19:** 6–7
rent allocation, **14:** 235
Smith's idea of, **19:** 302
socialism in, **19:** 251–55
socialist order, replaced by, **16:** 226–27;
   19: 231–33
spontaneous coordination of, **19:**
   166–68, 264–66, 279, 302
welfare transfers in, **19:** 255–58
See also exchange; exit options; liberty
market equilibrium and Keynesian
   economics, **8:** 26–27
market exchange, **12:** 34–35; **16:** 223; **17:**
   316–17; **18:** 268–70

choices in, **16:** 249–50
in constitutional politics, **16:** 249–50
consumption in, **19:** 229–31
dependence with, **18:** 229–31
exploitation in, **16:** 269
goods and services and, **15:** 132
interdependence in, **18:** 230
liberty to choose in, **18:** 69, 206, 239, 268
market failure from perspective of, **19:**
   137
politicized interferences, effect of, **19:**
   315
prisoners' dilemma in, **17:** 87–89, 90–91
process, distribution in, **17:** 298
production in, **19:** 229–31
property rights and, **18:** 236–39
self-interest in, **13:** 73: of Smith, **19:** 358
Smith's understanding of, **19:** 289–91,
   293–96
social value absent in, **12:** 117
trade and, **19:** 103–5, 289–91, 293–96,
   315
value transfer outside, **19:** 103–5
market failure, **7:** 47–50, 216
conditions for, **19:** 130
correcting for, **15:** xv; **18:** 279–85; **19:** 56
defined, **13:** 116; **19:** 137
diagnosis of, **19:** 137
diagnostics and identification of, **12:**
   135–36
discovery of, **13:** 37
exchange, from perspective of, **19:** 137
extent of, **15:** xv
government and, **7:** 216; **13:** 113; **15:**
   xi–xii, xiv–xv
in *Homo economicus,* **12:** 133–34; **13:**
   116–18
identification of, **18:** 277–78; **19:** 143–44
model of, **18:** 279–80
public expenditure with, **15:** xi–xv
public goods and, **15:** xiii–xiv, 188
Smith's conception of, **15:** 290–91

market failure (*continued*)
  theories of, **19:** 129
  in welfare economics, **13:** 113–14, 173; **15:** 286; **19:** 56, 129, 130–31
  welfare economics theory of, **13:** 113–14; **17:** 276
market order
  bureaucratic discretion, effect on, **16:** 264
  critique of, socialist, **16:** 5–6
  emergence of, **16:** 260
  exit option, **16:** 269–70
  extended, Hayek's influences on, **12:** 429–30
  generation of, **19:** 214
  government powers with, limits on, **19:** 176–77
  ignorance, subverted by, **19:** 220
  natural liberty, system of (Smith), **19:** 359
  opponents of, **19:** 165–70
  spontaneous coordination of market economy, **19:** 166–68, 264–66, 279, 302
market price, **16:** 254–61
  tax-price and, compared, **4:** 23–24, 87–90, 182–83
market restriction and generality, **11:** 101–12
markets
  adjustments in, **15:** 137–40
  agreement on, **1:** 219
  allocationist view, **19:** 7
  allocative function, **13:** 113
  behavior in, **1:** 35–42, 75–88, 346–59; **13:** 72–73; **17:** 81–87, 208, 243
  Buchanan's interest in, **1:** 29, 37–38, 42
  catallactic view of, **19:** 7–9
  choice in, individual choice in voting compared with, **1:** xvi, 16, 64–66, 69, 75–88, 93, 100–102
  choices exploited by, **19:** 230

competition exploited by, **19:** 261
competitive, **1:** 363–67; **13:** 405–6; **19:** 255: rational morality of (Gauthier), **17:** 452–54
in constitutional politics, **16:** 62–63, 68, 71, 249–50
consumer choice in, **13:** 162–64
costs, **19:** 190
critique of market order, Knight's ethical, **12:** 117–23
defined, **1:** 37–38
democracy and, **16:** 226–28
distribution in, **17:** 298, 316–27; **18:** 287–88, 310
economic rent and, **1:** 105, 106
economy and dispersion of property, **1:** 316
efficiency, **13:** 122–23; **16:** 5, 253–54
entrepreneurship, in Kirzner's theory of, **18:** 298–304
equal treatment and, **17:** 335–37
equilibrium, **1:** 168
ethics and, **1:** 368–73
evaluation, **18:** 287–88
exit options, **12:** 439–41; **18:** 68–70
exploitation, **19:** 232
extent of, **12:** 378–81
externalities, **15:** 132
failure of, **1:** 38, 45, 60–63; **5:** 80, 179; **10:** 16; **16:** 5–6
freedom in, **1:** 89–102, 182–84, 202, 282, 346–59
functions of, **16:** 257–58, 261–62; **19:** 358–59
goods and services, for exchange of, **15:** 132
government intervention in, **15:** 291–92; **17:** 307–10
individual equality, influence on, **12:** 275
as institutional process, **13:** 72–76
intertemporal divergences between, **18:** 300–301

intervention in, **19:** 189–90, 216
justice of, **16:** 354
knowledge (Hayek), as users of, **16:** 135; **19:** 210
labor supply on, impact of, **1:** 346–59
in laissez-faire economy, **15:** 10
maximization in idealized, **12:** 114
morality, **1:** 360–67; **12:** 439; **19:** 131
mutuality of gain in, **17:** 298–99
nonteleological perspective, **18:** 307
order of, **1:** 244–45, 276–77, 457
ownership rights in, **13:** 74
Pareto-efficient results generated by, **17:** 100
politicization of, **19:** 191–92, 216, 220
politics and, difference between, **1:** 455–68
politics as, **17:** 166
predictive theory of, **17:** 254
prices, **16:** 254–61
as process, **19:** 214
production and consumption in, **19:** 229–31
properties of, coordinating, **19:** 264–65
public goods theory, identity with, **5:** 49–50
of radical subjectivism, **18:** 293–98, 304–5
rationing function of, **16:** 257
restrictions, **13:** 389–91
role of, primary, **16:** 354
rules of, **10:** 16–18; **17:** 81–91
size: division of labor and, **1:** 346–59; **12:** 378; **19:** 299; specialization and, **12:** 392
as social decision rule, **16:** 202
social order of, **19:** 198
specialization and, **1:** 348–49, 351, 352, 357; **12:** 392
spontaneous coordination in, **16:** 7; **18:** 267–68, 311–17; **19:** 7–8, 166–67, 264–66, 279

spontaneous order in, **17:** 96–101, 243–45; **18:** 304–6, 311–17
state and, the, **3:** 18
success and political failure, **1:** 45, 46, 185–86
teleological conceptualization of, **18:** 306–8
theory, **1:** 29, 40; **5:** 78
underground, shadow, and black, **19:** 193–94
voluntary exchange, restraints on, **16:** 35–36
See also behavior; exchange; exit options; incentives; individual choice; interdependence; prices; trade; transfers
market space, **13:** 230–36
Marshallian economics, **12:** 142
demand curve, **12:** 54–55
external economies, **1:** 351–52
quasi-rents, **1:** 106
tax schemes, **1:** 62
time and economic theory, **1:** 444–46, 454
Marshallian geometry, **5:** 23, 29, 43, 45
Marxism, **3:** 12; **4:** 128; **13:** 174–75
maximin principle. *See* difference principle of distribution (Rawls)
maximization
exchange value and, **10:** 28–29
in idealized market, **12:** 114
subjectively defined norm, **12:** 14
maximization criteria, **1:** 194
maximization paradigm
adherence to, **12:** 127
market order in, Knight's criticism of, **12:** 117–23
social value scale in, **12:** 121
in study of economics, **12:** 22–23
maximizing-economizing paradigm, **12:** 116
means testing
classical liberalism and, **11:** 206

means testing (*continued*)
  for pensions, **11:** 173
  for transfers, **11:** 164
"meddlesome preferences," **1:** 284, 382
median income symmetry, **5:** 130–32
median preference, delegation of power, **5:**
  106, 112
median voter, **4:** 143–56, 158, 163–67; **9:** 102
  Black's theory, **14:** 12
  defined, **13:** 200
  earmarked or nonearmarked public
    goods, choices for, **14:** 75–83
  generality in taxation, with constraint
    of, **14:** 310–11
  model, **1:** 54–55, 425; **9:** 220
  preferences satisfied in yes-no voting,
    13: 200–207
median voter theorem, **11:** 37, 49, 89–90,
  120–21, 161–62
medical insurance, **11:** 178. *See also*
  National Health Service, Britain
medical services
  abrogation of individual choice, **15:** 365
  individual vouchers to purchase, **15:**
    356–57
  preferences and demand for, **15:** 363–73
membership
  exclusion and, **7:** 53
  preferred, **15:** 194
  rights, **7:** 94
mercantilism
  in modern economic order, **19:** 289,
    314–16
  Smith's criticism of, **19:** 291–300
merger as private response to externalities,
  13: 359
meta-rules, **10:** 117
methodological error, **2:** 24, 42, 46
methodological individualism, **3:** xvi, xvii,
  3, 11–15, 316–17
methodology
  of debt theory, **2:** 18–25

in economics, **3:** xv
error, **2:** 23
fallacy in, **2:** 60
of incidence theory, **2:** 21 n. 4
Ricardian, **2:** 90
microeconomics, **8:** 30; **16:** 106
migration
  externalities created by, **18:** 49
  fiscal behavior, in Tiebout's model of,
    18: 44–64, 148, 163
  fiscal constraints and, **9:** 200–203
  fiscal equalization to limit, **18:** 38–40
  fiscal incentives for, **18:** 29–32, 38,
    41–43, 48–56, 63–64
  fiscally induced (Samuelson), **18:** 46
  fiscal surpluses on, effect of, **18:** 40–42
  freedom of, **18:** 61
  as individual choice, **18:** 33–38, 42–43
  public and private goods, with
    provision of, **18:** 29–42
  sources of excessive, **18:** 40
Miller et al. v. Schoene (1928), **1:** 440; **16:**
  99; **17:** 112, 133; **18:** 342–57
minimal state, **1:** 52, 293, 389; **10:** 26, 129
  Nozick's, **17:** xx, 416–22, 424–28, 432,
    434–35
minimax strategy, **9:** xxiii, 220
minimum wage, **1:** 302; **13:** 58
minority exploitation, **7:** 195–97
minority rule, **3:** 254–56
mobility costs and fiscal surplus, **9:**
  209–10; **11:** 19–21
models, political, **9:** 3, 18; **13:** 293–95; **17:**
  268–70, 276–79; **18:** 186–96, 254–56
  analysis of, democratic, **4:** 181–211
  benevolent despot, **1:** xvi, 15–16, 72,
    74, 144, 203, 362, 456; **9:** 7, 14, 220; **14:**
    176
  contractarian, **16:** 215; **17:** 270–71
  demand-driven, **9:** 18; **13:** 58–59
  direct democracy, **13:** 403
  economic, **1:** 168; **4:** 171–72; **8:** 83–84; **9:**

16–17; **12:** 390–91, 395–96; **13:** 307–12, 468–73
incumbency, **13:** 284–87, 293
Italian, **1:** 17; **9:** 18 n. 1; **15:** 69–70, 76–77, 84
Leviathan, **1:** 21–22, 57–59; **9:** 33–37, 46–48, 152, 219; **14:** 97–100; **19:** 317
one-person, **19:** 135–36
voluntary exchange, **9:** 7, 10; **16:** 247, 374–79; **19:** 313, 315–16
monetarism, **1:** 20, 167
monetarist paradigm and inflation, **8:** 115
monetarists
  Keynesian analysis, challenge to, **19:** 325
  inflation, causes of, **8:** 59–60
  influence of, **19:** 324
monetary authority
  bureaucracy and, **8:** 122–23
  independence, **8:** 114–17; **13:** 438–39
  inflationary bias, **8:** 123
  predictions, **8:** 123
monetary constitution, **8:** 122, 189–90
  continuous equilibrium, **1:** 400–401
  efficiency, **1:** 398–401
  for European Union, **18:** 110–12
  inflation and, **8:** 60
  institutions and money and, **1:** 167–68
  for monetary stability, **18:** 257
  of New Deal, **18:** 385–88, 399–410
  social contract arising from, **18:** 411–15
  See also currencies; gold; gold standard; money
monetary policy, **4:** 279–80
  antirecession, **13:** 447
  asymmetrical application, **8:** 44
  exchange rates and, **8:** 126
  idealized, **13:** 441–42
  inflation and, **8:** 43–45
  interest rates, **8:** 123
  in Keynesian economics, **8:** 86
  in political democracy, **8:** 117–25
  politics, influence of on, **13:** 439–40

reform, **8:** 8–9
restrictive, **13:** 446
stabilization policy, as instrument of, **13:** 435–37
World War II, rediscovery after, **8:** 44
monetary system
  managed versus automatic, **1:** 403–7
  predictability and, **1:** 396–418
  stability and, **1:** 169, 397–98
monetary system, international, **2:** 64–65
  fractional reserve base, **18:** 388
  gold standard, pre-1933, **18:** 388–89, 418
monetary system, U.S.
  changes in, contractarian view of, **18:** 386–87
  dollar/gold link, post-1934, **18:** 396–97, 423–24
  failure of, **18:** 422–26
  fractional reserve base, **18:** 388
  managed and automatic, mix of, **18:** 415
  New Deal changes and, **18:** 387–95, 402, 418, 423
money
  in command economy, **12:** 417–20
  competitive, **9:** 130
  free market and, **9:** 130
  gold and paper currency used as, **18:** 390–91
  legal characteristics of U.S., **18:** 400–402
  nominal value and, **9:** 140
  in private-goods exchange, **5:** 75
  protection of, **18:** 247–49
  public good characteristics, **18:** 412
  quantity of, **12:** 60, 61
  real value and, **9:** 133
  rediscovery in 1950s, **8:** 85
  as standard of preferred payment, **18:** 394–95
  transactions services, **9:** 133
  value of, effect of inflation on, **18:** 247–49

money creation, **1:** 170, 171–72, 173; **4:** 271
  budget deficits and, **4:** 98, 103–8; **8:**
    110–28, 147–49; **14:** 390
  debt and, **2:** 99, 101, 104–5, 132, 144–48;
    14: 349–51, 355, 360
  default through, **14:** 452
  disguising, **14:** 350
  as form of tax, **14:** 457
  government's power of, **14:** 355
  inefficiency in early Keynesianism, **1:**
    167
  under Keynesian theory, **14:** 363–64
  labor standard of value, **1:** 415–16
  as monopoly franchise, **9:** 129–30
  optimal, **9:** 155
  public spending, to finance, **14:** 351,
    359–60
  as revenue source, **9:** 131–32
money economy
  asymmetric reciprocity, **12:** 413–16
  idealized exchange in, **12:** 412–13
money illusion, **1:** 150
money income
  Friedman demand curve, **12:** 199
  on Hicks's orthodox demand curve, **12:**
    198
  on marginal evaluation curve, **12:** 198
money supply
  budget deficits and, **8:** 118–20; **14:**
    479–80
  consols, **2:** 162–63
  national debt, **2:** 155–59
  public debt, **2:** 78, 101, 132
monopolist
  gains-from-trade, **12:** 206
  pricing strategy of profit-maximizing,
    12: 227–32
  in "welfare triangle" example, **12:** 207–9
monopoly, **1:** 57, 107–8, 109; **15:** 23–24
  benefits, capitalization of, **12:** 214–15
  bureaucracy, power of, **9:** 28–29

  competitive, **13:** 336–37
  discriminatory, **9:** 81–82
  distortions, allocative and
    nonallocative, **13:** 333–35
  efficiency and, **1:** 274–75
  government, model of, **4:** 128–38; **9:**
    20–32, 52–53, 231
  government as, **18:** 150–63, 192–94
  in market and in taxation, **9:** 90
  models creating, **12:** 213–14
  natural, regulation of, **13:** 261n. 3,
    316–17
  power of, **12:** 206–7
  price, orthodox theory of, **12:** 219–20
  problems of, **12:** 216–18
  profits of, **12:** 215
  prosecution of, **1:** 201
  public debt, analogy to deadweight, **12:**
    211–16
  in reaction-curve construction, **18:**
    438–46
  regulated, **13:** 318–23, 327, 331–32
  restrictions, burden of, **12:** 212–13
  solutions, discriminatory and
    nondiscriminatory, **13:** 320–21,
    333–35
  state as, power of the, **18:** xi–xii,
    xv–xvi
  technological innovation, as outcome
    of, **12:** 213–14
  unregulated, predictable actions of, **13:**
    321
  value of firm, capitalized, **12:** 209–10
  welfare costs of, **13:** 251
  See also ruling-class model
monopoly theory
  price in, **12:** 221–35
  time in, **12:** 221–35
monopsony
  bias toward, **13:** 323–26
  consumer with, power of, **13:** 319–21

industry and, **13:** 320–21

marginal, demand curve (Weintraub),
  12: 195–97

nondiscriminatory, **13:** 320 n. 4

power of, **12:** 192 n. 2

unrestricted, behavior of, **13:** 321

monopsony solution: in regulated
  monopoly, **13:** 320–21, 332

moral anarchy

defined, **17:** 190

individuals under, behavior of, **17:**
  190–91

moral community and moral order
  subverted by, **17:** 200

in U.S., **17:** 197

moral community

Buchanan's notion of, **17:** xiii–xiv

defined, **17:** 188

in Japan, **17:** 198–99

justice and fairness, **17:** 195

limits of, extension of, **17:** 205–7

membership in, **14:** 488, 522–23; **17:**
  203–4

society under, **17:** 192–96

in U.S., **17:** 196–97

moral conduct and institutional form, **1:**
  xx, 360–67

"moral free zone," **1:** 350–51

moralist, constitutional, **16:** 363–64

morality

agreement on, **1:** 86

cooperative behavior as form of, **17:**
  230–31, 461

legislation, **1:** 327

of market behavior, **12:** 439

Nozick on, **17:** 431, 433

in politics, **3:** 108

rational, **17:** 453, 461–68

of rights of free trade, **19:** 193

in social order, **19:** 130–34

moral law, **1:** 312, 313, 314–22

moral norms

in exchange relationship, **17:** 82–83

learned and self-imposed, **17:** 221

promulgation of, **17:** 223–26

moral order

in anarchy, **7:** 8

defined, **1:** 244–45; **17:** 189–90

governance under, implications of, **17:**
  200

individual behavior under, **17:** 191–92,
  194–95

justice and fairness in, **17:** 195

Keynesian theory, shift in norms under,
  14: 490–91

legal order, moral value of, **14:** 523

moral community superseded by, **17:**
  208–10

norms, **14:** 488; **17:** 226–28

participation in, **14:** 48

public bad and, **7:** 153

public spending and consumption,
  norms related to, **14:** 496

rules necessary for, **17:** 227–31

in U.S., **17:** 197–98

moral philosophy

contributions of eighteenth-century, **17:**
  45–46, 56–57

defined, **17:** 25

economics and, compared, **19:** 70–72

of Knight, **19:** 82–83, 92

of Smith, **19:** 289–91

social order, in maintenance of, **19:**
  131–32

most-favored-nation, **11:** 111–12

Mt. Pelerin Society, **19:** 117–18, 119, 120

multi-issue space, **13:** 195 n. 1

multilateral agreement, **5:** 9. *See also*
  agreement; costs

multiplier, balanced-budget, **2:** 77

multiplier effect, **4:** 275–76

Munn v. Illinois, **16:** 340

Nash equilibrium, **11:** 55–59, 61–62, 65, 89, 91, 92, 93–94

National Commission on Social Security Reform (Greenspan Commission), **15:** 388–89

national debt. *See* public debt

National Health Service, Britain, **4:** 193
　Buchanan-Kafoglis analysis, **15:** 357–59
　choice under model of, **15:** 347–49
　external economies in, **15:** 344
　failure explained, **15:** 340–42, 347
　under model of democratic individual choice, **15:** 347–49
　neoclassical prediction, **15:** 345–47
　price elasticity of demand in, **15:** 342–44
　public and private services, **15:** 350–52
　reform, directions for, **15:** 353–60
　structure in, **15:** 341–42
　weakness of, **15:** 359–60

national income and public debt, **2:** 139. *See also* money; public debt

national planning. *See* budgets and budgeting; economic policy

nation-states, **17:** 132; **18:** 123–30

natural and artifactual man, **1:** 246–59

natural distribution, **1:** 434; **7:** 19, 75

naturalistic fallacy, **1:** 47

natural liberty
　equal liberty, **1:** 293, 298, 299, 309: Rawls on, **1:** 298 n. 13, 299, 301–4, 306, 307–8, 309–10; **17:** 355–56, 385–86, 413; violation of, **1:** 307
　justice and, **1:** 292–310; **17:** 327
　as public goods, **15:** 290–92
　Smith's system of, **1:** 298–301, 303, 304–8, 309–10; **12:** 431–32; **19:** 359

natural-rate hypothesis, **1:** 170

natural rights, **3:** 314; **11:** 8
　origins of state and, **10:** 27
　rules and, **10:** 25

natural science
　applications of, organization of, **12:** 46

economic science and, compared, **19:** 200–202, 215–16, 218–19, 293–94
　predictions of, **12:** 31–32
　social science and, compared, **19:** 21–22

neoclassical economics
　choice analysis, **19:** 155, 156
　cost, **2:** 30
　defined, **1:** 191
　expectations, **18:** 295
　general equilibrium theory in, criticism of, **18:** 293–98, 299, 308, 309–10
　Knight's contribution to, **19:** 88–89
　Marshall's theory, **12:** 142
　radical subjectivism from, departure of, **18:** 304
　teleological perspective of, **18:** 296–98

net worth
　of bond purchaser, **2:** 41
　debt repayment and, **2:** 93
　of taxpayer-borrower, **2:** 45

neutrality
　intertemporal, tax rates with, **14:** 403–4
　of public debt (Barro), **14:** 410–13
　See also Barro neutrality theorem

neutrality, allocational
　administrative-decision model, extension to, **13:** 307–11
　Coase theorem of, **13:** 299–306, 312
　extensions, **13:** 298–99
　in Hume's villager example, **13:** 303
　limits on, **13:** 299
　property rights and liability rules under, **13:** 300
　state under, theory of the, **13:** 311–15
　valid and invalid, **13:** 307–11, 314

neutrality, full: in decision rules, **4:** 152–63 passim

neutrality theorem. *See* Coase theorem

New Deal, **1:** 175
　centralized government, **16:** 339–42
　changes and U.S. monetary system, **18:** 387–95, 402, 418, 423

Constitution, U.S., changes to, **18:** 399–410

constitutional revolution of, **16:** 350; **18:** 385

constitutional rules, **16:** 346–47

economic constitution, **16:** 339, 345–47

economic policy of, **16:** 340–41

gold under, **18:** 395–410

Great Depression, economic policy during and after, **16:** 339–42

implications for reform, **16:** 353–55

Keynesian economic theory and, **16:** 345–46

monetary constitution of, **18:** 385–88, 399–410

monetary policy, **18:** 389, 395–410, 423–26

policies with absence of, **16:** 341

Roosevelt administration, policies of, **18:** 385–87, 395–410

"new" economics, **2:** 5, 14, 66; **8:** 31, 79

in Camelot, **8:** 37

in practice, **8:** 50–51

New Frontier and economic policy, **8:** 49–50

Nixon administration, **18:** 425

Nobel Prize. *See* Alfred Nobel Memorial Prize in Economic Sciences

nonauction, noncontract method, **13:** 261–62

noncontractarian constitutionalism, **10:** 24–25

nonexclusion, **5:** 35, 48, 60, 67, 191

"non-Tuism," **3:** 17, 18

Norman v. Baltimore and Ohio Railroad Co. (1935), **18:** 400n. 7

normative behaviors in Rawlsian economics, **1:** 432

normative individualism, **1:** 281–91; **3:** xvii; **11:** 21

normativism, **17:** 121–23, 133; **18:** 177

North American Free Trade Agreement (NAFTA), **12:** 42

Nortz v. United States (1935), **18:** 400n. 7

numbers, relevance of, **1:** 318–22

objectivity
in economic behavior, **12:** 8, 23–24
in identifying costs and benefits, **12:** 19

offer curves (Marshall), **12:** 255

Old-Age, Survivors, and Disability Insurance (OASDI), **15:** 407, 443

oligopoly behavior
competitive outcome, conditions for less than, **15:** 241–42
cooperative, independent, and strategic, **15:** 240–42
free-rider strategy and, compared, **15:** 242

omniscience assumption, critique of, **1:** 193–94

open economy, fiscal policy in, **4:** 272–77

opportunity cost(s), **1:** 18, 103, 105, 263; **2:** 30; **7:** 128, 167–69; **4:** 59n. 2; **6:** 17–36
alternative-product value and, **6:** 19–20
alternatives, **12:** 8–9
Austrian origins, **6:** 21
choice and, **6:** 16, 19, 32
definitions of, **12:** 280, 285, 337–38
as displaced value, **6:** 20
in economic depression, **2:** 95; **6:** 17–36
emergence of, **13:** 358
with internalization, **12:** 297
legal institutions, effect on, **12:** 286–87
legal uncertainty, in context of, **12:** 296
of lenders, **14:** 438
measurement of, **12:** 285
nonmarket value and, **6:** 15
proxies for, **12:** 285
public goods, decision on quantity of, **4:** 59–60, 68–70
of public spending, **6:** 57–59; **8:** 34–35
sacrifice of value and, **6:** 43–44

opportunity cost(s) (*continued*)
   theory of, misconceptions in, **12:**
      329–30
   valuation of a life, **12:** 278–81
   See also costs
opportunity cost theory
   in Knight, **19:** 89–90
   London School of Economics,
      contributions of, **12:** 335–39
   in Smith's deer-and-beaver model, **12:**
      337, 349
optimality, **1:** xix, 61, 71, 72, 139, 140, 203,
      208, 300, 426; **3:** 172
   of competitive equilibrium, **1:** 350
   conditions, **1:** 192–93, 194–95, 211–12
   critique of, **1:** 210–29
   defined, **1:** 192
   in federal structure, **9:** 201–12
   in monetary rules, **9:** 157–58
   rules, **1:** 211–14
   of rules, **1:** 219–24
   in size of government, **3:** 113–14
   usefulness of, **1:** 210–11
   See also efficiency; Pareto criterion;
      Pareto optimality
optimal-mix path (ray), **5:** 61–62, 63, 68,
      71, 73
order, public, **7:** 153
order, spontaneous, **1:** 109, 244–45; **17:** 101
   application of, Polanyi's, **17:** 98
   of development of law, **18:** 179
   economic inefficiency, to explain, **17:**
      101
   in economics, **12:** 22–23
   in economic theory, **13:** 17
   of Hobbes's anarchy, **13:** 73
   justifications for, **17:** 97–99
   legal institutions and, **17:** 101–2
   market process and, **13:** 72–73; **18:**
      311–12, 314–17
   normative element in, **17:** 244–45
   prediction, **17:** 100

principle of, **17:** 242–45, 274
   "scientific," **12:** 28
   of subjectivist paradigm, **12:** 27
organic theory of the state, **1:** 119, 120–22,
      132, 204; **2:** 29; **3:** 11–12, 31–32; **11:** 207
organizational choice, theory of, **5:** 175
organizations
   Coase on, **1:** 223n. 7
   constitution of, **14:** 431
   as decision-making unit, **14:** 430–31
   functions of, **5:** 168
   market form of, Knight on, **1:** 219
   nature of, **1:** 222–23
organizations, private
   entry and exit, freedom of, **14:**
      439–40
   lending to, **14:** 440–41
   right to vote, **14:** 442
orthodox public finance. *See* public
   finance
orthodoxy
   in commodity-tax theory, **9:** 68–69
   fiscal, **9:** xxi
   fiscal federalism, in theory of, **9:** 203–5
   in income and capital-tax theory, **9:**
      101–3
   inflation as a tax, in analysis of, **9:**
      150–53
   new, **2:** 5–17, 50
   in tax reform advocacy, **9:** 225–26
   in tax theory, **9:** 15
output
   heterogeneous input combination
      model, **12:** 262–65
   optimum, **12:** 99
ownership
   centralized, road construction with, **12:**
      315–23
   under collective action, **15:** 308–18
   common, **15:** 14
   competitive, road construction with, **12:**
      323–24

decentralized, road construction with,
12: 322–23
private, absence of, **15:** 14
See also property rights
ownership-consumption
of club theory, **15:** 194–207
private and public range of, **15:** 193–94
ownership rights
assignment of, **13:** 256–57, 261–62
auctioning, **13:** 257–62
of external diseconomies, **13:** 252–55
law establishing, **12:** 290–91
lobbying for, **13:** 58–66
in politics and the market, **13:** 74
rent seeking and, **13:** 275–76
rents with, **13:** 253, 256–57
value of, **12:** 404–6
See also property rights

pain-cost doctrine, **2:** 30
paradox of government, **7:** 116–35
paradox of voting, **7:** 182
Pareto classifications, **13:** 239–41; **16:** 81–82
Pareto criterion, **1:** 256, 300, 431, 439; **3:** 92;
11: 69; **13:** 8–9
changes, applied to, **3:** 173–74, 284
efficiency (*see* Pareto efficiency)
emergence of, point of, **17:** 78–79
empirical status of, **17:** 129
externalities and, **1:** 262, 263, 350
for income redistribution, **13:** 135–36,
141–47
Lindahl and, **1:** 426, 434
objections to, **17:** 237–40
optimality (*see* Pareto optimality)
paradox, **1:** 211–29
Pareto's interpretation of, **17:** 136, 138
relevance of, **1:** xvii, xix, 210–29
Sen's rule and, **17:** 72–79
for social improvement, **15:** 30
of superiority, **1:** 268, 434; **16:** 248
transfers, in analysis of, **13:** 139–49

unanimity and, **3:** 92n. 3; **17:** 259–60
utility, **1:** 309
welfare economics and, **1:** 36, 191–209,
210–29
Wicksellian unanimity and, **16:** 10, 71
See also welfare economics
Pareto efficiency, **1:** 61, 71, 72, 137, 139, 140,
142, 195, 300, 306, 350; **5:** 11, 88, 190; **10:**
22; **11:** 83, 88, 90, 143
agreement on, **16:** 374–75
defined, **1:** 192
Pareto equilibrium, **15:** 115
Pareto frontier, **5:** 88–89, 92
Pareto inferiority, **11:** 92
Pareto-optimal area (set), **5:** 108, 112, 114,
115, 116
Pareto optimality, **1:** xix, 61, 71, 72, 137, 139,
140, 194–95, 203, 205, 210–20, 222–29,
256, 261, 300, 306, 350, 426, 434, 453; **3:**
93, 201; **5:** 79, 91–92, 107–8, 112, 146; **7:** 52;
9: 26, 38; **10:** 22, 33; **11:** 91, 100; **13:** 134–35
agreement on, **16:** 374–75
Coase on, **1:** 221
conditions for, **12:** 347–49
corporation income tax and, **4:** 55
defined, **1:** 192
departures from, **4:** 119, 290–93
under equal-preference models, **4:**
159–68
externality and, **3:** 190–99
fiscal justice and, **4:** 296
full neutrality and, **4:** 153–54
majority rule and, **3:** 172–89
marginal conditions for, **12:** 301–2
monopoly power and, **12:** 206
normative, **4:** 286–87
with public goods, **4:** 113–14
side payments and, **3:** 187–89
three-person, world of equals model, **4:**
145
in valuation of a life, **12:** 281
Wicksellian, conditions for, **4:** 287–89

Pareto-optimal move, **5:** 107n. 4, 132
Pareto-optimal point (position), **5:** 107n.
    4, 108, 116, 127, 132
Pareto regions, **1:** 210, 211, 434
Pareto relevance, **11:** 109; **12:** 362; **15:**
    119–20
Pareto rule, **3:** 94
Pareto set, **13:** 240, 242–44
Pareto superiority, **10:** 151–52, 154; **11:** 62,
    65, 69, 77, 155, 156, 164
Pareto-superior reform, **11:** 69
Pareto welfare economics, **3:** 8; **5:** 45; **11:** 69
Pareto-Wicksell construction, **16:** 410–11
park as a quasi-collective good, **4:** 19
parliamentary democracy, **1:** 448
partial equilibrium analysis, **12:** 53–57, 66
party platforms, political
    issues in, **13:** 236–37
    in two-dimensional issue space, **13:**
        228–29, 231–36
paternalism, benevolent, **1:** 284
payoffs: prisoners' dilemma with
    nonsymmetrical, **11:** 43; **13:** 349–51
payroll tax, social security, **9:** 60
    favoritism and penalties, **15:** 451–52
    repeal of, **15:** 413–14
    shifting and incidence of, **14:** 22
    vulnerability of, **15:** 451
    See also social security system
peak-load pricing, **5:** 46; **12:** 298–307,
    309–10
penalty tax, **13:** 420–29, 431
pensions, **11:** 167–69, 173
perception and reality, **1:** 165–66, 393–94.
    See also Keynesian economic theory;
    political philosophy: Nietzsche
perfect competition. *See* competition
Perry v. United States (1935), **18:** 400n. 7
personal income tax. *See* income tax,
    personal
Phillips curve, **1:** 169, 170; **8:** 87–90,
    173–74; **10:** 91

physical capital, incentives to accumulate,
    14: 402–3
Pigou effect, **2:** 49
Pigovian analysis, **3:** 201n. 4
Pigovian welfare economics, **1:** 296; **6:** 65,
    72–74; **13:** 37–38; **19:** 129
    analytics, **1:** 60–74
    Coase's criticism of, **1:** 60n. 1
    defined, **1:** 60
    margins, **1:** 60–74, 104
    See also welfare economics
Pike and Brouwer v. United States (1965),
    18: 424n. 31
Polanyi, economics of: Knight's critique
    of, **1:** 230–43; **7:** 48n. 3, 234; **10:** 47; **16:**
    91; **17:** 98, 153n, 155; **18:** 303n. 51, 305–6,
    312; **19:** 41, 52, 118, 262
police protection. *See* law enforcement
political agenda and generality, **11:**
    66–78
political agents
    benevolent, **19:** 332–33
    constraints on, **19:** 334–43
    monolithic and nonbenevolent, **19:**
        333–40
    nonmonolithic and nonbenevolent, **19:**
        337
    political choice model, discretion in, **14:**
        50–52, 92
    politics, in conceptualization of, **14:** 505
    repudiation of commitments made by,
        14: 526
    Smith's mistrust of, **19:** 300
    Tax Reform Act (1986), interests related
        to, **14:** 50–52
political behavior: public choice analysis,
    14: 490; **16:** 152, 154; **19:** 314
political biases and Keynesian economics,
    8: 26
political choice
    analysis, **4:** 170–71; **13:** 9–10
    collective-, **19:** 216

consensus model, taxpayers in, **14:** 46–48

constitutional rules, constrained by, **16:** 45

defined, **1:** 362

discretion in, **14:** 50–52

economic model, **4:** 171–72

economics in, **19:** 214–15, 219–20

economics of politics, **4:** 171–72

generalization in, **19:** 281–82

group size on, effect of, **1:** 362–63

implementation of, **1:** 62

individual behavior theory in, **13:** 6–7

of individual voter, **13:** 162–64

of institutions, **19:** 212–13

nonconsensus (conflict) model, taxpayers in, **14:** 48–50

political-constitutional, **19:** 220

public choice, influence of, **13:** 82–85

public choice theory to analyze, **14:** 490

rule for making, **5:** 145–50

rules, made within or among, **14:** 500–501

stochastic results and, **16:** 72

theory of, **5:** 117, 182–83

Tullock on, **1:** 40 n. 10

in two-dimensional model, **13:** 228–29

unanimity rule in, **13:** 10–11

Wicksellian, **16:** 72–73

See also economic behavior; individual choice

political-choice institutions, **5:** 75

political constitution, **5:** 146–47

defined, **16:** 45

democratic polities under, reform in, **16:** 268–76

economic theory of, **13:** 45–46; **16:** 307–8

laws in, **16:** 44

revision of (Wicksell), **16:** 71–72

theory of, Tullock on, **1:** 39 n. 9, 50 n. 3

political economists, role of, **1:** 191–92,

200–202, 205, 207–8, 269. *See also* economists

political economy

analysis, **1:** 63–66

applicability, **1:** 208

art and science of, **1:** 164–66

artifactual, **19:** 239

British (Hutt), **19:** 138

Buchanan's criticism of, **19:** 23–24

classical, **1:** 40–42, 182–83, 386–90; **7:** 214–15; **14:** 26; **16:** 5–7; **17:** 243–44; **19:** 191, 264–66, 310–11: development of, **13:** 123; *Homo economicus* in, **10:** 53; **12:** 83–85; with introduction of capital, **14:** 329–34; purposes of, **12:** 89; normative principles of, **13:** 122–23; in Smith's economics, **1:** 387, 389

under constant returns, **14:** 322–26

constitutional (*see* constitutional political economy)

as constitutional order, **16:** 418–21

constraints of, **16:** 250–52

contractarian, **17:** xiv–xv; **19:** 63

criteria, **1:** 196; **8:** 4–5

efficiency and, **1:** 193–96

emergence, **19:** 310, 359

errors in, **12:** 42

under generalized increasing returns, **14:** 326–29

markets, intervention in, **19:** 189–90

methodological revolution in, **19:** 48

methodology, **1:** 200

"new," **1:** 4, 45

normative, **1:** 207, 269, 275, 442–54, 462–65: positive and, **19:** 23–24, 140–45, 240; Wicksell on, **19:** 140–42

policy reform of, **19:** 343

positive, **1:** 200, 207, 208–9

purposes of, **17:** 51

role, **1:** 208

science of, **12:** 50; **17:** 40–41, 44–45, 47–48, 50–51, 53–54

political economy (*continued*)
  scope, **1:** 200–202
  social philosophy, role in, **17:** 242–43,
    247, 249–50
  spontaneous order principle in, **17:**
    244–45, 247
  See also public choice
political economy, Virginia school of, **1:**
  25–26; **9:** 7; **19:** 41–44, 50–63
  constitutionalist-contractarian
    methodology in, **19:** 62
  normative purpose of, **19:** 63
  research program, **19:** 50–51, 59–60
  Tullock's contribution to, **19:** 54–55
  at University of Virginia, **19:** 40–44,
    50–63
  at Virginia Polytechnic Institute and
    State University, **19:** 44–45
  See also constitutional political
    economy; George Mason University,
    Center for Study of Public Choice;
    University of Virginia; Virginia
    Polytechnic Institute and State
    University
political exchange, **1:** 262–64, 265, 267,
  272, 275–76; **3:** x, 18–22; **10:** 29–31; **11:**
  20–24; **12:** 442–43; **13:** 16–24, 71–76; **16:**
  62–63, 68, 71; **19:** 9
  bargaining in, **18:** 186
  choices in market and, **16:** 249–50
  constitutional aspects of, **18:** 189–92
  in constitutional democracy, **18:** 195
  defined, **1:** 50; **11:** 58–68
  generality and, **11:** 52–54
  between individual and collectivity, **18:**
    186–89
  between individual and sovereign, **18:**
    192–94
  model, **19:** 135–36
  normative, **18:** 196
  paradigm, centrality of, **1:** 24, 26–27, 29,
    34, 35–36, 49, 181–82, 384, 456, 460–61
  in postconstitutional politics, **1:** 52–57
  in public goods model, **18:** 186–87
  in Rawlsian economics, **1:** 50
  rights and efficiency, **1:** 260–72
  role of government, **18:** 188–89
  unanimity, **3:** 248–51
  voluntary (*see* voluntary exchange)
political failure, **1:** 45, 46
political games, 284–87, 404–5. *See also*
  games
political-legal order
  contractarian, **16:** 222–23
  functions, **16:** 63; **17:** 274
  the state as, **16:** 244–45
political obligation, **3:** 309, 313–15; **7:**
  69–70
political order, **1:** 276
  Buchanan's interest in, **1:** xix
  Knight's and Polanyi's conception of, **1:**
    230–43
  legitimacy of, **1:** 51–52
  See also social order
political parties, **3:** xvi, 9
political philosophy, **1:** 452–54, 456–57
  Hegel, **13:** 170–72
  Hobbes, **1:** 26, 51, 59, 389, 433
  Hume, **1:** 361, 424, 451
  Kant, **1:** 67, 312
  Knight, **1:** 251, 253–54, 451
  Lenin, **1:** 183, 285
  Locke, **1:** 51, 389
  Madison, **1:** xx, 19, 372, 468
  Marx, **1:** 148, 183, 285, 387
  Nietzsche, **1:** 34, 46, 179, 180, 393
  Rawls, **1:** 23–24, 292–93, 296–99, 301–4,
    306, 307–10, 439, 465
  Rousseau, **1:** 100
  Smith, **1:** xxii, 28, 114, 186, 292–301,
    303–10, 387, 389
  Wicksell, **1:** 15–16, 20, 74, 98, 125–26,
    135, 140–42, 144–45, 204, 217–18, 362,
    421, 455–57, 459–61, 463–66, 468

political process, **7:** 3; **9:** 3, 7, 18n. 1, 33, 37;
  10: 51; **17:** 154, 162, 168
  analysis of, **1:** 63–66
  collective outcomes from, **14:** 21
  constraints on, **14:** 482–83
  economic policy emerging from, **14:**
    483–84
  market analysis and, compared, **1:**
    75–88
political rules. *See* behavior; constitutional
  political economy; individual choice;
  rules
political science, **3:** 310; **7:** 216n. 4
  economics, contributions of, **17:** 9,
    15–16
  methodological setting for, **1:** 230
  political philosophy, as separate from, **1:**
    242–43
  See also constitutional political
    economy
political structure
  economics and, **8:** 4–5
  taxation and, **11:** 118
  See also economic policy; government
political systems
  competitive federalized, **18:** 69–70
  parliamentary and nonparliamentary,
    18: 195
  power in, **18:** 134–37
politicians
  behavior of, in politics and the
    bureaucracy, **13:** 11–13, 62–70
  competition among, **8:** 98–100
  distributive politics, role in, **19:** 277–83
  incentives of, **19:** 327
  rational expectations about rules, **16:**
    65–67
  self-interest, **19:** 279
  tax trade-offs, response to, **13:** 473–74
politicization
  behavior, to impose preferences on, **13:**
    413–18

cartel restrictions, enforcement of, **13:**
    390–96
  of choice, **18:** 68
  of economic policy, **19:** 319
  of the economy, **19:** 139, 189
  external diseconomies, taxation for
    control of, **13:** 366–70
  externalities and, **12:** 182–85; **13:** 360–66;
    18: 279–85
  legal rights, abrogation of, **13:**
    359–60
  of markets, **19:** 216, 220, 271
  of money prices in command economy,
    12: 417–20
  saving and, **12:** 467–68
  of social interdependence, **13:** 413
  under socialism, **19:** 189
  of voluntary exchange, **19:** 313
  welfare economics for, **12:** 292–93; **19:**
    292
politics
  agreement in, **16:** 155–56; **17:** 165
  assumptions of, **18:** 68
  behavior and, **13:** 418
  boundaries for, **13:** 101
  budgetary, **8:** 95–96
  of bureaucracy, **19:** 97–99
  choice and, **11:** 27–28, 72–74
  classical, **1:** 234
  as class struggle, **3:** 26
  coercive, **18:** 69, 81
  conflict resolution through, **13:** 414–17;
    17: 163–64
  of constituency response, **19:** 191
  constitutional function in, **17:** 163
  constitutional perspective, **13:** 19–20
  constitutional rules, within, **14:** 381–82;
    17: 275–76
  constraints on, **1:** 447–48
  contractarian model for, **16:** 215, 249; **17:**
    269–70
  cooperative, **3:** 266; **18:** 186

politics (*continued*)

decision making in (*see* decision
making, political)

defined, **1:** 40, 235, 236, 237–38; **13:** 3–4;
16: 216–17, 221, 228; **19:** 346, 353

democratic, **1:** 21; **16:** 381

democracy, of modern, **19:** 311–12

as discovery, **11:** 15

discrimination and, **11:** xix, 14–16, 67,
68; **19:** 351

of disorder, **19:** 194–97

distributive, **16:** 148–54; **19:** 200–206,
271–73, 277–83, 344–45

distributive justice and, **10:** 126–48

distributive process in, **18:** 287–88

as economic exchange, **3:** 16–30; **10:**
29–31, 41–42

economic theory of, **12:** 49–50; **13:**
20–21, 41–44, 50–51, 54; **19:** 44

electoral fallacy in, **19:** 347, 350–51

elitist mentality in, **17:** 241–42

empirical reality of, **18:** 68

evaluation and choice, **16:** 45–46

as exchange, **1:** 460–61; **10:** 29–31; **11:**
20–24, 58–68; **12:** 442–43; **13:** 16–24,
71–76; **16:** 62–63, 68, 71; **18:** 185–97;
19: 9

exit option in, **18:** 69, 81–82

exploitation in, **16:** 269

fiscal and monetary policy, influence
on, **13:** 439–40

free riders and, **10:** 33, 41

generality in, **11:** 3–16, 65–67; **19:** 352

government, role in business of, **13:** 4

Homo economicus in economic theory
of, **19:** 59

improvement of, **13:** 19

individualistic approach to, **17:** 251–52,
254–55, 260–61, 264, 269–70

inflation and, **8:** 171–72

interactions limited in, **17:** 162

interest and values, as market in, **17:** 166

interest-group theory of, **19:** 59–60

interest in, absence of, **19:** 209

Keynesian economics and, **8:** 95–109

Keynesian model of, **19:** 326

Keynesian neglect of, **14:** 470–71

law and, **11:** 9–11, 66–67

majoritarian, **16:** 319–20, 381; **19:** 352

mapping using federal jurisdictions,
18: 85

market failure, to correct, **19:** 56

market features in, **18:** 81–82

mercantilist-protectionist, **1:** 186–87

modeling by public choice perspective,
13: 18–19

model of unconstrained majoritarian,
12: 443–48

monetary policy and, **8:** 117–25

nonindividualistic view of, **17:** 263

operation of, constitutional constraints
on, **12:** 436–37

opposing conceptions of, **16:** 364–70

ordinary: disregard for, **1:** 174–76; rules
for operation within, **16:** 228–31

ownership rights in, **13:** 74

Platonic, **7:** 3

political agents conceptualized in, **14:**
505

political science and, **7:** 216n. 4

pork-barrel, **11:** 129

as positive sum, **3:** 23; **11:** 32–33

postconstitutionalist politics, **1:** 52–57

as power struggle, **3:** 23

pragmatic, **7:** 213–16

predatory, **13:** 75

predictive model of, **17:** 276–79

predictive theory of, requirements for,
17: 253–54

profit and, **7:** 218

public choice perspective applied to, **13:**
15–16, 18–21

public choice theory, interpretation by,
14: 46

of public debt, **14:** 424–25
public good and, **10:** 46
"publicness" and, **10:** 32–33, 41
realist concept of, **19:** 346
relationship of economics to, **17:** 166
role for, fundamental, **17:** 275
without romance, **1:** 45–59, 60–74,
  75–88, 89–102, 103–15, 421
romantic image of, **19:** 345–47, 353–54
as rules, **1:** 276; **10:** 18–19
within rules, **16:** 229–31
science and, **1:** 230–43; **10:** 27–31, 43–46;
  17: 153–54, 168
scientific, **13:** 14, 68
in social choice theory, **19:** 9
socialist, failure of, **1:** 57–59, 185–86,
  187; **12:** 471–72; **16:** xii, 244; **18:** 90–91,
  107; **19:** 198, 217, 221–23, 227, 249–51,
  261
in socialist philosophy, **18:** 106
social purpose and, **11:** 14–15
time horizons and, **8:** 166
trading process in, **14:** 11
from transcendentalist perspective, **13:**
  174
transfers and, **10:** 127, 129
truth discovery model of, **17:** 268–70
truth in, **1:** 234–37, 242–43; **11:** 4
as truth judgment, **3:** 4; **7:** 20–21, 124;
  16: 18, 175–76, 367–70
unanimity rule in, **13:** 10
United Kingdom, analyses in, **13:** 40–41
U.S., in modern, **16:** 232–33
voluntary cooperation in, **13:** 101
as zero-sum game, **3:** 23, 252
politics, constitutional, **16:** 62–63
  with complex interdependence, **13:**
  406–9
  democratization of, **16:** 230–31
  function in, **17:** 163
  market exchange in, **16:** 249–50
  overriding interest-group, **13:** 405–6

parametric framework of, **16:** 229
perspective, **13:** 19–20
rules within, **14:** 381–82; **17:** 275–76
of a unitary policy, **16:** 232
politics, two-party, **13:** 227–28, 231–37
pollution, **7:** 144 n. 5, 153–55
population, Malthusian theory of, **6:** 7
population migration. *See* migration
pork-barrel politics, **3:** 22; **7:** 197; **11:** 129
positive and normative theory, barrier
  between, **5:** 8
positive economics, **6:** 38
positive science, defined, **1:** 207
positivism, **1:** 191–92, 195–96, 200, 207,
  208–9, 450
  of Buchanan, **17:** 114–15, 117–18,
  121–22
  legal, **7:** 70; **18:** 176, 177
  of Samuels, **17:** 115–17, 122
poverty relief, **15:** 410
power, division of, **3:** xvi
power indices, **13:** 200–207
praexeology (praxiology), **3:** 27–30; **17:**
  32–34
pragmatism, **7:** 208–28
precommitment as constraint, **10:** 81–82
predictions, **1:** xxi, 77, 178, 246–47, 312, 313
  conditions for making, **12:** 7
  in economics, **5:** 3–5; **6:** 37–40; **16:** 353
  from economic science, **19:** 200, 208,
  263–75, 295, 328–29
  Hayek on, **1:** 416; **3:** 7 n. 5, 58 n. 8, 78 n. 6
  individual's responses, related to, **16:**
  403–7
  joint supply and, **5:** 35
  monetary authority, **8:** 123
  monetary constitutions and, **1:** 396–418
  of natural science, **12:** 31–32
  neoclassical, **15:** 345–47
  price-level, **1:** 400–409, 416–18
  public choice and, **13:** 60, 166; **14:** 471
  in rules, **10:** 10–11

predictions (*continued*)
  in science of economic behavior, **12:**
    10–12
  spontaneous order, **17:** 100
  about sustainability of institutions, **16:**
    296–304
  in theory of exchange, **12:** 23
  in theory of externalities, **12:** 135
  trading equilibrium, **5:** 77
  veil of ignorance, from behind, **16:**
    287–91; **17:** 376
  veil-of-ignorance notion, using Rawls's,
    16: 74
preference
  capacities, equal and differing, **17:**
    286–89, 301–2
  in choice behavior, **16:** 156–59
  concealing, **4:** 14, 33, 112–13, 117–22; **5:**
    81; **15:** 186–88, 227–28, 231–32,
    238–39
  constraints, distinct from, **17:** 160 n. 5
  derived, **16:** 158
  equality in, **17:** 283–86
  equal-preferences hypothesis, **17:** 295
  evaluative and cognitive components,
    16: 157
  free riders concealing, **15:** 186–88,
    227–28, 231–32, 238–39
  identity in, **17:** 283
  for impartial rules, **16:** 163
  imposition of, politics used for, **13:**
    414–18
  of individuals in economic theory of
    politics, **13:** 41–44
  individuals' "true," **14:** 61–62, 86–87
  intensity, **3:** 125, 131; **5:** 109, 110, 112
  intertemporal, **14:** 462–64
  lexicographical, ethics of, **15:** 368–73
  majority cycle: in decision for binding,
    13: 186–92; in establishment and
    discontinuance of, **13:** 181–86
  in markets and politics, **3:** 109–12

  median restrictions on, **12:** 37–40, 381;
    13: 199–200
  ordering of, **12:** 5, 7, 18: modification of,
    17: 227–31; restrictions on individual,
    16: 208–10
  in public choice theory, **13:** 174
  in rational choice theory, **16:** 156
  revealed, **3:** 109–12; **13:** 167–68; **16:** 71
  science of economics restricts, **12:**
    35–40
  single-peaked, **13:** 44, 179, 198–99,
    364–65
  subjective values, **16:** 157
  symmetric and asymmetric, **13:** 94–97,
    102–7
  temporary preference theory, **16:** 401–2
  time: choice and, **16:** 399–401; of
    Leviathan, **9:** 116–17; of taxpayer, **9:**
    121–22
  veil of ignorance or uncertainty,
    behind, **15:** 370
  vote buying/selling model, **14:** 13
  in voting behavior, **13:** 156–69
  See also choices
pressure groups, **3:** 22, 282–94
  ethics and, **3:** 293–94
  size of government and, **3:** 285
  See also coalitions, special interest
price, marginal supply (Marshall), **12:**
  67–69
price change, Knight on dilemma of, **12:** 55
price discrimination
  among buyers, **5:** 37–38
  joint supply, analogous to Marshall's
    theory of, **5:** 38
  in joint supply of services, **15:** 214
  marginal, among consumers of public
    goods, **5:** 38
  marginal prices, **12:** 300–301
  in orthodox price theory, **5:** 37
  possibility of, over quantity to a single
    buyer, **5:** 37

in public goods, absence of institutions
to prevent, **5:** 39
among quantities, **5:** 37
quantity discount, as profit-
maximizing, **12:** 204–5
questionability of term, **5:** 38
in tax-prices, **15:** 153–55
trading process, as outcome of, **5:**
37, 39
See also discrimination
price elasticity
of demand, **12:** 219–20, 246–47: in
National Health Service, Britain, **15:**
342–44
in demand and supply, **12:** 254
demand curves, application to, **12:**
246–47
goods and services and, **15:** 343–44
income allocation, in Crusoe model of,
12: 247–50
labor-supply curve, in backbending, **12:**
257
in public finance theory, **15:** 342–43
price level
absolute, **2:** 76–78
debt, effects of, **2:** 75–78
predictability, **1:** 400–409, 416–18
price neutrality, relative, **11:** 151–52
prices
as common denominator of value, **12:**
114–15
equilibrium, **12:** 25
equilibrium analysis, in general, **12:**
56–57
function for the individual, **12:** 114
Hicksian demand curve, in analysis of,
12: 56
homogeneous inputs, theory of pricing
of, **12:** 261
marginal, uniformity in, **12:** 300–302
marginal supply price (Marshall), **12:**
67–69

market: in context of the, **12:** 25; in
idealized, **12:** 114–15
Marshallian demand curve, in analysis
using, **12:** 55
money prices in command economy,
12: 417–20
in monopoly theory, **12:** 221–35
tax-prices, **14:** 39–40, 75, 362: effect of
penalty tax on, **13:** 420–21; in fiscal
exchange contract, **14:** 93–94; to
satisfy preferences, **13:** 413
and wages, controls of, **8:** 93
prices, Lindahl, **11:** 156
prices, political, **16:** 254–59, 261–62
bureaucracy in, role of, **16:** 257–59
effect of, **16:** 257–59
regimes using, characteristics of, **16:** 258
regimes with, bureaucratic discretion
in, **16:** 258
prices, relative, **2:** 75
price setting
for heterogeneous inputs, **12:** 265–69,
276
monopolist, of profit-maximizing, **12:**
227–32
monopolist's, buyers' expectations of,
12: 232–33
monopolist's, model of, **12:** 227–31
multiple price offers, **12:** 302–6
theory of peak load (Steiner, Boiteux),
12: 298–307, 309–10
price stability and unemployment, **8:** 169
price theory
Chicago, **6:** 13
neoclassical, **5:** 77
penalty tax and direct regulation
alternatives, applied to, **13:** 422–23
summary of, **1:** 444
price uniformity, small-number model,
5: 44
pricing
monopsony, **13:** 321

pricing (*continued*)
   multi-part, **13:** 386
   theory of public utility pricing, **13:** 377
pricing, average-cost: public utility, **13:** 373–77, 381–86
pricing, marginal-cost, **6:** 29 n. 23
   public utility, **13:** 317–23, 373–83
pricing rules and cost, **6:** 31
prisoners' dilemma, **1:** 217–18, 266, 321, 362, 422–23, 435; **5:** 95, **7:** 35, 37, 84, 211; **9:** 23; **10:** 5–8; **11:** 31–32, 55, 89, 93, 96, 98
   economic and noneconomic behavior, **12:** 132–33
   in exchange relationship, **17:** 90–91
   externalities in, Pareto-relevant and -irrelevant, **17:** 217–18
   of Gauthier's rational morality, **17:** 461–62
   in incumbency, **13:** 284–87
   incumbency analogue to, **13:** 295–96
   in labor negotiations, **17:** 91
   large-number, **5:** 95
   laws, change of rules to reform, **12:** 288–89
   majority rule voting in setting of, **13:** 91–94
   in market exchange, **17:** 87–89, 90–91
   n-person analogue to, **5:** 10
   payoff structure, **12:** 13–18: classical, **13:** 348–49; with collective action, **16:** 150–52; nonsymmetrical, **13:** 349–50; symmetrical, **13:** 348–49; in two-person/two-strategy, **16:** 149–50
   without personal overtones, **5:** 84
   policy norms, in derivation of, **12:** 13–18
   preferences: illustrating restrictions on, **12:** 37–40; with symmetric and asymmetric individual, **13:** 94–110
   preform regulatory setting in, **16:** 422
   public good benefits, of individuals sharing, **15:** 227–43

rent-seeking behavior, applied to, **13:** 350–52
rules: individual departure from, **16:** 92–95; institutional, change in, **12:** 287–92; nonsymmetrical, **14:** 274–78
Smith's system of natural liberty, interpretation of, **12:** 431–32
standard illustration, **16:** 411
tax competition and, **9:** 200
in trade or exchange relationship, **17:** 87–89
voluntary exchange of rights in, **16:** 206–9
private bads, **1:** 236
private behavior
   under corporation income tax, **4:** 46–50
   under general sales tax, **4:** 50–52
   under personal income tax, **4:** 30–36, 38–43
   under specific excise tax, **4:** 52–54
   tax-price of, effect on, **4:** 16, 25–28
private choice, outcomes different from public choice, **14:** 478–79
private-cost–social-cost analysis, **1:** 70 n. 11
private debt, **2:** 5, 8, 26, 38–57, 149–51
private economy compared with public economy, **8:** 130–31
private goods, **1:** 136, 236, 326–27; **5:** 3
   as collective goods, **4:** 21
   costs to collectivize, **13:** 455
   defined, in identifiable units, **5:** 50
   equilibrium marginal prices of, in neoclassical setting, **5:** 32
   gains-from-trade in, **15:** 472–75
   impure, **5:** 49, 163–64
   individual demand curve for, derivation of, **5:** 38–39
   as numeraire, **5:** 74–75, 96–97, 107
   as public goods, **5:** 49–50, 65
   public goods, compared with, **1:** 361
   public provision of, **15:** 322–26
   pure, **5:** 70, **15:** 267, 271–73

pursuit of, **15:** 303–7
redistribution as, **15:** 483
rival and excludable, **15:** xii
private goods and services: consumption
   exchanges, private nonjoint, **15:** 211
privatization
   classical economics for, argument of,
     19: 292
   of the commons, **18:** 216, 217, 220–21
   the commons, tragedy of: rules change
     to overcome, **12:** 289–92
   in former socialized economies, **19:**
     191–92
   process of, **18:** 97–98
probabilistic distributional formulas, **11:**
   179
probability
   of choice under cognitive certainty, **12:**
     145–49
   entrepreneurial choice, in
     understanding, **12:** 150–51
   Shackle on, **12:** 147
probability of rights, **7:** 64
probability theory, **1:** 23
producer interests
   capture of regulatory agency by, **13:**
     322–23
   cartel restrictions, for government
     enforcement of, **13:** 389–99
   with general inflation, **13:** 323–26
   seeking politicized protection, **13:** 388–91
   in theory of public regulation, **13:** 319–20
producer liability
   accident differentials in, **18:** 358–63
   assignment of, **18:** 363–64
   strict, economic rationale for, **18:** 364–68
production
   consumer or household, **16:** 157–58
   consumption and, **1:** 161, 346–47,
     348–49, 415; **5:** 33; **19:** 221–25
   in deer-beaver model, **15:** 159–67
   effort attributes, **19:** 224

exchange equivalent to, **12:** 116
factors of: allocation in, **12:** 311–26;
   heterogeneous inputs, model of, **12:**
   262–65; homogenization of
   heterogeneous, **12:** 265–69; team
   production with, **12:** 269–72 (*see also*
   labor supply)
goods and services, in private exchange
   of, **15:** 211
of government services, **11:** 149–50
heterogeneous input (*see* inputs,
   heterogeneous)
of joint supply, **15:** 212–14, 217–22
joint supply theory, in Marshallian, **15:**
   212–14
in market exchange, **19:** 229–31
in public goods theory, **15:** 274
under socialism, **19:** 221–23, 226–29,
   231–37
value created by, **19:** 223–24, 234, 268
See also output
production economy, efficient: Stolper-
   Samuelson condition, **15:** 166
production function, **7:** 72
   monopolistic competition, in model of,
     12: 390–91
   substitutable heterogeneous inputs, **12:**
     275
production team, **12:** 269–72, 356
production units, **15:** 267, 274
productive state, **1:** 52; **7:** 88–90, 121,
   123–25; **11:** 143–45. *See also* protective
   state
productivity, internal and external, **14:**
   234–35
products, external and internal marginal,
   14: 235 n. 8
profits
   of entrepreneur, **12:** 163, 166
   in entrepreneurial choice, **12:** 151–52
   factor returns (Knight), distinct from,
     12: 142

profits (*continued*)
  inflation and, **8:** 68
  Knight's explanation of, **19:** 87
  maximization, standard criterion for,
    12: 219
  monopoly, **12:** 207, 211–15
  opportunity cost and, **6:** 28
  political, **7:** 218
  potential, emergence in markets of, **19:**
    106
profit seeking. *See* rent seeking
progressive tax, **1:** 129–30, 148, 198; **9:** 44,
    54–55, 227–28
  choice calculus and, **4:** 38–42, 148–66,
    227–42
  constant-share, **4:** 39
  constitutional choice and, **4:** 227–42
  equality before law and, **9:** 185
  fiscal illusion and, **4:** 139
  Flint v. Stone Tracy Co., **18:** 18 n. 28
  full neutrality and, **4:** 153–54
  ignorance of tax liability under, **4:**
    38–43
  inflation and, **8:** 72, 147 nn. 17,18
  institutional choice of, **4:** 227–42,
    250–51
  model, **4:** 240–42; **14:** 197–211
  redistribution under, **4:** 227–28, 238–40
  revenue potential, **9:** 58
  rule of law and, **9:** 223
  uncertainty and, choice between, **4:**
    236–38
prohibitionists, **11:** 65
property
  common: government role related to,
    15: 13–15; implicit ownership to, **15:**
    309–18
  commons as, **18:** 216, 220–22
  economics of, **7:** 29, 69 n. 1
  laws to protect, **15:** 286
  liberty and, relationship between, **18:**
    222–26
  property law as enacted by Virginia
    legislature, **18:** 343–46, 353–55
  public, public policy to conserve, **15:** 319
  See also commons, the; liberty
property, private
  Aristotelian defense of, **1:** 319; **6:** 87
  asset accumulation, **18:** 245–47
  as asset yielding money income, **18:**
    244–45
  defense of, *Rerum Novarum*, **18:** 252–54
  liberty with, protection of, **18:** 240, 246,
    258–59
  money or money claims, protection of,
    18: 247–49
  ownership of: incentives with, **19:** 360;
    necessity of, **18:** 256–57; self-
    production with, **18:** 241–44;
    specialization with, **18:** 230
  protection of, **1:** 343
  under socialism, **18:** 249–51, 254
  social rent in, **18:** 220–21
property rights, **11:** 84
  anarchy, distribution under, **7:** 31–32,
    19: 174
  assignment of: under Coase theorem,
    12: 291, 293–94; **13:** 300; in
    determining alternative institutions,
    15: 176–88; effect of inefficient, **15:**
    286–87; enforcement and, **18:** 370–73,
    19: 360–61; value of, **13:** 411–13
  bureaucratic behavior, relation to, **13:**
    48–49
  in club theory, adjustment for
    exclusion, **15:** 208–9
  in Coase theorem, **13:** 300; **15:** 174–75
  collective action, with and without, **13:**
    304–5
  conflict over, potential for, **13:** 411–13
  constitutional protection of, **16:** 260,
    364
  in constitutional structure, **16:** 260
  defined, values with, **17:** 163–64

disarmament and, **7:** 76–77

economics of, **1:** 260–77, 383; **15:** 288 n. 12; **16:** 8, 107–8; **17:** 61: Knight's introduction of, **19:** 16, 82

efficiency and, **7:** 27–28

enforcement of, **5:** 172: community's role in, **18:** 379–81; erosion of, conditions for, **18:** 377–79; investment required for, **18:** 373–77; nominal and actual, **18:** 373–77

evolution of, **11:** 93–94

exchange, basis for, **7:** 22–24

externality and, **7:** 30–31; **15:** 20, 27–28

functions, **7:** 13–14

government and, **7:** 107; **15:** 13–15

incentives in economics of, **19:** 235–36

institutions, proposed modification of, **15:** 306–7

law and, **7:** 22–24

laws define, **15:** 28

legal structure defines market power of, **15:** 10–11

in legal system, **15:** 7

in modern economic system, **14:** 278–79

in natural distribution of goods, **16:** 91–96

origins, **7:** 12–15, 29–30, 33–35

Pareto-relevance under assignments of, **18:** 370–73

partial redefinition, **15:** 29

penalty tax, change under, **13:** 425

in Pigovian framework, **12:** 18

protected by property rule, **12:** 175

protection for, **18:** 236, 239

protection of private rights under U.S. Constitution, **17:** 305

public, **7:** 224; **17:** 297–98, 306–9

reform to establish or reassign, **12:** 289–92

rents in orthodox theory of, **13:** 266–67

scarce resources, function in allocation of, **18:** 38

social cost (Coase), in theory of, **12:** 170, 172

in status quo, **7:** 111–15

structure of, **5:** 167–68; **16:** 99

trades and exchanges with specified, **17:** 112

trading of, **13:** 304

value of, **18:** 236–37

in voting franchise, **13:** 147

voting right as, **13:** 147

See also Coase theorem; exclusion rights; ownership rights; rights

property rule

bargaining under, **12:** 171

defined, **13:** 301 n. 2

entitlements protected by (Coase), **12:** 170–76

established and enforced, setting of, **13:** 300–301

institutionalization of, **12:** 178–82

liability rule (Calabresi-Melamed), differences from, **12:** 170–72

social cost theory, protection under, **12:** 172–74

in valuation of a life, **12:** 280

property tax, **9:** 229–31; **16:** 104

proportional tax, **1:** 129; **4:** 30–38, 48–66

Hayek's conception of, **14:** 196, 250–51, 257–58

Proposition 13 (California), **1:** 58; **9:** xxi, 31, 221, 229–31

limits on property tax, **16:** 104

rules limiting new tax enactment, **16:** 311–12

protection, legal

for property and property rights, **16:** 260, 364

of voluntary exchange, **16:** 39–40

protectionist-mercantilist regime

interventions in markets under, **19:** 315

with majoritarian democracy, **19:** 316

protective state, **1:** 52; **7:** 88–90, 121–23; **10:** 26
  defined, **7:** 121
  democracy and, **7:** 90
  legislation and, **7:** 89
  as referee, **7:** 121–23
  See also productive state
public bads, **1:** 236; **5:** 129
  disorder and, **7:** 11
  environmental quality, **7:** 153–54
  erosion of order, **7:** 153
  failure to eliminate, **15:** 301–2
  generation without collective action, **15:** 310
  laws as, **15:** 288
  liberty as, restrictions on, **15:** 290
  political interference with trade as, **15:** 289
  private goods, produced from pursuit of, **15:** 304–5
  public goods and, **18:** 447: erosion of, **15:** 302; reciprocity of, **15:** 301, 309–11; trade-off among, **16:** 412
  rule breaking, **7:** 20
  tax evasion, **7:** 152–53
  theory of, **7:** 11
public capital, **16:** 321–23
  constitutions as, **7:** 156–60
  laws as, **7:** 136–64; **18:** 340–41
  moral constraints as, **14:** 461
  tax system as, **14:** 269–83
public choice, **3:** ix; **9:** 35–36; **11:** xxi, 19, 27–29, 36–37, 67–68, 72–73, 120
  administrative-decision model, **13:** 307
  of benevolent political agents in, **19:** 333–34
  Buchanan's approach to, criticism of, **17:** 129–31
  contribution of, **16:** 12–13
  defined, **8:** 131; **13:** 39; **19:** 8, 44
  fiscal institutions, effects of, **14:** 18–19, 28–30
  future direction, **13:** 60

individual behavior with externality as, **13:** 29–30
  internationalization of (1970s), **19:** 44–45
  Keynesian policy and, **8:** 96
  model of government, **9:** 18
  political actors, influence on, **13:** 82–85
  political institutions, effects of, **14:** 19–20, 30–31
  politics as exchange, **16:** 71
  private choice, outcomes different from, **14:** 478–79
  United Kingdom, ideas neglected in, **13:** 40–41, 54
Public Choice (journal), **3:** xiii; **19:** 57
public choice analysis, **11:** 29
  institutional arrangements, **13:** 164–68
  multi-issue space, **13:** 195n. 1
  political behavior, **14:** 490; **16:** 152, 154; **19:** 314
  political decisions rules, **16:** 105–7
  political institutions, **12:** 100
  predictions of, **13:** 60, 166
  public finance in, **14:** 20–24
  Samuelsonian, **11:** 155
  social interaction, **13:** 173
  social security system, U.S., **15:** 446
  view of politics, **13:** 85
public choice economists, **11:** 19. *See also* economists; political economists, role of
Public Choice Society, **1:** 19; **3:** xiii; **19:** 44, 57
public choice theory, **1:** 4, 45–59, 156; **8:** 7–8; **9:** 8–9
  analysis of, **17:** 61
  applicability, **1:** 21
  Buchanan's interest in, **1:** xv–xvi, 3–5, 19–21, 45–59
  Calculus of Consent and, **1:** 19
  catallactics approach to economics, **13:** 15–21
  constitutional approach, **14:** 34–35
  constitutional economics and, **1:** 377–95

constitutionalist-contractarian position, **13:** 176
in constitutional perspective, **13:** 87–89
of constitutions, **1:** 51–52
constraints and, **1:** 462–65
contribution of, **19:** 56
contributions to, **1:** 16
controversy related to, **13:** 80
criticism of (Musgrave), **14:** 66–67
decision making, mode of, **1:** 136, 138–40; **13:** 29
defined, **1:** 47–48, 114; **13:** 53, 86, 153, 170; **19:** 8–9
explanatory power of, **13:** 38
of government failure, **13:** 59, 113–14, 173; **15:** 288n. 13
Hobbes's influence on, **19:** xvi
Hobbes's view, compatible with, **13:** 175
Homo economicus aspect, **12:** 85–86; **13:** 15–16, 21–24, 118–21
impact of, **12:** 357
implications, **12:** 292–93; **19:** 343
individual behavior in, **13:** 26, 29–30, 174
in Japan, **1:** 419
lessons of, **16:** 353
Leviathan and, **1:** 57–59
markets and politics, conditions for failure of, **12:** 432
Marxism, compared to, **13:** 174–75
methodological individualism, **1:** 24, 48–49, 390–91, 456, 457–58
methodological thrust, **13:** 118–19
Nobel Memorial Prize for, **1:** 3–5
noncontract, nonauction methods of regulation, **13:** 261–62
normative implications, **1:** 47; **19:** 61
people at margins, actions of, **14:** 479
policy instruments, individual's choice of, **13:** 419–32
political business cycles in, **13:** 51–52
political economy: divorced from, **19:** 56–57; as subdiscipline of, **14:** 265; **16:** 7–8, 46, 85, 105–7

political failure and, **1:** 21, 45, 46; **19:** 56–57, 276
political outcomes, emergence of, **13:** 408–9
of politics, **13:** 18–19, 39–40, 419; **14:** 46; **16:** 80; **19:** 59–60, 346
predictive, **15:** 391
predictive model of politics in, **17:** 276–79
predictive science of politics, **13:** 164–68
property rights and, **1:** 276
public consumption, prediction about financing of, **14:** 471
public debt different from taxation, **14:** 476–77
public finance and, **1:** 54; **14:** 25–27
public interest and, **1:** 275
rational ignorance hypothesis, **16:** 132–34
reform implications emerging from, **16:** 46–47
rent seeking in, **19:** 63
romantic illusions, exposing, **17:** 467
rules, attention and emphasis on, **13:** 20
social choice theory, differences from, **19:** 8–9
social evolution view, compatible with, **13:** 175–76
socialism, and failure of, **1:** 185
social security provision and financing, **14:** 22–24
as subdiscipline of economics, **1:** 15–16, 19–21, 45–46, 296, 455–57, 459–60
Tax Reform Act (1986), normative evaluation of, **14:** 52–53
utility maximization in, **13:** 174
voting in, paradox of, **13:** 42–43, 119, 228n. 3
voting rules and, **1:** 50
welfare economics and, **1:** 296
Wicksell's influence on, **1:** 4, 5, 456–57, 459, 460, 461, 465–66; **13:** 20–21, 40–41; **19:** xvi–xvii, 4, 24, 140–41, 245

public choice theory (*continued*)
  See also bureaucracy; business cycles; individual choice; politics; rent seeking
public debt, **2:** 13; **9:** 122–26; **17:** 88–89
  abnormal expenditure and, **2:** 129
  amortization, **8:** 18–19
  analysis, **2:** 115–16
  anti-inflation, **2:** 111–14
  banking system, sold to, **2:** 104
  budget deficit used to finance, **4:** 107–8, 272
  burden of (*see* public debt burden)
  capital and, **11:** 135–37; **14:** 375–76
  capital outlay and, **2:** 121; **8:** 11, 18–19
  in classical economic theory, **2:** 26; **8:** 16–18; **13:** 443–44
  classification, **2:** 18
  collective choice and, **2:** 119–29
  cost and, **6:** 59–63
  cost of serving, annual, **2:** 134
  creation, issue, and retirement of, **14:** 343–44, 350
  creation of, **1:** 172; **4:** 107–8, 272; **6:** 59–63; **14:** 351 (*see also* budget deficit)
  currency outstanding, distinct from, **14:** 343
  current consumption, creation to finance, **14:** 369, 376–77, 458, 490
  debt/GNP ratio, irrelevance of, **14:** 477
  debt instruments of, **14:** 346–47, 357–58
  default, **13:** 442–43; **14:** 378–80, 469–70, 519–20
  defined, **1:** 151
  deflation and, **2:** 112
  depression and, **2:** 95–103
  domestic, **2:** 13–14
  economic policy and, **4:** 265
  economic theory and, **8:** 21–22
  external, **2:** 9–10, 11, 26, 58–66; **4:** 274–75, 279, 281; **9:** 125–26
  extraordinary outlay and, **9:** 124
  financing of, **1:** xviii, 6, 150–63, 172, 176; **14:** 455
  fiscal choice, effect on, **4:** 98–101
  fiscal device, creation as, **14:** 360
  fiscal illusion, **4:** 131–32: cost theory and, **1:** xviii, 150–63, 467
  fiscal policy, relation to, **14:** 349–50
  future burdens and, **8:** 12, 15
  future generations and, **8:** 20: claims against, **14:** 441; effect on, **12:** 211–12
  future tax liabilities in, **14:** 352–55, 357–64
  general theory of, **2:** 95
  governmental or quasi-governmental agencies, held by, **14:** 347–48
  idle balances and, **2:** 98
  illusion caused by, **4:** 266
  incentives and, **8:** 144–47
  individual shares, **2:** 154–55
  inflation and, **2:** 24, 111–14; **14:** 380, 452–53
  institutional choice of, **4:** 258–68
  interest charges on, **14:** 344, 519
  internal, **2:** 8–9, 26
  internal and external, **14:** 353–55, 433
  internally and externally held, servicing, **14:** 348
  investment expenditure and, **2:** 128
  involuntary transfer and, **2:** 104
  issue of, effects of, **14:** 362–63
  before Keynes's ideas, **14:** 365–67, 477
  life cycle and, **8:** 145–46
  limits, **4:** 100; **8:** 20, 146–47; **9:** 123
  liquidity and, **2:** 112
  local government, **4:** 100–101
  for long-term projects, **2:** 122
  management, **2:** 134; **14:** 348–49
  "marginal," **2:** 67–68
  maturity structure, **8:** 60n. 5
  measurement, **2:** 154–59; **14:** 344–46
  modern theory of, **13:** 444–46

monetary aspects, **2:** 66

monetary policy, associated with, **13:** 442–43

monetization of, **2:** 144–48; **8:** 116, 189; **14:** 349–51, 360

as money creation, **2:** 99, 101, 104–5, 132; **8:** 147

moneyness, **2:** 78, 132, 155–59

monopoly, **12:** 211–15

national government, **4:** 101–3

national income and (Domar), **2:** 139

orthodoxy, criticism of, **1:** 19

in overlapping-generations model, **14:** 386–87

ownership, **14:** 347–48

permanence, **14:** 377

for "physical" project, **2:** 128

planning horizon and, **4:** 265

principles of, **13:** 443; **14:** 350–51, 361

private debt and, analogy between, **2:** 5, 8, 26, 38–57; **14:** 369–70

productivity, **2:** 16

public choice theory of, **14:** 475–77

public debt illusion, converse of, **4:** 266–68

purchasing power and, reduction in, **2:** 111

pure, **2:** 27, 66, 78, 132 n. 6, 155, 158 n. 7, 159

recurring expenditure and, **2:** 129

retirement (*see* public debt, retirement of)

revaluation, **2:** 149–63

Ricardian equivalence theorem, **14:** 393, 477–79, 491

of selected countries, **14:** 344–46

for short-term projects, **2:** 120

size, **2:** 134

taxation: and borrowing, equivalence of, **14:** 436–38; difference from, **13:** 445–46; **14:** 476; equivalence of, **13:** 445

taxes to service, **2:** 127

tax imposition, to alter timing of, **14:** 394–403

taxing power and, **9:** 123

temporal effects, **8:** 20–21; **10:** 104–6

theory of, **1:** 119–32, 133–49, 150–63, 164–78, 179–88; **14:** 475–77: burden and cost, **8:** 36 n. 11; "classical," **2:** 9–10, 81; cost, **1:** xviii, 150–63, 467; **8:** 143 n. 14; general, **2:** 95; Keynesian, **8:** 16, 142–43; **14:** 445–46; modern, **13:** 444–46; pre-Keynesian, **2:** 79–94; **14:** 511

uncertainty and, **4:** 263–64

of U.S., **14:** 343, 346–47

as voluntary transfer, **2:** 104

war, **2:** 104–10

See also budget deficit; deficit finance; private debt; public debt issue; Ricardian equivalence theorem

public debt, default on

argument against, **14:** 521–22

capital value, effect on, **14:** 378–80

effect of, **14:** 378–80, 519–20

through inflationary financing, **14:** 380

through repudiation, **14:** 470

risk premium, **14:** 531–32

public debt, retirement of: **2:** 134–42; **8:** 18–19, 189–90; **11:** 138–39; **13:** 446–47

bank-held debt, **2:** 143–44

conceptual, **2:** 155–59

de Viti de Marco's model, **2:** 92–94

diminishing marginal utility and, **2:** 138–39

economic growth and, **2:** 140–42

economic stabilization and, **2:** 143–48

equity grounds, **2:** 137–38

of existing public debt, **14:** 376–78

Federal Reserve held, **2:** 112

financing, **2:** 134–35

net worth and, **2:** 93

revenue surplus, by generation of, **14:** 469

public debt (*continued*)
  for self-liquidating projects, **2:** 127–28
  stabilization and, **2:** 143–48
public debt burden, **1:** 150–63, 467–68; **8:** 16–21, 142–43; **14:** 369
  borne by individuals, **15:** 86–88
  denial in Keynesian economic theory, **19:** 29
  disappointed borrowers and, **2:** 5, 6, 7, 8–9, 12–14, 26, 27–28, 32, 34, 73, 81, 98, 107–8
  goods and services, as sacrifice of, **15:** 86
  Keynesian theory, **14:** 475
  postponement, **14:** 362–64
  secondary, **2:** 7, 13–14
  temporal shift of, restricted, **14:** 442
public debt financing
  intergenerational effects, **14:** 496–97
  intergenerational transfer with, **14:** 532
  private investment by, crowding out of, **14:** 448–50
public debt issue
  alternatives to, **1:** 76–77, 81–82; **2:** 22
  under Barro neutrality, **14:** 409–13
  Barro's analysis, **14:** 386–90
  of classical public finance theory, **14:** 511
  to finance budget deficits, **14:** 390
  future taxes, **14:** 390, 394
  of Keynesian theory, **14:** 475
  long-term public projects, **2:** 122, 126–27
  money creation and, **1:** 170, 171–72, 173, 174
  objective costs, **1:** 153–56, 159, 160
  postponement of burden with, **14:** 362–64
  postponement of transfer of resource services, **14:** 352–55
  of Ricardian equivalence theorem, **14:** 409
  short-term public projects, **2:** 120

public debt orthodoxy, Tullock on analysis of, **1:** 19
public economy
  private economy and, compared, **8:** 130–31
  theory of, **5:** 6–11
public expenditure, **1:** 119, 120–22, 198; **9:** 190–92
  benefits of, **4:** 189–94
  bureaucracy, carried out by the, **15:** 33–35
  as capital investment, **14:** 370–73
  change in composition of U.S. (1960–75), **15:** 441
  constraints on, **14:** 260–61
  cost of, **14:** 357–62
  financing: through borrowing, **14:** 373–75, 446–47; with debt, **14:** 446–47; methods, **14:** 351, 353–54; by public loans, **14:** 357–58; by taxation, borrowing, and money creation, **14:** 352–55, 357–64
  generality in, **14:** 257–58
  increases, **14:** 476; **15:** 441
  in Italian fiscal theory, **15:** 75–79, 81–83
  Keynesian aggregation fallacies, **14:** 352–55, 373–75
  recurring, **2:** 129
  Ricardian theorem, in terms of, **14:** 476–77
  state-local, **8:** 58 n. 2
  transfer payment share of U.S., **15:** 441–42
  unproductive, **2:** 66, 81
  on welfare, **15:** 455–56
  See also government spending
public expenditure theory, **2:** 116–19
  with market failure, **15:** xi–xv
  of Samuelson, **15:** 124, 144
public finance, **1:** xvii–xviii, 15, 17–18, 20, 119–32, 134
  continental tradition in, **5:** 181–82

exchange paradigm and, theory of, **1:** 24
Italian tradition in, **1:** 20
after Marshall, **14:** 4–5, 22
neoclassical, **5:** 156–57
normative theory of, **5:** 182–86
orthodox, **1:** 15, 16
orthodoxy in, departure from, **5:** 6
positive analysis in, domain for, **14:**
    20–24, 27–35
positive theory of, **5:** 180, 182, 188–89
public choice theory in, origins of, **14:**
    25–27
pure voluntary exchange theory of, **5:** 10
Wicksell's contribution, **14:** 62–63
See also public debt; public debt issue;
    public sector; taxation
public finance, traditional
    description of, **4:** 5–6
    excess burden analysis of, **4:** 43, 54–55
    income tax progression and, **4:** 228
    individual choice in, **4:** 215
    individualist and democratic model
        and, **4:** 282
    rehabilitation of, **4:** 223–26
public finance theory, **13:** 44
    branch of scholarship, as separate, **15:**
        60–62
    classical Italian tradition, **15:** 60
    constitutions (voting rules), **14:** 13–14
    deficit financing, **19:** 204
    demand in, price elasticity of, **15:** 342–43
    European, **14:** 26
    Italian, **14:** 14–15, 155–56; **19:** 32–36
    Keynesian, **19:** 60
    of Musgrave, **14:** 54–68
    normative: Hutt, **19:** 141–46;
        Samuelson, **14:** 64–65; Wicksell-
        Buchanan, **19:** 140–43
    of Pigou, **14:** 91, 121
    post-Pigovian normative, **14:** 5, 8, 13, 121
    public debt (Buchanan), **19:** 28–30
    transformation of U.S., **14:** 8–17

voting, **14:** 11–13
    before World War II, **14:** 65
public goods, **1:** 70–71, 73, 154–56; **3:** 34–35;
    5: 3; **9:** 31, 33–34, 191; **11:** 27, 29–30, 50n.
    4, 58, 69–70, 143–46; **17:** 274
    allocation, **12:** 155–58
    all purely public, **15:** 221n. 15, 265–67,
        271–73
    basic theory of, extension of, **5:** 62,
        161–62
    behavior in production of, **5:** 24
    buyers of substitute, **18:** 203–4
    cases of, between polar limits, **5:** 55
    choice, unidimensional, **16:** 209–10
    classification, **13:** 451n. 1
    club-like arrangements, provided by, **5:**
        167
    club setting of, sharing in, **15:** 195–207
    collective goods and services, **1:** 70–71,
        73, 154–56
    collectively chosen, quantity of:
        corporation income tax, effect on, **4:**
        48–49; general-fund financing, effect
        on, **4:** 82–84; public debt issuance,
        effect on, **4:** 100–101; tax and
        spending decisions, effect on
        separation of, **4:** 96
    collective provision of, **18:** 24, 94
    complementary and substitute relations
        among, **5:** 96, 102–4, 106, 113
    consumption components in, **5:** 55
    consumption of, **5:** 121; **14:** 39–41, 75–76
    contract and, **7:** 40–41
    cost of, **5:** 31, 85–88, 123; **6:** 49–64; **14:** 75
    cost-sharing schemes of, **5:** 37, 121, 147,
        150
    cost-shifting of, **5:** 123
    demand and supply of, **14:** 9–10, 14–16,
        75–83: process of equilibrium in, **5:**
        11; in the simplest model, **3:** 36; **5:** 12,
        142 (*see also* equilibrium)
    democracy and, **7:** 217

public goods (*continued*)
  differential marginal prices for, **5:** 32,
    36–37, 121
  at different locations, **5:** 56, 58
  divisibility, **13:** 452
  efficient provision (Musgrave), **18:**
    26–27
  efficient supply of, determination of,
    5: 44
  enforcement and, **7:** 86–87
  in entrepreneurial process, **18:** 299
  equal availability of, defined, **5:** 52
  equilibrium supply of, error in locating,
    5: 42
  erosion of, **15:** 302
  exchange, **7:** 46
  excludability, absence of, **15:** 5
  first law of demand, application of, **5:**
    121, 122
  fiscal differentials even with efficiency
    (Buchanan), **18:** 26
  fiscal structures (Tiebout), in
    multilevel, **18:** 26
  gains-from-trade: in local, **15:** 475–77; in
    national, **15:** 478–82
  generality and, **11:** 58
  generalization of model of, **5:** 49, 53, 55,
    62, 72
  goods consumed in common, **15:** xii
  government as provider of, **15:** 303; **18:**
    4–7, 35–42
  impure, **4:** 18–21; **5:** 21, 46, 48, 51, 52, 56,
    60, 62–64, 70, 84, 152, 178; **11:** 144–48;
    18: 24, 35–36, 54: public provision of,
    15: 330–35
  income elasticity of, **5:** 14, 152
  indeterminacy in model of, **5:** 36
  individual demand schedule for,
    derivation of, **5:** 38–41, 44, 137–38
  indivisibility in, **5:** 70, 71, 87, 163–65, 176
  interdependence of, behavior in
    ignorance of, **5:** 29

joint consumption, advantages of, **13:**
    459–61
joint-supply characteristic of, **5:** 33, 46
large-number model, extension to, **5:**
    75–84 passim, 98–99, 113–17, 166–67
law and, **7:** 137–40
law enforcement as, **18:** 434n. 4
legal system as, **15:** 6
liberty as free good, **18:** 204–7
local, provision of, **18:** 44–64, 148
lumpiness in, **5:** 87
majority coalition, financed by, **16:** 271
markets to produce, failure in, **15:**
    301–2
mix of: under fixed proportions, **5:**
    57–59, 67; under variable
    proportions, **5:** 59–63, 67
multidimensional nature of, **5:** 54
natural liberty as, **15:** 290–92
neglect of, by socialist theorists, **5:**
    180–81
nonexcludability of, **9:** 191; **15:** 208
nonpolar, **5:** 48–49, 72
nonreciprocal supply of, **15:** 245–50
n-person trade in, **5:** 81
opportunity cost and, **6:** 52–55
optimality, conditions for: in mix of, **5:**
    59; in supply of, **5:** 22, 59, 122–23, 128,
    182
optimal sharing of, **15:** 194
order, **7:** 10
oversupply of, **5:** 179
polar, **5:** 48, 71–72, 162, 174
political exchange in model of, **18:**
    186–87
preferences, **14:** 61–62
pricing structure of, **5:** 121
private decisions and, **5:** 123
private goods and, compared, **13:**
    453–55
private goods features, exhibiting,
    18: 49

public bads and, reciprocity of, **15:** 301, 309–11
pure, **4:** 11–18; **5:** 21, 35, 48, 51, 58, 62, 70, 97, 101, 102, 116, 117, 152, 160, 163, 170, 171, 173, 174; **15:** 5
purely collective, public provision of, **15:** 326–30
questions about, **13:** 125–26
range of, **9:** 206–10
reciprocal supply of, **15:** 250–56
redistribution: as local, **15:** 483–84; as national, **15:** 486
revenue requirements and, **9:** 78
revolution as, **7:** 19
rival and excludable, degrees of, **15:** xii–xiii
rules, **7:** 20
Samuelsonian, **9:** 191; **11:** 29–30, 55, 74, 189, 203; **15:** xiii–xiv; **18:** 25, 31, 45, 51
seceding unit, provided by, **18:** 150
security to claims, **7:** 87
Smith's conception of, **15:** 283–88
Smith's laws and institutions as, **15:** 286
supply analysis, **13:** 46–49
supply of: and demand for, theory of, **14:** 9–10, 15–16, 31–32, 75–83; reciprocal and nonreciprocal, **15:** 250–56; under unanimity, **5:** 88
tax-price of, **14:** 75–83
technology of, **5:** 54
trade in, prospect for, **5:** 30
transfer of income to the poor as, **13:** 130
user pricing of, **4:** 19–21; **5:** 171–72
with variable mix, **5:** 56
Wicksellian contribution to theory of, **5:** 93
Wicksellian solution to allocation of, **5:** 128, 131, 135
See also publicness
public goods and services, **14:** 230–31
final, **15:** 42–48, 53

government supply of divisible, **15:** 342–43
intermediate, **15:** 52–53: evaluation of, **15:** 42–48; excluded from estimates of national product, **15:** 48–51
theory of supply, **1:** 53, 56, 352
public goods–ethical choice models, **1:** 325
public goods models, **15:** 229–39
public goods theory, **1:** xviii, 20, 119–33, 138, 146, 160, 192, 238, 271, 323–24; **4:** 285–89; **7:** 11, 46–68
classification of, **1:** 326–27
Coase neutrality theorem, **13:** 302–3
constraints, dimensionality and convexity, **15:** 277n. 8
dilemma, **1:** 363, 365
external economy or diseconomy in, **15:** 217–18
laws and institutions in, **15:** 284–88
local government finance, applied to, **5:** 178
Marshallian joint supply theory, as extension of, **15:** 262
modern, **5:** 22, 27, 59, 117, 120, 140, 144, 160, 176, 182
normative, **5:** 182–89
orthodox, **5:** 48, 69
positive, **5:** 180, 186–89
production and consumption units in, **15:** 274
relevance of, **5:** 49
Samuelsonian efficiency, **1:** 136, 137, 426
services and, **1:** 154–56
Wicksell-Lindahl, **15:** 292
public interest, **3:** 12, 14, 19 n. 3, 99, 275, 283–85, 308; **4:** 221–22; **7:** 127; **11:** 19, 44; **13:** 107
public loans, internal and external, **2:** 58–66
publicness
degree of, **5:** 72, 164–65
free riders and, **10:** 160

publicness (*continued*)
  organizational policy implication of, **5:** 161
  in organization of supply, **5:** 120
  partial, **5:** 169
  of political decisions, **5:** 120
  politics and, **10:** 32–33, 41
  pure, world of, **5:** 96
  See also public goods
public policy
  agreement on and within rules, **16:** 73–74
  choice of, organizational forms for, **13:** 464–65
  constitutional policy actions, analysis of alternative, **16:** 331–33
  constitutional political economy, applications from, **19:** 60
  economic theory: analysis of alternative policies, **16:** 331–32; deriving policy using, **12:** 13–18
  economists' role in, **16:** 101–2
  external diseconomies, **13:** 420–32
  monopoly problem implications for, **12:** 216–18
  ordering of options for, **19:** 332–43
  Pigovian norms, **12:** 18–19
  Smithian, **12:** 18
  state-level tax, **12:** 238–41
  See also economic policy; fiscal policy; monetary policy
public sector
  inefficiency of shift of rights to, **13:** 314–15
  normative theory of, **5:** 11, 162
  size of, **3:** 200–209: and inflation, **8:** 71–73; side payments and, **3:** 208–9; special interest groups and, **3:** 285
  See also bureaucracy; discretion, bureaucratic; government; public finance; public goods

public services
  demand for, **11:** 141–42
  discriminatory pricing with, **15:** 152–53
  needs for, **4:** 90–91
  as productive factors (de Viti–Einaudi), **15:** 73–79, 81, 84, 92
  rationing of, **15:** 143–44
  tax-prices, discrimination in, **15:** 153–55
public spending. *See* government spending; public expenditure
public utility pricing, theory of, **5:** 45–46
public utility regulation, **13:** 316–17
punishment
  components, **7:** 176–77
  in constitutional dimension, **7:** 172–80
  costs of, **7:** 167–69
  in democracy, **7:** 184–85
  deterrence of, **7:** 170
  dilemma, **7:** 165–85; **17:** 446
  generality, **7:** 177–78
  as public choice, **7:** 180–84
  as retribution, **7:** 170 n. 4
  strategy, **7:** 172–80
  theory, **7:** 174 n. 6
  time dimension, **7:** 169–72
Puritan ethic, **1:** 343–44

qualified majority rule, **3:** 210–30; **7:** 64
quasi-collective goods, **4:** 18–21
quasi-rents, **6:** 69, 80–81
quotas, **11:** 107
  as alternative to penalty tax, **13:** 431
  among groups or classes, **17:** 343

rational choice
  in collective decision making, **16:** 84, 394–95
  constitutional alternatives, deference to people informed about, **16:** 186
  at constitutional stage, **16:** 39
  of constraints, **17:** 463

freedom, in indivisible and exhaustible, **16:** 392–94, 396
  under full knowledge conditions, **17:** 69–70
  under ignorance or uncertainty, **17:** 69–70
  restrictive model, **16:** 387–92
  in voting choice theory, **16:** 185–86
rational choice behavior models
  constraints in, **17:** 55, 60–66
  extensions of, **17:** 66–69
  of individual choice behavior, **17:** 55–58
  methodological individualism in, **17:** 55–58
  utility maximization in, **17:** 55, 58–60
rational choice theory, **16:** 156
rational deference theory, **16:** 185–86, 189–95
rational expectations
  hypothesis, **14:** 478
  in macroeconomic theory (Barro neutrality), **14:** 408–9, 413–14
  public-debt theory extended to, **14:** 478
  about rules, of citizens and politicians, **16:** 65–67
rational expectation theory, **1:** 173
rational ignorance
  circumventing, **16:** 135
  constitutional experts, link to, **16:** 135–39
  in fiscal choice, **8:** 137
rational ignorance theory, **16:** 185–86
  conflicting interests, with absence of, **16:** 188–89
  in constitutional choice, **16:** 130, 132–39
  defined, **16:** 131–33
  rational deference theory as variation of, **16:** 191–95
rationalism, constructivist (Hayek), **16:** 140
rationality, **3:** xvi, 31–39
  bounded, **17:** 3–95

constitutional economics and, **1:** 391–92
constitutions and, **3:** 81–83
in decision making, **1:** 85, 86, 88, 90, 102, 152, 391–92
extended, **17:** 230
in game theory, **3:** 161–63
individual, in social decisions, **2:** 120–21
in market choice, **3:** 33–34
postulate, **1:** 335
social, **3:** 32
in social decisions, **2:** 120–21
See also social rationality
rationality of choice under cognitive certainty, **12:** 149
rationing, **12:** 417–20; **16:** 257, 261
real balance effects, **2:** 49–50
real-bills doctrine, **8:** 115 n. 3
real burden, **2:** 5, 6, 8–9, 26, 32
real debt. *See* public debt: pure
reciprocity, **18:** 206–7
  asymmetry in money economy, **12:** 413–14
  in command economy, **12:** 417–20
  in exchange relationship, **12:** 410
  in external diseconomies, **13:** 426–30
  generality and, **11:** 8
  interdependence of demand and supply, **12:** 57–59; **15:** 250–56
  in moral order, **14:** 488–89
  in social interdependencies, **13:** 410–13
  between supply and demand, **12:** 254–56
redistribution, **4:** 297–99
  constitutional, **3:** 197; **15:** 485–89
  under corporation income tax, **4:** 49–50
  difference principle (Rawls), **9:** 192; **17:** 326
  generality and, **11:** 159–75
  in initial contract, **7:** 83
  as insurance, **3:** 193–99
  as local public good, **15:** 483–84
  in modern state, **19:** 312

redistribution (*continued*)

as national public good, **15:** 485

norm, **15:** 435

Pareto optimality and, **3:** 190–99; **15:** 481

politics of, **19:** 282–83, 311–12

as a private good, **15:** 483

under progressive income tax, **4:** 227–28, 238–40

rectificatory, **17:** 450–51

rent seeking in game of, **19:** 31

status quo and, **10:** 155–60

Tullock on, **1:** 438

See also distribution

referenda, **9:** 21

reform. *See* constitutional reform; economic reform; fiscal reform; institutional reform; Pareto-superior reform; tax reform

refunding, treasury, **2:** 159–63

Regents of the University of California v. Bakke (1978), **17:** 344, 347, 348

regressive tax rates, **1:** 130, 148; **4:** 163–64; **9:** 44–45, 51, 54

discrimination and, **9:** 86

full neutrality and, **4:** 154–55

regulation

external diseconomy, of industry producing, **13:** 421–24

monopoly solution, **13:** 319–21

monopsony solution, **13:** 320–21

noncontract, nonauction methods, **13:** 261–62

ownership rights, in assignment of, **13:** 261–62

political, **13:** 416

as political response to externalities, **13:** 360–61

practical objective of, **13:** 319–20

water-quality standards, government-imposed, **1:** 303

See also laws; rules

regulation, direct

imposed by persons on themselves, **13:** 426–30

penalty tax and, **13:** 420–26

regulatory agency

consumer interest, captured by, **13:** 322

with general inflation, **13:** 323–26

politically sensitive, problems of, **13:** 321–22

producer interests, captured by, **13:** 322–23

time in analysis of, **13:** 324–26

relatively absolute absolute(s), **1:** 233, 360, 369, 418, 442–54

constitutional rules, as, **16:** 66, 230–31

Knight on, **1:** 443; **19:** 93

in political interaction, **19:** 14

principle of, **19:** xi–xiii, 13–14, 78

rules as, **19:** 14, 81

relevant comparisons, importance of, in analysis, **2:** 21, 42, 46, 60–62

religion

analogous to science, **17:** 158–59

Christian ethics, **6:** 72–74

Christian hypothesis behavior, **13:** 33–34

individual choice behavior prescribed by Christianity, **13:** 33–34

Knight's attitude toward, **19:** 92–93

orthodox, decline of, **19:** 132–33

religious choice, **17:** 176–81

rents

bureaucratic, **7:** 197–204

cartelization, after enforcement of, **13:** 403–6

from claim enforcement, **18:** 221

combining of resources to produce, **12:** 160–62

competitive industry, in model of goods produced by, **15:** 159–60

composite quasi-rents, **18:** 213n. 9

consumer's, **18:** 200–203
demand-for-money rents, **13:** 50
dissipation, **13:** 258–60
Ferrara's theory of, **15:** 63
from firms, **13:** 319–21
in incumbency model, **13:** 284–87
of incumbent legislators, **13:** 292–93
in market economy, allocation to, **14:** 235
in market failure model, **18:** 279
market restrictions, of producers from, **13:** 389–91
with ownership rights, **13:** 253–55, 257–58
political agents maximize, **14:** 50–52
producer's, **18:** 204
profit distinct from (Knight), **19:** 87
in relationships among and between persons, **13:** 18
rent-protecting interest, **18:** 203, 208, 210, 213
resources in theory of, specialization of, **18:** 212–14
social rent in private property, **18:** 219–21
spatial, **18:** 50 n. 8
special interest groups, secured by, **19:** 315
transfers, in uncompensated, **13:** 263, 277
See also social rent
rents, locational
defined, **18:** 58
fiscal surplus and, **9:** 201
government's knowledge of, **18:** 62
in individuals' incomes, **18:** 58–60
shares of, relationship of total tax shares to, **18:** 59–60
in theory of the firm, **18:** 58
rent seeking, **1:** xvii, 103–15, 186; **9:** 40; **11:** 84, 86, 151, 181, 195

cartel restrictions, of firms seeking government enforcement of, **13:** 398–402
circumstances for, **13:** 265–69, 275–77
in command and market economies, **12:** 423
in competition for access to scarce goods, **16:** 258–59
competitive, effect on cartel coalitions of, **13:** 403
constitutional contract, in model of, **14:** 246–47
in constrained polity, **11:** 202–3; **18:** 138 n. 8
defined, **1:** 104–6; **13:** 49, 50
eliminating, conditions for, **13:** 269–72
entrepreneurship and, **1:** 105, 106–7
evolution and potential for reforms to change, **13:** 352–54
in foreign trade, **11:** 107
generality and, **1:** 426–27; **11:** 46 n. 3, 53 n. 6, 122–23
government and, **10:** 134
institutions, in unconstrained, **19:** 63
investment in, conditions for, **13:** 251
levels of, **1:** 112–14
literature of, **16:** 160–61
majoritarian, **11:** 45–46
market discipline limits, **19:** 206
motive force in, **1:** 110
in nonattenuated rights settings, **13:** 275–76
nonmarket settings, as profit seeking in, **19:** 106
ownership rights, **13:** 253–55, 260
political allocation without, **1:** 111–12
political (re)allocation and rent seeking, **1:** 110–12
of politics of churning state, **19:** 312
prisoners' dilemma with nonsymmetrical payoffs, **13:** 350–52

rent seeking (*continued*)
  private ownership with resources on
    common facilities, **13:** 257–58
  profit seeking equivalent to, **13:** 277
  in public choice theory, **19:** 60, 63
  in redistributional game, **19:** 312
  social inefficiency of, **1:** 107–8; **13:** 277,
    346; **19:** 259
  social return and, **1:** 167–68
  tax treatment and reform, related to, **16:**
    323–26
  transfers of value: under restricted rules
    of, **13:** 271–73; in uncompensated, **13:**
    265–66
  Tullock's theory of, **1:** 163; **19:** 105–6
  wasteful, **13:** 265, 269, 272, 276–77
  in welfare state, **19:** 259
  See also economic rent
rent theory, Ricardian, **6:** 5
repayment of public debt. *See* public debt,
  retirement of
resource allocation
  advertising promotion, gains from, **13:**
    338–39
  under Coase theorem, **18:** 370
  competitive structure for, **13:** 334
  defined (Robbins), **12:** 330
  distorted, **13:** 336
  efficient, **13:** 314, 334–35
  by entrepreneurs, **12:** 155–68
  in federal system, **18:** 10–13, 24–25
  by firm to market product, **13:** 335
  generalized increasing returns, in model
    of, **12:** 392–93
  legal uncertainty, in context of, **12:** 296
  in market economy, **18:** 92; **19:** 229–31
  of mobile units, **13:** 256–60
  monopoly achieving Pareto optimality,
    conditions for, **13:** 333–35
  neoclassical welfare economics for,
    conditions in, **12:** 397
  optimal, **12:** 24–25

  optimum, ownership and pricing for,
    12: 311–26
  ownership rights, efficiency in
    assignment of, **12:** 290–91
  positive feedback model, choices in, **12:**
    393
  property rights, as function of, **18:** 38
  with public and private goods, **18:** 49
  public finance, efficiency in, **18:** 25
  of rent seeking, **13:** 346
  with rent seeking related to
    uncompensated transfers, **13:**
    278–80
  in road construction models, **12:**
    311–26
  social cost, in Coase's theory of, **13:**
    298–300
  under socialist system, **19:** 226–29,
    231–34, 249
  state, the: in Coase's conception of, **13:**
    312; Pigovian model of, **13:** 311–12
  technological external diseconomies, in
    context of, **12:** 316–17
  in welfare-transfer state, **19:** 257–58
  See also distribution; efficiency; Pareto
    criterion; redistribution; scarcity
resource allocation theory, **1:** 35, 355
  criticism of, **1:** 29, 30, 32–33, 34, 37, 41,
    227–28, 273, 382
  distribution and, **7:** 67–68
resources
  external diseconomies: with specialized,
    13: 255–58; with unspecialized, **13:**
    252–55
  idle, **12:** 367–68
  idleness of nonlabor, **12:** 371–73
  labor and nonlabor, **12:** 368
  natural, scarce, **11:** 99–100
  transfer of, **2:** 96
resource utilization, **1:** 275
  barriers to, **1:** 267–73
  "free-rider" constraints, **1:** 268–72

information-communication
constraints, **1:** 267–68
strategic behavior, **1:** 272–73
retribution, **7:** 170n. 4
revenue and demand for public goods, **9:**
77–78
revenue earmarking. *See* earmarked
revenue; earmarking
revenue maximization, **1:** 22; **9:** 33–37,
46–48
revenues
disposition versus level, **9:** 160
general-fund, to finance public goods
with earmarked revenues, **14:** 76–86
limits, **9:** 233–34
from money creation, **9:** 111–13
nontax sources, **16:** 54–55
not earmarked, **14:** 73–74
penalty tax revenues, significance of, **13:**
425–29
tax-rate, tax-revenue relationship, **13:**
468–74
revenue sharing, **8:** 48n. 10; **9:** 214
federal-state, examples of, **18:** 143–44
reverse, **18:** 138–46
under supranational federalism, **18:**
136–37
revolutionary behavior (Tullock), **19:**
101–3
Ricardian economics of
abstract analysis, **1:** 387
choice, **1:** 158
equivalence, **1:** 156
life-cycle model extension, **1:** 248
Ricardian equivalence theorem, **2:** 34–37;
6: 61–63; **8:** 139–41; **9:** 101; **11:** 132; **14:** xv,
352, 393, 475–77, 491, 510
Barro neutrality theorem, difference
from, **14:** 409–13
Barro neutrality under, **14:** 409–13
conditions necessary for, **14:** 393–94,
406

consumption and savings streams
under, **14:** 411
feasible tax institutions, in context of,
14: 395–403
on financing of public outlay, **14:**
409–10, 510
generality and, **11:** 134–35
lump-sum taxes condition, **14:** 93–95
Ricardo-Barro model
pension payments, of intergenerational
financing of, **15:** 444–45, 446–47
savings habits, estimates of, **15:** 449
Ricardo-Barro proposition, **11:** 135–36
rights
amenity rights, **15:** 28, 179–80
in anarchy, **15:** 4
assignment of, **16:** 207–11; **18:** 205,
208–11: under allocational neutrality
theorem, **13:** 301–11; individual, **17:**
78–79; in market economy, **12:** 34–35;
uncertainty in, **12:** 296
changes in, **7:** 105–8; **16:** 91–93
under constitution, **19:** 174–75
constitutional, disintegration of, **16:**
99–100
contract and, **7:** 28–31
of creditors against public debt default,
14: 530–32
defined, **3:** 47; **16:** 23–25
differences, **7:** 15
distribution of, **18:** 208, 211–12
legal system, wrongs in, **15:** 5–7
liberties distinct from, **18:** 208
as limits, **7:** 14–15, 111–12
membership, **7:** 94
natural, **11:** 8
ownership, **19:** 360
ownership-consumption, **15:** 194
personal, enforcement of, **19:** 282
of poor, **7:** 94
of rich, **7:** 94–95
separated, enforcement of, **18:** 221

rights (*continued*)
    social stability and, **7:** 26–27
    in status quo, **7:** 111–15, 224; **16:** 117–22
    transfer in exchange of, **16:** 29–31
    See also Coase theorem; constraints;
        exchange; exclusion rights; individual
        rights; laws; ownership rights;
        property rights; rules; transfer rights;
        voluntary exchange; voting rights
risk
    under cognitive certainty, **12:** 145–49
    defined (Knight), **12:** 142
    taken by entrepreneurs, **12:** 162–64
    uncertainty and, **12:** 142–45; **19:** 87–88
risk aversion, **11:** 182
Robinson Crusoe models, **1:** 27, 35–36,
    364; **17:** 42–46, 48–49, 362–64
Roosevelt administration
    devaluation of currency under (1934),
        18: 405–8
    New Deal policies of, **18:** 385–87,
        395–410
    See also New Deal; Supreme Court, U.S.
Royal Swedish Academy of Sciences
    (Stockholm), **1:** xiv, 3–7
rule of action, Kantian, **1:** 67
rule of law, **9:** 184–200; **11:** xix, 10–11, 67,
    96; **12:** 99
    applied to economics, **19:** 282–83
    centrality of, **1:** 420
    constitutional limits under, **16:** 274–75
    fairness and, **11:** 13–14
    generality principle in, **19:** 351
    idea of equal treatment under, **16:** 275
    justice requires, **19:** 312–13
    personal rights, to enforce, **19:** 282
    for privatized common property, **18:**
        222–26
    protection of liberty under, **18:** 172,
        173–75
    taxation and, **9:** 223; **11:** 130
    veil of ignorance/uncertainty and, **19:**
        281–83

    See also laws; liability rule; property
        rule
rules
    agreement and, **3:** 78: depends on
        alternative, **17:** 325–26; as essence of
        rule making, **16:** xii
    as artifacts, **11:** 4–5
    authorities versus, **1:** 224–25
    for balanced budget, **8:** 153–66; **14:**
        500–504
    basic, design and implementation of,
        16: 228–31
    for behavior, **1:** 313, 334
    for budget deficits, **14:** 501
    changed by legislation, **18:** 339–41
    choice alternatives, to constrain, **17:**
        92–94
    choice of, **1:** 235, 237–40, 269, 383–84,
        395; **3:** ix; **10:** 11–13, 33–34; **16:** 419
    choice under a constitution of, **16:**
        157–59; **18:** 175–78
    for collective choice (Wicksell), **1:** 15, 23,
        217–19; **3:** 6, 63–84
    competitive market distributive, **17:** 326
    compliance related to long- and short-
        term, **16:** 164
    as constitution, **9:** 5; **10:** 9; **16:** 45
    constitutional (*see* constitutional rules)
    constitutional change and, **10:** 153–54
    constitutional choice and, **7:** 90–92
    constitutional reform, **16:** 64
    constraints imposed by, **10:** 20; **18:**
        270–74
    conventions as, **10:** 12–13
    costs: of change in, **10:** 14; to violators
        of, **17:** 228–29
    criterion, **1:** 216–19
    decision-making: outcomes, **14:** 503–4;
        procedures, **14:** 503–4
    defecting from, **16:** 164
    defined, **1:** 211–14
    distributional, **16:** 286
    distributional conflict and, **10:** 15

enforcement, **7:** 118–21; **10:** 7; **18:** 174–76

evolution of, **10:** 13, 16–17, 24, 160–61

expectations and, **10:** 110–11, 115–16

failure to achieve, **1:** 141, 201, 204, 205, 235, 276

fair, **16:** 103, 188

of fair game, **1:** 211–16, 432, 448–50, 453

fairness in, **10:** 21; **17:** 327–29

fairness of and compliance with, **16:** 163–64

for fiscal choice (Wicksell), **19:** 142

fiscal constitution, **14:** 272–73: in proposed, **16:** 314

fiscal institutions and: choice of, **5:** 159; collective outcomes, **4:** 201–7; derivation of, **5:** 155; imposition of, **5:** 150, 151; theory of, **5:** 142–43, 149

fiscal justice and, **4:** 295–96

in fiscal theory (Wicksell), **16:** 9–10

of games, **10:** 8–10; **16:** 44

general and durable, **16:** 162

for human behavior, **18:** 317–21

human characteristic, **7:** 118–21

hypothetical consent and, **10:** 115

importance of, **1:** 19–22; **16:** xi–xii

incidence of, **10:** 131–35

individual, **3:** 97

information and, **10:** 10–11

as institutions, **10:** 18–19

justice, **10:** 108–24

less-than-unanimity, **4:** 120

of majority (*see* majority rule)

majority voting (*see* majority rule voting)

of the market, **1:** 35, 276; **10:** 16–18

market economy, required for, **19:** 266–67

meta-rules and, **10:** 105

monetary, potential change in, **16:** 424–25

for money supply, **4:** 111

moral, choice behavior constrained by, **17:** 93–94

of moral order, **17:** 189–90, 200, 227–28

natural rights and, **10:** 20

nonsymmetrical, **14:** 274–78

optimal, **1:** 219–20

of order, **7:** 157

of an organization, **14:** 431

organization and authority of the state, defining, **18:** 169–70

Pareto optimality and, **1:** 210–29

as plans, **7:** 118–21

political, fairness in, **17:** 327–29

political choice, related to, **14:** 500–501

in political constitution, **16:** 45

political economy and, **1:** 202

of political order, **1:** 276; **10:** 18–19

politics carried out within, **16:** 64

predictability in, **10:** 10–11

as process, **10:** 16

as promises, **10:** 111–13

prospective, **10:** 153–54

quality of, **16:** 188

as relatively absolute absolutes, **19:** 14, 81

relative unanimity, **4:** 116

relevance of numbers and, **1:** 318–22

as rights, **7:** 90–92; **14:** 271–73

of road, **10:** 7–15

samaritan's dilemma and, **1:** 329–45

as self-government, **7:** 119–20

of social-economic-political game, **19:** 24–25

of social order, **10:** 4

strategies within, **16:** 127

symmetrical self-enforcing, **14:** 273–74

tacit consent and, **10:** 115–16

tax institutions and, **4:** 219–21

temporal aspects of, **10:** 76–91

of trade, **1:** 265; **10:** 30

truth judgment conception of, **11:** 4–7

of unanimity, **1:** 5, 15, 64, 72, 98, 99–100, 145, 208, 270, 421, 423, 463, 464; **4:** 115–16, 288–89

unanimity as, **11:** 118–19

rules (*continued*)
  understanding of, principle from, **14:** 278
  unwritten, **10:** 13
  See also balanced-budget rule; constitutional rules; fiscal rules; voting rules
rules, alternative
  constitutional choice among, **16:** 11–12, 45, 127–28
  evaluation of, **16:** 4, 44–45
  political choice among (Wicksell), **16:** 72–74
  in public choice theory, **16:** 105
  ranking of, individual's informed, **16:** 186–87
  social choice, as objects of, **16:** 211
  sub-constitutional choice within, **16:** 127–28
rule-utilitarianism, **5:** 160
ruling-class model, **4:** 174–76
  Italian analysis, **4:** 127–36 passim
  progressive income tax and, **4:** 240–42
ruling-class theory of state, **3:** 12

sacrifice
  debt creation, involved in, **2:** 29
  on group, **2:** 30
  savings bonds, **2:** 78
sacrifice principle of taxation
  Barone's argument against, **15:** 69–70
  Einaudi's minimum, **15:** 80–81
sales tax, general, **4:** 50–52, 251
  incidence of, **4:** 50
samaritan's dilemma, **1:** 329–45, 439–40; **17:** 446
Samuelsonian economics
  analysis, **11:** 155
  attributes of public behavior, **1:** 381, 426
  conditions for public goods efficiency, **1:** 136, 137

configuration of economic systems, **1:** 120n. 2
free-rider problem, **1:** 324n. 7
model, **11:** 70
social welfare function, **1:** 193, 197, 202
"solution" to public expenditures, **1:** 72n. 12
saving
  act of, **12:** 462
  under Barro neutrality theorem, **14:** 411–13
  Crusoe model of, **12:** 250–51
  debt financing, in response to, **14:** 476
  ethic of, **12:** 466–69
  government debt issue, relation to, **14:** 417–21
  incentives to save, modified, **12:** 467
  inflation on, effect of, **12:** 468
  interest-rate changes (Bailey), response to, **12:** 245–52
  interest rates, relation to, **12:** 245–52
  intergenerational ethics, norms based on, **12:** 460–61
  Keynes's interpretation of, **12:** 458–59, 462, 466–67
  rates in U.S., **12:** 456–57
  real saving, defined, **12:** 251–52
  under Ricardian equivalence theorem, **14:** 411
  spillover benefits, **12:** 464
  welfare-transfer state, influence of, **12:** 467–69
savings
  double taxation in Italian fiscal theory, **15:** 83–84
  increase motivated by transfer burden, **15:** 449
  social security, reduced under, **15:** 446, 448
  taxation of, **11:** 127
Say's law, **1:** 352; **8:** 97n. 1

scarcity, **1:** 30, 81, 379–80
   artificial, conditions for, **19:** 194
   choice among alternatives with, **12:** 114
   necessity of choice with, **19:** 223
Schelling point, **7:** 79
science
   abstract, **12:** 10–11
   beliefs and social function of, **17:**
      156–57, 174–75
   decision making in, **1:** 234, 237
   economics as, **13:** 16–21, 57–59,
      68–69
   freedom in, **1:** 230–43
   human and nonhuman, **13:** 82–83
   normative, defined, **1:** 208
   of political economy, **1:** 164–66
   politics and, **1:** 230–43; **10:** 27–31,
      41–42
   politics interpreted as, **17:** 153
   positive nature of, **17:** 41
   predictive, **12:** 10–11; **17:** 48–49
   process of, **17:** 154–55, 157, 167
   raison d'être of, **17:** 40
   religion analogous to, **17:** 158–59
   scientific method and, **1:** 230–31, 232,
      239, 295
   social order, refutation of, **1:** 230–31
   spontaneous coordination principle to,
      application of, **17:** 98
   truth in, **1:** 232–34, 385; **17:** 157–58
   See also economic science; natural
      science; political economy
scientific choice versus political choice, **1:**
   237
scientific decision, defined, **1:** 234
scientific freedom, defense of, **1:** 230–43
scientific methodology, **1:** 230–31
   defined, **1:** 165–66
"scientific" socialism, **1:** 285
scientism, criticism of
   Hayek's, **12:** 12, 24
   Knight's, **12:** 24

scientists
   choices of, **17:** 174–76
   Crusoe and Friday as, **17:** 42–45, 48–49
Scottish method, **1:** 295–96, 297. *See also*
   scientific methodology; Smithean
   economics
secession
   European Union, option in proposed,
      18: 105, 114
   forms of, **18:** 149
   by internal exit, **18:** 149–51
   liberty of, **14:** 225–26, 241n. 15, 242
   as lost option, **18:** 104
   political, **1:** 367; **14:** 220–27, 242–43
   right of, **18:** 103
   as threat, **18:** 70–71, 103
   See also exit options; internal-exit model
second-best, theory of, **1:** 296; **4:** 55–56
   commodity taxes and, **9:** 69–70
   See also welfare economics
security
   justice as, **1:** 297, 298
   as public good, **7:** 87
   See also law enforcement; laws;
      property, private
self-government, **7:** 119–20. *See also* rules
self-interest, **3:** 16
   assumption, **1:** 66, 72, 360
   bureaucrats acting in, **13:** 12
   of butcher (Smith), **18:** 446
   channeling to socially desired direction,
      18: 448
   in collective decision making, **17:**
      255–57
   constitutional choice and, **3:** ix, 95–96
   of criminals, **18:** 446–48; **19:** 103
   in exchange (Smith), **19:** 358
   as human nature, **3:** 27
   individual behavior, in Kantian
      hypothesis of, **13:** 35–37
   in individual market behavior, **13:** 37,
      72–73, 124

self-interest (*continued*)
limits of, **19:** 130–32
narrow and enlightened, **12:** 132
of politicians, **19:** 279
of revolutionaries, **19:** 101–2
Smith's concept of, **19:** 297–98, 358,
361
of Smith's tradesmen, **12:** 363–65
in social norms, **17:** 231
as utility maximization, **3:** 3
in voting behavior, **19:** 99–100
in work, **1:** 357–59
See also individual choice; market
order; political choice
self-liquidating projects, **2:** 127–28. *See
also* public debt
sellers
in barter economy, **12:** 411–12
in command economy, **12:** 417–20, 422
in competitive structure, **13:** 334
as consumers and buyers, **13:** 389–91
income transfer in quantity discount
transactions to, **12:** 200–202
liberty for, value of, **18:** 205
under marginal evaluation curve, **12:**
197–200
in money-goods exchange, **12:** 412–16
offering quantity discounts, **12:** 192–95
without perfect information, **13:** 335–36
rent-protecting interests of, **18:** 210
replacing monopoly, **13:** 334–35
substitute, **18:** 201–3
in vote market, **13:** 214–26
See also buyers
service levels, origins of uniform, **11:** 192
services
consumption: with nonreciprocal
external economies, **15:** 245–50; with
reciprocal external economies, **15:**
250–56
in Marshallian joint supply theory, **15:**
214

See also goods and services; public
services
sharing, cooperative-collective
activities organized under, **15:** 205n. 11
in clubs, **15:** 194, 201–5
exclusion in, **15:** 208
See also public goods; public goods and
services; social rent
side payments, **5:** 92, 98, 107
in majority voting, **3:** 154–58
Pareto optimality and, **3:** 187–89
public sector size and, **3:** 208–9
unanimity and, **3:** 90–91
"silent majority," **1:** 439
single-peaked preference, **3:** 343; **4:**
146–47; **5:** 99, 101, 105; **11:** 37, 121
sinking fund, **8:** 11, 20
for debt amortization, **14:** 477
tax rates, to ensure intertemporal
equality of, **14:** 404
slavery, **1:** 289–91; **7:** 77–78
contract under state power, **18:** 170–72
defined, **13:** 66
exchange process in, **13:** 66–67
government, effect on, **18:** 104
model, **16:** 203
serfs and, relationships of, **13:** 66–67
Smithean economics
alternative vision of, **12:** 28
benign deity, **1:** xxii
classical political economy and, **1:** 387,
389
classical tradition of, return to, **12:** 387
economic value, on increases in, **1:** 348
on exchange, **1:** 29, 37, 251, 357
gains-from-trade, mutual, **12:** 369,
430–31
on incentive, **12:** 32
influence of, **1:** 292; **12:** 481
on "invisible hand," **1:** 35, 458
on justice, **1:** 297
labor: division of, **1:** 387–88; **12:** 350, 378;

productive and unproductive,
distinction between, **12:** 77–78;
specialization of, **19:** 299;
unproductive, menial service as, **12:**
385–86
labor supply, **1:** 346–47, 415
market order, understanding and
explanation of, **12:** 429
market size and specialization,
relationship between, **12:** 392
mercantilist-protectionist politics,
attack on, **1:** 186
natural liberty, **1:** 298–301, 303, 304–8,
309–10
opportunity cost theory in deer-beaver
model, **12:** 337, 349, 399–400
profit seeking, **1:** 104
self-interest of tradesmen, **12:** 35, 363, 439
social interaction, model for, **1:** 292–96
social capital. *See* public capital
social change criteria, **16:** 89–91
social choice, **18:** 268
alternative assignment of rights, made
among, **16:** 205–6
Arrow on individual versus social
(collective) choice, **1:** 53–54, 79 n. 11,
86 n. 24
assigned rights as objects of, **16:** 207–11
choices different than outcomes, **16:** 419
entails multidimensional behavior, **16:**
201–3
individual rationality and, **3:** 31–39
master-slave behavior, in outcome of,
16: 204, 207
rational (*see* social rationality)
Tullock on, **1:** 362 n. 3
See also collective choice
social choice theory, **1:** 54, 246–69; **12:** 41
of Arrow, Black, Downs, and
Schumpeter, **16:** 68–69
Buchanan's critique of, **17:** xvi–xix
collective rationality in, **16:** 84

democracy and free markets and, **1:**
89–102
Homo economicus in, **19:** 9
implications of, **16:** 84
individual choice versus, **1:** 75–88
individual evaluations related to social
outcomes, **16:** 369 n. 12
public choice theory, differences from,
19: 8–9
See also collective choice; impossibility
theorem (Arrow); social welfare
function; utility maximization;
welfare economics
social contract, **3:** 248–51, 310; **11:** 5, 8
agreement in context of, **16:** 165
anarchy as alternative to, **17:** 405, 408
early discussion, **7:** 187
efficiency and, **7:** 51
evolutionism as alternative to, **17:**
405–6, 408
function of, **17:** 404–5
Marxism as alternative to, **17:** 406, 408
monetary constitution, arising from, **18:**
411–15
as myth, **16:** 89
postconstitutional, **7:** 37 n. 13, 38
renegotiating of, **7:** 97–98
social function of, **16:** 87–89
stages, **7:** 37
theory of, **1:** xix, 24–25, 39, 50, 51, 204,
269–70, 298, 429–31, 465–68
transcendentalism as alternative to, **17:**
406–8
violation of, conditions for, **16:** 97
See also anarchy; contractarian
perspective; contracts; socialist
economies
social contract theories, agreement in, **16:**
155–56, 159–60, 165
social cost, **6:** 32, 65–76
Coase on, **1:** 261, 262–64, 267, 276; **12:**
35; **13:** 297–98

social cost (*continued*)
  in decision making, **13:** 358
  Knight's interpretation of, **12:**
    311–15
  Pigovian concept, **12:** 335
  of private correction for negative
    externality, **13:** 358
social cost theory
  of Coase, **12:** 169–70, 172
  liability rule under, **12:** 173–74
  See also Coase theorem
social discount rate, **10:** 93–94
social disorder, **19:** 194–98
social engineer, **11:** 40–41
  classical liberal as, **19:** 211
  idea of (Knight), **19:** 92
  social philosopher, distinct from, **19:**
    307–8
  in totalitarian model, **19:** 306
social evolutionary process, **7:** 211
social insurance, **4:** 141n. 12; **11:** 180–82; **15:**
  407, 443
social interaction
  agreement in, **19:** 306–7
  as artifact, **19:** 315
  collective choice, from perspective of,
    17: xvii–xviii
  individual choice in, **17:** 56
  moral order in, **17:** 189–90
  objective attitude toward (Strawson),
    17: xiii
  order of, economy as an, **19:** 243
  participant's attitude in, Buchanan's
    notion of, **17:** xiii–xv
  structures of, differing, **19:** 20–23
  Wiseman's approach to, **19:** 115
social interaction theory, **12:** 329
  agreement in, **16:** 155–56, 159–60
socialist economies, **1:** 368; **7:** 187–88, 214,
  215
  anti-libertarian socialist, **19:** 166–69
  attitudes in formerly, **19:** 193

behavioral dichotomy in, assumption
  of, **1:** 70
Buchanan's criticism of, **19:** xvii
bureaucratic control in, **19:** 192–93
centralized decision making and, **1:** 75
challenge to the individual in, **1:** 285
collective ownership under, **19:** 249
collectivization of production under, **19:**
  226–29
competition under, **19:** 255, 261
criticism of (Hayek-Mises), **19:** 120, 197,
  221, 232, 234, 250
critique by Pope Leo XIII (*Rerum
  Novarum*), **18:** 252–54
death of, Hayek and, **1:** 180, 185
defined, **1:** 181; **19:** 242–43, 255–56
democratic, **13:** 452
differences from welfare state, **19:**
  256–58
distributional experiments of, **19:** 311
distributional objectives in, **19:** 236
distribution under, **19:** 236, 249–50, 311
early literature on, **1:** 70
economic structure (1930s), **12:** 329
ensures poverty, **19:** 222
entrepreneurship under, **19:** 251
failure of, **1:** 57–59, 179–88; **12:** 471–72;
  16: xii, 244; **18:** 90–91, 107; **19:** 198,
  217, 221–23, 227, 249–51, 261
as fatal conceit (Hayek), **18:** 310; **19:**
  120–21, 189, 267–69
federalism, opposition to idea of, **18:** 79
former socialist countries, **16:** xii,
  226–27; **19:** 193
Hayek and, **1:** 180, 185
incentives under, **19:** 235–36, 250–51,
  360, 363
individualism and, compared, **1:** 181–82
inefficiency of, **19:** 192
laws of economics in, **19:** 216
Leviathan and, **1:** 57–59, 179–80,
  186–87; **7:** 227–28

libertarian socialist, **19:** 166–68
loss of independence under, **18:** 107
in market economies, **19:** 251–55
market economy, as replacement for,
   19: 231–33
market order, criticism of, **5:** 139
Marxist, **16:** 207
Marxist model of economic
   development, **18:** 254–56
mystique of, **1:** 47
politically determined prices under, **16:**
   25–56
political order, as system of, **18:** 88
politicization under, **19:** 189
private property under, ownership of,
   18: 249–51, 254
production and consumption under,
   19: 221–23, 226–29, 231–33, 234–37
public good and, **1:** 47
public philosophy of, **18:** 106–8
recommended refutation of, **18:** 101
"reform" of, **19:** 227–28
restrictions on liberty, **18:** 249–51
romance of, **19:** 194, 317
"scientific," **1:** 285
socialist calculation, **6:** 21–23, 87–89
in Soviet Union, **1:** 183–84
See also consumption; distribution;
   production; welfare state
social marginal cost, **13:** 329
social order, **12:** 135
   analysis of, **1:** 61
   anarchy or contractual, **16:** 19–21
   Buchanan's interest in, **1:** xix
   conceptual origins of, **17:** 433–34
   conditions generating, **19:** 198
   constitutionalist-contractarian, **16:** 16–21
   decline in U.S., **16:** 350
   generalizing from individual
      maximization to, **16:** 106–7
   Knight's and Polanyi's conception of, **1:**
      230–43

liberal vision of, **16:** 178
maintenance of viable, **19:** 131
moral standards required for, **19:**
   130–34
necessity of, **1:** 59, 452–54
in nontotalitarian regimes, **19:** 306–7
Rawls's comparison of alternative, **17:**
   385
Rawls's notion of rule selection for, **16:**
   103
reform of (Knight), **19:** 93
rules of, **10:** 4
stability and vulnerability of, influences
   on, **19:** 132–34
without a state, **18:** 167
theory of, **19:** 124–26
university as a, **16:** 179–80
See also liberty; order
social philosophy
   Buchanan as social philosopher, **19:** 173
   dependent on equality, **17:** 295
   of Knight, **19:** 82, 91–93
   law and, **11:** 13
   political economy in, role of, **17:**
      242–43, 247, 249–50
   politics and, **11:** 14–15
   scientific economics as by-product of,
      17: 235
   social philosopher, role of, **19:** 307–8
social rationality, **1:** 89, 92–95, 102. *See also*
   rationality
social reform, samaritan's dilemma in, **1:**
   329–45
social rent
   distributive fairness in (Rawls and
      Gauthier), **17:** 452
   entitlement, conception of (Nozick), **17:**
      422–23
   owners of, **14:** 233–36
   with reduced level of transfer taxes, **14:**
      242–43
   sharing of, **14:** 235

social rent (*continued*)
  valued product as, **14:** 231–32, 233n. 7,
    237, 247–48
social science and natural science,
  compared, **19:** 21–22
social security reform, **15:** 387–88, 391–92,
  404–5, 413–18
  private investment, proposed voluntary
    withdrawal for, **15:** 392
  social insurance bonds, proposed, **15:**
    414–19, 451n. 8
  as tax-transfer scheme, **15:** 392–94, 408,
    411–13
social security system
  constituencies supporting payment of
    claims, **15:** 395
  crisis in, sources of, **15:** 410
  current pension payments, proposed
    financing of, **15:** 414
  demographic change, effect of, **15:**
    448–49
  existing, strategies for support of, **15:**
    392–93, 403–4
  financing, **12:** 467; **14:** 389–90
  future obligations, of effect of, **14:** 392
  generality of, departures from, **15:**
    450–52
  implicit debt, **15:** 392–97
  incomes of later periods, claims against,
    15: 448
  investment within, rates of return to, **15:**
    392
  modeling relevant alternative, **15:**
    394–98
  net indebtedness, **15:** 447–48
  nominal debt, **15:** 393, 397n. 8
  Old-Age, Survivors, and Disability
    Insurance (OASDI), **15:** 407, 443
  option to opt out of, **15:** 394n. 4
  payroll taxes, **9:** 60; **14:** 22; **15:** 413–14,
    451–52
  predicted survival, **15:** 405–6
  private saving (Feldstein), effect on, **14:**
    390
  taxes, **4:** 139–41
  trust fund revenues to balance fiscal
    budget, **14:** 512
social states, **1:** 123–32
  choice among, **11:** 27; **16:** 204–7, 211
  defined, **11:** 27n. 4; **16:** 205n. 6
  domains of, restrictions on, **16:** 205–8
  emerging from separate choice, **16:** 202,
    211
  as objects for choice, **11:** 27
  ordering of, **1:** 313–18
  as outcome in exchange of rights
    strategy, **16:** 206–11
social structures theory, **17:** 264–65
social surplus, **1:** 104, 105
social utility, **1:** 120, 122, 135
social value
  ethical weight in, absence of, **12:** 125
  judgments, **1:** 210, 229
  market exchange, absence in, **12:** 117
  maximization of, **1:** 263
social value scale, **1:** 93, 182; **12:** 114–15
social waste, **1:** 104
social welfare, **1:** 32, 87, 120–32, 137, 138; **3:**
  84; **10:** 20
  in eighteenth-century moral
    philosophy, **17:** 46
  See also welfare economics
social welfare function, **1:** 32, 33, 53, 90–92,
  95, 100–101, 102, 137, 138, 193, 202–4,
  210, 218, 229, 256, 335; **2:** 120–21; **3:** 14,
  283; **4:** 296–97; **5:** 128, 183–84; **6:** 52; **9:**
  17; **10:** 27; **14:** 12–13, 251
  Arrow's, **13:** 8–9, 43–44; **15:** 288n. 13;
    16: 84
  Bergson's, **16:** 80
  constructions in welfare economics, **16:**
    248
  defined, **1:** 90, 202–3
  does not exist, **16:** 107

introduction of, **17:** 240
of modern welfare economists, **17:** 255
Pareto criterion in, **17:** 240
for planner in centralized economy, **16:**
    241–42
used by economists, **16:** 81–83
in welfare economics, **17:** 240;
    economists using, **16:** 81–83;
    Samuelsonian economics and, **1:** 193,
    197, 202; terms of the economy, **16:**
    248
society
absence of authority system in, **14:** 431
character of, **1:** 252
defined, **1:** 32, 144
freely competitive, organization of, **12:**
    117, 125
moral anarchy in, **17:** 190
moral community in, **17:** 188, 196
moral erosion in U.S., **17:** 197
moral order in, **17:** 189–90, 196
Smith's paradigm for, **1:** 292–95
social functions of, **1:** 31
state provides legal umbrella for, **14:**
    432–33
See also laws; moral anarchy; moral
    community; moral order; social
    order
sovereignty
of consumers, **1:** 55; **15:** 363: Hutt on, **19:**
    139–41, 147–51
Hobbesian, **7:** 165–66, 208
of individuals, **1:** 288: creating and
    protecting, **18:** xv–xvi; maximization
    of, **18:** 88–89; the state as threat to,
    18: xi–xii, xv–xvi
partitioning in federalism of, **18:** 80,
    82–84
shared under federalism, **18:** 113
under socialist system, **18:** 108
with supranational economic
    integration, **18:** 119–23, 131

sovereignty, national: under federalism,
    18: 119–27
specialization
advantages of, **18:** 229–31
in complex modern economies, **18:**
    257
in consumption, **18:** 239–40
in economics, **17:** 20
exit from market dependency, as means
    of, **18:** 230–31
from extension of size of market, **12:**
    369–71, 378–79
forgetting encouraged by, **18:** 235–36
gains from, **18:** 234–35
generalized increasing returns, in model
    of, **12:** 392–93
of labor (Smith), **19:** 299
labor supply under increasing returns
    to, **12:** 379–81
markets and, **1:** 348–49, 351, 352, 357
market size and (Smith), **12:** 392
means to increase gains from, **12:** 365,
    379
private property, with ownership of, **18:**
    230
privatized common property, in setting
    of, **18:** 226–34
in production, **18:** 239–40
resources, **13:** 255–58: in ownership, **18:**
    212–14; in theory of, **18:** 212–14; in
    use of, **12:** 464–65
spending, public. *See* public expenditure
spending and taxation, approved: gap
    between, **4:** 91–95
spillover
beneficiary, **5:** 66
benefit, **5:** 30, 33, 55, 64, 67, 69, 171
effect, **1:** 80, 199, 269; **5:** 49, 173:
    exclusion from, **5:** 60; of idleness, **12:**
    368–71; of saving, **12:** 464; smoking-
    chimney model, **1:** 199–200
harm, **5:** 55

stability
    of a constitutional agreement, **16:**
        162–64
    constitutional choice, as consideration
        in, **16:** 164–65
    of majority-rule solution, **5:** 106
    in majority voting, **11:** 51–52
    monetary, need for in market economy,
        18: 257; **19:** 361–62
    monetary system and, **1:** 169, 397–98
    in rules for taxation, **16:** 315
    social, **7:** 26–27
    social order and, **19:** 132–34
    unemployment and, **8:** 169
    utility of (Stigler-Becker), **1:** 249
stabilization policy theory, **1:** 4, 6
Stackelberg model, **11:** 98
state, the
    adjudication and, **7:** 114
    as borrowing unit, **14:** 436
    change in man's vision of, **19:** 133
    churning state concept (de Jasay), **19:**
        63, 204, 312–13, 344
    Coase's model of, **13:** 312
    coercive power of, **19:** 271
    in constitutional contract, **17:** 434–35
    contract theory of, **16:** 87–88
    creditors lending to, **14:** 441
    defined, **3:** 306
    distinct from other organizations, **14:**
        432–33
    as enforcer, **17:** 304–5
    fiscal authority of, **14:** 90–92
    Hobbes's justification for powers of, **14:**
        278–79
    as idealized, **11:** xix
    individual in relation to, **18:** xi, 168–71
    individual sovereignty, as threat to,
        18: xi
    Italian conceptualization of, **1:** 17
    in laissez-faire regime, **16:** 244
    as Leviathan, **19:** 317

    macroeconomic policy theory of, **14:** 444
    maintaining and enforcing rules, **19:** 310
    man's dependence on, **14:** 228
    markets and, **3:** 18
    Marxist vision of, **3:** 12
    monopolistic model of the, **4:** 127–36
    monopoly power of, **18:** xi–xii, xv–xvi
    morals in, **1:** 360–67; **14:** 522–23
    nontransferability of membership
        rights, **14:** 440
    Nozick's invisible-hand explanation of,
        17: 430–31
    Nozick's minimal, **17:** xx, 416–22,
        424–28, 432, 434–35
    operation of, **18:** 168–69
    organic theory of, **1:** 119, 120–22, 132,
        204; **3:** 11–12, 31–32; **11:** 207
    as an organization, **14:** 430–33
    origins, **7:** 9
    Pigovian model of, **13:** 311–12
    as a political agency, **16:** 260
    as political-legal order, **16:** 244–45
    as political organization, **14:** 431
    potential for exploitation by, **18:** xvi,
        247–49
    power to take, limits on, **14:** 279
    as producer, **7:** 88–90
    productive, **18:** 120–23, 175
    protective, **7:** 88–90; **17:** 304–5; **18:**
        120–23, 175–76
    redistributive activity of modern, **19:** 312
    right to vote, **14:** 443
    rules defining organization and
        authority, **18:** 169–70
    rules limiting exercise of action by, **7:**
        17–20; **18:** 170
    ruling class theory of, **3:** 12
    slave contract as membership in, **18:** 171
    socialism, role in, **16:** 244
    taxes as coercive instrument of, **14:** 38,
        228–31
    tax limits of, **14:** 215–16

theories of, **1:** 16, 62; **19:** 120–22, 132,
204: contract, **1:** xix, 24–25, 39, 50, 51,
204, 269–70, 387, 388–90, 429–41,
465–68; individualistic, **1:** 119, 122–32,
468
See also government; political systems;
productive state; welfare state
state of nature
Hobbes's, **17:** 434
Locke's, **17:** 431, 433, 434
states in a federation
competition among, **18:** xii, 70–72
ethical ordering of, **1:** 313–18
fiscal systems of, differences in, **18:**
4–7
impurely public goods, provision of, **18:**
35–42
model of, **18:** 27–35
power to secede from, **18:** 70–71
status quo
assignment of rights and claims
describing, **17:** 245
Buchanan on, **17:** 122, 125–28, 130,
135–37
change and, **3:** 259–60
as contract, **7:** 96–115
contractual change and, **7:** 100–105
defense of, conditions for, **17:** 258
defined, **7:** 100; **17:** 127
existence of, **17:** 134–35
perpetuation of, example of, **17:** 129–30
possible changes from, **17:** 247–48
powerful in, **17:** 129
redistribution and, **10:** 155–60
Samuels on, **17:** 124, 127–28, 134–36
specification of rights and, **7:** 111–15
as starting point, **7:** 101
unanimity and, **3:** x
structure
defined, **12:** 144
properties distinct from properties of
choice, **12:** 144

risk and uncertainty as properties of
(Knight), **12:** 142, 144
See also public choice theory
subjectivism, **1:** 286–89
Austrian version, **18:** 293–94
as a body of thought, **18:** 293
economic, **6:** 10, 23–26; **12:** 23–24; **18:**
292–94
Friedman's objection to, **12:** 28
of Hayek, **12:** 8, 23
in logic of choice, **12:** 8
radical (Shackle), **18:** 293–98, 304–5
replaced by objective payoffs, **12:** 9
spontaneous order principle, **12:** 27
substitution
backbending labor-supply curve, effect
in, **12:** 255–57, 259
between decision rules and other
constitutional constraints, **16:** 308
between fiscal and nonfiscal
constraints, **9:** 192–96
of labor inputs, **12:** 262–65
between political decision rules and
fiscal rules, **5:** 153–56
sunk cost, **6:** 45–46
superiority, Pareto. *See* Pareto superiority
supply-side economics, **1:** 170; **10:** 94
Supreme Court, U.S., **17:** 347–49
Agricultural Adjustment Act (1936)
and, **18:** 355
decisions: in *Miller et al. v. Schoene*
(1928), **18:** 355–56; in *United States v.
Butler* (1936), **18:** 355
gold-clause abrogations (1935) and, **18:**
400, 404–5, 408–10, 419, 425, 428–30
surplus, taxpayer's, **5:** 39, 45, 89, 91
effect on migration, **18:** 40–42
locational rents and, **9:** 201
mobility costs and, **9:** 209–10
symmetry
debtor-creditor, **2:** 43
defined, **11:** 57

symmetry (*continued*)
  along diagonals, **11:** 38
  in individual choice behavior, **13:** 108–10
  in inputs, **11:** 56
  in Keynesian economic theory,
    application of, **8:** 52
  median income, **5:** 130–32
  in payoffs, **11:** 43
  public interest and, **11:** 44

tariffs, **11:** 107
  to finance decreasing-cost facilities, **13:**
    386
  optimal, **9:** 198
  tax exportation, **9:** 198–99
tax analysis, **14:** 307–10
  equilibrium and, **9:** 96–98
taxation
  application of constitutional economics
    to, **16:** 12–13
  in backbending labor-supply curve, **12:**
    257–58
  benefit theory of, **1:** 124–25, 135
  budget deficit to reduce, **14:** 499
  budget size and, **11:** 125
  of capital, **9:** 114–16, 178, 230
  capitalization, **2:** 43, 89–90; **6:** 63–64
  conception of modern economists, **13:**
    367n. 14
  in constitutional perspective, **9:** 221–24
  constitutional structure, **11:** 115
  to constrain government revenue-
    maximization, **14:** 154–64
  of consumption spending, **9:** 96–98,
    111–13
  contractarianism and, **1:** xviii
  discrimination in, inefficiency in, **11:**
    113–14, 119–20; **14:** 313–15
  economic growth and, **11:** 125
  efficiency in, **11:** 113–30
  equality in U.S. Constitution related to,
    14: 252–53

equality or inequality in, **1:** 128, 135–36,
    141–42
equal treatment in, **11:** 113–14, 119–20;
    14: 316–17
ethical limits, **14:** 214
exchange model, **11:** 117–18
externalities and, **8:** 132n. 2; **13:**
    360–61
externality-creating activities, to
    control, **13:** 366–67
financing government and, **1:** 170–71
fiscal constitution, as part of, **16:** 321
in fiscal exchange paradigm, **1:** 133–49;
    16: 317–18
of foreigners, **9:** 198–99
general, **14:** 315–18
generality in, **11:** 113–30; **14:** 250–51,
    256–58, 305–6
generality principle and, **1:** 424–25; **19:**
    353
government authority and, **1:** 22
government choice to reduce, **13:** 447
high, trap of, **13:** 480
incidence of, **9:** 3; **14:** 361–64
indirect, **4:** 44–56
individual behavior distorted by, **15:**
    135–36
inflation and, **2:** 132–33
intertemporal model, **14:** 104–8
justice in, **1:** 15–16, 98, 125, 126, 134, 141,
    142, 455–68
majoritarianism and, **11:** 113–30
majority rule, distribution under, **14:** 310
in marginal benefit principle, **1:** 71, 73
Marshallian incidence theory of, **14:**
    4, 65
nature of, **9:** 4–5
norms for, **14:** 5, 38–39; of cooperation,
    17: 230–31; cultural evolution of
    moral order, **17:** 226–28; theory of
    the state and, **1:** 16, 62, 119, 120–22,
    132, 204 (*see also* moral norms)

one-period model, **14:** 103–4
optimal, **9:** 17, 70, 81–82; **11:** 116
Pigovian-Edgeworthian normative
    principles, **14:** 65
political, **14:** 306–10
in political democracy, **14:** 310–15
political structure and, **11:** 118
post-Marshallian theory of, **14:** 4–5, 22
post-Pigovian theory of, **14:** 5, 22
principles of, **4:** 224; **9:** 3, 43; **14:** 217–21:
    Barone's argument against, **15:**
    69–70; traditional, **5:** 156–58
proportionality criterion, **14:** 258
proportionality in, **9:** 44, 51, 53, 54–55:
    equality before law and, **9:** 185;
    income tax, **4:** 160, 164, 166; model of
    government fiscal decisions, **14:**
    197–211; rule of law and, **9:** 223
public spending, to finance, **14:** 351,
    358–60
purpose of, **1:** 170–71
regulation, as preferred alternative to,
    13: 367
in Ricardian equivalence theorem, **14:**
    393, 409
rule of law and, **11:** 130
sacrifice principle of, **15:** 69–70, 80–81
sacrifice related to, Einaudi's view of,
    15: 80
shifting, effects of, **14:** 4–5
spending and, gap between approved,
    4: 91–95
stability in rules for, **16:** 315
structure distinct from levels of, **16:** 315
subsidy consequences and: in Crusoe
    model of income allocation, **12:**
    247–50; in Crusoe model of saving,
    12: 250–51
taking versus: constitutional limits on,
    16: 51, 67; power of, **9:** 11–12, 193–94
taxing-spending decisions (Wicksell),
    19: 140–42

tax norm, simplicity as, **11:** 124
uniformity, **14:** 39–41: impossibility of,
    11: 158; in taxes, **9:** 69, 184–85
wartime, **2:** 104–10, 132; **4:** 61–62
See also efficiency; fairness; fiscal
    constitution; government spending;
    incentives; public debt; regulation;
    revenues; Ricardian equivalence
    theorem; taxes; tax rates
tax base
    comprehensiveness in, **9:** 45–46, 49,
    59–60
    constitutional control over, **14:** 262–64
    constraints on, **9:** 48–55, 231–33
    erosion of, **9:** 60
    geographic limits on, **14:** 264
    income as, **11:** 127–28
    income elasticity of demand for, **9:** 167
tax burden, excess, **1:** 127–32; **5:** 174, 175; **6:**
    50; **11:** 116
    analysis and decision-making efficiency,
    4: 54–55
    analysis of traditional public finance, **4:**
    43, 54–55
    cost of, **14:** 357–64
    defined, **14:** 122
    discrimination in, **9:** 86
    in discussion of tax reform, **14:** 285
    distributional impact, **14:** 285–86
    elasticity of demand and, **9:** 54, 61, 76,
    176
    equal maximum revenue and, **9:**
    68, 74
    excise tax, of specific, **4:** 243–44
    with general and uniform tax rates, **14:**
    314
    inefficiency, **5:** 174; **14:** 313–14
    issues, **14:** 285
    Italian fiscal theory and, **15:** 74–75,
    84–85
    majoritarian rotation and, **11:** 34
    on majority coalition, **9:** 187–88

tax burden, excess (*continued*)
  maximization of revenues and, **9:**
    73–74, 78–79, 225
  in model of constitutional contract, **14:**
    245–46
  optimal taxation and, **9:** 70
  under perfect tax discrimination, **9:**
    85–86
  rates and, **9:** 54–55
  tax collection to finance public services,
    14: 122–25
  taxes and, **9:** 43–44; **11:** 116, 125
  tax institutions, and analysis of, **4:**
    43, 54
  with temporal shift, **14:** xv, 437, 475–76
  theorem, **14:** 101, 122
  See also costs; public debt
tax cartel. *See* cartels
tax constitution. *See* fiscal constitution
tax deduction
  categories of itemized, **14:** 134
  difference from tax credit, **14:** 135
  for individual taxpayer benefit, **14:**
    137–38
  justification for, **14:** 134–35
  for purely private good, **14:** 138–41
  substituting for public spending, **14:**
    142–44
tax distribution, equirevenue, **11:** 115–16
taxes, **10:** 94–101
  allocation and distribution of, **1:** 120,
    121–22, 123–32; **5:** 174; **7:** 67–68; **14:**
    75–86
  avoidance of, **9:** 109
  awareness of, **4:** 186, 187–89
  broad-based, **9:** 69, 228
  burden of payment, **4:** 254: distribution,
    1: 122–32; fragmentation of, **4:** 134
  capital gains, **11:** 127
  as coercive instruments, **14:** 38, 228–31
  commodities, **11:** 128
  consumption, **11:** 128

  credit different from tax deduction, **14:**
    135
  in Crusoe model: of income allocation,
    12: 247–50; of saving, **12:** 250–51
  direct, **4:** 22–43, 44–45
  as drainage on the economy, **14:** 125
  excise, **4:** 52–54, 63, 131, 187, 243–57
  expenditure, **2:** 67–71; **4:** 42–43; **9:** 49,
    111; **11:** 128
  exploitation of, **9:** 198–99
  fiscal illusion and incidence of, **4:**
    134–35, 283–85; **5:** 182
  flat-rate, **1:** 425; **11:** 114, 126, 128
  hailstorm, **5:** 157
  highway, **9:** 170
  income (*see* income tax, personal)
  inheritance, **1:** 307; **4:** 133, 300–301
  interest income, **9:** 111
  labor income, **9:** 111–12
  lump-sum (*see* lump-sum tax)
  on money balances in inflation, **9:**
    134–44
  new versus old taxes, **4:** 57–62
  payroll, **9:** 60; **14:** 22; **15:** 413–14, 451–52
  penalty tax, **13:** 420–30, 431
  Pigovian, **6:** 66
  policy implications of response to, **14:**
    126–28
  progressive (*see* progressive tax)
  property, **9:** 229–31; **16:** 104
  proportional, **1:** 129; **4:** 30–38, 48–66;
    14: 196, 250–51, 257–58
  public debt, **13:** 445–46; **14:** 394–403,
    476
  real-estate, **4:** 65–68
  redistributive, **1:** 130
  regressive tax rates, **1:** 130, 148; **4:**
    154–55, 163–64; **9:** 44–45, 51, 54, 86
  road-use, **9:** 170; **12:** 311–26
  on savings, **11:** 127
  state-level policy, **12:** 238–41
  tax exemption, **2:** 152–53; **11:** 128

transfer, **4:** 133; **14:** 242–43; **17:** 322–24

value-added, **9:** 60, 228

wealth, **4:** 27–29; **9:** 109–10 (*see also* taxation: of capital)

See also taxation; tax limits; taxpayers; tax rates; tax system; tax theory

tax incidence, **6:** 50–52

Black's analysis, **14:** 26–27

post-Marshallian theory, **14:** 12

social security, **14:** 22–24 (*see also* payroll tax, social security)

taxing and spending decisions, bridge between, **4:** 87–96, 115

Wicksell on, **19:** 140–42

See also balanced budget; public debt

tax institutions

constitutional choice among, **14:** 34–35, 151–74

efficiency ranking of, **14:** 305

elasticity of, **4:** 63–64

fiscal perceptions and, **8:** 131–38

individual modification of tax bases under, **14:** 86–87

influence on fiscal choice, **8:** 131–38

interdependencies between revenue demands and form of, **14:** 152

perceived permanence of, **14:** 153–54

proposals for reform, **14:** 128–32, 153–54

rank ordering of, **4:** 43

as rules, **4:** 219–21

threshold of response under, **4:** 60

See also fiscal institutions; social security system

tax law

costs to change, **14:** 279

pressure to change, **14:** 280–81

tax liability, ignorance of

under corporation income tax, **4:** 15–16, 47–50

under earmarking, **4:** 72

under excise tax, **4:** 52–54

under general sales tax, **4:** 50–52

under progressive income tax, **4:** 38–43

under proportional income tax, **4:** 30–36

public debt issue and, **4:** 99

rules of thumb, and use of, **4:** 37

with separate tax and expenditure decisions, **4:** 92–96

undervaluation, **1:** 151–56

tax limits

alternative forms of, **14:** 181–94

constitutional, **14:** 179

constitutional choice related to, **14:** 229–49

ethical, relevance of, **14:** 213–15

ethical justification for upper, **14:** 225

ethical norms, derivation from, **14:** 213–14, 225–26

implied by maximal equal liberty, **14:** 217–20

imposed by liberty of secession on, **14:** 220–22

limits on, **9:** 196

objective, **14:** 176

setting, parameters in, **14:** 222–25

of the state, **14:** 215–16

on tax base, **14:** 181, 184–89

on tax rates, **14:** 181, 189–94

tax reform and, **9:** 59–60, 224–28

tax loopholes, **7:** 210 n. 11; **9:** 57, 232

taxpayers

agreement related to transfer taxes, **14:** 242–43

in alternative models of political choice, **14:** 46–53

as bearer of cost of public debt, **14:** 357–64

choice calculus of, **4:** 12–14, 90–95, 172–73, 216

collective choice and, **13:** 382–86

conditions for imposing costs on, **14:** 499

counterequity model of tax reform, **14:** 288–98

taxpayers (*continued*)

equity model of tax reform, **14:** 288–98

expectations of, **13:** 477–78

individual choice and, **13:** 382–86

marginal rates and high-income, **4:** 186

median-voter, **4:** 143–56, 158, 163–67

in model of government fiscal decisions, **14:** 197–211

net worth, **2:** 45

predicting tax-rate, tax-revenue equilibrium, **13:** 477–78

rationality of, **4:** 8–9, 27, 60, 92–93, 122–23, 126–27, 262–63

responses to alternative tax rates, **13:** 470–73, 477–78

surplus, **5:** 39, 45, 89, 91

tax burden with temporal shift, **14:** 475–76

tax deduction benefit for, **14:** 137–38

tax reform with marginal rate reduction, **14:** 298–303

time preference, **9:** 121–22

tax-prices, **14:** 39–40, 75, 362

budget deficits and, **8:** 107

in collective decision models, **4:** 149–51

decision-making efficiency of invariant, **4:** 23–27

discrimination and, **9:** 38, 87–88, 185; **15:** 153–55

equilibrium set of, determination of, **5:** 44–45

in fiscal exchange contract, **14:** 93–94

invariant, **4:** 23–27

Lindahl, **1:** 137–38; **9:** 43n. 2; **11:** 29, 153–57

marginal valuation curve relation to, **5:** 137

market price and, compared, **4:** 23–24, 87–90, 182–83

penalty tax on, effect of, **13:** 420–21

price discrimination in, **15:** 153–55

private behavior on, effect of, **4:** 16, 25–28

of public goods, **14:** 75–83

to satisfy preferences, **13:** 413

supplementing of direct user pricing by, **5:** 173

surplus symmetrical shifts in, **4:** 149–50, 155–56, 163–68

uniformity in, **5:** 44

variability of, **4:** 39–41

tax rates

announcement of, effects of, **9:** 103–10

constitutional constraints on, proposal to impose, **13:** 53–54

constraints on, **9:** 48–55

excess tax burden and, **14:** 314

fiscal policy and, **13:** 442–43, 445

harmonization of European Union, **18:** 146

intertemporal neutrality, **14:** 403–4

limits of, **9:** 229–31

regression in, **9:** 44–45, 51, 54

setting, Hayek's suggestion for, **14:** 259

in short-term Laffer curve, **13:** 314

sinking fund and, **14:** 404

structure, degression in, **9:** 54

taxpayers' response to alternative, **13:** 470–73, 477

tax revenue, relationship to, **13:** 466–68

uniform, **9:** 57, 79–84

tax reform, **9:** xxii, 14, 15; **11:** 123

costs of and pressure for, **14:** 279–83

counterequity model, **14:** 288–98

in democracy, **9:** 223

discussion (late 1970s), **16:** 328–29

excess tax burden and, **14:** 285

equirevenue comparison, **9:** 225–26

equity model, **14:** 288–98

Leviathan model of government and, **9:** 219

with marginal rate reduction, **14:** 298–303

orthodoxy in, **9:** 225–26
prospects, **9:** 224–38
rent seeking related to, **16:** 323–26
revenues and, **9:** 225–26
tax base, analysis of, in decisions for, **14:** 171–74
tax limits and, **9:** 59–60, 224–28
Tax Reform Act (1986)
generality in, **14:** 318–19
political agents' interest in, **14:** 50–52
public choice theory evaluation of, **14:** 52–53
rate reduction and base-broadening, **14:** 46–50
tax revolt, **9:** xxi, 14, 31, 220–21, 226
tax rules
as constitutional rules, **9:** 222
in open economy, **9:** 200–203
as social overhead capital, **14:** 269–83
tax-sharing arrangements, **5:** 45, 124–25, 127–41 passim, 144, 150–53, 156, 158
constitutional rules on, **5:** 153
in federalist system, **18:** 23
under fiscal exchange, **16:** 318
fiscal externalities, in internalization of, **18:** 58–60
inflexibility in, **5:** 149–50
in local government units, **18:** 60–62
locational rents and, **18:** 59–60
nature of, **5:** 122–24
proposal for downward shift in, **5:** 137
publicness in, **5:** 122, 138
in tax theory, **14:** 212–13
vectors, lexicographic ordering of, **5:** 133
tax surveys:, **4:** 187–88 (Ferber); Institute of Economic Affairs, **4:** 188, 193–97, 202–4; University of Cologne, **4:** 185–86 (Schmölders); University of Michigan, **4:** 186 (Gensemer, Lean, Neenan); University of Virginia, **4:** 183–84 (Enrick), 184–85 (Wagstaff)

tax system
in constitutional perspective, **14:** 269–71; **16:** 314
criteria, **16:** 314–18, 320–21
in European Union, with reverse revenue sharing, **18:** 145–46
neutral, **15:** 78
public finance, in orthodox, **14:** 269
quasi-constitutional status, **14:** 270
rules, predictable and stable, **16:** 321–23
as social capital, **14:** 269–83
structure, **14:** 309–10; **16:** 321–23
tax theory
ability-to-pay, **4:** 156–57; **5:** 158
commodity, orthodoxy in, **9:** 68–69
contractarianism and, **1:** xviii
equirevenue and, compared, **9:** 42–43
income and capital, orthodoxy in, **9:** 101–3
of Italian fiscal theorists, **15:** 64–65, 81–97
normative, **14:** 31–35, 152
orthodoxy in, **9:** 15
tax share allocation in, **14:** 212–13
teams, theory of, **3:** 10
technology
information-communication revolution, **19:** 201, 206, 247, 261–62
of public goods, **5:** 54
temporary preference theory, **16:** 401–2
term limits
constraints imposed by, **13:** 283–84
legislative initiative for, **13:** 281
terms of trade, **3:** 101–2
manipulation of, **18:** 239, 247–49
Thomas Jefferson Center for Studies in Political Economy (and Social Philosophy), **1:** 7, 26; **19:** 38–44, 51–52, 54, 118
Tiebout adjustment, **11:** 190–91
Tiebout competition, **11:** 191
Tiebout efficiency, **11:** 191

Tiebout mobility, **11:** 19–21
Tiebout model, **14:** 226, 241n. 15
    citizens in, **18:** 81, 163
    of dividend income, **18:** 62
    individuals in idealized, **18:** 47–48
    of local government fiscal behavior, **18:**
        44–64, 148, 163
    in multilevel fiscal structures, **18:** 26
time, **10:** 76–91
    arbitrage-through-time, **12:** 164–67
    choice of excise tax and, **4:** 245–52
    entrepreneurs holding assets through,
        12: 164–65
    in fiscal decisions, **4:** 57–70
    in household production function, **12:**
        219–20
    in Kirzner's theory of entrepreneurship,
        18: 300–303
    in monopolist-consumer exchanges, **12:**
        211–12
    in monopoly theory, **12:** 221–35
    in ownership of private property, **18:**
        245–47
    in subjectivist theory, **18:** 297, 300, 304
    taxes and, **10:** 94–101
time, theories of
    choice and, neo-Austrian, **1:** 251
    economics, Marshallian, **1:** 444–45,
        454
trade
    bargaining in, **5:** 77, 82
    via collective-coercive arrangements,
        5: 80
    commencement of, **5:** 25
    after contract, **7:** 78–83
    determination of, by comparative
        advantage, **5:** 16; **6:** 8
    determining efficient, **5:** 15–16, 19
    ethics and, **3:** 267–70
    exit from exchange relationship, **12:**
        437–41
    external, **11:** 104–7

final goods: allocation of, **12:** 155–56
foreign, and generality, **11:** 104–7
free, and generality, **11:** 101–12
freedom of, **18:** 77–78, 97; **19:** 193
gains-from-trade (*see* gains-from-trade)
goods in exchange transaction of, **12:**
    33–34
interference with public bad, **15:** 289
in intermediate goods, **12:** 154–58
to internalize externalities, **12:** 169
market exchange, **19:** 103–5, 289–91,
    293–96, 315
prisoners' dilemma in, **17:** 87–89
in private goods, **5:** 75–76, 79–80, 121
in public goods, **5:** 30, 75, 79–80, 121,
    186
rules, **1:** 265; **10:** 30
with specified property rights, **17:** 112
terms of, **5:** 76, 83
in theory of social cost (Coase), **12:** 154,
    169–70
in votes, **3:** 38, 123
See also buyers; fiscal exchange; sellers
trade-off
    alternative tax-rate, tax-revenue,
        politicians' response to, **13:** 473–74
    choice sets of individuals in
        intertemporal, **16:** 411–12
    among "goods" and "bads," **16:** 412
    between unemployment and inflation,
        8: 87–90, 172–74
Trading with the Enemy Act (1917), **18:**
    396
tragedy of the commons. *See* commons,
    the
transaction costs, **1:** xix, 260–77; **3:** 90; **7:**
    48; **9:** 10
    in Coase theorem, **12:** 295; **13:** 298; **15:**
        174–75
    collective action to reduce, **15:** 13–14
    in contractarian concept of collective
        action, **13:** 302–3

in economic theory, **12:** 137

in economy: with money, **12:** 414; without money, **12:** 417

in exchanges, **15:** 12–13

externalities: in agreements for dealing with, **13:** 359–62; in small- and large-number, **15:** 175

externality-creating, **13:** 360–64

free-rider responsibility and, **15:** 12–13

Pareto relevance of externality, in determining, **12:** 362

in potential exchanges, **15:** 175

role in government organization of activities, **13:** 314–15

See also borrowing; buyers and sellers; Coase neutrality theorem

transfer payments, **2:** 46

demographic change, effect of, **15:** 448–49

as share of U.S. GNP, **15:** 442–43

under social security system, **15:** 392–94, 408, 411–13, 447

to veterans and to unemployed, **15:** 456

welfare transfers under social security, **15:** 455–56

transfer rights

inefficiency of uncompensated, **13:** 263

Pareto criterion to evaluate potential, **17:** 78–79

transfers

in budget, **11:** 162–63

of churning state, **19:** 204

collective or governmental, **19:** 104–5

constitutional, **10:** 145

under contractual distribution, **16:** 278–80

economic growth and, **11:** 163–64

in federal system, **18:** 12–13

financed by majority coalition, **16:** 271

fiscal, using equity principle to determine, **18:** 13–25

for fiscal equalization in federal system, **18:** 39–40

in-kind, **11:** 171

intergenerational, **17:** 322–24: overlapping-generations model (Barro), **14:** 386–87; public debt financing on, effects of, **14:** 496–97, 532

interpersonal, **19:** 103–5

interregional, **2:** 63

in market economies, **19:** 255–58

means testing for, **11:** 164

as nonproductive public spending, **18:** 126

old-age, **11:** 167–69

Pareto criterion in analysis of, **13:** 139–49

policy for interpersonal, **13:** 273–75

politics and, **10:** 127, 129

problem, Keynes-Ohlin sense, **2:** 63–65

of rights, **13:** 263, 274, 277; **16:** 29–31

supranational federalism, spending under, **18:** 126–27

targeted, **11:** 169–70

uncompensated: resource allocation with rent seeking related to, **13:** 278–80

of value, **13:** 264–77

voluntary cooperative for purpose of making, **13:** 135–36

in welfare states, **19:** 237, 255–60

in Western economies, **19:** 237–38

See also bequests; fiscal transfer; income transfer; intergenerational transfers

transfer tax, **17:** 322–24

fiscal illusion and, **4:** 133

social rent with reduced level of, **14:** 242–43

transfer welfare state. *See* welfare state

truth

in autobiography, **19:** 64

model of, **17:** 268–70

truth (*continued*)
mutual exclusivity of, **17:** 157, 162
in politics, **1:** 234–37, 242–43; **11:** 4; **17:**
165–66
provisional, **17:** 167–68
in science, **1:** 232–34, 242–43, 385; **17:**
154–55, 157–58, 167
tested by agreement, **16:** 175–76
test of, **2:** 4
values different from, **17:** 164, 169
vision of academic liberal, **16:** 175–78
truth judgment
constitutional agreement, in
interpretation of, **16:** 166–69
in judicial review, **16:** 63
in law enforcement, **16:** 217
in politics, **3:** 3; **7:** 20–21, 124; **16:** 18,
175–76, 367–70
student revolutionary, approach of, **16:**
178–79
tyranny, **1:** 373, 441
potential for, **17:** 153
See also Leviathan

unanimity, **1:** 5, 15, 64, 72, 98, 99–100, 145,
208, 270, 421, 423, 463, 464; **3:** x, 85–96;
4: 115–16, 288–89
bargaining costs and, **3:** 60, 69, 107
as benchmark, **3:** 6, 96; **9:** 9–10; **11:** 22
collective order and, **10:** 26
compensation and, **3:** 90–91
constitutional, **11:** 22–23
constitutional change and, **7:** 106
as contractual ideal, **10:** 31–33
costs of, **3:** 69
criterion, **1:** 216–19, 463, 464; **3:** 14–15,
92n. 3; **17:** 257–58
departures from, **7:** 55–67
efficiency and, **7:** 50
exchange and, **7:** 50–52
exclusion and, **7:** 52–55
failure to achieve, **1:** 141, 201, 204, 205,
235, 276

in fiscal choice, **9:** 182–83
majority rule and, **3:** 254–55; **11:** 39
Pareto criterion and, **3:** 92n. 3
political exchange and, **3:** 248–51
public goods under, supply of, **5:** 88
as rule, **4:** 116; **11:** 118–19
side payments and, **3:** 90–91
status quo and, **3:** x
voluntary behavior and, **7:** 52–55
unanimity criterion (consensus criterion)
conceptual, **17:** 379
in constitutional choice setting, **16:** 10,
220–21
at constitutional level, **17:** 257
at operational level of choice, **17:** 257–58
Pareto criterion defined by, **17:** 259–60
in Rawls's difference principle, **16:**
291–92
rules, applied to, **16:** 73
rules for change based on, **17:** 114–15
Samuels's criticism of, **17:** 129–30
unanimity rule
bargaining and, **3:** 69, 107
for cartel agreement, **13:** 341
changed to relative unanimity, **4:** 116
collective choice: absence of, **13:** 303–4;
operating under, **16:** 150
in constitutional reform, **16:** 270
criticism of, **12:** 185
for decision making, **5:** 90
entrepreneurial activity, effect on, **12:**
184–85
fiscal process with and without, **14:** 95
full, **5:** 92
in group decision making, **5:** 9, 10, 101;
15: 464
implicit, in private goods trade, **5:** 79
market institutions, analogy to, **5:** 7–8
in model of Pareto-optimal income
redistribution, **13:** 137
near-, **5:** 95
Pareto optimality and, **5:** 91–92, 114,
116

political choice, as basis for discussion of, **13:** 10

in politics, **13:** 10

"relative," **5:** 90–91, 92, 147

replaced by majority rule, **16:** 270

status quo, and **3:** x

vote trading and, **3:** 276–77

"workable," **5:** 9, 10

See also collective action; majority rule voting; neutrality, allocational; voting rules

unanimity rule (Wicksell), **1:** 5, 98, 140, 145, 204, 421, 464; **3:** xix, 85–96; **4:** 116–17, 287–89; **5:** 50, 88, 127, 132, 146–48, 154, 155; **7:** 124, 127, 188–90; **10:** 151–52; **13:** 10, 75, 93, 94, 110, 301–3; **14:** 309; **16:** 72; **18:** 351–53

collective choice and, **1:** 15, 23, 217–19; **3:** 6, 63–84

consensus test and, **1:** 269, 431, 432, 466

constitutions and, **14:** 259–60

constructual criteria, **14:** 228–29

contribution to theory of, **5:** 93

in fiscal choice, **19:** 142

in fiscal exchange model, **14:** 92–95

in fiscal theory, **16:** 9–10

government debt and spending under, **14:** 259–60, 463–64

imposition of tax charges, **14:** 228–29, 233

Pareto criterion and, relationship between, **16:** 10, 71

in public finance theory, **14:** 62–63

for taxing and spending proposals, **16:** 319

unanimity test, **12:** 281

of voting on public sector decisions, **14:** 7, 11–13

See also voting rules

uncertainty, **1:** 23, 370

alternative choice under, **4:** 107–8; **17:** 38, 172–73

in assignment of rights, **12:** 296

choice between debt and currency creation, effect on, **4:** 107–8

choice of progressive income tax institution and, **4:** 236–38

choice of public debt institution and, **4:** 263–64

choice of specific excise tax institution and, **4:** 253

in choice theory, **12:** 142–43

choice under: Arrow on, **1:** 77 nn. 2,5; Shackle on, **12:** 143, 150, 163

in collective choice, **3:** 37

about constitutional issues, **16:** 161–62

in decision-making process, **4:** 157–58

decision making under (Wiseman), **19:** 113, 115

entrepreneurial choice and, **12:** 150, 163

increasing, facilitating agreement by, **16:** 162 n. 10

individual choice and, **12:** 149, 151; **14:** 113–16

in inflation, **8:** 67–68

information and (Knight), **12:** 145

Knight on, **1:** 77

opportunity costs and, **12:** 296

rational choice behavior under, **17:** 69–70

risk and, **12:** 279; distinction between (Knight), **12:** 142–45; **19:** 87–88; as properties of structure (Knight), **12:** 142, 144

rules and, **3:** 78; **16:** 162

See also certainty; choice; veil of ignorance; veil of uncertainty

uncertainty, cognitive, **12:** 145, 149–52

unemployment, **4:** 104–6; **8:** 3, 8–9

debt theory and, **2:** 96–97

in Great Depression, **12:** 458

historical record, **8:** 169–70

inflation and, **2:** 96; **8:** 87–90, 172–77

involuntary, **8:** 178–79; **12:** 366

unemployment (*continued*)
  in Keynesian macroeconomic theory, **2:**
    24; **12:** 366, 458–59
  natural rate, **8:** 91, 161, 174–75
  price-level stability and, **8:** 169n. 4
  structural, in Keynesian economics, **2:**
    24; **8:** 97n. 2
uniform service levels, origins of, **11:** 192
unitary polity
  constitutional politics of, **16:** 232
  modern U.S. as, **16:** 232–33
United Artists Television, Inc. v. Fortnightly
  Corp. (1966), **15:** 261n. 2
United States v. Briddle and Mitchell
  (1962), **18:** 424n. 31
United States v. Butler (1936), **18:** 355
United Steelworkers, etc. v. Weber (1979),
  17: 344, 347–49
universal benevolence assumption, **1:** 72
universalization principle, **1:** 312–13. *See
  also* generality principle
University of Chicago
  economics department (1940s), **19:**
    10–13, 51, 77, 88–89
  intellectual excitement of, **19:** 6
  Knight's influence at, **19:** 52–53,
    77–85
University of Virginia
  economics program (1950s), **19:** 39–40,
    52–54
  Hayek's visit to, **19:** 118–19
  Thomas Jefferson Center for Studies in
    Political Economy (and Social
    Philosophy), **1:** 7, 26; **19:** 38–44,
    51–52, 54, 118
  Virginia school of political economy
    (*see* political economy, Virginia
    school of)
unknowability
  of choice (Shackle), **19:** 159–60
  Wiseman's thesis of, **19:** 110, 114
use rights, **11:** 84–85

utilitarianism, **16:** 28; **17:** 236–38
  individualism in, **1:** 94
  influence on economic theory, **1:** 191,
    256, 282, 389
  nineteenth-century, **11:** 116
  rejection of, **1:** 17, 32, 87, 250, 298, 301
  taxation and, **11:** 116
utilitarian tradition, **2:** 29
utility
  cost and, **6:** 41
  in equirevenue model, **11:** 115–16
  of income, **1:** 294
  of nonlabor resources, **12:** 371–72
  Pareto criterion and, **1:** 309
  principles of, **1:** 194, 298
  samaritan's dilemma and, **1:** 329, 335–37
  Stigler-Becker stability of, **1:** 249
  value of leisure, **12:** 371
  See also economic theory; marginal-
    utility economics; public debt; social
    utility; value
utility function, **1:** 34, 244, 246, 260, 282,
    286, 287, 349, 457
  in explanatory sense of economic
    theory, **12:** 134–36
  of *Homo economicus,* **13:** 116–17
  of individual (Alchian), **12:** 129–32
  individual behavior and, **1:** 286
  of individual with public and private
    goods, **15:** 195–96
  in predictive sense of economic theory,
    12: 134–35
  tax-rate, tax-revenue model of, **13:**
    468–73
utility maximization, **1:** 191, 245, 251, 333,
    338, 339, 343, 344, 349, 356, 362; **17:**
    99–101
  of Arrow, Black, Downs, and
    Schumpeter, **16:** 68–70
  in choices, **13:** 116; **15:** 362–63
  circumstances for departing from, **17:**
    229–31

criticism of, **16:** 108, 239–40
dictating choice behind veil of
  uncertainty, **16:** 74
difference from contractarian
  paradigm, **16:** 85
generalizing from individual, **16:** 106–7
in exchange relationship, **17:** 81
limits of individual, **17:** 99–101
man and (Stigler), **12:** 74–75
in neoclassical economics, **17:** 236–39
in politics, **3:** 26
preference of rational actor, **16:** 156–57
in prisoners' dilemma, **17:** 440
in private individual behavior, **15:** 303–4
in public choice theory, **13:** 174
in rational choice model, **17:** 55, 58–60
self-interest, **3:** 3
small- versus large-number settings, **1:**
  363, 371
utility theory as forerunner, **3:** 330. *See also*
  game theory
utopian future state, **1:** 233; **7:** 5–9

valuation
  of life, **12:** 278–79
  marginal evaluation curve (Hicks), **12:**
    196–99
  role of information in process of, **12:**
    144
  of traded intermediate and final goods,
    12: 155–56
  of traded items, **12:** 154–55
  See also marginal evaluation curve
value
  attempts by rent seekers to secure, **19:**
    106
  bequests as transfers of, **13:** 265
  capital, **9:** 99; **14:** 381, 456, 461–62,
    368–73, 376–80, 447
  Coase theorem, in statement of, **12:**
    154–55
  in choice among alternatives, **12:** 114

decision rules restricting transfer of, **13:**
  271–73
determining, **12:** 25
economic, of voting franchise, **13:** 147
exchange, **10:** 28–29; **13:** 264–65; **17:** 30,
  31
of external and internal marginal
  products, **14:** 235 n. 8
of firm and monopoly, **12:** 209–10
gifts as transfers, **13:** 265
individuals as sources of, **10:** 25–27; **17:**
  267–73
interest and, as market in politics, **17:**
  166
interpersonal transfers of, **19:** 103–5
labor standard of, **1:** 415–16
of legislators as agents, **13:** 283–84
of leisure, **1:** 349; **12:** 371
of liberty for buyers and sellers, **18:** 205
loss in rent-seeking activities, **13:**
  346–47
marginal utility and, **6:** 9
markets, created by, **19:** 268–69
money and, **9:** 133, 140; **18:** 247–49
of opportunity foregone, **12:** 285–86
of ownership rights, **12:** 404–6
production cost and, **6:** 17
production creates, **19:** 223–24, 234, 268
profit seeking, created by, **13:** 277
in public choice theory, **13:** 174
social rent as, **14:** 231–32, 233 n. 7, 237,
  247–48
of social security benefit payments, **15:**
  451–52
socialist economy, generation in, **19:** 237
social standards (Knight), in setting, **12:**
  111–12
social value: ethical weight in, absence
  of, **12:** 125; judgments, **1:** 210, 229;
  market exchange, absence in, **12:** 117;
  maximization of, **1:** 263
in spontaneous order, **13:** 72–73

value (*continued*)
  in trade relationship, **12:** 33–34
  of work, **1:** 415–16
  See also capital value; costs; market
    exchange
value relativism, **1:** 451–52
values
  collectivists' positive, **17:** 296
  democratic, basis for, **14:** 37
  electoral process as expression of, **17:**
    269–70
  ensured, **13:** 75
  equality and, as premise for
    individualism, **16:** 19, 24, 27
  individualists' positive, **17:** 296
  of liberty, prosperity, and peace, **19:**
    309–10
  moral value of legal order, **14:** 523
  relative and absolute, **17:** 167–69
  relativism and individualism of, **17:**
    169–70
  in traditional economic theory, **14:** 479
  truth different from, **17:** 164, 169
  in uncompensated transfers, **13:** 277
  See also ethics; opportunity cost(s);
    preference
value scale
  criticism of Knight's, **12:** 113
  economic, **12:** 114
  of an economic system (Knight), **12:**
    111–13, 116
  for efficiency, **1:** 194–95
  establishment of, **12:** 113
  individual, **1:** 93, 194
  individual's, role of prices in, **12:** 114–15
  individual's internal, **12:** 114–15
  social, **1:** 93, 182; **12:** 121
value theory (Ferrara), **15:** 62
veil of ignorance, **9:** 6, 15, 16, 38; **10:** 33–35,
  155; **11:** 7–9, 16, 64, 68, 77, 99, 176, 185,
  192, 194 n. 6; **14:** 13 n. 16, 236–37; **16:** 128,
  160, 326–27, 334, 407–8; **18:** 180, 192,
  272–73

agreement made from behind, **16:** 187;
  17: 364–66
bargaining behind, **16:** 294–95, 300–301
choice from behind, **14:** 255, 527–28; **15:**
  370; **16:** 187, 287–96; **17:** 365–66,
  388–95: Rawls's, choice made behind,
  1: 24, 146 n. 7, 301, 365, 432, 465, 466;
  14: 464; **16:** 103, 129
choice from behind partial, **16:** 327–28
choice of rules or institutions from
  behind, **16:** 38, 285–92
choice under, **16:** 129
constraints and, **9:** 41
in contractual process, **17:** 380
criticism of, **19:** 281
fiscal policy from behind, **19:** 61–62
institutions chosen from behind, **16:**
  287–96; **17:** 388–90
intergenerational, **15:** 372
interpretation and use of, **19:** 280–81
intertemporal choices behind, **14:** 464,
  532–33
justice and agreement from behind, **16:**
  103
lagged implementation and, difference
  between, **16:** 409
legal rules chosen from behind, **16:** 32
lexicographical preferences from
  behind, **15:** 370
maximal equal liberty behind,
  acceptance of, **14:** 226
original position, **10:** 36
predictions from behind, **16:** 287–91,
  294–96; **17:** 376
preferences behind, **15:** 370
rule of law, relationship to, **19:** 281–83
values assigned from behind, **17:** 386–87
See also difference principle of
  distribution (Rawls); justice
veil of insignificance, **13:** 371
veil of uncertainty, **1:** 23, 464, 466; **3:**
  78–79; **11:** 7–9, 23, 64, 68, 77; **16:** 128–29,
  333–34, 407–8; **18:** 180, 192, 272–73

choice and agreement behind, **16:** 187–88

choice of rules behind, **16:** 74

criticism of, **19:** 281

fiscal policy from behind, **19:** 61–62

interpretation and use of, **19:** 280–81

lexicographical preferences from behind, **15:** 370

preferences behind, **15:** 370

rule of law, relationship to, **19:** 281–83

utility maximization and, **16:** 74

variation in thickness of, **16:** 161–62

veto, **3:** xvi

Vietnam era

draft during, **11:** 59–60

war, financing of, **11:** 121n. 10

Virginia Polytechnic Institute and State University

Center for Study of Public Choice, **19:** 44–45, 108–9

public choice program, **19:** 57–58

Virginia school of political economy. *See* political economy, Virginia school of

voluntary agreement emerging from decision-making efficiency, **18:** 322–23

voluntary exchange

absent in individual-government exchange, **18:** 187

agreement in, **19:** 141, 150–51

constitutional protection of, **16:** 39–40

constraints, **19:** 241

economic reform, **16:** 376–79

exchange economy coordination, **15:** 8–10

externalities, influence on, **16:** 37–38

as fiscal choice (Wicksell), **19:** 141–42

of goods and services, **16:** 36–39

government as, **9:** 7

among individuals, **18:** 186–87

labor market for, restraints in, **16:** 35–36

legal protection of, **16:** 39–40

liberty to enter, **16:** 29–32

majority rule and, **16:** 39

multi-person, **16:** 31–32

political models, **9:** 7, 10

politicization of, **5:** 7; **19:** 313

politicized interference in, **16:** 374–79; **19:** 315–16

in prisoners' dilemma, **16:** 206–9

restrictions on, **13:** 387–88; **19:** 314–15

rights in, **16:** 29–32; **18:** 210

state intervention, potential for, **16:** 247

theory of pubic finance, pure, **14:** 62–63

two-person, **16:** 29–31

See also behavior; collective choice; exchange; exit options; freedom of choice; individual choice; rights; trade; transfers

voluntary exchange behavior, **1:** 41, 182, 198, 244, 266, 268, 275

unanimity and, **3:** 50–60; **7:** 52–55

voluntary exchange process, **5:** 7–9, 94; **16:** 29–32; **18:** 210

voluntary exchange theory, **5:** 8–9, 27, 45, 186

vote market, **13:** 213–26

voter behavior, **13:** 156–59; **19:** 99–100

choices and, **10:** 86

consumer behavior and, differences in, **13:** 162–64

in election for incumbent, **13:** 283–87

explanation of, **13:** 155, 170

expressive voting, **13:** 294–96

Hegel's recognition of, **13:** 170–72

in incumbency model, **13:** 284–87

with majority rule, **19:** 99–101

in model of electoral choice, **13:** 293–95

paradox of, **13:** 119; **19:** 99–101

participation of individual, **13:** 170–71

perception of tax to correct external diseconomies, **13:** 366–71

political agents, **19:** 334–43

preferences, **13:** 166–69

rational, **13:** 156–62, 167–68

single-peaked preferences, **13:** 44

sports spectator analogy, **13:** 154–55

voter behavior (*continued*)
  transfer programs, related to, **19:** 104
  See also choice calculus; collective
    action; collective choice; individual
    choice; majority rule voting
voter-taxpayer, rationality of
  costs of decision making and, **4:** 219
  in decision to vote, **4:** 122–23
  in fiscal choice, **4:** 8–9, 27, 60
  fiscal illusion and, **4:** 126–27
  public debt and, **4:** 262–63
  spending and tax decisions, with
    respect to gap between, **4:** 92–93
vote trading, **3:** 38, 123, 270–74; **5:** 102,
    109–13
  effect on preferences, **14:** 13
  equilibrium, **5:** 112
  explicit, **5:** 109
  large-number example, **13:** 223–26
  in legislature, **3:** 234
  in many-person model, **5:** 115
  of proxy form, **5:** 111
  small-number example, **13:** 216–18
  structure, **13:** 214–16
  unanimity and, **3:** 276–77
voting
  conflict resolution through, **13:** 414–15
  ethnic differences in, **1:** 321–22
  expressive, theory of, **1:** xvi; **13:** xii
  to impose preferences on behavior, **13:**
    415–18
  individual choice in, **1:** xvi, 16, 64–66,
    69, 75–88, 93, 100–102
  one-dollar–one-vote analogy, **1:** 75,
    83–85
  one-man–one-vote principle, **16:**
    181–82
  paradox of, **5:** 118; **13:** 7, 42–43, 119,
    228 n. 3
  political, **1:** 86
  rights in, **7:** 224
  theories of, and rules, **1:** 50, 53–55, 72,
    226–27; **10:** 85–87

  behind veil of insignificance, **13:** 371
  yes-no, **13:** 196–207, 213–26
  See also duopoly theory; majority;
    majority rule voting
voting, majority. *See* majority rule
  voting
voting choice theory, **16:** 185–86
voting franchise
  economic value of, **13:** 147
  ownership and rights in income
    redistribution, **13:** 139–49
  in Pareto-optimal income
    redistribution, **13:** 129–30
  in Pareto-optimal transfer of goods, **13:**
    139–49
  restriction for income redistribution
    issues, **13:** 130–33, 138–39
voting model
  power index defined, **13:** 202–7
  of yes-no with majority rule, **13:**
    196–201
voting rights, membership-voting, **13:**
  139–40
voting rules
  less-than-unanimity or nonunanimity,
    13: 304
  majority rule (Black), **14:** 12
  theory in public finance, **14:** 11–13
  theory of constitutions, **14:** 13–14
  Wicksell's replacement of strict
    unanimity, **14:** 260
  See also majority rule voting
vouchers to purchase health services, **15:**
  356–57

wages
  classical theory, **6:** 7
  equal pay for equal work, **12:** 272–73
  heterogeneous input, **12:** 262–72
  increased rate in backbending labor-
    supply curve, **12:** 257–59
  inflation and, **8:** 175
  interest group retention of, **13:** 58

minimum, **1:** 302; **13:** 58
prices and, control of, **8:** 93
wage standardization policy
  effect of national, **12:** 236–38
  proposed state-level tax policy to
    counteract, **12:** 238–41
Wagner's law of increasing government
  activity, **15:** 145–47
"waiting." *See* capital formation
wartime debt, **2:** 104–10, 132; **4:** 61–62.
  See also federalism; Hobbesian jungle;
  public debt burden
wartime taxation, **2:** 104–10, 132; **4:**
  61–62
Watergate, **7:** 152n. 10
wealth
  capitalization on, **4:** 29
  constraints on taxation of, **9:** 110
  decision-making efficiency, **4:** 27–29
  fiscal institutions transfers, **14:** 41–43
  illusion of, **2:** 49–50
welfare economics, **1:** 191–209, 210–29,
  256, 275, 453, 467; **3:** xviii, xix, 91–96; **5:**
  118, 139, 183; **6:** 25, 39–40, 65; **7:** 216; **10:**
  16–17; **11:** 69
  allocative norms of, extension to public
    goods, **5:** 161
  ambiguity in, **5:** 183
  applied, **17:** 241
  of Arrow, **1:** 89–92; **13:** 7–9, 43–44; **15:**
    288n. 13; **16:** 68–70, 84
  Buchanan's interest in, **1:** xviii–xix,
    20, 32
  classical and neoclassical economics,
    shift from, **12:** 135
  collective decisions and spending in
    U.S., **15:** 456–57
  compensation in, **1:** 196–202; **3:** 90–91
  contractarian perspective as superior to,
    17: 246–47
  costs in, **6:** 25
  criticism of, **1:** 60–74
  emphasis (1950s, 1960s), **19:** 56

equilibrium, conditions generating, **16:**
  396n. 15
externalities and, **1:** 196–200; **17:**
  142–44; neoclassical (Pigou), **12:**
  292–93; **14:** 121–23; technological and
  pecuniary, **12:** 177–78; **17:** 455
frontier, **1:** 203
function of, **1:** 202–4
government finance and, **1:** 120–32,
  137
individual choice behavior and, **1:** 20
majoritarianism and, **11:** 69–70
marginal-cost pricing, **13:** 317
market failure in, **13:** 113–14, 173; **15:** 286;
  19: 56, 129, 130–31
"meddlesome preferences" and, **1:** 284
neoclassical, **12:** 292–93, 397
normative content in, **17:** 237–40
Paretian, **1:** 192; **3:** 8; **11:** 69: logic of, **16:**
  380–81; Pareto criterion, **1:** 36,
  191–209, 210–29, 256, 300, 431, 439; **3:**
  92; **13:** 8–9; Pareto optimality and, **1:**
  210–29; **17:** 144
Pigovian, **1:** 60–74, 296; **3:** 200–201; **6:**
  65, 72–74; **13:** 29–30, 37, 366; **14:**
  121–23
politicization in, argument for, **19:** 292
post-Pigovian, **1:** 296; **13:** 37–38; **19:** 129
principles of, **13:** 347–48
private choice behavior, **13:** 29
public choice and, **1:** 296
relation of, with positive theory, **5:** 8
before Robbins, **1:** 93
of social choice theory, **16:** 201–10
social welfare function in, **17:** 240:
  economists using, **16:** 81–83;
  Samuelsonian economics and, **1:** 193,
  197, 202; terms of the economy, **16:**
  248
theoretical: development of, **14:** 121;
  theory of market failure in, **13:**
  113–14; **17:** 276
theory of, **13:** 317

welfare economics (*continued*)
  transfers in market economy and, **19:**
    255–58
  See also general impossibility theorem,
    Arrow's; social choice theory; social
    welfare function
welfare gains
  from joint supply of goods and services,
    13: 455–56
  in shift from market to collective
    supply, **13:** 456–57, 459–61
welfare losses
  in comparison between monopoly and
    other market organizations, **12:**
    89–98
  under monopoly, **13:** 251
  in shift from market to collective
    supply, **13:** 455
welfare state, **11:** 159–75
  altruism in (Tullock), **19:** 104–5
  constitutional, **11:** 172–74
  constraints of, **11:** 172–74
  democracies as modern, Western, **19:**
    350
  distribution of economic value under,
    19: 255–56
  distributive politics in, **19:** 272
  effect of Cold War on, **19:** 203, 205
  effect of modern, on fiscal account, **12:**
    433
  failure of, **1:** 60–74, 119–32, 137, 140, 142,
    184–85, 192, 195, 300, 306, 350
  general, **11:** 159–75
  incentives in, **19:** 257, 259
  market economy of, intrusions in, **19:**
    194
  production and consumption in, **19:**
    237–38
  resource allocation, **19:** 257–58
  saving in, influence of, **12:** 467–69
  socialism, differences from, **19:**
    256–58

transfer system in, **19:** 104–5, 237,
    255–60
  See also protective state; socialist
    economies
welfare theory, **1:** 210–11
  competition and, **1:** 61
welfare triangle, **11:** 116; **12:** 207–9
Wicksellian economics
  on benevolent despots, **1:** 15–16, 74, 144,
    362 n. 2, 456
  choice-setting, individuals in, **16:** 73
  choices made within rules, **1:** 15, 23,
    217–19; **3:** 6, 63–84; **16:** 9–10
  collective-decision model, **15:** 462–63,
    467
  collectively financed goods, on
    consumers of, **19:** 141
  constitutional reform, contribution to,
    1: 463–64; **16:** 71–72; **19:** xvi
  contractarian perspective, **17:** 245–47
  contractual consensus test, **1:** 269, 431,
    432, 466; **12:** 281; **14:** 228–29
  efficiency and, **11:** 143
  fiscal choice, rules for, **19:** 142
  fiscal exchange paradigm in, **1:** 134,
    138–40, 142, 144, 145, 147, 192 n. 2;
    14: 11
  fiscal policy, theory of, **1:** 458; **16:** 9–10
  on fiscal results from political
    institutions, **14:** 33
  on free riders, **1:** 323 n. 7; **4:** 114–16, 123,
    287–89
  on gains-from-trade, **19:** 141
  on ideal constitution, **14:** 11
  influence on Buchanan, **1:** 15–16, 20,
    455–57
  Leviathan and, **9:** 183–84
  normative, **1:** 140–42
  on Pareto optimality, conditions for, **4:**
    287–89
  political change, consensus for, **19:** 143
  political choice and, **16:** 72–73

political philosophy, **1:** 20, 204, 421,
    455–57, 459–61; **5:** 10; **11:** 143
public choice: influence on, **19:**
    xvi–xviii, 4, 24, 140–41, 245; as
    precursor to, **13:** 20–21, 40–41
public finance: contribution to, **14:**
    62–63; theory and, **19:** 140–43
public goods: contribution to theory of,
    5: 93; **15:** 292; solution to allocation
    of, **5:** 128, 131, 135
rules of unanimity for collective choice,
    1: 5, 15, 23, 98, 140, 145, 204, 217–19,
    421, 464; **5:** 50, 88, 127, 132, 146–48,
    154, 155; **7:** 124, 127, 188–90; **10:**
    151–52; **13:** 10, 75, 93, 94, 110, 301–3;
    14: 259–60; **16:** 10, 72; **18:** 351–53 (*see
    also* unanimity rule [Wicksell])
taxing-spending choice, **1:** 98, 125, 126 n.
    12, 135, 141, 142, 455, 468; **16:** 319; **19:**
    xvii, 140–42
tax system, internal criteria for, **16:**
    317–18, 320–21
on voluntary exchange as fiscal choice,
    19: 141–42
voting rules and, **14:** 260
Wicksell-Pareto construction
constitutional change within, strategy
    for, **16:** 411
failure of rules within, interpretation of,
    16: 411–12
Wicksell-Pareto criterion, **16:** 10, 71; **17:**
    134, 135
Wicksteed model, **1:** 41
work
benevolent self-interest in, **1:** 357–59
value of, **1:** 415–16
work ethic, **1:** xx, 355–57
as constraint on preferences, **12:** 381
economic content in, **12:** 343, 363–65,
    373
importance of, **12:** 469

influenced by markets, **12:** 275
supply externality, **1:** 353–55, 358, 359
validity in some settings, **12:** 344–45
in work-leisure choice, **12:** 359
See also idleness; labor supply
work-leisure choice
ethical irrelevance of, **12:** 347–49
externality in, **12:** 353–55, 379
margin of, **12:** 364–65, 379
presence of ethical norm in, **12:**
    359–61
See also idleness
work supply
externality similar to trade-extension
    externality, **12:** 365
factors limiting or influencing, **12:**
    357–58
work week: length of, **4:** 35
World War II, **11:** xx, 112
errors in economic forecast after, **8:**
    31–40
public choice theory after, **1:** 45, 58
public finance theory before, **14:** 65
rediscovery of monetary policy after,
    8: 44
socialism and, **1:** 70, 184

yes-no voting
majority rule voting models and, **13:**
    196–200
median voter preferences satisfied in,
    13: 200–207
power indices in, **13:** 200–207
under simple majority rule, **13:** 196–97
voting market related to, **13:** 213–26

zero sum in politics, **3:** 23, 252
zero-transactions cost, **1:** 261, 267; **13:**
    297–315. *See also* Coase theorem
zoning, **3:** 56–57
external costs and, **3:** 71

Title Index

"The Achievement and the Limits of Public Choice in Diagnosing Government Failure and in Offering Bases for Constructive Reform," **13:** 112–26

"Achieving Economic Reform," **16:** 372–83

"Adam Smith as Inspiration," **19:** 289–302

"An Ambiguity in Sen's Alleged Proof of the Impossibility of a Pareto Libertarian," **17:** 71–79

"America's Third Century in Perspective," **19:** 173–86

"Analysis, Ideology and the Events of 1989," **19:** 187–98

"Asymmetrical Reciprocity in Market Exchange: Implications for Economies in Transition," **12:** 409–25

"The Backbending Supply Curve of Labor: An Example of Doctrinal Retrogression?" **12:** 253–59

"The Balanced Budget Amendment: Clarifying the Arguments," **14:** 493–518

"Barro on the Ricardian Equivalence Theorem," **14:** 385–91

"The Bases for Collective Action," **15:** 3–38

"Before Public Choice," **1:** 429–43

"Belief, Choice and Consequences: Reflections on Economics, Science and Religion," **17:** 171–84

"Better than Plowing," **1:** 11–27

"Born-Again Economist," **19:** 3–17

"Boundaries on Social Contract," **16:** 87–100

"Breton and Weldon on Public Goods," **15:** 265–70

"Budgetary Bias in Post-Keynesian Politics: The Erosion and Potential Replacement of Fiscal Norms," **14:** 455–72

"The Budgetary Politics of Social Security," **15:** 376–89

The Calculus of Consent: Logical Foundations of Constitutional Democracy (with Gordon Tullock), **3**

"Can Policy Activism Succeed? A Public Choice Perspective," **19:** 331–43

"Cartels, Coalitions, and Constitutional Politics" (with Dwight R. Lee), **13:** 387–409

"*Ceteris Paribus:* Some Notes on Methodology," **12:** 52–66

"Choosing What to Choose," **17:** 80–95

"The Coase Theorem and the Theory of the State," **13:** 297–315

"Coercive Taxation in Constitutional Contract," **14:** 228–49

"Cognition, Choice, and Entrepreneurship" (with Alberto di Pierro), **12:** 141–53

"Comment," **18:** 338–41

"Commentary," **15:** 421–24

"Confessions of a Burden Monger," **14:** 357–60

"Constitutional Choice, Rational Ignorance, and the Limits of Reason" (with Viktor J. Vanberg), **16:** 127–47

"Constitutional Constraints on Governmental Taxing Power," **14:** 250–65

"Constitutional Democracy, Individual Liberty, and Political Equality," **17:** 266–80

"Constitutional Design and Construction: An Economic Approach," **16:** 101–10

"Constitutional Economics," **16:** 3–14

"The Constitutional Economics of Earmarking," **14:** 80–100

"Constitutional Implications of Alternative Models of Increasing Returns" (with Yong J. Yoon), **12:** 388–96

"Constitutional Restrictions on the Power of Government," **16:** 42–59

"The Constitution of Economic Policy," **1:** 455–68

"Constructivism, Cognition, and Value," **17:** 459–68

"Consumerism and Public Utility Regulation," **13:** 316–32

"Consumption without Production: The Impossible Idyll of Socialism," **19:** 221–38

"Contractarianism and Democracy," **16:** 215–24

"The Contractarian Logic of Classical Liberalism," **16:** 28–41

"A Contractarian Paradigm for Applying Economic Theory," **16:** 79–86

"A Contractarian Perspective on Anarchy," **16:** 15–27

"Contractarian Political Economy and Constitutional Interpretation," **16:** 60–67

"Convexity Constraints in Public Goods Theory" (with António S. Pinto Barbosa), **15:** 271–81

"Cooperation and Conflict in Public-Goods Interaction," **15:** 227–43

Cost and Choice: An Inquiry in Economic Theory, **6**

"Criteria for a Free Society: Definition, Diagnosis, and Prescription," **18:** 173–84

"Cultural Evolution and Institutional Reform," **18:** 311–23

"The 'Dead Hand' of Monopoly" (with Gordon Tullock), **12:** 206–18

"Debt, Public," **14:** 343–56

"A Defense of Organized Crime?" **18:** 432–48

The Demand and Supply of Public Goods, **5**

"Democracy and Duopoly: A Comparison of Analytical Models," **13:** 227–38

Democracy in Deficit: The Political Legacy of Lord Keynes (with Richard E. Wagner), **8**

"Democracy within Constitutional Limits," **16:** 225–34

"Democratic Values in Taxation," **14:** 36–45

"Dialogues Concerning Fiscal Religion" (with Richard E. Wagner), **14:** 473–85

"Dismantling the Welfare State," **16:** 449–57

"Distributional Politics and Constitutional Design," **16:** 267–76

"Distributive and Redistributive Norms: A Note of Clarification," **15:** 434–39

"The Domain of Constitutional Economics," **1:** 377–95

"The Domain of Subjective Economics: Between Predictive Science and Moral Philosophy," **17:** 24–39

"Easy Budgets and Tight Money," **13:** 435–49

"Economic Analogues to the Generalization Argument" (with Gordon Tullock), **17:** 142–45

"The Economic Consequences of the Deficit," **14:** 445–54

"The Economic Constitution and the New Deal: Lessons for Late Learners," **16:** 339–55

"Economic Freedom and Federalism: Prospects for the New Century," **18:** 90–98

"Economic Interdependence and the Work Ethic," **12:** 343–65

"Economic Origins of Ethical Constraints," **17:** 215–31

"Economics and Its Scientific Neighbors," **17:** 3–23

"The Economics and the Ethics of Idleness," **12:** 366–76

"Economics as a Public Science," **12:** 44–51

"Economic Science and Cultural Diversity," **12:** 426–34

"Economics in the Post-Socialist Century," **19:** 239–47

"The Economics of Earmarked Taxes," **14:** 71–88

"Economic Theory in the Postrevolutionary Moment of the 1990s," **12:** 470–85

"An Economic Theory of Clubs," **15:** 193–209

"Economists and the Gains from Trade," **19:** 135–52

"An Economist's Approach to 'Scientific Politics,'" **13:** 3–14

"The Economizing Element in Knight's Ethical Critique of Capitalist Order," **12:** 110–27

"An Efficiency Basis for Federal Fiscal Equalization" (with Richard E. Wagner), **18:** 23–43

"Efficiency Limits of Fiscal Mobility: An Assessment of the Tiebout Model" (with Charles J. Goetz), **18:** 44–64

"Entrepreneurship and the Internalization of Externalities" (with Roger Faith), **12:** 169–87

"The Epistemological Feasibility of Free Markets," **19:** 210–20

"Equality as Fact and Norm," **17:** 281–96

"The Ethical Limits of Taxation," **14:** 212–27

"Ethical Rules, Expected Values, and Large Numbers," **1:** 311–28

"The Ethics of Constitutional Order," **1:** 368–73

"The Ethics of Debt Default," **14:** 519–33

"Europe's Constitutional Opportunity," **18:** 99–117

"The Evaluation of Public Services" (with Francesco Forte), **15:** 39–58

"External Diseconomies, Corrective Taxes, and Market Structure," **15:** 169–73

"External Diseconomies in Competitive Supply" (with Charles J. Goetz), **15:** 156–68

"Externality" (with Wm. Craig Stubblebine), **15:** 109–25

"Externality in Tax Response," **14:** 121–33

"Fairness, Hope, and Justice," **17:** 311–49

"Federalism and Fiscal Equity," **18:** 79–89

"Federalism and Individual Sovereignty," **18:** 79–89

"Federalism as an Ideal Political Order and an Objective for Constitutional Reform," **18:** 67–78

"Fiscal Choice through Time: A Case for Indirect Taxation?" (with Francesco Forte), **14:** 101–20

Foreword to *The Politics of Bureaucracy,* **13:** 62–70

"Foundational Concerns: A Criticism of Public Choice Theory," **13:** 90–111

"The Foundations for Normative Individualism," **1:** 281–91

"Frank H. Knight, 1885–1972," **19:** 74–85

"From Private Preferences to Public Philosophy: The Development of Public Choice," **13:** 39–56

"From the Inside Looking Out," **19:** 18–27

"The Gauthier Enterprise," **17:** 437–58

"General Implications of Subjectivism in Economics," **12:** 22–29

"Generality as a Constitutional Constraint," **1:** 419–28

"Gold, Money and the Law: The Limits of Governmental Monetary Authority" (with T. Nicolaus Tideman), **18:** 385–431

"Good Economics—Bad Law," **18:** 327–37

"Government Transfer Spending," **15:** 440–59

"Hegel on the Calculus of Voting," **13:** 170–72

"A Hobbesian Interpretation of the Rawlsian Difference Principle," **17:** 360–78

"The Homogenization of Heterogeneous Inputs" (with Robert D. Tollison), **12:** 260–77

"How Can Constitutions Be Designed So That Politicians Who Seek to Serve 'Public Interest' Can Survive and Prosper?" **16:** 148–54

"The Icons of Public Debt," **14:** 361–64

"Ideas, Institutions, and Political Economy: A Plea for Disestablishment," **19:** 318–30

"I Did Not Call Him 'Fritz': Personal Recollections of Professor F. A. v. Hayek," **19:** 116–22

"The Incidence and Effects of Public Debt in the Absence of Fiscal Illusion" (with Jennifer Roback), **14:** 408–26

"The Inconsistencies of the National Health Service," **15:** 340–60

"The Incumbency Dilemma and Rent Extraction by Legislators" (with Roger D. Congleton), **13:** 281–96

"In Defense of Advertising Cartels," **13:** 333–45

"In Defense of *Caveat Emptor*," **18:** 358–68

"The Individual as Participant in Political Exchange," **18:** 185–97

"Individual Choice in Voting and the Market," **1:** 75–88

"An Individualistic Theory of Political Process," **17:** 251–65

"Individual Rights, Emergent Social States, and Behavioral Feasibility," **16:** 201–11

"The Institutional Structure of Externality," **15:** 174–89

"Interests and Theories in Constitutional Choice" (with Viktor Vanberg), **16:** 155–71

"Introduction: L.S.E. Cost Theory in Retrospect," **12:** 327–39

"Is Economics a Science of Choice?" **12:** 3–21

"Is Public Choice Immoral? The Case for the 'Nobel' Lie" (with Geoffrey Brennan), **13:** 78–89

"Italian Retrospective," **19:** 28–37

"Jack Wiseman: A Personal Appreciation," **19:** 110–15

"Joint Supply, Externality, and Optimality," **15:** 210–24

"The Justice of Natural Liberty," **1:** 292–310

"Justification of the Compound Republic: The *Calculus* in Retrospect," **16:** 68–75

"Keynesian Follies," **1:** 164–78

"Knight, Frank H.," **19:** 86–94

"Lagged Implementation as an Element in Constitutional Strategy," **16:** 398–416

"Law and the Invisible Hand," **17:** 96–109

"The Libertarian Legitimacy of the State," **17:** 415–28

"Liberty, Market and State," **19:** 165–70

The Limits of Liberty: Between Anarchy and Leviathan, 7

"The Logic of Tax Limits: Alternative Constitutional Constraints on the Power to Tax" (with Geoffrey Brennan), **14:** 175–95

"The Logic of the Ricardian Equivalence Theorem" (with Geoffrey Brennan), **14:** 392–407

"Majoritarian Logic," **13:** 239–48

"Man and the State," **18:** 167–72

"The Market as a Creative Process" (with Viktor J. Vanberg), **18:** 289–310

"Market Failure and Political Failure," **18:** 276–88

"Markets, States, and the Extent of Morals," **1:** 360–67

"Marshall's Mathematical Note XIX" (with Charles Plott), **12:** 67–69

"The Matrix of Contractarian Justice" (with Loren E. Lomasky), **17:** 379–402

"Methods and Morals in Economics: The Ayres-Knight Discussion," **19:** 123–34

"The Minimal Politics of Market Order," **16:** 253–64

"Monetary Research, Monetary Rules, and Monetary Regimes," **17:** 146–49

"Moral Community and Moral Order: The Intensive and Extensive Limits of Interaction," **17:** 202–10

"Moral Community, Moral Order, or Moral Anarchy," **17:** 187–201

"The Moral Dimension of Debt Financing," **14:** 486–92

"National Politics and Competitive Federalism: Italy and the Constitution of Europe," **18:** 118–30

"Natural and Artifactual Man," **1:** 246–59

"The Normative Purpose of Economic 'Science': Rediscovery of an Eighteenth Century Method" (with Geoffrey Brennan), **12:** 70–86

"A Note on Public Goods Supply" (with Milton Z. Kafoglis), **15:** 244–58

"Notes for an Economic Theory of Socialism," **13:** 450–65

"Notes on Irrelevant Externalities, Enforcement Costs and the Atrophy of Property Rights," **18:** 369–81

"Notes on Justice in Contract," **17:** 403–14

"Notes on Politics as Process," **13:** 71–76

"Notes on the History and Direction of Public Choice," **13:** 57–61

"Notes on the Liberal Constitution," **16:** 439–48

"On a Fiscal Constitution for the European Union" (with Dwight R. Lee), **18:** 131–47

"On Monopoly Price" (with Geoffrey Brennan and Dwight Lee), **12:** 219–35

"On Some Fundamental Issues in Political Economy: An Exchange of Correspondence" (with Warren J. Samuels), **17:** 110–41

"On the Incidence of Tax Deductibility" (with Mark V. Pauly), **14:** 134–48

"On the Structure of an Economy: A Re-emphasis of Some Classical Foundations," **18:** 263–75

"Opportunity Cost and Legal Institutions," **12:** 285–97

"The Optimality of Pure Competition in the Capacity Problem: Comment," **12:** 308–10

"Order Defined in the Process of Its Emergence," **1:** 244–45

"Organization Theory and Fiscal Economics: Society, State, and Public Debt" (with Viktor Vanberg), **14:** 429–44

"Peak Loads and Efficient Pricing: Comment," **12:** 298–307
"Political Constraints on Contractual Redistribution" (with Winston C. Bush), **16:** 277–84
"Political Economy: 1957–82," **19:** 38–49
"Political Economy and Social Philosophy," **17:** 235–50
"The Political Economy of Franchise in the Welfare State," **13:** 129–52
"The Political Efficiency of General Taxation," **14:** 305–20
"Political Equality and Private Property: The Distributional Paradox," **17:** 297–310
"The Politicization of Market Failure" (with Viktor J. Vanberg), **13:** 357–71
"Politicized Economies in Limbo: America, Europe and the World, 1994," **19:** 199–209
"Politics and Meddlesome Preferences," **13:** 410–18
"Politics and Science: Reflections on Knight's Critique of Polanyi," **1:** 230–43
Politics by Principle, Not Interest: Toward Nondiscriminatory Democracy (with Roger D. Congleton), **11**
"Politics, Policy, and the Pigovian Margins," **1:** 60–74
"Politics, Property, and the Law: An Alternative Interpretation of *Miller et al. v. Schoene*," **18:** 342–57
"Politics without Romance: A Sketch of Positive Public Choice Theory and Its Normative Implications," **1:** 45–59
"Polluters' Profits and Political Response: Direct Controls versus Taxes" (with Gordon Tullock), **13:** 419–32
"Positive Economics, Welfare Economics, and Political Economy," **1:** 191–209
"Post-Socialist Political Economy," **19:** 248–62
"The Potential for Politics after Socialism," **19:** 303–17
"The Potential for Tyranny in Politics as Science," **17:** 153–70
The Power to Tax: Analytical Foundations of a Fiscal Constitution (with Geoffrey Brennan), **9**
"Pragmatic Reform and Constitutional Revolution" (with Alberto di Pierro), **16:** 384–97
"Predictability: The Criterion of Monetary Constitutions," **1:** 396–418
"Predictive Power and the Choice among Regimes" (with Geoffrey Brennan), **12:** 87–109
"Preface to *Essays on Unorthodox Economic Strategies: A Memorial Volume in Honor of Winston C. Bush*," **19:** 108–9
"Principles of Urban-Fiscal Strategy," **15:** 321–39
"Private Ownership and Common Usage: The Road Case Re-examined," **12:** 311–26

"Procedural and Quantitative Constitutional Constraints on Fiscal Authority," **16:** 307–12

"Professor Alchian on Economic Method," **12:** 128–38

"Prolegomena for a Strategy of Constitutional Revolution," **16:** 417–27

"Property as a Guarantor of Liberty," **18:** 216–59

"Proportional and Progressive Income Taxation with Utility-Maximizing Governments" (with Roger Congleton), **14:** 196–211

"Public and Private Interaction under Reciprocal Externality" (with Gordon Tullock), **15:** 126–55

"Public Choice after Socialism," **19:** 276–85

"Public Choice and Ideology," **13:** 173–76

"Public Choice and Public Finance," **14:** 25–35

"A Public Choice Approach to Public Utility Pricing," **13:** 372–86

"The Public Choice Perspective," **13:** 15–24

"Public Debt and Capital Formation," **14:** 365–82

"Public Debt, Cost Theory, and the Fiscal Illusion," **1:** 150–63

"Public Finance and Public Choice," **14:** 3–24

Public Finance in Democratic Process: Fiscal Institutions and Individual Choice, **4**

"Public Goods and Natural Liberty," **15:** 282–97

"Public Goods and Public Bads," **15:** 301–20

"Public Goods in Theory and Practice: A Note on the Minasian-Samuelson Discussion," **15:** 259–64

Public Principles of Public Debt: A Defense and Restatement, **2**

"The Pure Theory of Government Finance: A Suggested Approach," **1:** 119–32

"The Qualities of a Natural Economist," **19:** 95–107

"Rational Choice Models in the Social Sciences," **17:** 55–70

"Rational Majoritarian Taxation of the Rich: With Increasing Returns and Capital Accumulation" (with Yong J. Yoon), **14:** 321–39

"Rawls on Justice as Fairness," **17:** 353–59

The Reason of Rules: Constitutional Political Economy (with Geoffrey Brennan), **10**

"Reform in the Rent-Seeking Society," **13:** 346–54

"Reform without Romance: First Principles in Political Economy," **19:** 356–63

"A Regional Countermeasure to National Wage Standardization" (with John E. Moes), **12:** 236–41

"The Related but Distinct 'Sciences' of Economics and of Political Economy," **17:** 40–54

"The Relatively Absolute Absolutes," **1:** 442–54

"The Relevance of Constitutional Strategy," **16:** 330–35

"The Relevance of Pareto Optimality," **1:** 210–29

"Rent Seeking and Profit Seeking," **1:** 103–15

"Rent Seeking, Noncompensated Transfers, and Laws of Succession," **13:** 263–80

"Rent Seeking under External Diseconomies," **13:** 251–62

"Resource Allocation and Entrepreneurship," **12:** 154–68

Review of *Imagination and the Nature of Choice,* by G. L. S. Shackle, **19:** 158–61

Review of *Politics and Markets: The World's Political Economic Systems,* by Charles E. Lindblom, **19:** 162–64

"Richard Musgrave, Public Finance, and Public Choice," **14:** 64–68

"Rights, Efficiency, and Exchange: The Irrelevance of Transactions Cost," **1:** 260–77

"The Samaritan's Dilemma," **1:** 329–45

"Saving and the Rate of Interest: A Comment," **12:** 245–52

"'La scienza delle finanze': The Italian Tradition in Fiscal Theory," **15:** 59–105

"Secession and the Limits of Taxation: Toward a Theory of Internal Exit" (with Roger L. Faith), **18:** 148–63

"Shackle and a Lecture in Pittsburgh," **19:** 153–57

"The Simple Economics of the Menial Servant," **12:** 377–87

"Social Choice, Democracy, and Free Markets," **1:** 89–102

"Social Insurance in a Growing Economy: A Proposal for Radical Reform," **15:** 407–20

"Socialism Is Dead, but Leviathan Lives On," **1:** 179–88

"Social Security Survival: A Public-Choice Perspective," **15:** 390–406

"Society and Democracy," **19:** 344–55

"Sources of Opposition to Constitutional Reform," **16:** 356–71

"Structure-Induced Behaviour in Markets and in Politics," **12:** 435–52

"The Structure of Progress: National Constitutionalism in a Technologically Opened World Economy," **16:** 428–38

"Student Revolts, Academic Liberalism, and Constitutional Attitude," **16:** 172–84

"Subjective Elements in Rawlsian Agreement on Distributional Rules" (with Roger L. Faith), **16:** 285–304

"The Supply of Labour and the Extent of the Market," **1:** 346–59

"Taxation in Fiscal Exchange," **1:** 133–49

"Tax Rates and Tax Revenues in Political Equilibrium: Some Simple Analytics" (with Dwight R. Lee), **13:** 466–80

"Tax Reform as Political Choice," **14:** 46–53

"Tax Reform in 'Constitutional' Perspective," **16:** 313–29

"Tax Reform without Tears" (with Geoffrey Brennan), **14:** 284–304

"The Tax System as Social Overhead Capital: A Constitutional Perspective on Fiscal Norms" (with Geoffrey Brennan), **14:** 269–83

"Technological Determinism Despite the Reality of Scarcity: A Neglected Element in the Theory of Spending on Medical and Health Care," **15:** 361–75

"A Theory of Leadership and Deference in Constitutional Construction" (with Viktor Vanberg), **16:** 185–200

"The Theory of Monopolistic Quantity Discounts," **12:** 191–205

"The Theory of Public Finance," **14:** 54–63

"A Theory of Truth in Autobiography" (with Robert D. Tollison), **19:** 64–73

"There *Is* a Science of Economics," **12:** 30–43

"Toward Analysis of Closed Behavioral Systems," **13:** 15–38

"Towards a Tax Constitution for Leviathan" (with Geoffrey Brennan), **14:** 151–74

"Towards a Theory of Yes-No Voting" (with Roger L. Faith), **13:** 195–212

"Towards the Simple Economics of Natural Liberty: An Exploratory Analysis," **18:** 198–215

"The Triumph of Economic Science: Is Fukuyama Wrong and, If So, Why?" **19:** 263–75

"Trying Again to Value a Life" (with Roger L. Faith), **12:** 278–81

"A Two-Country Parable," **17:** 211–14

Untitled, **16:** 237–52

"The Use and Abuse of Contract," **16:** 111–23

"Utopia, the Minimal State, and Entitlement," **17:** 429–36

"Virginia Political Economy: Some Personal Reflections," **19:** 50–63

"Vote Buying in a Stylized Setting" (with Dwight R. Lee), **13:** 213–26

"Voter Choice: Evaluating Political Alternatives" (with Geoffrey Brennan), **13:** 153–69

"We Should Save More in Our Own Economic Interest," **12:** 453–69

"What If There Is No Majority Motion?" **13:** 179–94

"What Kind of Redistribution Do We Want?" **15:** 427–33

"What Should Economists Do?" **1:** 28–42

"Who Cares Whether the Commons Are Privatised?" **12:** 397–406

"Who Should Distribute What in a Federal System?" **15:** 471–90

"Who 'Should' Pay for Common-Access Facilities?" **15:** 460–70

Curriculum Vitae

BOOKS

James M. Buchanan, C. L. Allen, and M. R. Colberg, *Prices, Income, and Public Policy* (New York: McGraw-Hill, 1954). Second edition (1959).

Public Principles of Public Debt: A Defense and Restatement (Homewood, Ill.: Richard D. Irwin, 1958).

Fiscal Theory & Political Economy (Chapel Hill: University of North Carolina Press, 1960). Translated into Turkish (1965); Japanese (1972).

The Public Finances (Homewood, Ill.: Richard D. Irwin, 1960). Second edition (1965); third edition (1970); fourth edition, with Marilyn Flowers (1975); fifth edition, with Marilyn Flowers (1980); sixth edition, with Marilyn Flowers (1986). Translated into Spanish (1968); Japanese (1972).

James M. Buchanan and Gordon Tullock, *The Calculus of Consent: Logical Foundations of Constitutional Democracy* (Ann Arbor: University of Michigan Press, 1962). Paperback edition (1965). Translated into Japanese (1979); Spanish (1980); Romanian (1996); Russian (1997); Italian (1998).

Public Finance in Democratic Process: Fiscal Institutions and Individual Choice (Chapel Hill: University of North Carolina Press, 1967). Translated into Japanese (1971); Spanish (1973); Chinese (1993); Polish (1997).

The Demand and Supply of Public Goods (Chicago: Rand McNally, 1968). Translated into Italian (1968); Japanese (1974).

Cost and Choice: An Inquiry in Economic Theory (Chicago: Markham, 1969). Reprinted by University of Chicago Press, Midway Reprint (1978). Translated into Japanese (1988); Portuguese (1993).

James M. Buchanan and Nicos Devletoglou, *Academia in Anarchy: An Economic Diagnosis* (New York: Basic Books, 1970).

James M. Buchanan and Robert D. Tollison, eds., *Theory of Public Choice: Political Applications of Economics* (Ann Arbor: University of Michigan Press, 1972).

James M. Buchanan and G. F. Thirlby, eds., *L.S.E. Essays on Cost* (London: London School of Economics, 1973). Reprinted by New York University Press, Institute for Humane Studies (1981).

The Limits of Liberty: Between Anarchy and Leviathan (Chicago: University of Chicago Press, 1975). Translated into Japanese (1977); Italian, partial (1979); German (1984); Czechoslovakian (1996); Romanian (1997); Russian (1997); Italian (1998).

James M. Buchanan and Richard E. Wagner, *Democracy in Deficit: The Political Legacy of Lord Keynes* (New York: Academic Press, 1977). Translated into Japanese (1979); Korean (1981); Spanish (1983).

Freedom in Constitutional Contract: Perspectives of a Political Economist (College Station: Texas A&M University Press, 1978). Translated into Italian (1990).

What Should Economists Do? (Indianapolis: Liberty Fund, 1979).

Geoffrey Brennan and James M. Buchanan, *The Power to Tax: Analytical Foundations of a Fiscal Constitution* (Cambridge: Cambridge University Press, 1980). Translated into German (1988).

James M. Buchanan, Robert D. Tollison, and Gordon Tullock, eds., *Toward a Theory of the Rent-Seeking Society* (College Station: Texas A&M University Press, 1980).

James M. Buchanan and Robert D. Tollison, eds., *The Theory of Public Choice—II* (Ann Arbor: University of Michigan Press, 1984).

Geoffrey Brennan and James M. Buchanan, *The Reason of Rules: Constitutional Political Economy* (Cambridge: Cambridge University Press, 1985). Translated into Japanese (1989); Italian (1991); German (1993).

Liberty, Market and State: Political Economy in the 1980s (Brighton, England: Wheatsheaf Books, 1986; New York: New York University Press, 1986). Translated into Chinese (1990).

James M. Buchanan, Charles K. Rowley, and Robert D. Tollison, eds., *Deficits* (New York: Blackwell, 1987). Translated into Japanese (1991).

Essays on the Political Economy (Honolulu: University of Hawai'i Press, 1989).

The Economics and the Ethics of Constitutional Order (Ann Arbor: University of Michigan Press, 1991). Translated into Japanese, partial (1992); Korean (1996).

Better than Plowing: And Other Personal Essays (Chicago: University of Chicago Press, 1992).

Ethics and Economic Progress (Norman: University of Oklahoma Press, 1994). Translated into Catalan, partial (1995); Spanish, partial (1995); Korean (1996); Spanish (1996); Japanese (1997).

James M. Buchanan and Yong J. Yoon, eds., *The Return to Increasing Returns* (Ann Arbor: University of Michigan Press, 1994).

Post-Socialist Political Economy: Selected Essays (Cheltenham, U.K.: Edward Elgar, 1997).

James M. Buchanan and Roger D. Congleton, *Politics by Principle, Not Interest: Toward Nondiscriminatory Democracy* (New York and Cambridge: Cambridge University Press, 1998.)

JOURNAL ARTICLES AND CONTRIBUTIONS TO BOOKS

"Regional Implications of Marginal Cost Rate Making," *Southern Economic Journal* 16 (July 1949): 53–61.

"The Pure Theory of Government Finance: A Suggested Approach," *Journal of Political Economy* 57(December 1949): 496–505. In *Fiscal Theory & Political Economy: Selected Essays* (Chapel Hill: University of North Carolina Press, 1960), 8–23.

"Communication: Note on the Differential Controversy," *Southern Economic Journal* 17 (July 1950): 59–60.

"Federalism and Fiscal Equity," *American Economic Review* 40 (September 1950): 583–99. In *Fiscal Theory & Political Economy: Selected Essays* (Chapel Hill: University of North Carolina Press, 1960), 170–89; *The Economics of Federalism,* ed. B. S. Grewal, G. Brennan, and R. L. Mathews (Canberra: Australian National University Press, 1980), 183–200; *The Economics of Fiscal Federalism and Local Finance,* ed. Wallace E. Oates (Cheltenham, U.K.: Edward Elgar, 1998), 347–63.

"A Rejoinder," *Journal of Political Economy* 59 (August 1951): 358–59.

"Knut Wicksell on Marginal Cost Pricing," *Southern Economic Journal* 17 (October 1951): 173–78.

"Criteria for Government Expenditure: Comment," *Journal of Finance* 6 (December 1951): 440–42.

"Federal Grants and Resource Allocation," *Journal of Political Economy* 60 (June 1952): 208–17. "A Reply," *Journal of Political Economy* 60 (December 1952): 536–38. In *Perspectives on the Economics of Education,* by G. C. S. Benson (New York: Houghton-Mifflin, 1963).

"The Pricing of Highway Services," *National Tax Journal* 5 (June 1952): 97–106.

"The Theory of Monopolistic Quantity Discounts," *Review of Economic Studies* 20 (June 1953): 199–208.

"Social Choice, Democracy, and Free Markets," *Journal of Political Economy* 62 (April 1954): 114–23. In *Fiscal Theory & Political Economy: Selected Essays* (Chapel Hill: University of North Carolina Press, 1960), 75–89; *Public Finance: Selected Readings,* ed. Helen Cameron and William Henderson (New York: Random House, 1966), 158–74; *Economics: Between Predictive Science and Moral Philosophy,* comp. Robert D. Tollison and Viktor J. Vanberg (College Station: Texas A&M University Press, 1987), 171–83; *The Aggregation of Preferences,* vol. 1, *Social Choice Theory,* ed. Charles K. Rowley (London: Edward Elgar, 1993), 418–27. Translated into Italian (1972).

"Decisions Affecting Economic Growth," *American Economic Review* 44 (May 1954): 228–31.

"Individual Choice in Voting and the Market," *Journal of Political Economy* 62 (August 1954): 334–43. In *Fiscal Theory & Political Economy: Selected Essays* (Chapel Hill: University of North Carolina Press, 1960), 90–104; *Economics: Between Predictive Science and Moral Philosophy,* comp. Robert D. Tollison and Viktor J. Vanberg (College Station: Texas A&M University Press, 1987), 185–97; *The Aggregation of Preferences,* vol. 1, *Social Choice Theory,* ed. Charles K. Rowley (London: Edward Elgar, 1993), 428–37. Translated into Spanish (1982).

"Professor Maxwell and Fiscal Equity," *Journal of Finance* 10 (March 1955): 70–71.

"Private Ownership and Common Usage: The Road Case Re-examined," *Southern Economic Journal* 22 (January 1956): 305–16. In *Explorations into Constitutional Economics,* comp. Robert D. Tollison and Viktor J. Vanberg (College Station: Texas A&M University Press, 1989), 344–58.

"The Capitalization and Investment Aspects of Excise Taxes under Competition: Comment," *American Economic Review* 46 (December 1956): 974–77.

"External and Internal Public Debt," *American Economic Review* 47 (December 1957): 995–1000.

"*Ceteris Paribus:* Some Notes on Methodology," *Southern Economic Journal* 24 (January 1958): 259–70. Translated into German (1971).

"Saving and the Rate of Interest: A Comment," *Journal of Political Economy* 67 (February 1959): 79–82.

"The Real Debt," *Challenge* 7 (July 1959): 58–61.

"Positive Economics, Welfare Economics, and Political Economy," *Journal of Law and Economics* 2 (October 1959): 124–38. In *Fiscal Theory & Political Economy: Selected Essays* (Chapel Hill: University of North Carolina Press, 1960), 105–24; *Economics: Between Predictive Science and Moral Philosophy,* comp. Robert D. Tollison and Viktor J. Vanberg (College Station: Texas A&M University Press, 1987), 3–19.

James M. Buchanan and John E. Moes, "A Regional Countermeasure to National Wage Standardization," *American Economic Review* 50 (June 1960): 434–38.

"The Methodology of Incidence Theory: A Critical Review of Some Recent Contributions," in *Fiscal Theory & Political Economy: Selected Essays* (Chapel Hill: University of North Carolina Press, 1960), 125–50. Substantially modified version of Italian translation (1955).

"Politica economica, libere istituzioni e processo democratico" (Economic policy, free institutions and democratic process), *Il Politico* 25 (1960): 265–77; Italian translation.

"'La scienza delle finanze': The Italian Tradition in Fiscal Theory," in *Fiscal Theory & Political Economy: Selected Essays* (Chapel Hill: University of North Carolina

Press, 1960), 24–74. In *Public Debt and Future Generations,* ed. J. M. Ferguson (Chapel Hill: University of North Carolina Press, 1964), 47–54; *Altro Polo: Italian Economics, Past and Present,* ed. Peter Groenewegen and Joseph Halevi (Sydney: Frederick May Foundation for Italian Studies, University of Sydney, 1983), 79–116; *Economics: Between Predictive Science and Moral Philosophy,* comp. Robert D. Tollison and Viktor J. Vanberg (College Station: Texas A&M University Press, 1987), 317–56. Translated into Italian (1980).

Francesco Forte and James M. Buchanan, "The Evaluation of Public Services," *Journal of Political Economy* 69 (April 1961): 107–21. In *Explorations into Constitutional Economics,* comp. Robert D. Tollison and Viktor J. Vanberg (College Station: Texas A&M University Press, 1989), 176–93. Translated into German (1969).

"Simple Majority Voting, Game Theory, and Resource Use," *Canadian Journal of Economics and Political Science* 27 (August 1961): 337–48.

"A Pricing Approach to Motor Vehicle Taxation," *Automobilissimo* (October 1961): 1–19.

"Comment on Musgrave and Tiebout Papers," in *Public Finances: Needs, Sources and Utilization* (Princeton: Princeton University Press, 1961), 122–29. National Bureau of Economic Research, Special Conference Series, 12.

Introduction to *Public Finances: Needs, Sources and Utilization* (Princeton: Princeton University Press, 1961): xi–xiv. National Bureau of Economic Research, Special Conference Series, 12.

"Politics, Policy, and the Pigovian Margins," *Economica* 29 (February 1962): 17–28. In *Externalities: Theoretical Dimensions of Political Economy,* ed. Robert Staaf and Francis Tannian (New York: Dunellen, 1972), 179–90; *Theory of Public Choice: Political Applications of Economics,* ed. James M. Buchanan and Robert D. Tollison (Ann Arbor: University of Michigan Press, 1972), 169–82; *Economics: Between Predictive Science and Moral Philosophy,* comp. Robert D. Tollison and Viktor J. Vanberg (College Station: Texas A&M University Press, 1987), 83–95.

"Easy Budgets and Tight Money," *Lloyds Bank Review* 64 (April 1962): 17–30. In *Monetary Theory and Policy,* ed. Richard Ward (Scranton: International Textbook, 1966), 164–77; *Theory of Public Choice: Political Applications of Economics,* ed. James M. Buchanan and Robert D. Tollison (Ann Arbor: University of Michigan Press, 1972), 62–75; *Readings in Macroeconomics,* ed. William E. Mitchell, John H. Hand, and Ingo Walter (New York: McGraw-Hill, 1974), 235–44. Translated into Spanish (1962).

James M. Buchanan and Wm. Craig Stubblebine, "Externality," *Economica* 29 (November 1962): 371–84. In *A. E. A. Readings in Welfare Economics,* ed. Kenneth J. Arrow and T. Scitovsky (Homewood, Ill.: Richard D. Irwin, 1969), 199–212; *Externalities: Theoretical Dimensions of Political Economy,* ed. Robert Staaf and Fran-

cis Tannian (New York: Dunellen, 1972), 277–90; *Economics: Between Predictive Science and Moral Philosophy,* comp. Robert D. Tollison and Viktor J. Vanberg (College Station: Texas A&M University Press, 1987), 97–111.

"The Relevance of Pareto Optimality," *Journal of Conflict Resolution* 6 (December 1962): 341–54. In *Freedom in Constitutional Contract: Perspectives of a Political Economist* (College Station: Texas A&M University Press, 1977), 215–34.

James M. Buchanan and Gordon Tullock, "The Costs of Decision Making," in *The Calculus of Consent* (Ann Arbor: University of Michigan Press, 1962), 97–116. In *Economic Theories of International Politics,* ed. Bruce M. Russett (Chicago: Markham, 1968), 455–71.

James M. Buchanan and Gordon Tullock, "A Generalized Economic Theory of Constitutions," in *The Calculus of Consent* (Ann Arbor: University of Michigan Press, 1962), 63–84. In *The Economic Approach to Politics,* ed. René Frey and Bruno Frey (Tübingen: J. C. B. Mohr, 1972), 63–84. Translated into Italian (1972); German (1974).

James M. Buchanan and Gordon Tullock, "The Orthodox Model of Majority Rule," in *The Calculus of Consent* (Ann Arbor: University of Michigan Press, 1962), 249–62. In *Public Finance in Canada: Selected Readings,* ed. A. J. Robinson and James Cutt (Toronto: Methuen, 1968), 60–73.

"Predictability: The Criterion for a Monetary Constitution," in *In Search of a Monetary Constitution,* ed. Leland B. Yeager (Cambridge: Harvard University Press, 1962), 155–83; *Money and Finance,* ed. Deane Carson (New York: Wiley, 1966), 52–57.

James M. Buchanan and Gordon Tullock, "Qualified Majority Voting Rules, Representation, and the Interdependence of Constitutional Variables," in *The Calculus of Consent* (Ann Arbor: University of Michigan Press, 1962), 211–31. Translated into Italian (1972).

James M. Buchanan and Gordon Tullock, "Simple Majority Voting," in *The Calculus of Consent* (Ann Arbor: University of Michigan Press, 1962), 131–45. In *The Economic Approach to Politics,* ed. René Frey and Bruno Frey (Tübingen: J. C. B. Mohr, 1972), 131–45. In *Economic Foundations of Property Law,* ed. B. A. Ackerman (Boston: Little, Brown, 1975), 238–47.

James M. Buchanan and Milton Z. Kafoglis, "A Note on Public Goods Supply," *American Economic Review* 53 (June 1963): 403–14. In *Explorations into Constitutional Economics,* comp. Robert D. Tollison and Viktor J. Vanberg (College Station: Texas A&M University Press, 1989), 194–207.

"The Economics of Earmarked Taxes," *Journal of Political Economy* 71 (October 1963): 457–69. As "Earmarked Taxes," in *Public Finance,* ed. R. W. Houghton (London: Penguin, 1970), 277–95; *Theory of Public Choice: Political Applications of Econom-*

ics, ed. James M. Buchanan and Robert D. Tollison (Ann Arbor: University of Michigan Press, 1972), 106–22.

"Taxation: The Other Side of the Budget," *Newsletter, Joint Council on Economic Education* (November 1963): 1–2, 6.

"Staatliche Souveränität, nationale Planung und wirtschaftliche Freiheit" (National sovereignty, central planning and economic freedom), *ORDO* Band 14 (Düsseldorf: Verlag Helmut Kupper, 1963), 249–58; German translation.

"What Should Economists Do?" *Southern Economic Journal* 30 (January 1964): 213–22. In *What Should Economists Do?* (Indianapolis: Liberty Fund, 1979), 17–37; *Economics: Between Predictive Science and Moral Philosophy*, comp. Robert D. Tollison and Viktor J. Vanberg (College Station: Texas A&M University Press, 1987), 21–33; *The Aggregation of Preferences*, vol. 1, *Social Choice Theory*, ed. Charles K. Rowley (London: Edward Elgar, 1993), 438–47. Translated into Spanish (1984).

"Fiscal Institutions and Efficiency in Collective Outlay," *American Economic Review* 54 (May 1964): 227–35. In *Economics: Between Predictive Science and Moral Philosophy*, comp. Robert D. Tollison and Viktor J. Vanberg (College Station: Texas A&M University Press, 1987), 357–66.

James M. Buchanan and Francesco Forte, "Fiscal Choice through Time: A Case for Indirect Taxation?" *National Tax Journal* 17 (June 1964): 144–57. In *Explorations into Constitutional Economics*, comp. Robert D. Tollison and Viktor J. Vanberg (College Station: Texas A&M University Press, 1989), 228–45.

James M. Buchanan and Gordon Tullock, "Economic Analogues to the Generalization Argument," *Ethics* 74 (July 1964): 300–301.

"Confessions of a Burden Monger," *Journal of Political Economy* 72 (October 1964): 486–88. *The Bobbs-Merrill Reprint Series in Economics*, 68311 (Indianapolis: Bobbs-Merrill).

"Are Rational Economic Policies Feasible in Western Democratic Countries?" *Il Politico* 29 (1964): 801–8.

"Concerning Future Generations," in *Public Debt and Future Generations*, ed. James M. Ferguson (Chapel Hill: University of North Carolina Press, 1964), 55–63.

"Public Debt, Cost Theory, and the Fiscal Illusion," in *Public Debt and Future Generations*, ed. James M. Ferguson (Chapel Hill: University of North Carolina Press, 1964), 150–63.

"An Economic Theory of Clubs," *Economica* 32 (February 1965): 1–14. *The Bobbs-Merrill Reprint Series in Economics*, 68155 (Indianapolis: Bobbs-Merrill). In *Economic Theories of International Politics*, ed. B. Russett (Chicago: Markham, 1968), 50–63; *Readings in Microeconomics*, 2d ed., ed. William Breit and Harold Hochman (New York: Holt, Rinehart and Winston, 1971), 547–56; *Externalities: Theo-*

retical Dimensions of Political Economy, ed. Robert Staaf and Francis Tannian (New York: Dunellen, 1972), 321–33; *Municipal Expenditures, Revenues, and Services*, ed. W. Patrick Deatin (New Brunswick: Center for Urban Policy Research, Rutgers University, 1983), 20–30; *Economics: Between Predictive Science and Moral Philosophy*, comp. Robert D. Tollison and Viktor J. Vanberg (College Station: Texas A&M University Press, 1987), 207–21; *The Theory of Market Failure*, ed. Tyler Cowen (Fairfax, Va.: George Mason University Press, 1988), 193–208; *The Economics of Fiscal Federalism and Local Finance*, ed. Wallace E. Oates (Cheltenham, U.K.: Edward Elgar, 1998), 456–69.

James M. Buchanan and Charles Plott, "Marshall's Mathematical Note XIX," *Economic Journal 75* (September 1965): 618–20.

"Ethical Rules, Expected Values, and Large Numbers," *Ethics 76* (October 1965): 1–13. In *Freedom in Constitutional Contract: Perspectives of a Political Economist* (College Station: Texas A&M University Press, 1977), 151–68. Translated into Italian (1972).

"A Note on Semantics," *The Exchange* 26 (November 1965): 5–6.

"Critique of the Public Debt," in *Economic Issues and Policies*, ed. A. L. Grey and J. E. Elliott (New York: Houghton-Mifflin, 1965), 185–90.

Foreword to *The Politics of Bureaucracy*, by Gordon Tullock (Washington: Public Affairs Press, 1965), 1–9. As the foreword to Tullock's *The Politics of Bureaucracy*, in *What Should Economists Do?* (Indianapolis: Liberty Fund, 1979), 161–73; foreword to *The Politics of Bureaucracy*, in *Economics: Between Predictive Science and Moral Philosophy*, comp. Robert D. Tollison and Viktor J. Vanberg (College Station: Texas A&M University Press, 1987), 199–206.

James M. Buchanan and Gordon Tullock, "Public and Private Interaction under Reciprocal Externality," in *The Public Economy and the Urban Community*, ed. Julius Margolis (Washington, D.C.: Resources for the Future, 1965), 52–73. In *Economics: Between Predictive Science and Moral Philosophy*, comp. Robert D. Tollison and Viktor J. Vanberg (College Station: Texas A&M University Press, 1987), 113–39. Translated into Spanish (1982).

"Externality in Tax Response," *Southern Economic Journal 33* (July 1966): 35–42.

James M. Buchanan and Gordon Tullock, "Gains-from-Trade in Votes," *Ethics 76* (July 1966): 305–6.

"Peak Loads and Efficient Pricing: Comment," *Quarterly Journal of Economics 80* (August 1966): 463–71.

"The Icons of Public Debt," *Journal of Finance 21* (September 1966): 544–46.

"Joint Supply, Externality, and Optimality," *Economica 33* (November 1966): 405–15.

"Economics and Its Scientific Neighbors," in *The Structure of Economic Science: Essays on Methodology*, ed. Sherman Roy Krupp (Englewood Cliffs: Prentice-Hall,

1966), 166–83. In *What Should Economists Do?* (Indianapolis: Liberty Fund, 1979), 115–42. Translated into German (1971); Spanish (1981).

"'Fiscal Policy' and Fiscal Choice: The Effects of Unbalanced Budgets," in *Public Finance in Democratic Process* (Chapel Hill: University of North Carolina Press, 1966), 98–112. As "Fiscal Policy and Fiscal Preference," in *Theory of Public Choice: Political Applications of Economics*, ed. James M. Buchanan and Robert D. Tollison (Ann Arbor: University of Michigan Press, 1972), 76–84.

"An Individualistic Theory of Political Process," in *Varieties of Political Theory*, ed. David Easton (Englewood Cliffs: Prentice-Hall, 1966), 25–37. In *Economics: Between Predictive Science and Moral Philosophy*, comp. Robert D. Tollison and Viktor J. Vanberg (College Station: Texas A&M University Press, 1987), 223–35.

"Monetary and Fiscal Policies for Economic Growth in a Free Society," *Il Politico* 31 (1966): 801–7. Translated into German (1967).

"Breton and Weldon on Public Goods," *Canadian Journal of Economics and Political Science* 33 (February 1967): 111–15. In *Explorations into Constitutional Economics*, comp. Robert D. Tollison and Viktor J. Vanberg (College Station: Texas A&M University Press, 1989), 208–12.

"Cooperation and Conflict in Public-Goods Interaction," *Western Economic Journal* 5 (March 1967): 109–21.

"Fiscal Policy and Fiscal Preference," *Papers on Non-Market Decision Making* 1 (March 1967): 1–10.

"Politics and Science: Reflections on Knight's Critique of Polanyi," *Ethics* 77 (July 1967): 303–10.

"Public Goods in Theory and Practice: A Note on the Minasian-Samuelson Discussion," *Journal of Law and Economics* 10 (October 1967): 193–97.

"The Optimality of Pure Competition in the Capacity Problem: Comment," *Quarterly Journal of Economics* 81 (November 1967): 703–5.

"Can Federal Funds Save Our Cities?" in *Our Cities in Crisis: Review and Appraisal (Proceedings of the Fourth Annual Conference on Economic Affairs)* (Department of Economics, Georgia State College, Atlanta, Ga., May 1968), 29–36.

"Democracy and Duopoly: A Comparison of Analytical Models," *American Economic Review* 58 (May 1968): 322–31. Translated into Spanish (1980).

"What Kind of Redistribution Do We Want?" *Economica* 35 (May 1968): 185–90.

James M. Buchanan and Gordon Tullock, "The 'Dead Hand' of Monopoly," *Antitrust Law and Economics Review* 1 (summer 1968): 85–96. In *Theory of Public Choice: Political Applications of Economics*, ed. James M. Buchanan and Robert D. Tollison (Ann Arbor: University of Michigan Press, 1972), 277–87.

"A Public Choice Approach to Public Utility Pricing," *Public Choice* 5 (fall 1968): 1–17. In *Theory of Public Choice: Political Applications of Economics*, ed. James M.

Buchanan and Robert D. Tollison (Ann Arbor: University of Michigan Press, 1972), 153–66.

"Student Revolts, Academic Liberalism, and Constitutional Attitude," *Social Research* 35 (winter 1968): 666–80. In *Freedom in Constitutional Contract: Perspectives of a Political Economist* (College Station: Texas A&M University Press, 1977), 110–22.

James M. Buchanan and Marilyn Flowers, "An Analytical Setting for a Taxpayers' Revolution," *Western Economic Journal* 6 (December 1968): 349–59.

"A Behavioral Theory of Pollution," *Western Economic Journal* 6 (December 1968): 347–48.

"Congestion on the Common," *Il Politico* 33 (December 1968): 776–86.

"Social Insurance in a Growing Economy: A Proposal for Radical Reform," *National Tax Journal* 21 (December 1968): 386–95. Exerpts in *Poverty, Inequality and the Law*, ed. B. Brudno (St. Paul: West, 1976), 557–58.

"Debt, Public," in *International Encyclopedia of the Social Sciences*, vol. 4 (London and New York: Macmillan, 1968), 28–34. In *The Reference Shelf*, vol. 57 (no. 4), *The Federal Deficit*, ed. Andrew C. Kimmens (New York: H. W. Wilson, 1985), 11–23.

"An Economist's Approach to 'Scientific Politics'," in *Perspectives in the Study of Politics*, ed. Malcolm B. Parsons (Chicago: Rand McNally, 1968), 77–88. In *Coursebook for Economics: Private and Public Choice*, ed. Richard Stroup, A. Studenmand, and James Gwartney (New York: Academic Press, 1976), 34–36; *What Should Economists Do?* (Indianapolis: Liberty Fund, 1979), 143–59. Translated into Spanish (1987).

"Knight, Frank H.," in *International Encyclopedia of the Social Sciences*, vol. 17, ed. David L. Sills (New York: Macmillan and Free Press, 1968), 424–28.

James M. Buchanan and Alberto di Pierro, "Pragmatic Reform and Constitutional Revolution," *Ethics* 79 (January 1969): 95–104. In *Freedom in Constitutional Contract: Perspectives of a Political Economist* (College Station: Texas A&M University Press, 1977), 271–86.

"External Diseconomies, Corrective Taxes, and Market Structure," *American Economic Review* 59 (March 1969): 174–77. In *Externalities: Theoretical Dimensions of Political Economy*, ed. Robert Staaf and Francis Tannian (New York: Dunellen, 1972), 269–72.

"An Outside Economist's Defense of Pesek and Saving," *Journal of Economic Literature* 7 (September 1969): 812–14. Translated into German (1974).

"A Future of Agricultural Economics," *American Journal of Agricultural Economics* 51 (December 1969): 1027–36.

"The Calculus of Consent," in *Law and the Behavioral Sciences*, ed. Lawrence M. Friedman and Stewart Macaulay (Indianapolis: Bobbs-Merrill, 1969), 56–75.

"Financing a Viable Federalism," in *State and Local Tax Problems,* ed. H. Johnson (Knoxville: University of Tennessee Press, 1969), 3–19.

"In Defense of Advertising Cartels," in *Pubblicita e Televisione* (Rome: RAI, 1969), 84–93; Italian translation.

"Internal and External Borrowing," in *Public Finances,* ed. R. W. Houghton (London: Penguin, 1969), 338–45.

"Is Economics a Science of Choice?" in *Roads to Freedom: Essays in Honour of Friedrich A. von Hayek,* ed. Erich Streissler (London: Routledge & Kegan Paul, 1969), 47–64. As "Is Economics the Science of Choice?" in *What Should Economists Do?* (Indianapolis: Liberty Fund, 1979), 39–63; *Economics: Between Predictive Science and Moral Philosophy,* comp. Robert D. Tollison and Viktor J. Vanberg (College Station: Texas A&M University Press, 1987), 35–50.

"Notes for an Economic Theory of Socialism," *Public Choice* 8 (spring 1970): 29–43. In *Economics: Between Predictive Science and Moral Philosophy,* comp. Robert D. Tollison and Viktor J. Vanberg (College Station: Texas A&M University Press, 1987), 238–50.

James M. Buchanan and Mark V. Pauly, "On the Incidence of Tax Deductibility," *National Tax Journal* 23 (June 1970): 157–67. In *Theory of Public Choice: Political Applications of Economics,* ed. James M. Buchanan and Robert D. Tollison (Ann Arbor: University of Michigan Press, 1972), 288–301.

"In Defense of Caveat Emptor," *University of Chicago Law Review* 38 (fall 1970): 64–73.

"The 'Social' Efficiency of Education," *Il Politico* 25 (fall 1970): 653–62. Translated into German (1971).

"Political Economy and National Priorities," *Journal of Money, Credit, and Banking* 11 (November 1970): 486–92.

James M. Buchanan and Gordon Tullock, "The Democratic Calculus," in *Frontiers of Democratic Theory,* ed. Henry S. Kariel (New York: Random House, 1970), 78–80.

James M. Buchanan and Richard E. Wagner, "An Efficiency Basis for Federal Fiscal Equalization," in *The Analysis of Public Output,* ed. Julius Margolis (New York: National Bureau of Economic Research, 1970), 139–58. In *The Economics of Federalism,* ed. B. S. Grewal, G. Brennan, and R. L. Mathews (Canberra: Australian National University Press, 1981), 235–53.

James M. Buchanan and C. M. Lindsay, "The Organization and Financing of Medical Care in the United States," in *Health Service Financing* (London: British Medical Association, 1970), 535–85.

"Public Goods and Public Bads," in *Financing the Metropolis: Public Policy in Urban Economies,* vol. 4, ed. John P. Crecine (Beverly Hills: Sage, 1970), 51–71.

"Taxpayer Constraints in Educational Finance," in *Economic Factors Affecting the Financing of Education*, vol. 2, ed. Roe L. Johns and others (Gainesville, Fla.: National Educational Finance Project, 1970), 265–90.

"Equality as Fact and Norm," *Ethics* 81 (April 1971): 228–40. In *What Should Economists Do?* (Indianapolis: Liberty Fund, 1979), 231–52.

"The Backbending Supply Curve of Labor: An Example of Doctrinal Retrogression?" *History of Political Economy* 3 (fall 1971): 383–90. "The Backbending Supply Curve of Labor: Comment on Buchanan, with His Reply," *History of Political Economy* 5 (spring 1973): 266–67. In *Pioneers in Economics: Harold Hotelling, Lionel Robbins, Clark Warburton, John Bates Clark, Ludwig von Mises*, vol. 40., ed. Mark Blaug (Hants, England: Edward Elgar, 1992), 1–8.

"Principles of Urban-Fiscal Strategy," *Public Choice* 11 (fall 1971): 1–16.

"Violence, Law, and Equilibrium in the University," *Public Policy* 19 (winter 1971): 1–18.

Charles J. Goetz and James M. Buchanan, "External Diseconomies in Competitive Supply," *American Economic Review* 61 (December 1971): 883–90. "External Diseconomies in Competitive Supply: Reply," *American Economic Review* 63 (September 1973): 745–48. Translated into Japanese (1972).

"Economists, Government, and the Economy," in *Economic Policies in the 1970's*, ed. A. K. Ho, Michigan Business Papers, No. 57 (Ann Arbor: Bureau of Business Research, 1971), 1–14.

"How 'Should' Common-Access Facilities Be Financed?" in *Toward Liberty: Essays in Honor of Ludwig von Mises on the Occasion of His 90th Birthday, September 29, 1971*, vol. 2, ed. F. A. Hayek and others (Menlo Park: Institute for Humane Studies, 1971), 75–87.

"Public Finance and Academic Freedom," *AGB Reports* 14 (January 1972): 9–18. In *What Should Economists Do?* (Indianapolis: Liberty Fund, 1979), 253–70.

James M. Buchanan and Wm. Craig Stubblebine, "Pareto Optimality, Trade and Gains-from-Trade: A Comment," *Economica* 39 (May 1972): 203–4.

"Rawls on Justice as Fairness," *Public Choice* 13 (fall 1972): 123–28. In *Social Justice and Classical Liberal Goals*, vol. 3, *Social Choice Theory*, ed. Charles K. Rowley (London: Edward Elgar, 1993), 75–80.

"Wicksell on Fiscal Reform," *American Economic Review* 42 (September 1972): 599–602.

"Politics, Property, and the Law: An Alternate Interpretation of *Miller et al. v. Schoene*," *Journal of Law and Economics* 15 (October 1972): 439–52. In *Freedom in Constitutional Contract: Perspectives of a Political Economist* (College Station: Texas A&M University Press, 1977), 94–109; *The Economic Foundations of Property*

Rights: Selected Readings, ed. Svetozar Pejovich (Cheltenham, U.K.: Edward Elgar, 1997), 66–79.

"Before Public Choice," in *Explorations in the Theory of Anarchy,* ed. Gordon Tullock (Blacksburg, Va.: Center for Study of Public Choice, 1972), 27–37. In *The Economics of Legal Relationships,* ed. H. B. Manne (St. Paul: West, 1975), 67–77; *Freedom in Constitutional Contract: Perspectives of a Political Economist* (College Station: Texas A&M University Press, 1977), 81–93.

"Comment on Shoup," in *Public Expenditures and Taxation* (New York: National Bureau of Economic Research, 1972), 62–66.

James M. Buchanan and Charles J. Goetz, "Efficiency Limits of Fiscal Mobility: An Assessment of the Tiebout Model," *Journal of Public Economics* 1 (1972): 25–43. In *The Economics of Federalism,* ed. B. S. Grewal, G. Brennan, and R. L. Mathews (Canberra: Australian National University Press, 1980), 71–88.

"Laissez-Faire, Locational Patterns, Local Public Finance, and National Policy," in *The Family and Rural Community Development,* ed. S. J. Richey (American Home Economics Association, 1972), 13–22.

"Notes on Irrelevant Externalities, Enforcement Costs and the Atrophy of Property Rights," in *Explorations in the Theory of Anarchy,* ed. Gordon Tullock (Blacksburg, Va.: Center for Study of Public Choice, 1972), 77–86.

"Preliminary Notes on the Samaritan's Dilemma," in *Economic Freedom, Growth, and Stability* (Kalamazoo: Western Michigan University Press, 1972), 15–23.

"Scelta sociale, democrazia e mercati," in *Economia del benessere e democrazia,* ed. F. Forte and G. F. Mossetto (Milan: Franco Angeli Editore, 1972), 285–300.

"Toward Analysis of Closed Behavioral Systems," in *Theory of Public Choice: Political Applications of Economics,* ed. James M. Buchanan and Robert D. Tollison (Ann Arbor: University of Michigan Press, 1972), 11–23.

"Who 'Should' Pay for Common-Access Facilities?" *Public Finance/Finance Publiques* 27 (no. 1, 1972): 1–9.

"The Institutional Structure of Externality," *Public Choice* 14 (spring 1973): 69–82.

"Reply to Leijonhufvud," *History of Political Economy* 5 (spring 1973): 266–67.

"The Coase Theorem and the Theory of the State," *Natural Resources Journal* 13 (October 1973): 579–94. In *The Theory of Public Choice—II,* ed. James M. Buchanan and Robert D. Tollison (Ann Arbor: University of Michigan Press, 1984), 159–73.

"America's Third Century in Perspective," *Atlantic Economic Journal* 1 (November 1973): 3–12.

"A Defense of Organized Crime?" in *The Economics of Crime and Punishment,* ed. Simon Rottenberg (Washington, D.C.: American Enterprise Institute, 1973), 119–32.

"Inflation, Progression and Politics," in *The Impact of Economic Growth on Taxation* (Madrid: International Institute of Public Finance, 1973), 45–56.

"Introduction: L.S.E. Cost Theory in Retrospect," in *L.S.E. Essays on Cost,* ed. J. M. Buchanan and G. F. Thirlby (London: London School of Economics and Political Science, 1973), 1–16.

"Social Choice and Freedom of Inquiry: The Internal and External Institutions for Decision Making in Higher Education," in *Grenzen der Demokratie? Probleme und Konsequenzen der Demokratisierung von Politik, Wirtschaft und Gesellschaft,* ed. L. Erhard, K. Bruss and B. Hagemeyer (Düsseldorf: Econ-Verlag GmbH, 1973), 387–406.

"Hegel on the Calculus of Voting," *Public Choice* 17 (spring 1974): 99–101.

James M. Buchanan and Winston C. Bush, "Political Constraints on Contractual Redistribution," *American Economic Review* 64 (May 1974): 153–57. In *Essays on Unorthodox Economic Strategies: A Memorial Volume in Honor of Winston C. Bush,* ed. A. T. Denzau and R. J. Mackay (Blacksburg, Va.: Center for Study of Public Choice, 1976), 57–64. In *Freedom in Constitutional Contract: Perspectives of a Political Economist* (College Station: Texas A&M University Press, 1977), 186–93.

James M. Buchanan and T. Nicholaus Tideman, "Gasoline Rationing and Market Pricing: Public Choice in Political Economy," *Atlantic Economic Journal* 2 (November 1974): 15–26.

"Federalne podatki akcyzowe i transfedowe," in *Politische Okonomie Kapitalizmie,* ed. J. Gluchowski (Toru'n, Poland: 1974), 116–21.

"Podatki od zatrudnienia i system ubezoieczen spolezhych," in *Polityka Finansowa w Kapitalizmie,* ed. J. Gluchowski (Toru'n, Poland: 1974), 122–29.

"Public Choice and Public Policy," in *Increasing Understanding of Public Problems and Policies* (Chicago: Farm Foundation, 1974), 131–36.

"Who Should Distribute What in a Federal System?" in *Redistribution through Public Choice,* ed. H. Hochman and G. Peterson (New York: Columbia University Press, 1974), 20–42.

James M. Buchanan and Warren J. Samuels, "On Some Fundamental Issues in Political Economy: An Exchange of Correspondence," *Journal of Economic Issues* 9 (March 1975): 15–35. In *The Methodology of Economic Thought,* ed. Warren Samuels (New Brunswick: Transactions Books, 1980), 517–40.

James M. Buchanan and Gordon Tullock, "Polluters' Profits and Political Response: Direct Controls versus Taxes," *American Economic Review* 65 (March 1975): 139–47. "Reply," *American Economic Review* 66 (December 1976): 983–84. In *The Political Economy of Environmental Protection: Analysis and Evidence,* ed. Roger D. Congleton (Ann Arbor: University of Michigan Press, 1996), 31–42.

"A Contractarian Paradigm for Applying Economic Theory," *American Economic Review* 65 (May 1975): 225–30. In *Freedom in Constitutional Contract: Perspectives of a Political Economist* (College Station: Texas A&M University Press, 1977), 235–42; *Social Choice Theory*, vol. 2, *Utilitarian and Contractarian Goals*, ed. Charles K. Rowley (London: Edward Elgar, 1993), 267–72. Translated into Spanish (1984).

"Boundaries on Social Contract," *Reason Papers* 2 (fall 1975): 15–28.

"Utopia, The Minimal State, and Entitlement," *Public Choice* 23 (fall 1975): 121–26. In *Social Choice Theory*, vol. 3, *Social Justice and Classical Liberal Goals*, ed. Charles K. Rowley (London: Edward Elgar, 1993), 550–55.

"Public Finance and Public Choice," *National Tax Journal* 28 (December 1975): 383–94. Translated into Turkish (1990).

"The Bases for Freedom in Society," in *The Limits of Liberty: Between Anarchy and Leviathan* (Chicago: University of Chicago Press, 1975), 17–34. Translated into Yugoslavian (1989).

"Consumerism and Public Utility Regulation," in *Telecommunications, Regulation, and Public Choice*, ed. Charles F. Phillips, Jr. (Lexington, Va.: Washington and Lee University Press, 1975), 1–22.

James M. Buchanan and T. Nicolaus Tideman, "Gold, Money and the Law: The Limits of Governmental Monetary Authority," in *Gold, Money and the Law*, ed. Henry G. Manne and Roger Leroy Miller (Chicago: Aldine, 1975), 9–70.

James M. Buchanan and James Dean, "Inflation and Real Rates of Income Tax," in *Proceedings of the 67th Conference on Taxation, St. Louis, October 14–17, 1974* (Columbus, Ohio: National Tax Association, 1975), 343–49.

James M. Buchanan and Marilyn Flowers, "Local Government Expenditures: An Overview," in *Management Policies in Local Government Finance*, ed. J. R. Aronson and E. Schwartz (Washington, D.C.: 1975), 25–41. In *Local Government Finance*, ed. J. Richard Aranson and Eli Schwartz (Washington, D.C.: International City Management Association, 1981), 25–43.

"The Political Economy of Franchise in the Welfare State," in *Capitalism and Freedom: Problems and Prospects*, ed. Richard T. Selden (Charlottesville: University Press of Virginia, 1975), 52–77. In *The Economics of Legal Relationships*, ed. H. B. Manne (St. Paul: West, 1975), 78–97. As "The Political Economy of the Welfare State," in *The Theory of Public Choice—II*, ed. James M. Buchanan and Robert D. Tollison (Ann Arbor: University of Michigan Press, 1984), 174–93.

James M. Buchanan and T. Nicolaus Tideman, "Response to Comment," in *Gold, Money and the Law*, ed. Henry G. Manne and Roger L. Miller (Chicago: Aldine, 1975), 125–30.

"The Samaritan's Dilemma," in *Altruism, Morality and Economic Theory*, ed. E. S. Phelps (New York: The Russell Sage Foundation, 1975), 71–85. In *Freedom in*

Constitutional Contract: Perspectives of a Political Economist (College Station: Texas A&M University Press, 1977), 169–85.

"The Justice of Natural Liberty," *Journal of Legal Studies* 5 (January 1976): 1–16. In *Adam Smith and the Wealth of Nations: Bicentennial Essays 1776–1976*, ed. Fred Glahe (Boulder: Colorado Associated University Press, 1978), 61–81; *Adam Smith and Modern Political Economy*, ed. Gerald O'Driscoll (Ames: Iowa State University Press, 1979), 117–31; *Economics: Between Predictive Science and Moral Philosophy*, comp. Robert D. Tollison and Viktor J. Vanberg (College Station: Texas A&M University Press, 1987), 253–68.

"Adam Smith on Public Choice," *Public Choice* 25 (spring 1976): 81–82.

"Barro on the Ricardian Equivalence Theorem," *Journal of Political Economy* 84 (April 1976): 337–42. In *The International Library of Macroeconomic and Financial History*, vol. 3, *Debt and Deficits: Debt Neutrality and the Theory of Fiscal Policy 1970s to 1990s*, ed. Lakis C. Kaounides and Geoffrey E. Wood (Hants, England: Edward Elgar, 1992), 74–87. Translated into Spanish (1982).

"Taxation in Fiscal Exchange," *Journal of Public Economics* 6 (July–August 1976): 17–29. In *Freedom in Constitutional Contract: Perspectives of a Political Economist* (College Station: Texas A&M University Press, 1977), 254–70. Translated into Spanish (1979).

"Government Transfer Spending," in *Government Controls and the Free Market: The U.S. Economy in the 1970s*, ed. Svetozar Pejovich (College Station: Texas A&M University Press, 1976), 122–40.

"A Hobbesian Interpretation of the Rawlsian Difference Principle," *Kyklos* 29, fasc. 1 (1976): 5–25. In *Freedom in Constitutional Contract: Perspectives of a Political Economist* (College Station: Texas A&M University Press, 1977), 194–211; *Economics and Social Institutions*, ed. Karl Brunner (Boston: Martinus Nijhoff, 1979), 59–78; *Social Choice Theory*, vol. 3, *Social Justice and Classical Liberal Goals*, ed. Charles K. Rowley (London: Edward Elgar, 1993), 127–46.

"Methods and Morals in Economics: The Ayres-Knight Discussion," in *Science and Ceremony: The Institutional Economics of C. E. Ayres*, ed. William Breit and William Patton Culbertson, Jr. (Austin and London: University of Texas Press, 1976), 163–74. In *What Should Economists Do?* (Indianapolis: Liberty Fund, 1979), 202–17.

James M. Buchanan and Gordon Tullock, "The Politics and Bureaucracy of Planning," in *The Politics of Planning: A Review and Critique of Centralized Economic Planning*, ed. A. Lawrence Chickering (San Francisco: Institute for Contemporary Studies, 1976), 255–73.

Preface to *Essays on Unorthodox Economic Strategies: A Memorial Volume in Honor*

of Winston C. Bush, ed. Arthur T. Denzau and Robert J. Mackay (Blacksburg, Va.: Center for Study of Public Choice, 1976), vi.

"Public Goods and Natural Liberty," in *The Market and the State: Essays in Honour of Adam Smith*, ed. Thomas Wilson and Andrew S. Skinner (Oxford: Clarendon Press, 1976), 271–86.

"School User Taxes and Economic Efficiency," in *Non-Public School Aid*, ed. E. G. West (Lexington, Mass.: Lexington Books, 1976), 116–20.

James M. Buchanan and Gordon Tullock, "The Expanding Public Sector: Wagner Squared," *Public Choice* 31 (fall 1977): 147–50.

"Tax Reform in 'Constitutional' Perspective," *Invited Essay* (September 1977): 1–5. In *Congressional Record*, vol. 197, pt. 2 (Washington, D.C.: Government Printing Office, 15 December 1977), S–19929–19933; *Law and Economics*, ed. G. Skogh (Lund: Juridiska Foreningen, 1978), 103–20.

Geoffrey Brennan and James M. Buchanan, "Towards a Tax Constitution for Leviathan," *Journal of Public Economics* 8 (December 1977): 255–73. In *The Theory of Public Choice—II*, ed. James M. Buchanan and Robert D. Tollison (Ann Arbor: University of Michigan Press, 1984), 71–89; *Economics: Between Predictive Science and Moral Philosophy*, comp. Robert D. Tollison and Viktor J. Vanberg (College Station: Texas A&M University Press, 1987), 367–87; *The International Library of Critical Writings in Economics*, vol. 2, *Modern Public Finance*, ed. A. B. Atkinson (Hants, England: Edward Elgar, 1991), 353–60. Translated into Spanish (1979).

"Commentary," in *Income Redistribution*, ed. Colin D. Campbell (Washington, D.C.: American Enterprise Institute, 1977), 99–101.

"A Contractarian Perspective on Anarchy," in *Freedom in Constitutional Contract: Perspectives of a Political Economist* (College Station: Texas A&M University Press, 1977), 11–24; *Anarchism*, ed. J. Roland Pennock and John W. Chapman (New York: New York University Press, 1978), 28–42; *Schools of Thought in Politics 3*, vol. 1, *The State and Its Critics*, ed. Andrew Levine (Hants, England: Edward Elgar, 1992), 3–16.

"Law and the Invisible Hand," in *The Interaction of Economics and Law*, ed. Bernard H. Siegan (Lexington, Mass.: D. C. Heath, 1977), 127–38. In *Freedom in Constitutional Contract: Perspectives of a Political Economist* (College Station: Texas A&M University Press, 1977), 25–39.

"Political Equality and Private Property: The Distributional Paradox," in *Markets and Morals*, ed. Gerald Dworkin, Gordon Bermant, and Peter Brown (Washington, D.C.: Hemisphere, 1977), 69–84.

"Politics and Science," in *Freedom in Constitutional Contract: Perspectives of a Political Economist* (College Station: Texas A&M University Press, 1977), 64–77.

"Die Verfassung der Freiheit" (The constitution of freedom), in *Zu den Grenzen der Freiheit,* ed. Otto Molden (Vienna: Fritz Molden, 1977), 57–67; German translation.

"Why Does Government Grow?" *Budgets and Bureaucrats,* ed. Thomas Borcherding (Durham: Duke University Press, 1977), 3–18.

"Markets, States, and the Extent of Morals," *American Economic Review* 68 (May 1978): 364–78. In *What Should Economists Do?* (Indianapolis: Liberty Fund, 1979), 219–29; *Economics: Between Predictive Science and Moral Philosophy,* comp. Robert D. Tollison and Viktor J. Vanberg (College Station: Texas A&M University Press, 1987), 269–75.

Geoffrey Brennan and James M. Buchanan, "Tax Instruments as Constraints on the Disposition of Public Revenues," *Journal of Public Economics* 9 (June 1978): 301–18. Translated into Spanish (1979).

James M. Buchanan and Richard E. Wagner, "Dialogues concerning Fiscal Religion," *Journal of Monetary Economics* 4 (August 1978): 627–36. Translated into Spanish (1984).

James M. Buchanan and Richard E. Wagner, "Contemporary Democracy and the Prospect for Fiscal Control," in *Fiscal Responsibility in Constitutional Democracy,* ed. James M. Buchanan and Richard E. Wagner (Leiden/Boston: Martinus Nijhoff, 1978), 1–9.

"From Private Preferences to Public Philosophy: The Development of Public Choice," in *The Economics of Politics* (London: Institute of Economic Affairs, 1978), 1–20. In *Constitutional Economics,* IEA Masters of Modern Economics Series (Oxford: Basil Blackwell, 1991), 29–45. Translated into Spanish (1980); Italian (1984).

Introduction to *The Anatomy of Public Failure,* by William Mitchell (Los Angeles: International Institute for Economic Research, 1978), 1–3.

James M. Buchanan and Richard Wagner, "The Political Biases of Keynesian Economics," in *Fiscal Responsibility in Constitutional Democracy,* ed. James M. Buchanan and Richard E. Wagner (Leiden/Boston: Martinus Nijhoff, 1978). In *Economics: Between Predictive Science and Moral Philosophy,* comp. Robert D. Tollison and Viktor J. Vanberg (College Station: Texas A&M University Press, 1987), 309–408. Translated into Spanish (1984).

"Summing Up," in *The Economics of Politics* (London: Institute of Economic Affairs, 1978), 155–58.

"The Potential for Taxpayer Revolt in American Democracy," *Social Science Quarterly* 59 (March 1979): 691–96.

"Constitutional Design and Construction: An Economic Approach," *Economia* 3 (May 1979): 293–314.

Geoffrey Brennan and James Buchanan, "The Logic of Tax Limits: Alternative Constitutional Constraints on the Power to Tax," *National Tax Journal* 32 (June 1979):

11–22. In *Municipal Expenditures, Revenues, and Services,* ed. W. Patrick Deatin (New Brunswick: Center for Urban Policy Research, Rutgers University, 1983), 91–111.

James M. Buchanan and Roger L. Faith, "Trying Again to Value a Life," *Journal of Public Economics* 12 (October 1979): 245–48.

"Commentaries," in *Financing Social Security,* ed. Colin Campbell (Washington: American Enterprise Institute, 1979), 208–12.

"Constitutional Constraints on Governmental Taxing Power," *ORDO* Band 30 (Stuttgart: Gustav Fischer Verlag, 1979), 334–59. In *Wirtschaftspolitische Blatter,* Heft 2 (Vienna, Austria, 1989), 183–93.

"The Economic Constitution and the New Deal: Lessons for Late Learners," in *Regulatory Change in an Atmosphere of Crisis: Current Implications of the Roosevelt Years,* ed. Gary Walton (New York: Academic Press, 1979), 13–26.

"Politics without Romance: A Sketch of Positive Public Choice Theory and Its Normative Implications," Inaugural Lecture, Institute for Advanced Studies, Vienna, Austria, *IHS-Journal, Zeitschrift des Instituts für Höhere Studien,* Wien 3 (1979): B1–B11. In *The Theory of Public Choice—II,* ed. James M. Buchanan and Robert D. Tollison (Ann Arbor: University of Michigan Press, 1984), 11–22. Translated into Turkish (1990).

James M. Buchanan and Roger Congleton, "Proportional and Progressive Income Taxation with Utility-Maximizing Governments," *Public Choice* 34 (1979): 217–30.

"Public Choice and Public Finance," in *What Should Economists Do?* (Indianapolis: Liberty Fund, 1979), 183–97. In *Public Choice and Public Finance,* Proceedings of 34th Congress, International Institute of Public Finance, Hamburg, 1978, ed. Karl W. Roskamp (Paris: Editions CUJAS, 1980), 11–18. Translated into Turkish (1989).

"Sector Publico versus Sector Privado" (The public sector versus the private sector in a market economy), in *El Sector Publico en Las Economias de Mercado* (Madrid: Espasa-Calpe, 1979), 88–100; Spanish translation.

James M. Buchanan and Alberto di Pierro, "Uncertainty, Subjective Probabilities, and Choice," in *Studi e Richerche,* Scuola Superiore "Enrico Mattei" (Torino: Gialichelli, 1979).

James M. Buchanan and Alberto di Pierro, "Cognition, Choice, and Entrepreneurship," *Southern Economic Journal* 46 (January 1980): 693–701.

James M. Buchanan and Roger L. Faith, "Subjective Elements in Rawlsian Agreement on Distributional Rules," *Economic Inquiry* 18 (January 1980): 23–38.

"Comment on Lindsay and McKean Papers," in *Research in Law and Economics,* Supplement No. 1, *The Economics of Non-Proprietary Organizations,* ed. R. O. Zerbe, Jr. (Greenwich: JAI Press, 1980), 234–37.

James M. Buchanan and António S. Pinto Barbosa, "Convexity Constraints in Public Goods Theory," *Kyklos* 33, fasc. 1 (1980): 63–75.

Foreword to *The Birth of the Transfer Society,* by Terry L. Anderson and P. J. Hill (Stanford: Hoover Institution, 1980).

Geoffrey Brennan and James M. Buchanan, "The Logic of the Ricardian Equivalence Theorem," *Finanzarchiv* 38, no. 1 (1980): 4–16. In *Deficits,* ed. James M. Buchanan, Charles K. Rowley, and Robert D. Tollison (New York: Blackwell, 1987), 79–92; *The International Library of Macroeconomic and Financial History,* vol. 3, *Debt and Deficits: Debt Neutrality and the Theory of Fiscal Policy 1970s to 1990s,* ed. Lakis C. Kaounides and Geoffrey E. Wood (Hants, England: Edward Elgar, 1992), 74–87.

"Procedural and Quantitative Constitutional Constraints on Fiscal Authority," in *The Constitution and the Budget: Are Constitutional Limits on Tax, Spending, and Budget Powers Desirable at the Federal Level?* ed. W. S. Moore and Rudolf G. Penner (Washington, D.C.: American Enterprise Institute, 1980), 80–84.

"Reform in the Rent-Seeking Society," in *Toward a Theory of the Rent-Seeking Society,* ed. James M. Buchanan, Robert D. Tollison, and Gordon Tullock (College Station: Texas A&M University Press, 1980), 359–67. Translated into German (1987).

"Resource Allocation and Entrepreneurship," The Arne Ryde Symposium on the Economic Theory of Institutions, *Statsvetenskaplig Tidskrift (The Swedish Journal of Political Science)* 5 (1980): 285–92.

James Buchanan and Geoffrey Brennan, "Tax Reform without Tears," in *The Economics of Taxation,* ed. Henry J. Aaron and Michael J. Boskin (Washington, D.C.: Brookings Institution, 1980), 33–53.

James M. Buchanan and Robert D. Tollison, "The Homogenization of Heterogeneous Inputs," *American Economic Review* 71 (March 1981): 28–38. "The Homogenization of Heterogeneous Inputs: Reply," *American Economic Review* 74 (September 1984): 808.

James M. Buchanan and Roger Faith, "Entrepreneurship and the Internalization of Externalities," *Journal of Law and Economics* (April 1981): 95–111.

"Revenue Implications of Money Creation under Leviathan," *American Economic Review* 71 (May 1981): 347–51.

Geoffrey Brennan and James Buchanan, "The Normative Purpose of Economic 'Science': Rediscovery of an Eighteenth Century Method," *International Review of Law and Economics* 1 (December 1981): 155–66. In *The Theory of Public Choice—II,* ed. James M. Buchanan and Robert D. Tollison (Ann Arbor: University of Michigan Press, 1984), 382–94; *Economics: Between Predictive Science and Moral*

Philosophy, comp. Robert D. Tollison and Viktor J. Vanberg (College Station: Texas A&M University Press, 1987), 51–65.

James M. Buchanan and Gordon Tullock, "An American Perspective: From 'Markets Work' to Public Choice," in *The Emerging Consensus? Essays on the Interplay between Ideas, Interests and Circumstances in the First 25 Years of the IEA* (London: Institute of Economic Affairs, 1981), 79–97. In *Constitutional Economics,* IEA Masters of Modern Economics Series (Oxford: Basil Blackwell, 1991), 17–28. As "L'Europe attend son James Madison," *Le libéral européen,* 14 (July–August 1990): 32–36; modified French translation.

"Democracy and Keynesian Constitutions: Political Biases and Economic Consequences," in *Solutions to Unemployment,* ed. David C. Colander (New York: Harcourt Brace Jovanovich, 1981), 27–31; *Constitutional Economics,* IEA Masters of Modern Economics (Oxford: Basil Blackwell, 1991), 91–112; *The Politics of American Economic Policy Making,* 2d ed., ed. Paul Peretz (Armonk, N.Y.: M. E. Sharpe, 1996), 249–61. Translated into Italian (1979, 1984).

"Equal Treatment and Reverse Discrimination," in *Social Justice,* ed. Randolph L. Braham (Boston: Martinus Nijhoff, 1981), 79–94. In *Economics: Between Predictive Science and Moral Philosophy,* comp. Robert D. Tollison and Viktor J. Vanberg (College Station: Texas A&M University Press, 1987), 277–88.

"A Governable Country?" in *Japan Speaks* (Osaka, Japan: Suntory Foundation, 1981), 1–12.

"Möglichkeiten institutioneller Reformen im Rahmen kulturell geformter abstrakter Verhaltensregeln" (Prospects of institutional reform through changes in behavioral rules), in *Evolutionismus oder vertragstheoretischer Konstitutionalismus?* by Viktor Vanberg (Tübingen, Germany: J. C. B. Mohr, 1981), 45–48; German translation.

Roger L. Faith and James M. Buchanan, "Towards a Theory of Yes-No Voting," *Public Choice* 37 (1981): 231–45. In *The Theory of Public Choice—II,* ed. James M. Buchanan and Robert D. Tollison (Ann Arbor: University of Michigan Press, 1984), 90–104. Translated into Japanese (1982).

Geoffrey Brennan and James M. Buchanan, "Der verteilende Staat: Ansätze zu einer Theorie der Umverteilung" (The transfer state: toward a theory of redistribution), *Zeitschrift für Wirtschaftspolitik* 30 (1981): 103–28; German translation.

"What If There Is No Majority Motion?" in *Toward a Science of Politics: Papers in Honor of Duncan Black,* ed. Gordon Tullock (Blacksburg, Va.: Center for Study of Public Choice, 1981), 79–90.

"The Related but Distinct 'Sciences' of Economics and of Political Economy," special issue, *Social Psychology and Economics,* ed. Wolfgang Stroebe and Willi Meyer,

British Journal of Social Psychology, vol. 21, pt. 2 (June 1982): 175–83. In *Liberty, Market and State: Political Economy in the 1980s* (Brighton, England: Wheatsheaf Books, 1986), 29–39.

James M. Buchanan and Dwight R. Lee, "Tax Rates and Tax Revenues in Political Equilibrium: Some Simple Analytics," *Economic Inquiry* 20 (July 1982): 344–54. In *The Theory of Public Choice—II*, ed. James M. Buchanan and Robert D. Tollison (Ann Arbor: University of Michigan Press, 1984), 194–205.

James M. Buchanan and Dwight R. Lee, "Politics, Time, and the Laffer Curve," *Journal of Political Economy* 90 (August 1982): 816–19. In *Economics: Between Predictive Science and Moral Philosophy*, comp. Robert D. Tollison and Viktor J. Vanberg (College Station: Texas A&M University Press, 1987), 409–13.

"The Political Ambiguity of Reagan Economics: Marginal Adjustments or Structural Shift?" *Journal of Monetary Economics* 10 (November 1982): 287–96.

"Order Defined in the Process of Its Emergence," *Literature of Liberty* 5 (winter 1982): 5. In *Liberty, Market and State: Political Economy in the 1980s* (Brighton, England: Wheatsheaf Books, 1986), 73–74.

"Democracia Limitada o Ilimitada" (Limited or unlimited democracy), *Conferencia Mont Pelerin, Estudios Publicos* 6 (Santiago, Chile: Centro de Estudios Publicos, 1982), 37–52.

"The Domain of Subjective Economics: Between Predictive Science and Moral Philosophy," in *Method, Process, and Austrian Economics: Essays in Honor of Ludwig von Mises*, ed. Israel M. Kirzner (Lexington, Mass: D. C. Heath, 1982), 7–20. In *Economics: Between Predictive Science and Moral Philosophy*, comp. Robert D. Tollison and Viktor J. Vanberg (College Station: Texas A&M University Press, 1987), 67–80.

Foreword to *Demain le capitalisme* by Henri LePage (Lasalle: Open Court, 1982), vii–xi. Translated into Chinese.

Foreword to *Freedom and Reform* by Frank H. Knight (Indianapolis: Liberty Fund, 1982), ix–xiv.

"Kommentar" (Commentary), in *Ethik des Kapitalismus*, ed. Peter Koslowski (Tübingen: Mohr, 1982), 69–80; German translation. Reprinted (1991). Translated into Chinese (1996); English (1996); Japanese (1996); Russian (1996).

"The Limits of Taxation," in *The Constitutional Challenge*, ed. Michael James (St. Leonards, N.S.W.: Centre for Independent Studies, 1982), 113–30. In *Taxation: An International Perspective*, ed. Walter Block and Michael Walker (Vancouver, Canada: Fraser Institute, 1984), 41–54.

James M. Buchanan and Dwight R. Lee, "Where Are We on the Laffer Curve? Some Political Considerations," in *Supply-Side Economics in the 1980's* (Westport,

Conn.: Quorum Books, for Federal Reserve Bank of Atlanta and Emory University Law and Economics Center, 1982), 193–96.

"The Public Choice Perspective," *Economia delle scelte pubbliche* 1 (January–April 1983): 7–15. In *Liberty, Market and State: Political Economy in the 1980s* (Brighton, England: Wheatsheaf Books, 1986), 19–27; *Essays on the Political Economy* (Honolulu: University of Hawai'i Press, 1989), 13–24.

Geoffrey Brennan and James Buchanan, "Predictive Power and the Choice among Regimes," *Economic Journal* 93 (March 1983): 89–105.

"Monetary Research, Monetary Rules, and Monetary Regimes," *Cato Journal* 3 (spring 1983): 143–46.

"Rent Seeking, Non-Compensated Transfers, and Laws of Secession," *Journal of Law and Economics* 26 (April 1983): 71–85.

"Social Security Survival: A Public-Choice Perspective," *Cato Journal* 3 (fall 1983): 339–54.

"The Achievement and the Limits of Public Choice in Diagnosing Government Failure and in Offering Bases for Constructive Reform," in *Anatomy of Government Deficiencies,* ed. Horst Hanusch (Berlin: Springer-Verlag, 1983), 15–25.

"Constitutional Contract in Capitalism," in *Philosophical and Ethical Foundations of Capitalism,* ed. Svetozar Pejovich (Lexington, Mass.: Lexington Books, 1983), 65–69.

"Fairness, Hope, and Justice," in *New Directions in Economic Justice,* ed. Roger Skurski (South Bend, Ind.: University of Notre Dame Press, 1983), 53–89. ("Justice and Equal Treatment," in *Liberty, Market and State: Political Economy in the 1980s* [Brighton, England: Wheatsheaf Books, 1986], 140–58, and "Rules for a Fair Game: Contractarian Notes on Distributive Justice," in *Liberty, Market and State: Political Economy in the 1980s* [Brighton, England: Wheatsheaf Books, 1986], 140–58. Both papers originally part of "Fairness, Hope, and Justice.")

"The Flat-Rate Tax and the Fiscal Appetite," in *New Directions in Federal Tax Policy for the 1980's,* ed. Charles Walker and Mark Bloomfield (Washington, D.C.: American Council on Capital Formation, 1983), 314–16.

"I limiti alla fiscalita" (Limits of fiscal authority), in *La costituzione fiscale,* ed. A. Martino (Rome: CREA, 1983), 17–34; Italian translation.

"Moral Community and Moral Order: The Intensive and Extensive Limits of Interaction," in *Ethics and Animals,* ed. Harlan B. Miller and Willilam H. Williams (Clifton, N.J.: Humana Press, 1983), 95–102.

Geoffrey Brennan and James M. Buchanan, "Normative Tax Theory for a Federal Polity," in *Tax Assignment in Federal Countries,* ed. C. McLure (Canberra: Australian National University Press, 1983), 52–65.

Geoffrey Brennan, James Buchanan, and Dwight Lee, "On Monopoly Price," *Kyklos* 36, fasc. 4 (1983): 531–47. "On Monopoly Price: Reply," *Kyklos* 38 (1985): 274–75.

Geoffrey Brennan and James Buchanan, "The Tax System as Social Overhead Capital: A Constitutional Perspective on Fiscal Norms," in *Public Finance and Economic Growth*, Proceedings of the 37th Congress of the International Institute of Public Finance, Tokyo, 1981, ed. Dieter Biehl, Karl Roskamp, and Wolfgang F. Stolper (Detroit: Wayne State University Press, 1983), 41–54.

"Verschuldung, Demos, und Wohlfahrtsstaat" (Debt, demos, and the welfare state), in *Chancen und Grenzen des Sozialstäts*, ed. Peter Koslowski, Philipp Kreuzer and Reinhard Löw (Tübingen: J. C. B. Mohr [Paul Siebeck], 1983), 117–32; German translation. In *Liberty, Market and State: Political Economy in the 1980s* (Brighton, England: Wheatsheaf Books, 1986), 210–22.

"Alternative Perspectives on Economics and Public Policy," *Policy Report* 6 (January 1984): 1–5.

"The Ethical Limits of Taxation," *Scandinavian Journal of Economics* 86 (April 1984): 102–14. In *Limits and Problems of Taxation*, ed. Finn R. Forsund and Seppo Honkapahya (London: Macmillan, 1985), 4–16; *Liberty, Market and State: Political Economy in the 1980s* (Brighton, England: Wheatsheaf Books, 1986), 165–77.

James M. Buchanan and Loren E. Lomasky, "The Matrix of Contractarian Justice," *Social Philosophy and Policy* 2 (autumn 1984): 12–32.

Geoffrey Brennan and James Buchanan, "Voter Choice: Evaluating Political Alternatives," *American Behavioral Scientist* 28 (November–December 1984): 185–201.

"Democracy in Deficit," *Manhattan Report* 4 (1984): 6–9.

"La ricerca di rendite parassitazie e la ricezca dei profitti" (Rent seeking and profit seeking), in *Scelte Pubbliche*, ed. S. Carrubba and Domenico Da Empoli (Florence: L. Monnier, 1984), 245–60; Italian translation.

"Rights, Efficiency, and Exchange: The Irrelevance of Transactions Cost," in *Ansprüche, Eigentum und Verfügungsrechte* (Berlin: Duncker and Humblot, 1984), 9–24. In *Liberty, Market and State: Political Economy in the 1980s* (Brighton, England: Wheatsheaf Books, 1986), 92–107; *Economics: Between Predictive Science and Moral Philosophy*, comp. Robert D. Tollison and Viktor J. Vanberg (College Station: Texas A&M University Press, 1987), 153–68.

"Schumpeter as Precursor to Non-Constitutional Public Choice," *Economia delle scelte pubbliche* 1 (1984): 51–53.

James M. Buchanan and Dwight Lee, "Some Simple Analytics of the Laffer Curve," in *Public Finance and the Quest for Efficiency*, Proceedings of the 38th Congress

of the International Institute of Public Finance, Copenhagen, 1982 (Detroit: Wayne State University Press, 1984), 281–95.

"Sources of Opposition to Constitutional Reform," in *Constitutional Economics: Containing the Economic Powers of Government,* ed. Richard B. McKenzie (Lexington, Mass.: D. C. Heath, 1984), 21–34. In *Liberty, Market and State: Political Economy in the 1980s* (Brighton, England: Wheatsheaf Books, 1986), 55–69.

"The Moral Dimension of Debt Financing," *Economic Inquiry* 23 (January 1985): 1–6. In *Liberty, Market and State: Political Economy in the 1980s* (Brighton, England: Wheatsheaf Books, 1986), 189–94; *A Nation in Debt,* ed. Richard Fink and Jack High (Frederick, Md.: University Publications of America, 1987), 102–7.

"Constitutional Democracy, Individual Liberty, and Political Equality," *Jahrbuch für neue politische Ökonomie* Band 4 (1985): 35–47. In *Liberty, Market and State: Political Economy in the 1980s* (Brighton, England: Wheatsheaf Books, 1986), 248–60. Translated into German (1987).

"Political Economy and Social Philosophy," in *Economics and Philosophy,* ed. Peter Koslowski (Tübingen: J. C. B. Mohr [Paul Siebeck], 1985), 19–36. In *Liberty, Market and State: Political Economy in the 1980s* (Brighton, England: Wheatsheaf Books, 1986), 261–74.

"Politics and Meddlesome Preferences," in *Smoking and Society: Toward a More Balanced Assessment,* ed. Robert D. Tollison (Lexington, Mass.: D. C. Heath, 1985), 335–42. In *Clearing the Air,* ed. Robert D. Tollison (Lexington, Mass.: D. C. Heath, 1988), 107–16.

Viktor Vanberg and James M. Buchanan, "Organization Theory and Fiscal Economics: Society, State, and Public Debt," *Journal of Law, Economics, and Organization* 2 (fall 1986): 215–27.

"The Relevance of Constitutional Strategy," *Cato Journal* 6 (fall 1986): 513–17.

"Better than Plowing," *Banca Nazionale del Lavoro Quarterly Review* 159 (December 1986): 359–75. In *Recollections of Eminent Economists,* vol. 2, ed. J. A. Kregel (London: Macmillan, 1989), 279–96; *Essays on the Political Economy* (Honolulu: University of Hawai'i Press, 1989), 67–85; *Better than Plowing: And Other Personal Essays* (Chicago: University of Chicago Press, 1992), 1–18.

"Bibliography," *Economia delle scelte pubbliche* 4 (December 1986): 125–48; *Scandinavian Journal of Economics* 89 (1987): 17–38.

"Can Policy Activism Succeed? A Public Choice Perspective," in *The Monetary versus Fiscal Policy Debate: Lessons from Two Decades,* ed. R. W. Hafer (Totowa, N.J.: Rowman and Allanheld, 1986), 139–50.

"The Constitution of Economic Policy," in *Les Prix Nobel* (Stockholm: Almquist and Wicksell International, 1986), 334–43. In *Economics: Between Predictive Science and Moral Philosophy,* comp. Robert D. Tollison and Viktor J. Vanberg (College Station:

Texas A&M University Press, 1987), 303–14; *Science* 236 (June 1987): 1433–39; *American Economic Review* 77 (June 1987): 243–50; *Public Choice and Constitutional Economics,* ed. James Gwartney and Richard Wagner (Greenwich, Conn.: JAI Press, 1988), 103–14; *The International Library of Critical Writings in Economics,* vol. 2, *Modern Public Finance,* ed. A. B. Atkinson (Hants, England: Edward Elgar, 1991), 353–60. Translated into Japanese (1988); Russian (1997).

"The Economic Consequences of the Deficit," *Economia delle scelte pubbliche* 3 (1986): 149–56. In *Symposium on Budget Balance,* ed. Carol Cox (Washington, D.C.: Committee for a Responsible Federal Budget, 1986), 11–18.

"First, the Academic Scribblers—*Democracy in Deficit: The Political Legacy of Lord Keynes,*" in *The Reference Shelf,* vol. 57 (no. 4), *The Federal Deficit,* ed. Andrew C. Kimmins (New York: H. W. Wilson, 1986), 42–54.

"Ideas, Institutions, and Political Economy: A Plea for Disestablishment," in *Real Business Cycles, Real Exchange Rates and Actual Policies, Carnegie-Rochester Series on Public Policy 25,* ed. Karl Brunner and Allan H. Meltzer (Amsterdam: North Holland, 1986), 245–57.

"La imposicion coativa en fase constitutiva" (Coercive taxation in constitutional contract), *Hacienda Publica Espanola* 100 (1986), 41–55; Spanish translation. In *Explorations into Constitutional Economics,* comp. Robert D. Tollison and Viktor J. Vanberg (College Station: Texas A&M University Press, 1989), 309–28.

"Liberty, Market and State," in *Liberty, Market and State: Political Economy in the 1980s* (Brighton, England: Wheatsheaf Books, 1986), 3–7. Translated into Polish (1987).

"Our Times: Past, Present, and Future," in *The Unfinished Agenda* (London: Institute of Economic Affairs, 1986), 29–38.

"Political Economy: 1957–1982," in *Liberty, Market and State: Political Economy in the 1980s* (Brighton, England: Wheatsheaf Books, 1986), 8–18. In *Ideas, Their Origins, and Their Consequences: Lectures to Commemorate the Life and Work of G. Warren Nutter* (Washington, D.C.: American Enterprise Institute, 1988), 119–30.

"Public Debt and Capital Formation," in *Taxation and the Deficit Economy: Fiscal Policy and Capital Formation in the United States,* ed. Dwight Lee (San Francisco: Pacific Research Institute for Public Policy, 1986), 177–94. In *Liberty, Market and State: Political Economy in the 1980s* (Brighton, England: Wheatsheaf Books, 1986), 195–209.

James M. Buchanan and Robert D. Tollison, "A Theory of Truth in Autobiography," *Kyklos* 39, fasc. 4 (1986): 507–17.

James M. Buchanan and Dwight R. Lee, "Vote Buying in a Stylized Setting," *Public Choice* 49 (1986): 3–16.

"Peut-on apprivoiser la democratie?" (Is social democracy possible?), *Commentaire* 9 (1986–87): 673–76; French translation.

"The Deficit and Obligations to Future Generations," *Imprimis* 16 (January 1987): 1–6. In *Champions of Freedom*, vol. 13, The Ludwig von Mises Lecture Series, *The Federal Budget: The Economic, Political, and Moral Implications for a Free Society*, ed. Joseph S. McNamara and Lynne Morris (Hillsdale, Mich.: Hillsdale College Press, 1987), 103–21.

James M. Buchanan and Jennifer Roback, "The Incidence and Effects of Public Debt in the Absence of Fiscal Illusion," *Public Finance Quarterly* 15 (January 1987): 5–25.

"Towards the Simple Economics of Natural Liberty: An Exploratory Analysis," *Kyklos* 40, fasc. 1 (January 1987): 3–20.

"Debt: An Economic and Moral Crisis," *IPA Review* (May–July 1987): 56–57.

"The Political Economy of the Deficit," *Florida Policy Review* 3 (summer 1987): 5–10.

"Tax Reform as Political Choice," *Journal of Economic Perspectives* 1 (summer 1987): 29–35.

"Justification of the Compound Republic: The *Calculus* in Retrospect," *Cato Journal* 7 (fall 1987): 305–12. In *Public Choice and Constitutional Economics*, ed. J. Gwartney and R. Wagner (Greenwich, Conn.: JAI Press, 1988), 131–38. As "Retrospective on *The Calculus of Consent*," *Citation Classics* 11 (January 1988); "The Justification of the Compound Republic: A Retrospective Interpretation of *The Calculus of Consent*," in *The Economics and the Ethics of Constitutional Order* (Ann Arbor: University of Michigan Press, 1991), 43–49.

"The Economizing Element in Knight's Ethical Critique of Capitalist Order," *Ethics* 98 (October 1987): 61–75.

"Some Remarks on Privatization," *Virginia Law Weekly* 40 (October 1987): 1–6.

James M. Buchanan and Roger L. Faith, "Secession and the Limits of Taxation: Toward a Theory of Internal Exit," *American Economic Review* 77 (December 1987): 1023–31.

"Im Wandel begriffene Idee vom Staat" (The changing idea of the state), *Neue Züricher Zeitung* 29 (December 1987). In *Wo Regeln Bremsen*, ed. G. Schwarz (Zürich: Verlag Neue Zürcher Zeitung, 1988), 115–19; German translation.

"Comment: Constitutional Strategy and the Monetary Regime," in *The Search for Stable Money*, ed. J. Dorn and A. Schwartz (Chicago: University of Chicago Press, 1987), 119–27.

"A Commentary: Liberty, Market and State," *Economic Impact* 58 (1987): 36–40.

"Constitutional Economics," in *The New Palgrave: A Dictionary of Economics*, vol. 1, ed. John Eatwell, Murray Milgate, and Peter Newman (London: Macmillan, 1987), 585–88. Translated into Turkish (1989).

"Constructivism, Cognition, and Value," in *Erkenntnis und Entscheidung: die Wertproblematik in Wissenschaft und Praxis, Europäisches Forum Alpbach, 1987*, ed. Otto Molden (Vienna: Österreichisches College, 1988), 36–48. In *The Economics and the Ethics of Constitutional Order* (Ann Arbor: University of Michigan Press, 1991), 231–38.

"The Fiscal Constitution," in *The Politics of American Economic Policy Making*, ed. Paul Peretz (New York: M. E. Sharpe, 1987), 225–28.

"Keynesian Follies," in *The Legacy of Keynes, Nobel Conference XII*, ed. David A. Reese (San Francisco: Harper & Row, 1987), 130–45.

"Man and the State," in *International Studies in Economics and Econometrics*, vol. 14, *Socialism: Institutional, Philosophical and Economic Issues*, ed. Svetozar Pejovich (Dordrecht/Boston/Lancaster: Kluwer Academic Publishing, 1987), 3–9. In *Explorations into Constitutional Economics*, comp. Robert D. Tollison and Viktor J. Vanberg (College Station: Texas A&M University Press, 1989), 51–56.

"Market Failure and Political Failure," in *Individual Liberty and Democratic Decision-Making: The Ethics, Economics and Politics of Democracy*, ed. Peter Koslowski (Tübingen: J. C. B. Mohr [Paul Siebeck], 1987), 41–52. In *Explorations into Constitutional Economics*, comp. Robert D. Tollison and Viktor J. Vanberg (College Station: Texas A&M University Press, 1989), 418–29; *Cato Journal* 8 (summer 1988): 1–14. Translated into German (1989).

"Opportunity Cost," in *The New Palgrave: A Dictionary of Economics*, vol. 3, ed. John Eatwell, Murray Milgate, and Peter Newman (London: Macmillan, 1987), 718–21.

(Public choice and fiscal theory), in *Collected Works of Nobel Prize Winners*, vol. 16 (Seoul: Korea Economic Daily, 1987); Korean translation.

"The Qualities of a Natural Economist," in *Democracy and Public Choice: Essays in Honor of Gordon Tullock*, ed. Charles Rowley (New York: Basil Blackwell, 1987), 9–19.

"Return to Constitutional Budgetary Reform," introduction to *The Constitutional Convention*, ed. James Bond, David Engdahl, and Henry Butler (Washington, D.C.: National Legal Center for the Public Interest, 1987), v–vi.

Geoffrey Brennan and James M. Buchanan, "Is Public Choice Immoral? The Case for the 'Nobel' Lie," *Virginia Law Review* 74 (March 1988): 179–89.

"The Economic Theory of Politics Reborn," *Challenge* 31 (March–April 1988): 4–10.

"The Gauthier Enterprise," *Social Philosophy and Policy* 5 (spring 1988): 75–94. In *The Economics and the Ethics of Constitutional Order* (Ann Arbor: University of Michigan Press, 1991), 195–213.

"Reining in the Deficit," *The Owen Manager* 9 (spring 1988): 27–31.

"Consecuencias economicas del estado benefactor" (Economic consequences of the welfare state), *Libertas* 8 (May 1988): 3–14; Spanish translation.

"Contractarian Political Economy and Constitutional Interpretation," *American Economic Review* 78 (May 1988): 135–39. In *The Economics and the Ethics of Constitutional Order* (Ann Arbor: University of Michigan Press, 1991), 81–87.

James M. Buchanan and Viktor J. Vanberg, "The Politicization of Market Failure," *Public Choice* 57 (May 1988): 101–13. In *The Economics and the Ethics of Constitutional Order* (Ann Arbor: University of Michigan Press, 1991), 67–79. Translated into Galician (1990).

"Prolegomena for a Strategy of Constitutional Reform," *Economic Education Bulletin* 28 (June 1988): 7–17.

"Post-Reagan Political Economy," *Christian Perspectives in Business and Government* 2 (summer 1988): 1–13. In *Reaganomics and After,* ed. Cento Veljanovski (London: Institute of Economic Affairs, 1989), 1–16; *Constitutional Economics,* IEA Masters of Modern Economics Series (Oxford: Basil Blackwell, 1991), 1–16.

"The Ethics of Work," *Scholar and Educator* 12 (fall 1988): 48–51.

"Economists and the Gains from Trade," *Managerial and Decision Economics,* special issue (winter 1988): 5–12. In *The Economics and the Ethics of Constitutional Order* (Ann Arbor: University of Michigan Press, 1991), 109–23.

"Hayek and the Forces of History," *Humane Studies Review* (winter 1988–89): 3–4. Translated into French (1989).

Viktor Vanberg and James M. Buchanan, "Rational Choice and Moral Order," *Analyse & Kritik* 10 (December 1988): 138–60. In *From Political Economy to Economics: And Back?* ed. James H. Nichols, Jr., and Colin Wright (San Francisco: Institute for Contemporary Studies, 1990), 175–237.

"Constitutional Imperatives for the 1990s: The Legal Order for a Free and Productive Economy," in *Thinking About America: The United States in the 1990s,* ed. Annelise Anderson and Dennis L. Bark (Stanford: Hoover Press, 1988), 253–64.

"The Simple Logic of Free Trade," *Proceedings of the First Annual Symposium of the Institute for International Competitiveness* (Radford, Va.: Radford University, 1988), iii–x.

"The Work Ethic," *Competing through Productivity and Quality,* ed. Y. K. Shetty and V. M. Buehler (Cambridge, Mass.: Productivity Press, 1988), 55–62.

"Camelot Will Not Return," *Reason* 20 (January 1989): 36–38.

Viktor Vanberg and James M. Buchanan, "Interests and Theories in Constitutional Choice," *Journal of Theoretical Politics* 1 (January 1989): 49–62. In *The Economics and the Ethics of Constitutional Order* (Ann Arbor: University of Michigan Press, 1991), 51–64.

"On the Structure of an Economy: A Re-emphasis of Some Classical Foundations," *Business Economics* 24 (January 1989): 6–12. In *The Economics and the Ethics of Constitutional Order* (Ann Arbor: University of Michigan Press, 1991), 19–28.

"Shackle and a Lecture in Pittsburgh," *Market Process* 7 (spring 1989): 2–4. In *The Economics and the Ethics of Constitutional Order* (Ann Arbor: University of Michigan Press, 1991), 217–20.

James M. Buchanan and Viktor Vanberg, "A Theory of Leadership and Deference in Constitutional Construction," *Public Choice* 61 (April 1989): 15–27. As "Leadership and Deference in Constitutional Construction," in *The Economics and the Ethics of Constitutional Order* (Ann Arbor: University of Michigan Press, 1991), 137–50.

"A Tale of Two Economies," *Durrell Journal of Money and Banking* 1 (August 1989): 12–15.

"Reductionist Reflections on the Monetary Constitution," *Cato Journal* 9 (fall 1989): 295–99.

"Nobelity," *Eastern Economic Journal* 15 (October–December 1989): 339–48. In *Better than Plowing: And Other Personal Essays* (Chicago: University of Chicago Press, 1992), 158–73.

James M. Buchanan and Dwight R. Lee (Cartels, coalitions, and constitutional politics), *Public Choice Studies* 13 (1989): 5–20; Japanese translation. *Constitutional Political Economy* 2 (1991): 139–61.

"Une chance unique pour l'Europe" (Europe's unique opportunity), *Le Figaro*, ed. W. Sichel (Kalamazoo: W. E. Upjohn Institute for Economic Research, 1989), 79–96.

"Contractarian Presuppositions and Democratic Governance," in *Politics and Process*, ed. Geoffrey Brennan and Loren E. Lomasky (Cambridge: Cambridge University Press, 1989), 174–82.

"The Ethics of Constitutional Order," in *Essays on the Political Economy* (Honolulu: University of Hawai'i Press, 1989), 25–31. In *The Economics and the Ethics of Constitutional Order* (Ann Arbor: University of Michigan Press, 1991), 153–57.

"Free Trade and Producer-Interest Politics," in *Essays on the Political Economy* (Honolulu: University of Hawai'i Press, 1989), 52–66. As "Cartels, Coalitions, and Constitutional Politics," James M. Buchanan and Dwight R. Lee, *Constitutional Political Economy* 2 (1991): 139–61. Translated into Japanese (1989).

"Message to the Young People," in *Nobel Laureates Forum in Japan, 1988* (Tokyo: Yomiuri Shimbun, 1989): 130–31.

"The Potential and the Limits of Socially Organized Humankind," in *Nobel Laureates Forum in Japan, 1988* (Tokyo: Yomiuri Shimbun, 1989), 85–94. In *The Economics and the Ethics of Constitutional Order* (Ann Arbor: University of

Michigan Press, 1991), 239–51; *Interdisciplinary Science Reviews* 16 (no. 2, 1991): 168–74.

"The Simple Economics of the Work Ethic," in *Mt. Pelerin Special Meeting in Taiwan, 31 August–2 September 1988, Conference Series, No. 9* (Taipei: Chung-Hua Institute for Economic Studies, 1989), 34–47.

Untitled, in *The State of Economic Science: Views of Six Nobel Laureates*, ed. Werner Sichel (Kalamazoo: W. E. Upjohn Institute for Economic Research, 1989), 78–95. As "The Economy as a Constitutional Order," in *The Economics and the Ethics of Constitutional Order* (Ann Arbor: University of Michigan Press, 1991), 29–41.

"Constitutional Manifesto," *Monetary Notes I* (May 1990): 2–5.

"Democrazia e libero Mercato" (Democracy and free markets), *Impresa e State* 10 (June 1990): 8–13; Italian translation.

"Kein Zentralismus" (No centralism), *Wirtschaftswoche* 39 (21 September 1990): 174–76; German translation.

"Elements d'une constitution pour l'Europe" (Elements of a constitution for Europe), *Liberté economique, et progres social* 59 (October 1990): 2–14; French translation.

"Born-Again Economist," in *Lives of the Laureates: Ten Nobel Economists*, ed. William Breit and Roger W. Spencer (Cambridge: MIT Press, 1990), 163–80. In *Better than Plowing: And Other Personal Essays* (Chicago: University of Chicago Press, 1992), 68–81.

"The Budgetary Politics of Social Security," in *Social Security's Looming Surpluses: Prospects and Implications*, ed. Carolyn L. Weaver (Washington, D.C.: AEI Press, 1990), 45–56.

"The Contractarian Logic of Classical Liberalism," in *Liberty, Property, and the Future of Constitutional Development*, ed. Ellen Frankel Paul and Howard Dickman (Albany: State University of New York Press, 1990), 9–21. In *The Economics and the Ethics of Constitutional Order* (Ann Arbor: University of Michigan Press, 1991), 125–35.

"The Domain of Constitutional Economics," *Constitutional Political Economy* 1 (1990): 1–18. In *The International Library of Critical Writings in Economics*, vol. 2, *The Philosophy and Methodology of Economics*, ed. Bruce J. Caldwell (Hants, England: Edward Elgar, 1993), 451–68. As "The Domain of Constitutional Political Economy," in *The Economics and the Ethics of Constitutional Order* (Ann Arbor: University of Michigan Press, 1991), 3–18. Translated into Czechoslovakian (1992).

"Europe's Constitutional Opportunity," in *Europe's Constitutional Future* (London: Institute of Economic Affairs, 1990), 1–20. Translated into French (1990); Italian (1991).

"Opportunity Cost of College Education," *Shaping the Future of Higher Education, Presidential Leadership: Proceedings, AASCU's 29th Annual Meeting, November 19–21, 1989, the Fairmont Hotel, San Francisco, California* (Washington, D.C.: American Association of State Colleges and Universities, 1990), 107–12.

"The Potential for Politics after Socialism," in *Geschichte end Gesetz, Europäisches Forum Alpbach, 1989,* ed. Otto Molden (Vienna: Österreichisches College, 1990), 240–56.

"Ricordo di un anno in Italia," introduction to Italian translation *Libertà nel contratto costituzionale,* ed. di Paolo Martelli (Milano: Arnoldo Mondadori Editore, 1990), xiii–xxii.

"Sovranita del consumatore e offerta di fattori" (Consumer sovereignty and the supply of factors), *Notizie di Politeia* 6 (1990): 8–9; Italian translation.

"Economics in the Post-Socialist Century," *Economic Journal* 101 (January 1991): 15–21. In *The Future of Economics,* ed. John D. Hey (Oxford: Blackwell, 1992), 15–21.

"The Minimal Politics of Market Order," special issue, *From Plan to Market: The Post-Soviet Challenge,* parts 1 and 2, *Cato Journal* 11 (fall 1991): 215–26. Translated into Russian (1993).

"Why the Soviets Cannot Understand the Market (and Why We Cannot Understand Why They Cannot Understand)," *Journal of Private Enterprise* 7 (fall 1991): 9–19. *Journal of Private Enterprise,* special issue, 13 (1997): 40–49.

James M. Buchanan and Viktor J. Vanberg, "The Market as a Creative Process," *Economics and Philosophy* 7 (October 1991): 167–86. In *Market Process Theories,* vol. 2, *Heterodox Approaches,* ed. Peter J. Boettke and David L. Prychitko (Cheltenham, U.K.: Edward Elgar, 1998), 579–98.

"An American Perspective on Europe's Constitutional Opportunity," *Cato Journal* 10 (winter 1991): 619–29. Translated into German (1991); Italian (1993).

"Belief, Choice and Consequences: Reflections on Economics, Science and Religion," in *Wege der Vernunft: Festschrift zum siebzigsten Geburtstag von Hans Albert,* ed. Alfred Bohnen and Alan Musgrave (Tübingen: J. C. B. Mohr [Paul Siebeck], 1991), 151–63.

Viktor J. Vanberg and James M. Buchanan, "Constitutional Choice, Rational Ignorance, and the Limits of Reason," *Jahrbuch für Neue Politische Ökonomie* 10 Band (1991): 61–78. In *The Constitution of Good Societies,* ed. Karol Edward Soltan and Stephen L. Elkin (University Park: Pennsylvania State University Press, 1996), 39–56.

"The Constitutional Economics of Earmarking," in *Charging for Government: User Charges and Earmarked Taxes in Principle and Practice,* ed. Richard E. Wagner (London and New York: Routledge, 1991), 152–62.

"The Constitutional Moment of the 1990s," *Economia delle scelte pubbliche* 3 (1991): 175–85. Translated into Italian (1993).

"Frank H. Knight, 1885–1972," in *Remembering the University of Chicago: Teachers, Scientists, and Scholars,* ed. Edward Shils (Chicago: University of Chicago Press, 1991), 244–52.

"From the Inside Looking Out," in *Eminent Economists: Their Life Philosophies,* ed. Michael Szenberg (Cambridge: Cambridge University Press, 1991), 98–106. In *Better than Plowing: And Other Personal Essays* (Chicago: University of Chicago Press, 1992), 147–57.

"Jack Wiseman: A Personal Appreciation," *Constitutional Political Economy* 2 (1991): 1–6.

Geoffrey Brennan and James M. Buchanan, "Konsumbesteuerung und demokratischer Prozess" (Consumption taxation and democratic process), in *Konsumorientierte Neuordnung des Steuersystems,* ed. Manfred Rose (Berlin: Springer-Verlag, 1991), 51–84; German translation.

James M. Buchanan and Dwight R. Lee, "Private Interest Support for Efficiency Enhancing Antitrust Policies," *Economic Inquiry* 30 (April 1992): 218–24.

"I Did Not Call Him 'Fritz': Personal Recollections of Professor F. A. v. Hayek," *Constitutional Political Economy* 3 (spring–summer 1992): 129–35.

James M. Buchanan and Dwight R. Lee, "Open Markets in the Transfer State," *Southern Economic Journal* 59 (July 1992): 1–8.

"Economic Science in the Future," *Eastern Economic Journal* 18 (fall 1992): 401–3. Translated into German (1992).

"Beyond Pragmatism: Prospects for Constitutional Revolution," in *Schools of Thought in Politics* 3, vol. 1, *The State and Its Critics,* ed. Andrew Levine (Hants, England: Edward Elgar, 1992), 290–304.

"Public Choice after the Revolutions: 1989–91," *Economia delle scelte pubbliche* 2 (1992): 93–101.

"The Supply of Labour and the Extent of the Market," in *Adam Smith's Legacy: His Place in the Development of Modern Economics,* ed. Michael Fry (London: Routledge, 1992), 104–16. In *The Return to Increasing Returns,* ed. James M. Buchanan and Yong J. Yoon (Ann Arbor: University of Michigan Press, 1994), 331–42.

"The Threat of Leviathan," in *Schools of Thought in Politics* 3, vol. 1, *The State and Its Critics,* ed. Andrew Levine (Hants, England: Edward Elgar, 1992), 271–89.

"Asymmetrical Reciprocity in Market Exchange: Implications for Economies in Transition," *Social Philosophy & Policy* 10 (summer 1993): 51–64. In *Liberalism and the Economic Order,* ed. Ellen Frankel Paul, Fred D. Miller, Jr., and Jeffrey Paul (Cambridge: Cambridge University Press, 1993), 51–64; *Legacies of the Col-*

lapse of Marxism, ed. John H. Moore (Fairfax, Va.: George Mason University Press, 1994), 149–64.

"How Can Constitutions Be Designed So That Politicians Who Seek to Serve 'Public Interest' Can Survive and Prosper?" *Constitutional Political Economy* 4 (winter 1993): 1–6.

"The Political Efficiency of General Taxation," *National Tax Journal* 46 (December 1993): 401–10.

"The Individual as Participant in Political Exchange," in *Social Theory and Social Policy: Essays in Honor of James S. Coleman,* ed. Aage B. Sørensen and Seymour Spilerman (Westport, Conn.: Praeger, 1993), 11–21.

James M. Buchanan and David Fand, "Monetary Policy: Malpractice at the Fed," *Critical Review* 6 (no. 4, 1993): 457–69. In *Wall Street Journal* 120 (no. 122, Monday, 21 December 1992): A8; modified version.

"Prólogo," prologue to *Hacia el Autogobierno: Una crítica al poder político* (Buenos Aires: Emecé, 1993); Spanish translation.

"Public Choice after Socialism," *Public Choice* 77, no. 1 (1993): 67–74.

"The Triumph of Economic Science: Is Fukuyama Wrong and, If So, Why?" *Journal of the Board of Audit* 3 (no. 7, 1993): 5–14. Translated into Portuguese (1993).

"We Should Save More in Our Own Economic Interest," in *Justice across Generations: What Does It Mean?* ed. Lee M. Cohen (Washington, D.C.: AARP, 1993), 269–82.

"Choosing What to Choose," *Journal of Institutional and Theoretical Economics* 150 (March 1994): 123–44.

James M. Buchanan and Roger D. Congleton, "The Incumbency Dilemma and Rent Extraction by Legislators," *Public Choice* 79 (April 1994): 47–60.

"Notes on the Liberal Constitution," *Cato Journal* 14 (spring–summer 1994): 1–9.

James M. Buchanan and Dwight R. Lee, "On a Fiscal Constitution for the European Union," *Journal des Economistes et des Etudes Humaines* 5 (June–September 1994): 219–32.

"Pareto Superior Tax Reform: Some Simple Analytics," *Eastern Economic Journal* 20 (winter 1994): 7–9.

"Economic Theory in the Postrevolutionary Moment of the 1990s," in *The Role of Economic Theory,* ed. Philip A. Klein (Boston/Dordrecht/London: Kluwer Academic Publishers, 1994), 47–60. As "Prospects for Economic Theory in the 1990s and Beyond," in *Prospects for Economic Theory in the 1990s and Beyond,* ed. Bodo B. Gemper (Siegen, Germany: Edition Ensis, 1993), 6–24.

Foreword to *Trust, Ethnicity, and Identity: Beyond the New Institutional Economics of Ethnic Trading Networks, Contract Law, and Gift-Exchange,* by Janet Landa (Ann Arbor: University of Michigan Press, 1994), vii–viii.

"Lagged Implementation as an Element in Constitutional Strategy," *European Journal of Political Economy* 10 (1994): 11–26.

"Federalism as an Ideal Political Order and an Objective for Constitutional Reform," *Publius* 25 (spring 1995): 19–27.

"Individual Rights, Emergent Social States, and Behavioral Feasibility," *Rationality and Society* 7 (April 1995): 141–50.

James M. Buchanan and Yong J. Yoon, "Rational Majoritarian Taxation of the Rich: With Increasing Returns and Capital Accumulation," *Southern Economic Journal* 61 (April 1995): 923–35.

"Clarifying Confusion about the Balanced Budget Amendment," *National Tax Journal* 48 (September 1995): 347–55.

"Economic Science and Cultural Diversity," *Kyklos* 48, fasc. 2 (1995): 193–200.

"Foundational Concerns: A Criticism of Public Choice Theory," in *Current Issues in Public Choice,* ed. José Casas Pardo and Friedrich Schneider (Cheltenham, U.K.: Edward Elgar, 1995), 3–20.

"A Two-Country Parable," in *Justice in Immigration,* ed. Warren F. Schwartz, *Cambridge Studies in Philosophy and Law* (New York: Cambridge University Press, 1995), 63–66.

Contribution to "In Celebration of Armen Alchian's 80th Birthday: Living and Breathing Economics," *Economic Inquiry* 34 (July 1996): 416–18.

"Economic Freedom and Federalism: Prospects for the New Century," special contribution to the inaugural issue, *Asian Journal of Business & Information Systems* 1 (summer 1996): 5–10.

"An Ambiguity in Sen's Alleged Proof of the Impossibility of a Pareto Libertarian," *Analyse & Kritik* 18 (September 1996): 118–25.

"Federalism and Individual Sovereignty," *Cato Journal* 15 (fall–winter 1996): 259–68.

(Adam Smith as inspiration), in *The Academic World of James M. Buchanan,* ed. Byeong-Ho Gong (Seoul: Korea Economic Research Institute, 1996); Korean translation.

"Distributional Politics and Constitutional Design," in *Economics and Political Institutions in Economic Policy,* ed. V. A. Muscatelli (Manchester, UK: Manchester University Press, 1996), 70–78.

"Economics as a Public Science," in *Foundations of Research in Economics: How Do Economists Do Economics?* ed. Steven G. Medema and Warren J. Samuels (Cheltenham, U.K.: Edward Elgar, 1996), 30–36. Paperback edition (1998).

"Europe as Social Reality," *Constitutional Political Economy,* special issue, *Europe: A Constitution for the Millennium,* 7 (1996): 253–56.

Introduction to *Economists of the Twentieth Century,* vol. 1, *Economic Analysis and*

Political Ideology: The Selected Essays of Karl Brunner, ed. Thomas Lys (Cheltenham, U.K.: Edward Elgar, 1996), xiii–xviii.

"Society and Democracy," in *The David Hume Institute—The First Decade,* ed. Nick Kuenssberg and Gillian Lomas (Edinburgh: David Hume Institute, 1996), 25–33. Translated into Spanish (1996).

"The Balanced Budget Amendment: Clarifying the Arguments," *Public Choice* 90 (March 1997): 117–38.

"Beyond Science: The Economist's Enterprise," in *Advances in Austrian Economics,* vol. 4, ed. Peter J. Boettke and Steven Horwitz (Greenwich, Conn.: JAI Press, 1997), 129–31.

"Can Democracy Promote the General Welfare?" in *The Welfare State,* ed. Ellen Frankel Paul, Fred D. Miller, Jr., and Jeffrey Paul (Cambridge: Cambridge University Press, 1997), 165–79. In *Social Philosophy and Policy* 14 (summer 1997): 165–79.

"Le crisi nelle democrazie del welfare" (The crises in welfare democracy), in *Globallizzazione dei mercati e orizzonti del capitalismo* (Rome: Editori Laterza, 1997); Italian translation.

"La scelta individuale nei ruoli decisionali" (Individual choice behavior in private, agency, and collective decision rules), in *Individuale e collettivo: decision e razionalità,* ed. Angelo M. Petroni and Riccardo Viale (Milan: Raffaello Cortina, 1997), 83–99; Italian translation.

"Structure-Induced Behavior in Markets and in Politics," in *Post-Socialist Political Economy: Selected Essays* (Cheltenham, U.K.: Edward Elgar, 1997), 136–50. Translated into Italian (1994).

"Konstitucionalna ograni enja politi kim aktivnostima" (Constraints on political action), *Ekonomska misao* 31 (July–September 1998): 167–78; Yugoslavian translation.

"Majoritarian Logic," *Public Choice* 97 (October 1998): 13–21.

"Agreement and Efficiency: Response to Guttman," *European Journal of Political Economy* 14 (1998): 209–13.

"Kommentar" (Commentary), in *Ethik des Kapitalismus: Mit einem Kommentar von James M. Buchanan,* Peter Koslowski (Tübingen: Mohr Siebeck, 1998), 79–90; German translation.

"Opportunity Cost and Legal Institutions," *The New Palgrave Dictionary of Economics and the Law,* vol.2, ed. Peter Newman (London: Macmillan, 1998), 710–15.

PAMPHLETS

The Inconsistencies of the National Health Service, Occasional Paper No. 7 (London: Institute of Economic Affairs, 1965). In *Theory of Public Choice: Political Appli-*

cations of Economics, ed. James M. Buchanan and Robert D. Tollison (Ann Arbor: University of Michigan Press, 1972), 27–45; *Constitutional Economics,* IEA Masters of Modern Economics (Oxford: Basil Blackwell, 1991), 113–32. Translated into Spanish (1966).

James M. Buchanan and Richard E. Wagner, *Public Debt in Democratic Society* (Washington, D.C.: American Enterprise Institute, 1966).

Academia in Anarchy: A Summary (Center for Independent Education, 1970).

The Bases for Collective Action (New Jersey: General Learning Press, 1971). Translated into Spanish (1980).

Natural Liberty and Justice: Adam Smith and John Rawls, C. A. Moorman Series (Canton, Mo.: Culver-Stockton College, 1976).

James M. Buchanan, Richard Wagner, and John Burton, *The Consequences of Mr. Keynes: An Analysis of the Misuse of Economic Theory for Political Profiteering, with Proposals for Constitutional Disciplines,* Hobart Paper 78 (London: Institute of Economic Affairs, 1978).

Constitutional Restrictions on the Power of Government, The Frank M. Engle Lecture, 1981 (Bryn Mawr, Pa.: The American College, 1981). In *The Theory of Public Choice—II,* ed. James M. Buchanan and Robert D. Tollison (Ann Arbor: University of Michigan Press, 1984), 439–52.

Geoffrey Brennan and James M. Buchanan, *Monopoly in Money and Inflation: The Case for a Constitution to Discipline Government,* Hobart Paper 88 (London: Institute of Economic Affairs, 1981). Translated into Spanish (1982).

Moral Community, Moral Order, or Moral Anarchy, The Abbott Memorial Lecture no. 17 (Colorado Springs: Colorado College, 1981). In *Liberty, Market and State: Political Economy in the 1980s* (Brighton, England: Wheatsheaf Books, 1986), 108–20; *Economics: Between Predictive Science and Moral Philosophy,* comp. Robert D. Tollison and Viktor J. Vanberg (College Station: Texas A&M University Press, 1987), 289–301; *The Market Economy: A Reader,* ed. James L. Doti and Dwight R. Lee (Los Angeles: Roxbury, 1991), 237–47.

Politiek Schuldbesef (Political debt consciousness), Rotterdamse Monetaire Studies, no. 16 (Rotterdam: Erasmus University, 1984); Dutch translation.

Staatsschuld en Politiek, Rotterdamse Monetarie Studies, no. 18 (Rotterdam: Erasmus University, 1984); Dutch translation.

Capitalism, Lectures in Social Philosophy and Policy (Bowling Green: Social Philosophy and Policy Center, 1988).

Socialism Is Dead, but Leviathan Lives On, the John Bonython Lecture, CIS Occasional Paper 30 (Sydney, Australia: Centre for Independent Studies, 1990). Excerpts in *Wall Street Journal* (18 July 1990): A8. Translated into Italian (1990).

Technological Determinism Despite the Reality of Scarcity: A Neglected Element in the Theory of Spending on Medical and Health Care (Little Rock: University of Arkansas Medical School, 1990). In *Health Care for an Aging Population,* ed. Chris Hackler (Albany: State University of New York, 1994), 57–68.

Analysis, Ideology and the Events of 1989 (Zürich: Bank Hofmann AG, 1991).

Market, Freiheit und Demokratie (Market, liberty, and democracy) (Vienna, Austria: Carl Menger Institute, 1992); German translation.

Consumption without Production: The Impossible Idyll of Socialism (Freiburg, Germany: Haufe, 1993), 49–75. Translated into German, (1993).

Property as a Guarantor of Liberty, The Shaftesbury Papers, vol. 1 (Hants, England: Edward Elgar, 1993). In *Property Rights and the Limits of Democracy: The Shaftesbury Papers,* vol. 1, ed. Charles K. Rowley (Hants, England: Edward Elgar, 1993), 1–64; *Nobelprizewinner James M. Buchanan in Jena, Munich and Bayreuth, 7–15 June 1994* (Munich: Herbert Quandt Stiftung, 1994).

Politicized Economies in Limbo: America, Europe and the World, 1994, Nobelprizewinner James M. Buchanan in Jena, Munich and Bayreuth, 7–15 June 1994 (Munich: Herbert Quandt Stiftung, 1994). Translated into Italian (1994); Spanish (1995).

The Metamorphosis of Western Democracies at the End of the Twentieth Century, Seventh Sinclair House Debate "Is Industrial Society Disintegrating?" (Bad Homburg: Herbert Quandt Foundation, 1997).

"The Structure of Progress: National Constitutionalism in a Technologically Opened World Economy," *Doctorado «Honoris Causa» del Excmo. Sr. D. James M. Buchanan* (Valladolid, Spain: University of Valladolid, 1997).

REVIEWS

A Financial History of Tennessee since 1870, by James E. Thorogood (Nashville: Tennessee Industrial School, 1950). *Southern Economic Journal* 17 (January 1951): 368–69.

Die Belastung durch die persönliche Einkommensteuer in Deutschland, England und den Vereinigten Staaten, by Rudolf Binder (Kiel: Institut für Weltwirtschaft, 1950). *Journal of Political Economy* 59 (February 1951): 78–79.

Creation of Income by Taxation, by Joshua C. Hubbard (Cambridge: Harvard University Press, 1950). *Journal of Political Economy* 59 (February 1951): 78.

A Reconstruction of Economics, by Kenneth E. Boulding (New York: Wiley, 1950). *Journal of Marketing* (July 1951): 104–5.

Economic Resources and Policies of the South, by C. B. Hoover and B. U. Ratchford

(New York: Macmillan, 1951). *Journal of Political Economy* 60 (February 1952): 81–82.

Berühmte Denkfehler der Nationalökonomie, by Ernst Wagemann (Bern: A. Francke, 1951). *Journal of Political Economy* 60 (June 1952): 261–62.

Federal Grants and the Business Cycle, by James A. Maxwell (New York: National Bureau of Economic Research, 1952). *Journal of Political Economy* 60 (October 1952): 457–58.

The Industrial Economy: Its Technological Basis and Institutional Destiny, by C. S. Ayres (Boston: Houghton Mifflin, 1952). *Journal of Political Economy* 60 (October 1952): 439–40.

The Tax System of Hawai'i, by R. M. Kamins (Honolulu: University of Hawai'i Press, 1952). *Journal of Political Economy* 61 (June 1953): 266.

L'Autofinancement des societes en France aux Etats-Unis, by Marcel Malissen (Paris: Librairie Dalloz, 1953). *Journal of Political Economy* 62 (August 1954): 353.

Monopoly and Competition and Their Regulation, ed. E. H. Chamberlin (New York: St. Martins Press, 1954). *Journal of Political Economy* 63 (February 1955): 77–78.

The Theory of Fiscal Economies, by E. R. Rolph (Berkeley: University of California Press, 1954). *Journal of Political Economy* 63 (December 1955): 538–39.

Materiale per una logica del Movimento Economico, by Giovanni Demaria, vols. 1 and 2 (Milan: La Goliardica, 1953, 1955). *American Economic Review* 46 (September 1956): 692–94.

Economic Commentaries, by Dennis Robertson (New York: John de Graff, 1956). *Southern Economic Journal* 23 (April 1957): 453–54.

Dundee Economic Essays, ed. J. K. Eastham (London: The Economists' Bookshop, 1955). *American Economic Review* 47 (June 1957): 402–3.

Teoria della Condotta economica dello stato, by Giuseppe Ugo Papi (Milan: A. Giuffre, 1956). *Journal of Political Economy* 65 (October 1957): 452.

Studi di scienza delle finanze e diritto finanziario, by Benvenuto Griziotti, vols. 1 and 2 (Milan: A. Giuffre, 1956). *American Economic Review* 47 (December 1957): 1037–38.

Humanist versus Economist: The Economic Thought of Samuel Taylor Coleridge, by W. F. Kennedy (Berkeley: University of California Press, 1958). *Southern Economic Journal* 25 (October 1958): 226.

Robert Torrens and the Evolution of Classical Economics, by Lionel Robbins (New York: St. Martins Press, 1958). *Southern Economic Journal* 25 (October 1958): 225–26.

Sales Taxation, by J. F. Due (Urbana: University of Illinois Press, 1957). *Journal of Political Economy* 66 (October 1958): 458–59.

The Economic Theory of Fiscal Policy, by Bent Hanson (London: Allen and Unwin, 1958). *Economica* 26 (August 1959): 266–67.

The Theory of Public Finance: A Study in Public Economy, by Richard A. Musgrave (New York: McGraw-Hill, 1959). "The Theory of Public Finance," *Southern Economic Journal* 26 (January 1960): 234–38.

Risparmio e ciclo economico, by Giancarlo Mazzocchi (Milan: Guiffr, 1957). *Journal of Political Economy* 68 (August 1960): 431.

Pareto-Walras: Da un carteggio inedito (1891–1901), introduction by Tommaso Giacalane Monaco (Padua: Cedam, 1960). *Economica* 27 (November 1960): 374–75.

The Trend in Government Activity in the United States since 1900, by Solomon Fabricant and R. E. Lipsey (New York: National Bureau of Economic Research, 1953). *American Economic Review* 43 (December 1960): 960–62.

Problemi Tributari nell' economica del benessere, by Giorgio Stefani (Padova, 1958). *Journal of Political Economy* 49 (February 1961): 99.

The Ideologies of Taxation, by Louis Eisenstein (New York: Ronald Press, 1961). *Journal of Political Economy* 70 (April 1962): 106–207.

United States Fiscal Policy, 1945–59: Its Contribution to Economic Stability, by A. E. Holmans (London: Oxford University Press, 1961). *Economic Journal* 72 (June 1962): 402–4.

Civilian Nuclear Power: Economic Issues and Policy Formation, by Philip Mullenbach (New York: 20th Century Fund, 1963). "Industrial Organization: Government and Business; Industry Studies," *American Economic Review* 53 (September 1963): 807–8.

Finanza Pubblica, by Celestino Arena (Torino: U.T.E.T., 1963). *Economica* 32 (February 1965): 118–19.

Nomos VII: Rational Decision, ed. C. J. Friedrich (New York: Atherton, 1964). *Annals* 359 (May 1965): 189–90.

Essays in the History of Economics, by George J. Stigler (Chicago: University of Chicago Press, 1965). "Economists—And Economists," *National Review* (7 September 1965): 77–78, 80.

Fiscal Neutrality toward Economic Growth, by E. S. Phelps (New York: McGraw-Hill, 1965). *Southern Economic Journal* 32 (April 1966): 492–93.

Politics, Economics and the Public: Policy Outcomes in the American States, by T. R. Dye (Chicago: Rand McNally, 1966). *Journal of Political Economy* 75 (December 1967): 896–97.

The Costs of Economic Growth, by E. J. Mishan (New York: Praeger, 1967). *American Economic Review* 58 (June 1968): 555–56.

Issues in Defense Economics, ed. R. N. McKean (New York: National Bureau of Economic Research, 1967). *Journal of Finance* (June 1968): 558–60.

Pollbooks: How Victorians Voted, by J. R. Vincent (Cambridge: Cambridge University Press, 1967). *Public Choice* 1 (1968): 87–88.

The Fiscal Revolution in America, by Herbert Stein (Chicago: University of Chicago Press, 1969). *Journal of Economic Literature* 7 (December 1969): 1202–4.

Public Finance, by Carl S. Shoup (Chicago: Aldine, 1969). *Journal of Business* (1969): 220–21.

The Quality of the Urban Environment: Essays on "New Resources" in an Urban Age, ed. H. S. Perloff (Washington, D.C.: Resources for the Future, 1969). *Journal of Economic Literature* 8 (June 1970): 496–97.

The New Towns: The Answer to Megalopolis, by F. J. Osborn and A. Whittick (Cambridge: MIT Press, 1969). *Public Choice* 10 (spring 1971): 109–10.

The Case for Participatory Democracy: Some Prospects for the Radical Society, ed. C. G. Benello and D. Roussopoulos (New York: Grossman, 1971). *Public Choice* 12 (spring 1972): 125–26.

Anarchism: From Theory to Practice, by Daniel Guérin (New York: Monthly Review Press, 1971, 1970). *Journal of Economic Issues* 7 (March 1973): 162–64.

Public Expenditure, by Jesse Burkhead and Jerry Miner (Chicago: Aldine, 1971). *Journal of Business* (April 1973): 305–6.

Competition, Collusion and Game Theory, by Lester Telser (Chicago: Atherton, 1972). James M. Buchanan and Winston C. Bush, *Public Choice* 16 (1973): 91.

Economic Analysis of Law, by Richard A. Posner (Boston: Little, Brown, 1972). "Good Economics–Bad Law," *Virginia Law Review* 60 (spring 1974): 483–92. In *Freedom in Constitutional Contract: Perspectives of a Political Economist* (College Station: Texas A&M University Press, 1977), 40–49.

The Machinery of Freedom: Guide to a Radical Capitalism, by David Friedman (London: Harper Colophon, 1973). *Journal of Economic Literature* 12 (September 1974): 914–15.

Economic Foundations of Political Power, by R. Bartlett (New York: Free Press, 1973). *American Political Science Review* 69 (June 1975): 702.

"The Independent Judiciary in an Interest-Group Perspective," by William M. Landes and Richard A. Posner, *Journal of Law and Economics* 18 (December 1975): 875. "Comment," *Journal of Law and Economics* 18 (December 1975): 903–5.

The Governmental Habit, by J. R. T. Hughes (New York: Basic Books, 1977). *Public Choice* 32 (winter 1977): 160–61.

Economic Institutions Compared, by P. J. D. Wiles (Oxford: Basil Blackwell, 1977). *Canadian Journal of Economics* 11 (February 1978): 160–62.

John Stuart Mill, *Essays on Politics and Society,* vols. 18 and 19, *Collected Works* (Toronto: University of Toronto Press, 1977). *Journal of Political Economy* 86 (June 1978): 546–48.

A Time for Truth, by William Simon (New York: Reader's Digest Press, 1978). *Reason* 10 (December 1978): 16–18.

Le regioni della giustizia, special issue of *Biblioteca della liberta* 65/66 (April–September 1977). *Public Choice* 33 (1978): 133.

Politics and Markets: The World's Political Economic Systems, by C. E. Lindblom (New York: Basic Books, 1977). *Journal of Economic Issues* 13 (March 1979): 215–17.

Adam Smith, Lectures on Jurisprudence, ed. R. L. Meek, D. D. Raphael, and P. G. Stein, vol. 5 (Oxford Press, 1978). *British Journal of Law and Society* 6 (summer 1979): 130–33.

Imagination and the Nature of Choice, by G. L. S. Shackle (Edinburgh: University of Edinburgh Press, 1979). *Austrian Economics Newsletter* 3 (summer 1980): 2–3.

Knowledge and Decisions, by Thomas Sowell (New York: Basic Books, 1980). *Public Choice* 36 (1981): 199–201.

Social Justice in the Liberal State, by Bruce Ackerman (New Haven: Yale University Press, 1981). *Public Choice* 37 (1981): 611–12.

Filosofia sociale e metodo della scienza economica, by Tiziano Raefelli (Bari: De-Donato, 1980). *History of Political Economy* 14 (spring 1982): 138–39.

The Nature and Logic of Capitalism, by Robert Heilbroner (New York: Norton, 1985). *Wall Street Journal,* 16 October 1985, 30.

Presidential Economics: The Making of Economic Policy from Roosevelt to Reagan and Beyond, by Herbert Stein (New York: Simon and Schuster, 1984). *Public Choice* 47 (1985): 531–32.

The State, by Anthony de Jasay (Oxford: Blackwell, 1986). "From Redistributive Churning to the Plantation State," *Public Choice* 51 (1986): 241–43.

Individual Interests and Collective Action: Studies in Rationality and Social Change, by James S. Coleman (Cambridge and New York: Cambridge University Press, 1986). *American Journal of Sociology* 92 (January 1987): 1024–26.

The Capitalist Revolution, by Peter Berger (New York: Basic Books, 1986). "The Facts Are Right, But the Facts Are Slight," *Reason* (February 1987): 50.

Crisis and Leviathan: Critical Episodes in the Growth of American Government, by Robert Higgs (New York: Oxford University Press, 1987). *Journal of Economic History* 48 (March 1988): 226–27.

The Economics of Rights, Cooperation, and Welfare, by Robert Sugden (Oxford/New York: Basil Blackwell, 1986). *Economics and Philosophy* 4 (1988): 341–43.

The New Palgrave: A Dictionary of Economics, ed. John Eatwell, Murray Milgate, and Peter Newman (London: Macmillan, 1987). "Public Choice Is New, Negligible, and beyond Mainstream Economics," *Public Choice* 59 (1988): 291–93.

Public Finance in a Democratic Society, by Richard A. Musgrave, vol. 1, *Social Goods,*

Taxation, and Fiscal Policy; vol. 2, *Fiscal Doctrine, Growth, and Institutions* (New York: New York University Press, 1986). "Richard Musgrave, Public Finance, and Public Choice," *Public Choice* 51 (June 1989): 289–92.

Theories of Surplus and Transfer: Parasites and Producers in Economic Thought, by Helen Boss (Boston: Unwin Hyman, 1990). *Constitutional Political Economy* 1 (spring–summer 1990): 92–93.

Constitutional Faith, by S. Levinson (Princeton: Princeton University Press, 1988). *Public Choice* 66 (1990): 196–97.

The Silence of Constitutions, by Michael Foley (London: Routledge, 1989). *Public Choice* 73 (January 1992): 132–33.

The Collected Works of F. A. Hayek, vol. 4, *The Fortunes of Liberalism,* ed. Peter G. Klein (Chicago: University of Chicago Press, 1992). *Public Choice* 75 (February 1993): 204.

Enlightenment's Wake: Politics and Culture at the Close of the Modern Age, by John Gray (Routledge: London and New York, 1995). "The Metamorphosis of John Gray," *Constitutional Political Economy* 6 (fall 1995): 293–35.

James M. Buchanan and Yong J. Yoon. *Increasing Returns and Path Dependence in the Economy,* by W. Brian Arthur (Ann Arbor: University of Michigan Press, 1994). "Constitutional Implications of Alternative Models of Increasing Returns," *Constitutional Political Economy* 6 (winter 1995): 193–98.

Value in Ethics and Economics, by Elizabeth Anderson (Cambridge and London: Harvard University Press, 1993). *International Studies in Philosophy* (1996): 107–8.

The Myth of Democratic Failure, by Donald A. Wittman (Chicago: University of Chicago Press, 1995). "The Best of All Possible Worlds? New Efforts to Prove That Political Institutions Work as Well as Markets," *Times Literary Supplement,* 26 January 1996, no. 4843, p. 13.

Democracy's Discontent: America in Search of a Public Philosophy, by Michael J. Sandel (Cambridge: Belknap/Harvard University Press, 1996). "Divided We Stand," *Reason* 28 (February 1997): 59–60.

Competitive Governments: An Economic Theory of Politics and Public Finance, by Albert Breton (Cambridge and New York: Cambridge University Press, 1996). *Public Choice* 93 (December 1997): 523–24.

TRANSLATIONS

Mauro Fasiani, "Di un particolare aspetto delle imposte sul consumo" (On a particular aspect of consumption taxes), *International Economic Papers* 6 (London: Macmillan, 1956), 34–49.

Knut Wicksell, *Finanztheoretische Untersuchungen* (A new principle of just taxation), *Classics in the Theory of Public Finance*, ed. Richard A. Musgrave and Alan T. Peacock (London: Macmillan, 1958), 72–118.

PUBLIC TESTIMONY AND SUBMITTED PAPERS

"Federal Expenditure and State Functions," in *Federal Expenditure Policy for Growth and Stability: Hearings before the Subcommittee on Fiscal Policy of the Joint Economic Committee, Congress of the United States, Eighty-fifth Congress, first session, pursuant to Sec. 5(a) of Public Law 304, 79th Congress, November 18–27, 1957,* United States Congress, Joint Economic Committee, Subcommittee on Fiscal Policy (Washington, D.C.: U.S. Government Printing Office, 1957), 174–79.

"Fiscal Policy Aspects of Report of Commission on Money and Credit," in *Review of Report of the Commission on Money and Credit,* United States Congress, Joint Economic Committee (Washington, D.C.: U.S. Government Printing Office, 1961).

"Fiscal Policy in the Decade Ahead," in *Fiscal Policy Issues of the Coming Decade; Statements by Individual Economists and Representatives of Interested Organizations. Materials Submitted to the Subcommittee on Fiscal Policy,* United States Congress, Joint Economic Committee (Washington, D.C.: U.S. Government Printing Office, 1965), 19–21.

"Short-Run Stabilization Tax Changes," in *The Investment Credit, the Case for Its Permanency; Statement to Subcommittee on Fiscal Policy of the Joint Congressional Economic Committee in Connection with Hearings on Short-Run Stabilization Tax Changes,* U.S. Congress, Joint Economic Committee, Subcommittee on Fiscal Policy, Council for Technological Advancement (Washington, D.C.: U.S. Government Printing Office, 1966).

"Indexation and Tax Rates," in *Tax Reform: Administration and Public Witnesses: Public Hearings before the Committee on Ways and Means, House of Representatives, Ninety-fourth Congress, First Session, on the Subject of Tax Reform,* United States Congress, House Committee on Ways and Means (Washington, D.C.: U.S. Government Printing Office, 1975).

"Sources of Government Growth," in *Fiscal Relations in the American Federal System: Hearings before a Subcommittee of the Committee on Government Operations, House of Representatives, Ninety-fourth Congress, First Session, 9 July 1975,* U.S. Congress, House Committee on Government Operations, Intergovernmental Relations and Human Resources Subcommittee (Washington, D.C.: U.S. Government Printing Office, 1975), 14–19.

"The Budget Balance Amendment: Statement to the New Hampshire House of Representatives, 2 April 1979," *Congressional Record,* 4 April 1979, S3858.

"In Defense of Budget Balance," *Congressional Record,* 125, 30 April 1979, no. 51, S4940–44.

MISCELLANEOUS

James M. Buchanan and Colin Campbell, "Voluntary Social Security," *Wall Street Journal* 14, 20 December 1966, 14.

Interview on Hutt's Role in Economics, *Manhattan Report* 3 (December 1983): 9–10.

Letter, *Times Literary Supplement* (London), 25 January 1985, 91.

Interview, *The Margin* 2 (February 1987): 9–11.

"Economic Priorities for the Next President," *Policy Review* 44 (spring 1988): 15.

Interview, *Revista de Occidente* 83 (April 1988): 120–35.

"Hemmnisse und Hindernisse Marktwirtschaftlicher Reformen" (Limits of economic reform), *Neue Zürcher Zeitung* (27–28 January 1990): 97; German translation.

"Awakening the New Leviathan," *The Australian,* 28 March 1990, 11.

Interview, *American Thought Leader* 7 (winter 1991): 1–10.

"'Public Choice' and Political Drives: A Talk with Professor James Buchanan," *We the People* 1 (January–February 1992): 4–7, 22–23 (inaugural issue).

Videotape interview by National Economic Educators Club Foundation, 10 March 1992.

Appearance on *MacNeil-Lehrer Newshour,* 16 March 1992.

Videotape interview, *NBC Nightly News with Tom Brokaw,* Mike Jensen, economic correspondent, 21 September 1992.

Contribution to "Books for Christmas," *The American Spectator* 25 (December 1992): 21.

Contribution to "What Should the President Read?" *Reason* 24 (December 1992): 22.

"Interview: James Buchanan," by Roger A. Arnold, *Economics,* 2d ed. (St. Paul: West, 1992), 733.

"L'economia elementare dell'etica: note da un viaggio in Italia" (The elementary economics of ethics: notes from an Italian journey), *Giornata della LUISS, 18 dicembre 1992 e cerimonia conferimento laurea "honoris causa," 26 gennaio 1993* (Rome: LUISS, 1993), 110–17; Italian translation.

"If Clinton Doesn't Botch It, Economy Could Be Perking in '96," *Richmond Times-Dispatch,* op. ed., 14 April, 1993, A14.

"The National Debt," videotape interview by Steve Lilienthal, National Educational Television, 14 August 1995.

". . . Here's His Take on the Flat Tax," op. ed., *Wall Street Journal* 127, 30 January 1996, A18.

"Economist James Buchanan: Taking Off Rose-Colored Glasses to Study Government," interview by Anna J. Bray, *Investor's Business Daily*, 26 August 1996, 1–2.

"Everyone for Himself and Each against All," interview by Claudio Carlone, *Capital*, 1 January 1997, 71–74.

James M. Buchanan and Yong J. Yoon, "Hong Kong's Real Threat May Come from Within," *Investor's Business Daily* 14, 5 August 1997, A28.

This book is set in Minion, a typeface designed by Robert Slimbach specifically for digital typesetting. Released by Adobe in 1989, it is a versatile neohumanist face that shows the influence of Slimbach's own calligraphy.

This book is printed on paper that is acid-free and meets the requirements of the American National Standard for Permanence of Paper for Printed Library Materials, z39.48-1992. ∞

Book design by Louise OFarrell, Gainesville, Fla.
Typography by Impressions Book and Journal Services, Inc., Madison, Wisc.
Printed and bound by Worzalla Publishing Company, Stevens Point, Wisc.